MW01194722

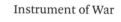
Instrument of War

Instrument of War

Music and the Making of America's Soldiers

DAVID SUISMAN

2/27/25

To Bob,

Best wishes —

THE UNIVERSITY OF CHICAGO PRESS

CHICAGO AND LONDON

The University of Chicago Press, Chicago 60637

The University of Chicago Press, Ltd., London

© 2024 by David Suisman

Published 2024

Printed in the United States of America

33 32 31 30 29 28 27 26 25 24   1 2 3 4 5

ISBN-13: 978-0-226-82292-1 (cloth)

ISBN-13: 978-0-226-82293-8 (e-book)

DOI: https://doi.org/10.7208/chicago/9780226822938.001.0001

Library of Congress Cataloging-in-Publication Data

Names: Suisman, David, author.
Title: Instrument of war : music and the making of America's soldiers /
    David Suisman.
Other titles: Music and the making of America's soldiers
Description: Chicago ; London : The University of Chicago Press, 2024. | Includes
    bibliographical references and index.
Identifiers: LCCN 2024016834 | ISBN 9780226822921 (cloth) | ISBN 9780226822938
    (ebook)
Subjects: LCSH: Music and war—United States. | Military music—United States—
    History and criticism. | War songs—United States—History and criticism. |
    Music—Social aspects—United States. | United States—Armed Forces—Bands.
Classification: LCC ML3917.U6 S83 2024 | DDC 781.5/990973—dc23/eng/20240416
LC record available at https://lccn.loc.gov/2024016834

♾ This paper meets the requirements of ANSI/NISO Z39.48-1992
(Permanence of Paper).

TO EILEEN

Contents

A Note to Readers

In this book, I use "soldier" in the generic sense, encompassing all members of the armed forces. Most of my examples are drawn from the army, the largest of the branches, but I also discuss service in the navy, marines, and air force where appropriate.

For the sake of readability, I have occasionally made silent corrections to spelling and punctuation when quoting from primary sources in order to avoid distracting repetition of "[*sic*]."

For playlists and links to music discussed in these pages, visit http://davidsuisman.net.

Making Music, Making War

In 2015, the U.S. Congress allocated some $437 million for military bands—an amount nearly three times the entire budget of the National Endowment for the Arts. Let that sink in a minute. Such funding represented only a drop in the bucket of the Pentagon's approximately $600 billion appropriation that year, but it far exceeded all other federal spending on music. In fact, this expenditure made the U.S. military the largest employer of musicians in the world, supporting not only traditional military brass bands but also rock groups, conservatory-trained jazz ensembles, and bluegrass combos. The armed forces even had a calypso band based in the Virgin Islands.[1]

Performing for both civilians and military personnel domestically and abroad, these ensembles enjoyed a reputation for delighting audiences that numbered in the millions each year. In the 2010s, though, the bands came under attack from congressional critics who sought to cut wasteful government spending. These "military musical units," Betty McCollum (D-MN) asserted, had little bearing on national security. Another representative, Martha McSally (R-AZ), herself a former air force fighter pilot, took aim at the sums spent on musical instruments, which, she charged, served no function but entertainment. These critiques drew many strenuous rebuttals. In an op-ed published in 2016, for example, Brian Dix, a retired major in the U.S. Marine Corps, opposed reductions in funding for bands that promoted American values around the world. "Now more than ever," he wrote, "military music needs to be on the front lines, vigorously showcasing and enlightening a global audience that continues [to] grappl[e] with the struggles of war." Military bands deserved congressional support, he urged, because they embodied "the clearest of messages of this nation . . . : Music is freedom."[2] The value of music did not end with its effectiveness as propaganda. John Carter, a Texas Republican who sat on the Defense Appropriations Subcommittee, claimed music had bearing on how the armed forces themselves functioned. "Military bands are vital to recruiting, retention and community relations," he argued, "and they provide patriotic and inspirational music to instill in soldiers, sailors, airmen, and marines the will to fight and win."[3]

These views represented only the latest iteration of a long-running debate over the value and significance of music in the military. Almost ninety years earlier, in 1927, Congress held hearings on the pay and rank of military bandsmen. Among the witnesses to testify was John Philip Sousa, composer of "The Stars and Stripes Forever," today the official march of the United States, and a figure of towering cultural authority in the early twentieth century. When one senator suggested that at least some military officials considered bands a "nuisance," Sousa scoffed, suggesting band music contributed to military might. "I do not believe that any nation that would go to war without a band would stand a chance of winning," he shot back. "You want something to put pep in a man, to make him fight."[4]

Ten years before that, military personnel at all levels had identified music in various forms as indispensable to the prosecution of World War I. "It sounds odd to the ordinary person when you tell him every soldier should be a singer, because the layman cannot reconcile singing with killing," Major General Leonard Wood, ex–Rough Rider and hero of the Indian Wars, explained as the Great War raged. "It is just as essential," he argued, "that the soldiers should know how to sing, as that they should carry rifles and learn how to shoot them."[5] His contemporary, General J. Franklin Bell, a former chief of staff of the army known for his ruthlessness in the Philippines at the turn of the century, put it more bluntly. "A singing army is a fighting army," he declared.[6] Further down the ranks, a soldier in the 305th Infantry, Frank Tiebout, recalled the impact of a military brass band that greeted recruits when they arrived at Camp Upton for basic training. "They had a band of music at the station playing the Star Spangled Banner, to get us to feel like fighting," he wrote. "It did— the way they played it." And a pilot in the Army Air Service, Elliott White Springs, called attention to the power of recorded music. "If you want to help win the war," he wrote to his father from Europe, "send me some phonograph records."[7]

Taken together, these remarks by generals and rank-and-file warriors alike attune our ears to a peculiar historical relationship between making music and making war. In the era of World War I, group singing, brass bands, and phonograph records not only resounded in the civilian world but also rang out in the military. And unlike the martial anthems that Tin Pan Alley churned out by the dozen for the home front, the music that these comments referred to was not just *about* the military, or adjacent to it, but intimately involved in the mission of the military itself.

To our twenty-first-century sensibility, the juxtaposition of music and war may be jarring—discomfiting, even—for we are more accustomed to positive associations with music. Whether linked to Apollonian majesty or Dionysian ecstasy, the very subject of music conjures up pleasures of the mind and body. Melodies enchant. Songs soothe and stimulate. In the right conditions, music can inspire, ennoble, elevate. "I want to take you higher," Sly and the Family Stone sang—and they did. The force of music can be emancipatory—both politically and libidinally. It can be a means of challenging or circumventing structures of authority and repression. It can stir us emotionally and can relocate us to idealized psychic places ("audiotopias," the scholar Josh Kun has called them). It can transport us, as the Mekons sang, to "that secret place we all want to go."[8]

Yet music has also coursed through the ascendency of the world's preeminent military force. Since the Civil War, the United States military has used music for everything from recruitment and training to signaling and mourning. Ceremonial music has welcomed fighters at the moment of induction and honored them at funerals. Reveille has roused soldiers in the morning, taps instructed them when to sleep. Chanting cadences ("Sound off! / One, two! / Sound off! / Three, four!" and so on) has been part of soldiers' physical and mental conditioning in boot camp. Musical strains have cheered soldiers in combat, and in a few cases, music has been deployed as a weapon. Soldiers have sung on the march, played pianos, harmonicas, and other instruments, listened to phonographs and armed forces radio, and filled the seats at live performances, both by fellow military personnel and by professional entertainers. Musical sounds have flowed through the history of American war-making, a "capillary" power (as philosopher Michel Foucault would call it) extending to the extremities of soldiers' service.[9]

Some of this musical activity has been improvised, but much of it has occurred by design. Both the makeshift and the intentional matter. In World War II, pianos were installed in the hulls of navy ships before they left the boatyards, and specially constructed, olive-green Steinways were airlifted to infantrymen overseas. Often soldiers sang parodies— new lyrics written to familiar tunes—while other times, their songs came directly out of military-issued songbooks. In Vietnam, they traded tapes of records recently released stateside. In Iraq, they swapped whole collections of MP3s via thumb drives. Frequently, military personnel have had access to the cutting edge of (music) technology, from wind-up phonographs in the trenches of World War I to hi-fi equipment purchased at post exchange stores in Vietnam. Whether it meant nightly brass-band concerts during the Civil War or individualized listening to an iPod in Iraq, military life has often been a musical life. "It would be a dreary service indeed without music," a Union officer concluded in 1862, "and I don't believe the men could be kept together without it."[10]

Through these and other musical practices, this book explores how music has enabled the waging of American wars, both as an instrument of discipline and control for the military and as a means of emotional expression and self-preservation for rank-and-file warriors. It shows that music has been involved in all stages of what we might call the "life cycle" of soldiering, from recruitment and training to firefights and funerals. In the course of this musical activity, both the institution of the military and the soldiers in its ranks have used music as a means to advance their respective wartime goals: defeating enemies of the state on the battlefield and maintaining their emotional and psychological integrity. Music energizes; it emboldens; it has special significance in the military context. The work of soldiers requires extraordinary emotional labor: coping with the strain of putting their lives at risk and killing other humans, as well as surviving the tedium, boredom, and homesickness concomitant with everyday life in the armed forces. Making and listening to music has helped render the performance of this emotional labor possible. These musical practices have prepared and directed soldiers as fighters and empowered them as humans, helping them withstand the demands made on them while doing their jobs.[11]

In some respects, all this music should not surprise us. Since time immemorial, peoples the world over have made deliberate use of music when taking up arms against others. Soldier-musicians appear in ancient Egyptian hieroglyphs. Sun Tzu gave instructions for drumming in *The Art of War*. Thucydides noted the effect of martial trumpets in *The Peloponnesian War*. Indeed, the Bible too had its own incident of musical warfare: Joshua's sonic assault on the city of Jericho. As novelist Arthur Koestler put it, "The most persistent sound which reverberates through man's history is the beating of war drums." The musicality of what is today the world's greatest military power, therefore, is hardly a sui generis American phenomenon. It belongs to a deeper history that one could trace back in time and across space.[12]

The sonic practices of the U.S. military since the Civil War have been distinct in several ways, however, and have taken an unprecedented number of forms. These have included not just singing and performing band music, practices found widely in other countries too. They have also involved, at various times, systematic distribution of songbooks, musical instruments, and phonographs; the establishment of armed forces radio, an unprecedented global network of the airwaves; and the integration of a vast system of professional live entertainment through the United Service Organizations (USO). Consequently, musical activity has been manifest in more ways, over more of the planet, in the U.S. military than in any other fighting force in history.

How this happened owes a great deal to the unusual relationship between the government and various kinds of nonstate actors— entanglements that scholars have called the "associational state."[13] Voluntarist and social welfare organizations like the YMCA have worked closely with the military to provide songbooks, pianos, phonographs, music instructors, and spaces for musical activity, as well as, in some cases, a stock of live performers. These relationships had extensive ramifications, giving the military musical capacities far greater than it otherwise would have had and amplifying the social impact of every available musical practice. Another distinctive American asset is the cooperation of the culture industry, various sectors of which have collaborated with the military extensively.[14] At different times, experienced personnel from the businesses of theater; music publishing; instrument manufacturing; and phonograph, radio, and film have all lent their expertise to one or another war effort, along with their vast operational capacities. No nation on earth has ever invested comparable industrial resources in scale and scope into furnishing its military with music.

Although library shelves groan under the weight of books about war, few of these books make more than passing reference to music. Conversely, books about music rarely mention war-making. Many of the works in which these subjects do intersect are mainly interested in the home front, not in the music of soldiers.[15] None has explored the complex work that music has been made to do in the processes of waging war over time. None has recognized the spectrum of musical modalities in military life. None has considered the sweep of music in war-making specifically in the United States.[16] Occasionally, one encounters isolated exceptions, like works on the outpouring of patriotic war songs in World War I, the staging of spectacular USO shows in World War II, or the mythic power of rock music in the war in Vietnam. Such touchstones often have the whiff of cliché, or they tell us more about civilians than about soldiers. Seldom are examples like these analyzed in relation to one another. Taken together, though, they illuminate something bigger, unfurling over time, a nearly ubiquitous subject hiding in plain sight. A synoptic history of music in the lives of American soldiers tells a story at once more complex and more important than a handful of dissociated, sometimes hackneyed examples can suggest. When we listen across wars, the musicality of the armed forces takes on new meanings.

The military, we recognize, is a musical institution. Whether the sounds come from brass instruments, the throats of weary soldiers, or a pair of heavily used earbuds, where there has been war, there has been music too. In 1863, as many as ten bands were present at the Battle of Gettysburg, at least one playing even in the full heat of combat.[17]

Around 1900, American soldiers in the Philippines battled boredom by crafting songs, both parodies and originals, to comment on their proximate concerns, which ranged from the sultry allure of Filipina women to the waterboarding of captured insurgents. In World War II, soldiers sang, played small instruments like kazoos and harmonicas, listened to government-issued phonographs and radios, and attended USO shows by the million. In the 1960s and '70s, homesick G.I.s in Vietnam were saturated with songs—not simply now-familiar rock anthems but, more often, copious amounts of Top 40 pop, easy listening, country, and soul. According to audience surveys, by 1968, nearly 80 percent of U.S. soldiers tuned in to armed forces radio for at least two hours every day (and 35 percent listened for five or more hours daily).[18] If the genres and technologies have changed over time, the presence of music in the making and maintaining of American soldiers has remained relatively constant.

•

Admittedly, rising to reveille, listening to brass-band concerts, attending USO shows, and plugging in to iPods represent very different practices, sonically and socially. To reconcile these differences, we will be attuned to what such practices share as much as to how they diverge. This entails thinking about what music is in an unusual way. Our primary concern will not be musical *works* but rather music as an activity, something people *do*—less a noun than a verb. In the spirit of musicologist Christopher Small, who called this practice *musicking* to emphasize its active nature, this approach enables us to talk about music in a general, inclusive way. It also helps us connect the manifold people involved in any experience of what is called "music."[19]

In the civilian world, for example, an event such as a concert depends simultaneously on composers, performers, and audience members—as well as instrument makers, managers, booking agents, critics, ticket takers and others. Small's approach sets in relief how all these actors are involved in the production of a single music event whose meaning rests not in disembodied sounds but in the interrelatedness of the sounds and other factors. Or, put differently, the idea of musicking allows us to think about music "in action" (as Bruno Latour did with science)—as situated social practice, grounded in particular times and places, with particular effects. With this in mind, our underlying concern is what musical activity makes possible (what it "affords," historians of technology might say), taking measure of music not only as an end in itself but also, as sociologist Tia DeNora has put it, as "a resource for getting things done."[20]

In the military context, centering *musical activity*, instead of, say, songs, as our primary concern also helps us circumvent the conventional but misleading division between performers and audiences, for often the line between them has been blurred. In the armed forces, buglers, bandsmen, singing soldiers, audience members, and iPod listeners have all been engaged in musical activity. Soldiers who start their day at the sound of reveille have likewise been involved in a musical practice, as have those tuning in to the latest popular hits on armed forces radio. So, too, have the military officials who have ordered or sanctioned performances, the contractors who have supplied military bands with sheet music and instruments, the music publishers who have granted the military permission to reprint lyrics in songbooks, and the civilians who have volunteered or made financial contributions to soldiers' musical recreation.

For our purposes, what matters most is the web of relationships, both social and sonic, in which all these actors are enmeshed. The value of musical activity in (and for) the military does not rest individually in the sounds, the repertoire, the musicians, or the way soldiers respond. Rather, it lies in the interconnectedness of these elements and the structure that binds them, within which music can have radically different functions. Their common context mutes the tensions between these functions, fusing them to one another. For example, a military brass band in the Spanish-American War might have given a ceremonial performance for new arrivals at a training camp, resounding as the embodiment of military order. The band was authorized, sanctioned, and regulated. Its musicians were highly disciplined, were organized hierarchically, and played on command—attributes which neither players nor audiences ever lost sight of. On the other hand, the same band might have also performed at other times to entertain soldiers, playing an eclectic mix of patriotic anthems, traditional songs, and current popular favorites. What soldiers experienced, then, was a polished, well-coordinated ensemble that could move easily—seamlessly—from one mode to the other, capable of creating a sonic world in which "The Star-Spangled Banner," "Home, Sweet Home," and "A Hot Time in the Old Town Tonight" each had its place, complementing and reinforcing the feelings elicited by the others.

The power of musical activity in the military has grown out of this multiplicity of meanings, harmonizing soldiers' numerous discrete identities—warrior; patriotic citizen; loyal son; eager consumer; young, male rabble-rouser; etc. This is possible because musical activity, in Christopher Small's words, has the power to "explore, affirm, and celebrate" multiple relationships at once.[21] In a single moment, it can affect soldiers individually, bond them to one another, and connect them to the institution they are all obligated to serve.

That music has done all this—that it has had these nuanced functions and multiple effects—is the result of an elaborate, dialectical process, which only music could animate, serving top-down and bottom-up ends, acting as an instrument of both military officials and the rank and file. Part of what has made *music* uniquely suited to do this is its protean, affective nature—its reach, versatility, and mutability; its capacity to be insinuated virtually anywhere, anytime; and its ability to move people, deeply, in mind and body. More than that, though, musical activity has been so valuable, so pervasive, so integral to war-making from above and below because it articulates—and allows soldiers to feel—the web of the relationships they are entangled in, and how those relationships, in turn, relate to one another. Only music can do this, because many of those relationships are of such immense subtlety and complexity that expressing and sorting them out verbally would be difficult or impossible. What words could adequately express a soldier's fear of killing a stranger or never seeing a loved one again? What language could do justice to a warrior's grief or resentment of the military? What other means could voice not only the simultaneity of these (and innumerable other) feelings but also the delicate, intricate ways they are interconnected?

At the same time, all this musical activity has existed in relation to other sounds, to the fighting of war itself—the cacophony of combat, the cries of the wounded and dying, the silences before and after battle. In response to these sounds, some musical activity has functioned as a means by which soldiers could exert control over their environment—a tool to displace, even for a few minutes, the soundscape governed by the military or by violence.[22] On the one hand, music has made possible a certain kind of psychic escape, a way to be somewhere else. Listening to Count Basie and Duke Ellington on armed forces radio, a World War II G.I. recalled, "You are not in the Army—you are not at home—in fact, you are not anywhere—just out in the world of memories."[23] On the other hand, musical activity could be a way soldiers have asserted authority over space, not just a way to be transported afar but also a means to redeem the place where they are. Through music, the distant can feel near and the near feel distant.[24] If sound mediates how we know and connect with the world, then in the sounds of music soldiers have found a valuable, meaningful way to reclaim some power over their immediate circumstances.

•

The chapters that follow move chronologically from the Civil War to the wars in Iraq and Afghanistan, exploring the multiple ways music has been involved in making and maintaining America's soldiers. It is tempting to say these pages demonstrate how musical activity from boot camp to battlefield has been a lubricant in the American war machine, enabling its gears to turn smoothly, regularly, with relatively little friction. In many respects this is so. Yet such a metaphor threatens to mislead, suggesting a mechanism driven by an independent motive force, which obscures that this is a book about people. Implying that warriors are gears may dehumanize war-making; flatten the complicated, three-dimensional experience of soldiering; and oversimplify the multifaceted work that musical activity has done in the lives of the men and women who have fought America's wars. Just as the military contains tensions, differences, and contradictions, the functions of music likewise are never monolithic. If music has been a lubricant in the war machine, it has also been more besides.[25]

Recognizing what music has done in American war-making over time can alter our historical perspective, for it reveals new pathways for understanding the relationship of war and society, of sound and the state. Predicated on not just looking at the past but listening too, this kind of history offers an alternative approach to some of the most radically transformative periods of the American experience, generating new questions about what made these pivotal chapters in the nation's history unfold as they did. For a nation to go to war, individuals must go to war—individuals who, it must be stressed, would generally rather not. Attending to music can help us comprehend the complex processes by which such individuals have been transformed into, and nourished as, soldiers. It can elucidate what has made the work of waging war possible on a personal, emotional, corporeal level. In so doing, this history connects diverse challenges faced by every country that goes to war: how to fill the ranks of the military; how to train ordinary civilians for the work of harming perfect strangers; how to maintain warriors, through not only the most strenuous, demanding aspects of soldiering but also the most boring and tedious; and how to prepare soldiers for the return to civilian life when they lay down their weapons. Introducing music into an analysis of large-scale state violence shows how tightly these issues are bound.

What music has done for soldiers complemented what it has done for the state, despite their discrete interests. Tuning in to the musical practices of the armed forces can enhance our grasp of what has motivated military personnel and kept them going. No less consequential than the ways music has made America's warriors are the ways it has enabled them to preserve a kind of affective autonomy, express themselves, exert control (however limited and ephemeral) over their circumstances, connect with others (comrades at their side, loved ones back home), and, in restricted but meaningful ways, push back against the state. If major military conflicts have been a consequential part of U.S. history—as undoubtedly they have—then their musical dimensions warrant our attention. Attending to these sounds can help us think anew about how wars happen.

Under the right circumstances, music can help us be our best selves, reach new heights, imagine new worlds. It can also embody and enact valuable, sometimes revolutionary, forms of resistance, contestation, and transgression. Appreciating these potentialities, however, requires that we confront how complicated the force of music can be. In numerous ways, musical activity has also enabled the complex machinery of war to function, helping people to kill and destroy—an agent of negation, not just creation. For all the innumerable, incalculable ways music has uplifted and inspired, for all it has done to challenge and circumvent structures of authority and repression, it has functioned to uphold and extend institutions of power too.[26] For all the joy and pleasure that music brings in the world every day, it has also contributed to the waging of America's wars. Taking measure of what this has meant may help us see both music and war in a new light.

CHAPTER ONE

A Great and Secret Power

Standing four and a half feet tall, with a slight build, Robert Henry Hendershot claimed to be the youngest soldier to have fought in the American Civil War—perhaps eleven years old when he joined the Union army as a drummer in October 1861. Armed only with wooden drumsticks, he was responsible for tapping out beats that instructed the soldiers of the Eighth Michigan Infantry where to go and what to do at different times—wake, eat, assemble, march, fight, stop fighting, sleep, and so on. According to Northern newspapers, Hendershot surpassed his normal musical duties in the Battle of Fredericksburg by assisting soldiers in crossing the Rappahannock River, exploits that soon became the stuff of lore. By late 1862, he was honorably discharged (on account of epileptic seizures), after which Horace Greeley, the well-known editor of the *New-York Tribune*, summoned him to Manhattan and presented him with a silver drum. His notoriety then led to eight weeks of performances at Barnum's Museum, which Hendershot parlayed into a scholarship at a business college upstate. His carte de visite featured a photograph by Mathew Brady's studio. He appears with a self-assured look on his face, one hand clutching an American flag, the other resting on his drum, his diminutive stature not filling the top quarter of the frame (figure 1.1).[1]

His tender age notwithstanding, Hendershot was not unique. In fact, the army relied on thousands of boys under the age of seventeen who joined the military in a similar capacity, some even younger than Hendershot. Reports indicate that as many as two dozen were under ten years old. Images sentimentalizing drummer boys' service circulated widely in popular culture, both during the war and after. They were the subject of songs, plays, biographies, poems, and illustrations in popular magazines. In each, the figure of the drummer boy was glorified as the embodiment of juvenile innocence, patriotism, and martial pride (figure 1.2).[2]

From our twenty-first-century perspective, these sorts of historical traces can make the past seem like a foreign country. To romanticize sending children to war flies in the face of our contemporary moral outlook. Remarkable, too, perhaps, is that these boys were *musicians*—for most people associate music primarily with pleasure and beauty, not

Figure 1.1. Robert Henry Hendershot, carte de visite. Photograph by the studio of Mathew Brady.

killing. Music seems out of place as a constituent part of military operations. If we look in the right places and listen for the right sounds, however, we find that the drummer boys represent only one of numerous ways that music enabled the prosecution of the Civil War. Alongside the drummers, there were fife players and buglers who also directed soldiers' movements. Whole brass bands traveled with the various armies for entertainment, playing concerts for warriors before, after, and sometimes even during battle. And the sound of fighters singing for amusement often rang out in camp or on the march. In short, music was present throughout the war from 1861, when a brass band played after the attack

THE DRUMMER BOY OF OUR REGIMENT—EIGHT WAR SCENES.

Figure 1.2. "The Drummer Boy of Our Regiment," by Thomas Nast, *Harper's Weekly*, December 19, 1863, is typical of the works romanticizing the service of young boys in the military.

on Fort Sumter, to 1865, when a bugler signaled the end of the fighting at Appomattox Court House and news of Lee's surrender led soldiers to erupt in song.[3]

"Music is almost as necessary for soldiers as rations," declared one Union officer. "Only the musician," wrote a cavalryman, "has the subtle power to bind . . . an army of men." "The men fight much better with music," a Union surgeon observed. More than just indispensable, music was ubiquitous. Every stage of military life had its own musical signature. In each case, the meaning of such music lay in the relationships it animated and the impact of the musical activity on the participants—regardless of whether they were playing instruments, singing along, or merely listening as audience members. Reflecting on the value of the brass bands in his encampment two miles from Confederate troops in 1862, a Union officer mused, "What would an army be without music? Music puts us in good humor, braces our nerves, and makes us cheerful and contented, whatever our surroundings may chance to be." He questioned whether the military could function without it, and he was hardly alone in this view. "Music exerts a great and secret power over us," another Union officer attested. "I have seen many a practical verification of this in the gathering freshness and quickness with which jaded men went on their march when the music called and cheered them."[4]

Indeed, it is unusual to find a volume of letters, a diary, or a memoir from the Civil War that does not make at least passing reference to music or to encounter a military manual that does not offer some prescription about its use.[5] Taken together, these historical traces do more than evoke an omnipresence of musical sound. They reveal the dual function that musical activity had in the military—as a top-down tool of the institution to make and maintain the soldiery, and as a bottom-up instrument enabling fighters to sustain themselves in mind and body. Music harmonized the divergent aims of the institution and its rank-and-file personnel. Galvanizing soldiers at once as warriors and as people, it was a dialectical force that helped make war possible. Admittedly, dissenters in the ranks did exist, but broadly, there was a consensus among military personnel at every level that music had a beneficial effect on soldiers physically, mentally, and even spiritually, affecting them both individually and as a group. If this helped soldiers reclaim a certain degree of psychic and emotional autonomy, it also helped the military wage war. As distant as the music of the Civil War can seem to today's ears, these musical practices can attune us to the ways music has enabled American war-making since.

The Sounds of "Total War"

By the time the Civil War broke out, observers both ancient and modern had attested to the significance of music for military action. "Trumpets pour an acid into the blood," wrote the British military theorist Campbell Dalrymple in 1761, "which rouses the spirits and elevates the soul above the fear of danger." Two years earlier, a British statesman named William Windham had observed soldiers marching in step: "The effects of the musick in regulating the step and making men keep their order [are] really very extraordinary." In the American Revolutionary War a few years later, General William Heath declared music essential for communicating orders and instructions—"not only ornamental to an army," he wrote in a letter to General George Washington, but "absolutely so essential that . . . manoever[s] cannot be performed in a regular manner without it." Meanwhile, Friedrich Von Steuben, the Prussian nobleman recruited by Washington to whip the ragtag Continental army into shape, included numerous drumbeats soldiers were supposed to know in what became the country's first military manual, *Regulations for the Order and Discipline of the Troops of the United States*, which remained in force until 1821.[6]

The Civil War, however, marked the start of a new epoch of war-making, with deep implications for musical activity in the ranks. Unlike previous American conflicts, the Civil War represented the mobilization of the modern nation-state, "organizing self-consciously *as such* for war," as the historian Richard English put it. With the vast expansion of power of the federal government, the Civil War was a military action of a different order, underpinned by novel ideological and material conditions. The centrality of slavery meant the war cut to the core of the nation's political and social identity. At the same time, the conflict heralded a seismic shift in warfare globally. In this new "age of systems" (as military historian and theorist Martin Van Creveld has called it), railroads, telegraphy, and other complex forms of logistical and technological organization remade how societies went to war. Other scholars have characterized it as the first instance of "total war"—a conflict pitting against one another not only military forces but entire societies and their resources.[7]

This "totality" involved a transformation in the way war sounded. Thanks to a range of novel weapons—louder, more accurate, more powerful—the Civil War represented a new kind of sensory experience, dense with meaningful sounds embedded in multiple, sometimes overlapping soundscapes. The most intense of these was the battlefield, an environment whose "keynotes" were gunfire, ordnance, and the screams and cries of the wounded and dying.[8] In the era before smokeless gunpowder, the air of the battlefield was often thick with swirling, pungent smoke, leaving soldiers with little more than sound to inform them about what was happening around them.[9] Amid this cacophony, recognizing and interpreting aural information correctly was a matter of survival. Learning which sounds to notice and make sense of—and which to ignore—could mean the difference between life and death, a peculiar system of listening that the scholar J. Martin Daughtry has called the "auditory regime" of wartime violence, that is, a conceptual grid for making sense of the peculiar embodied knowledge of combat.[10]

For this reason, many combatants took pains to describe what they heard. Future jurist Oliver Wendell Holmes Jr., who served in the Twentieth Massachusetts Infantry, characterized bullets as making "a most villainous greasy slide through the air." Charles Nott, a captain in the Fifth Iowa Cavalry, likened small-arms fire to "bundles of immense powder crackers." In small bursts, he recalled, "they would go r-r-r-r-rap; then came the scattered shots, rap, rap, rap—rap-rap, rap; then some more fired together, rrrrrap." Wilbur Fisk, an erstwhile Vermont schoolteacher, attempted a metaphorical taxonomy of sounds. "Some [bullets] come with a sharp 'clit,' like striking a cabbage leaf with a whiplash," he wrote to his hometown newspaper, while "others come with a sort of screech, very much like you would get by treading on a cat's tail. Then there are others, the sharpshooters' bullets we suppose, that whistle on a much higher key, and snap against a tree with as much force as if the tree had been struck by a heavy sledge hammer. Some strike the dirt with a peculiar 'thud,' others fly high in the air and make a noise similar to a huge bumble bee."[11]

Small-arms fire constituted only part of the din with which soldiers became intimately familiar. The scream of the Parrott cannon, the whine of Whitworth shells, the whistle of "Whistling Dick" siege guns, and the boom of thirty-two-pound howitzers—each of these also had a signature sound and inflected the auditory regime in a unique way. War correspondent Franc Wilkie characterized artillery coming in "with a diabolical shriek," while Charles Nott remembered shells approaching "with the rushing, clashing of a locomotive on a railroad." Another contemporary wrote that "some [artillery] sounded like wounded men crying; some like humming of bees; some like cats in the depth of the night; others cut through the air with only a 'Zip' like noise." In some instances, a combination of humidity, topography, ground cover, and wind could muffle the sound of battle, but often the sound was overwhelming, sometimes resulting in temporary or permanent hearing loss.[12] "The roar of artillery, the screaming of shells, and the sharp crack of musketry would have drowned a hundred thunders," wrote army surgeon George M. Staples in 1864.[13]

What soldiers experienced aurally in the crucible of combat tells only part of the story.[14] Clamorous clashes were often preceded by tense pre-battle lulls and followed by grim, otherworldly post-battle silences, out of which rose and fell moaning, wailing, begging for water, beseeching God, etc. Joshua Chamberlain of the Twentieth Maine Infantry recalled "the writhing concord broken by cries for help, pierced by shrieks of paroxysm" accompanied by the "deep bass notes from closed lips too hopeless or too heroic to articulate their agony." Filling the air, too, noted Captain William J. Seymour of the Sixth Louisiana, were "the unearthly cries of wounded horses," 3.5 million of which died during the war. Writing in his journal after the Battle of Chickamauga, Alva Griest of the Seventy-Second Indiana felt himself besieged by the sounds of the aftermath: "The thunder of battle has ceased . . . , but, oh, a worse, more heart-rending sound breaks upon the night air. The groans from thousands of wounded in our front crying in anguish and pain, some for death to relieve them, others for water. Oh, if I could only drown this terrible sound."[15] For many soldiers, such cries echoed in their heads long after the fact. John Wesley Powell recalled years later the aural experience of the hospital after the Battle of Shiloh as "a weight of horror on [my] ears that . . . [I] cannot throw off, cannot forget."[16]

Opposing Musical Forces

Sounds like these made up the aural backdrop of wartime musical activity, which military officials recognized could serve numerous ends. These included coordinating troop movements, energizing soldiers, intimidating enemies, commemorating ceremonies, and currying favorable relations with local civilians. The military divided this activity into two categories: *field music*, for communicating with troops in camp and in battle, and *bands of music*, for entertainment, esprit de corps, and other purposes. Alongside these, however, there also existed a third, more organic category—what we might call *soldiers' music*—directed and controlled not by the military but by the rank-and-file warriors themselves. None of the three was new in the 1860s. All had been part of war for centuries. Yet the Civil War marked the start of something new—a more systematic use of musical activity, more complex and extensive than ever before, both enabling and responding to the wrenching, traumatic experience of battlefield violence.

Field music was essential to military operations in both the Union and Confederate armies.[17] Before the advent of radio communications in the twentieth century, the very sonic properties of music—especially its loudness, its audibility above the cacophony of combat—made it among the most useful means of orchestrating when and where troops moved before, during, and after the physical action of fighting. In drills, field music helped synchronize soldiers marching in step. In camp, drumbeats and bugle calls told soldiers when to wake, eat, assemble, march, and go to bed. In battle, they told warriors when to advance, fight, and retreat. For this system to work, soldiers had to become adept at a disciplined kind of martial listening—instructions for which appear remarkable in their length and detail to most twenty-first-century readers. A typical Civil War military manual might include fifteen different beats that all soldiers had to know, from reveille, which woke them in the morning, to the "preparative," which signaled them to prepare to fire their weapons.[18]

On both sides of the conflict, soldiers had to be ready to recognize and respond to these sorts of sonic cues, making this peculiar kind of music part of the architecture of daily life. One Confederate prisoner of war detailed this aural acculturation in his diary. "The drum," he wrote, "tells us when to get up, when to go to our rooms, when to commence undressing, and when to put out the lights—I am getting quite accustomed to it." For most troops, this system for regulating time was wholly unfamiliar, but for some, these sounding practices would have echoed the growing use of horns, bells, and whistles to direct workers' bodies in factories and factory towns in the mid-nineteenth century.[19] (Indeed, the phenomenon of internalizing sonic signaling was not limited to humans. According to one well-known Civil War memoir, *Hardtack and Coffee* by John Billings, "even the horses became perfectly familiar with some of these calls, and would proceed to execute them without the execution of a driver. Cavalry horses, too, exhibited great sagacity in interpreting bugle signals."[20])

Industrialization affected musical activity in the military in another respect, too: it allowed scaling up the production of musical instruments, which also set the Civil War apart from previous conflicts. For the armies to standardize field music, they needed a great deal of musical equipment. Drums and fifes were relatively simple to make and therefore easy to procure, but bugles and other brass instruments were more complicated. For Union troops, many brass instruments were imported from Europe by merchants in New York, Chicago, and elsewhere, but the exponential surge in wartime demand favored the North's capacity to expand industrial manufacturing quickly. Numerous instrument suppliers capitalized on this opportunity, most notably John Stratton, a New York–based instrument maker and importer who became a wartime pioneer in the mass production of brass instruments. Beginning with eight employees in 1861, he quickly filled a factory with a capacity of two hundred after hostilities erupted. By the war's end, he had supplied the Union army with more than sixty thousand bugles and trumpets, as well as thousands of other brass instruments.[21] The Confederate army, by contrast, lagged far behind in manufacturing and was forced to rely primarily on imports.

As for the field musicians themselves, often they were boys, sixteen years old or younger, perhaps as many as forty thousand of them over the course of the war. Some received training at the U.S. military's School of Practice for U.S.A. Field Musicians, but most learned on the job. Many were older, too.[22] Regardless of age, these musicians often relied on an instruction manual cowritten by Daniel D. Emmett, the former principal fifer of the Union army's Sixth Infantry who was also the composer of "Dixie" (1860), the blackface minstrel song which became a Confederate anthem and was popular among Union soldiers too—meaning this one musician exerted an outsized influence on the wartime music of both the North and the South.[23]

Once trained, field musicians served under the command of an adult drum or fife major in infantry units or a chief bugler in cavalry and artillery units. The primary role of such field musicians was as the "mouthpiece" of a unit's commanding officer, communicating orders to the troops in camp or battle. Occasionally, they also were called upon to provide accompaniment for disciplinary rituals. The occasional execution of a deserter might be supported by a bugler or drum corps, for example, or a soldier who was to be dishonorably discharged might first be "drummed out" of camp—that is, forced to march while a drummer and fifer played the "Rogue's March."[24]

These ceremonial performances suggest the range of responsibilities that field musicians had and the degree to which using music to direct soldiers' bodies had more than mechanical effects. No matter how much it existed to be "functional," field music touched soldiers affectively too, as exemplified by the history of taps. As we know it today, this bugle call was composed (or perhaps adapted) in July 1862 by a Union general, Daniel A. Butterfield, who found the existing bugle call for "extinguish lights" too stuffy. Soon thereafter, Captain John C. Tidball ordered taps played at a funeral for the first time, recognizing its poignant metaphorical resonance. (This practice was adopted officially by the military after the war.)[25]

Then as now, music was primarily understood as a form of aesthetic expression, but we might also think of the sounds of drummers, buglers, and fifers in another way: as a military technology. That is, if we understand *technology* not just as hardware but as *the way things are made and done* (as one classic definition put it), we see music in a new light when we recognize it as a phenomenon that existed to *make war*.[26] Field music was an instrument crafted by, and at the disposal of, the state for achieving specific military objectives. In these circumstances, *what music did* was as important as *how it sounded*—which is not to say it was devoid of aesthetic "content," just that its presence depended on its effects within and for the military as an institution. In short, field music was a system of sounds and practices used to control and discipline soldiers' bodies—a "technology of power," the philosopher Michel Foucault would have called it—a way to get millions of individuals in very specific places, doing very particular things, at very exact times, even at the risk of their own lives.[27] Not all soldiers heard, understood, and respected every aural command, but generally, field music achieved these ends with a high degree of effectiveness.

•

In 2017, *Saturday Night Live* ran a skit titled "Civil War Soldiers." In it, a group of Union warriors sit around a campfire singing an earnest ballad about fighting for "old New York" when one of them breaks in and introduces a catchy modern hook and chorus, with lyrics about "a party at my parents' house" ("Skinny-dipping in the pool / Oh, oh, oh / All my friends are making out / Oh, oh, oh"). The gag is the anachronism, but the historical reference is more or less on point—soldiers did regularly sing to raise their spirits—and the sketch reflects how this practice still reverberates in popular culture, even if as a joke.[28]

In contrast to the strict discipline of the drums, fifes, and bugles, musical activity in the military also involved a great deal of singing and, to a lesser extent, instrument playing, which soldiers initiated independently and for their own benefit. This was *their* music. Driven from the bottom up, it was a means through which individuals conditioned and controlled their own bodies and behavior to achieve a certain level of happiness or well-being—what Foucault called a "technology of the self."[29] In the age before recorded music, amateur music-making was a common pastime for people from many backgrounds. Regardless of the part of the country soldiers came from, their class status, or the type of unit they fought in, music was a collective resource for addressing both social and psychic needs. Volunteers and regulars; infantry, artillery, and cavalry; army and navy—for all of them, music was at once versatile and accessible, capable of cultivating group cohesion and functioning as a tool of self-care. And it did these things with and through sound, reclaiming the auditory regime of war on soldiers' own terms, a valuable way they could exercise control over the world around them, even intangibly and ephemerally.

According to Bell Irvin Wiley, an authority on the social history of Civil War soldiers, no diversion except reading was as popular as music, and even reading, a surgeon in the Tenth Vermont Infantry suggested, had its limits. "If it was not for [music,] I do not know what we should do," he wrote. "We can't read nor write all the time, and playing cards is all played out, and we shall have hardships enough by and by—to warrant [that we] enjoy ourselves reasonably while we can." Although soldiers occasionally brought or crafted instruments (banjos, violins, guitars), most often music meant singing, either formally or informally.[30] In some units, soldiers formed glee clubs or minstrel troupes, and many sang in church services. Mostly, though, they sang around campfires at night, on marches during the day, or while riding trains or boats.

Sometimes, this singing was aided by the use of songsters—small, inexpensive, soft-bound songbooks, typically printed on cheap paper, with lyrics to fifty or perhaps seventy-five songs (without musical notation), which fit easily into a breast pocket.[31] More commonly, letters and diaries suggest, soldiers sang from memory, from a stock of songs widely known at the time, some of which were of recent vintage but many of which had older provenance. "The Star-Spangled Banner," "Yankee Doodle," and "Hail, Columbia" were traditional and patriotic. "John Brown's Body" and "The Battle Cry of Freedom" were current and topical. Others were neither, like parlor ballads or minstrel songs. Every fighter had identities other than "American" and "soldier" (like "son" or "young, urban roustabout"), and their singing reflected this diversity. That is, soldiers *in the midst of* war most often needed to sing about something *besides* war—to use music to get some distance from their immediate circumstances, or to form and express feelings about what they were living through. Especially popular were sentimental songs about home, mothers, and sweethearts, the most beloved of which was "Home, Sweet Home," written in the 1820s and popularized as a parlor ballad in the 1850s. (At times, however, the effect could be too strong. One Union soldier complained in a letter in 1863, "I don't like to hear ['Home, Sweet Home,'] for it makes me feel queer."[32])

The range of songs in soldiers' repertoire reflected the state of American musical culture, its relationship to the music industries, and soldiers' particular needs. At the time, there was a growing music publishing industry but as yet few professional songwriters or national "hits." "The Battle Cry of Freedom" was penned by a relatively well-known composer, George F. Root, while "John Brown's Body" was written by members of the Second Massachusetts Infantry Battalion. By contrast, many other songs popular among soldiers dated back to earlier periods, and often they were not American in origin. The Scots air "Auld Lang Syne" enjoyed much favor, as did "The Girl I Left behind Me," a folk song popular in the English army from at least the mid-eighteenth century. Another of the most widely sung ballads was "Annie Laurie," written by a Scottish songwriter and composer, Alicia Scott, in the 1830s (probably based on an eighteenth-century Scottish poem). Certainly, there were a few current favorites in soldiers' repertoire, but these commingled with numerous other kinds of songs, especially those from the world of blackface minstrelsy. And unlike the music of later conflicts, soldiers' songs in the Civil War had only a loose, informal connection to the music business, which was still small and decentralized.[33]

Undoubtedly, soldiers wrote their own songs too, but scant evidence of these survives. An 1892 survey of Civil War–era folklore found "the songs written by the soldiers and sailors themselves, descriptive of their engagements, or incidents of camp and march, or expressing their feelings, were not many." Notwithstanding the outpouring of song and verse on the home front, the study's author concluded, "the fact remains that there was . . . more singing than writing in the army and navy."[34]

One group of fighters, however, diverged from these patterns: soldiers of African descent who fought in the 175 segregated regiments of the United States Colored Troops and who, by 1865, made up 10 percent of the Union army. Numbering nearly 180,000 men over the course of the war, they included tens of thousands who fled enslavement when the war began and many others who had been born free or had escaped forced servitude earlier. As with white soldiers, their singing activities fell into two categories: formal and informal. Formal singing drew on a tradition of organized singing groups that had existed on slave plantations and in Northern free Black communities. Such groups performed both for purposes of entertainment and, in some cases, for more symbolic ends, to demonstrate and celebrate the value of the singers' culture, particularly when serenading officers (nearly all of whom were white). One performance that presumably served both ends was a "musical soiree" in honor of Thanksgiving in 1864 by the Shaw Glee Club of the Fifty-Fourth Massachusetts Volunteer Infantry, the first Black unit assembled during the war, in 1863. Named for the regiment's late commanding officer, Robert G. Shaw, who had been killed in battle, the singing group evidently was well known and held in high esteem, and its concert was announced by printed invitations. These left unstated the special meaning Thanksgiving might have for

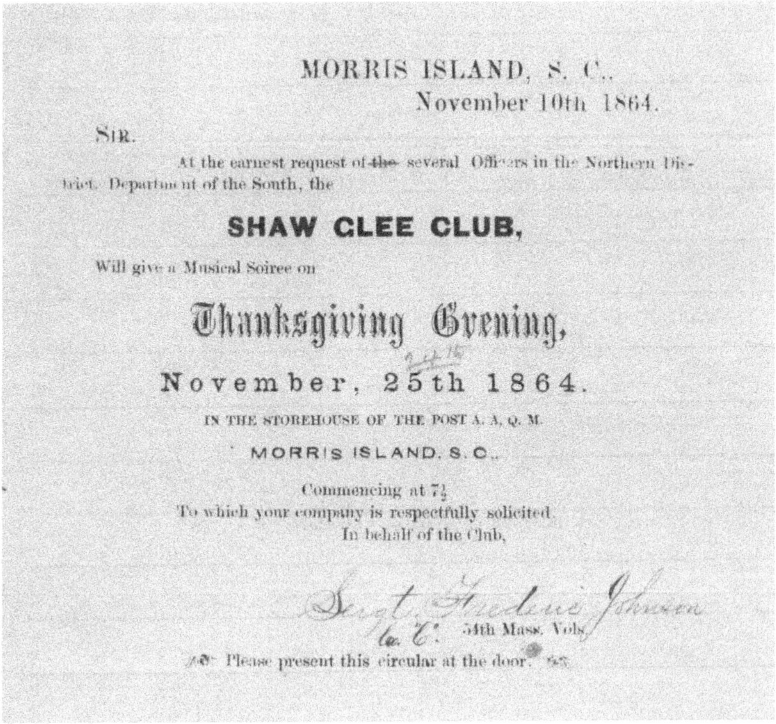

MORRIS ISLAND, S. C.,
November 10th 1864.

Sir.

At the earnest request of the several Officers in the Northern District, Department of the South, the

SHAW GLEE CLUB,

Will give a Musical Soiree on

Thanksgiving Evening,

November, 25th 1864.

IN THE STOREHOUSE OF THE POST A. A, Q. M.

MORRIS ISLAND. S. C..

Commencing at 7½
To which your company is respectfully solicited.
In behalf of the Club,

Sergt. Frederic Johnson
Co. C. 54th Mass. Vols.

Please present this circular at the door.

Figure 1.3. This invitation to a Thanksgiving concert by the Shaw Glee Club of the
Fifty-Fourth Massachusetts Volunteer Infantry Regiment represents not only a holiday celebration but also a claim to cultural citizenship.

Black soldiers. In the midst of a war to defeat slavery, the event asserted
a right to celebrate the most American of holidays, laying claim to a
form of cultural citizenship in a period when these soldiers' legal citizenship was not yet guaranteed.[35]

More prevalent than this kind of organized musical activity, however,
was informal singing around campfires at night by Black soldiers, especially those who had formerly been enslaved. "The black soldiers' life was
full of either music or religion," Captain George Sutherland remarked.[36]
He might have added that the two often commingled, a point not lost on
his superior, Colonel Thomas Wentworth Higginson, who took extensive
notes on the mores of the Black troops under his command and dedicated a whole chapter to their singing in his memoir *Army Life in a Black
Regiment*. Much of their singing involved spirituals, he noted, which the
fighters had sung when they were enslaved, frequently combined with a
circular dance known as a ring shout. Beyond the older material, their

repertoire also involved updated or new songs which made reference to the war in direct and indirect ways. Among the most moving was one Higginson titled "Many Thousand Go":

> No more peck o' corn for me,
>   No more, no more—
> No more peck o' corn for me,
>   Many thousand go.
>
> No more drivers' lash for me, (*Twice.*)
>   No more, &c.
>
> No more pint 'o salt for me, (*Twice.*)
>   No more, &c.
>
> No more hundred lash for me, (*Twice.*)
>   No more, &c.
>
> No more mistress' call for me,
>   No more, &c.
>
> No more mistress' call for me,
>   Many thousand go.

Commemorating the mass exodus from life under the lash, with meager food rations, and being bound to heed the "mistress's call," the song represented a plaintive statement on the war's personal stakes.[37]

With one of his soldiers acting as informant, Higginson was able to transcribe more than three dozen of these songs, and he was evidently sensitive to their range and power. Yet even he underestimated the complexity and richness of what he heard, as did other white officers. "These songs are but the vocal expression of the simplicity of their faith and the sublimity of their long resignation," Higginson concluded. Other uncomprehending officers attempted to dictate the music that their Black soldiers sang, as either a tool of moral uplift or a buoy for morale. Urging them to embrace songs like George F. Root's "Tramp, Tramp, Tramp" and Henry Clay Work's "Marching through Georgia," those officers failed to recognize that singing meant something different for their Black troops than it did for most white soldiers, being one of the most vital and valued forms of expression of the cultural, intellectual, and spiritual life of enslaved communities.[38]

This depth of meaning meant that songs like the one that Colonel Samuel Armstrong called the "Negro Battle Hymn" carried unusual weight. One of the favorite songs of the Eighth Colored Infantry, it fused Old Testament symbols with military imagery, held together by a chorus that stressed the soldiers' manhood:

> They look like men,
> They look like men,
> They look like men of war,
> All arm'd and dressed in uniform,
> They look like men of war.[39]

For fighters who, until recently, had been enslaved (as most of them had), a song evoking their status as armed, uniformed men carried the epic force of an anthem, calling forth not only their shared history but also their transcendence of emasculating, dehumanizing oppression.

Beyond the public assertion of power exemplified by the "Negro Battle Hymn," Black soldiers had a private side of their musical lives as well, most of which went unrecorded. Despite underestimating the complexity of what he heard, Higginson grasped that his soldiers had a secret culture they practiced out of earshot of white officers. Observing that occasionally his troops stopped singing when he approached, Higginson speculated that the full ambit of their songs included subjects and feelings to which he had no access—a "hidden transcript," in anthropologist James C. Scott's formulation, capable of commenting freely on the soldiers' conditions. Accordingly, a full account of Black soldiers' music-making would also likely include a greater amount of secular material, which some scholars have suggested is underrepresented in the surviving sources. Although Higginson did learn of one song whose lyrics protested against Black soldiers' unequal pay, it is probable that Black troops expressed critical views on many other issues as well.[40]

The Bands of War

"I don't believe we can have an army without music," General Robert E. Lee is reported to have said after a brass-band concert on the eve of the Battle of the Wilderness in 1864.[41] Indeed, the entertainment provided by such "bands of music" (as they were called) fell in between the top-down field music and bottom-up singing.[42] The bands belonged to both worlds, serving the needs of the military as well as the soldiers who filled its ranks. Over the course of the war, hundreds of brass bands served in the Union and Confederate armies, with far-reaching consequences. As the authors of a book titled *Enduring Military Boredom* have noted, the word *entertainment* is derived etymologically from the (Old) French *entretenir*, meaning "to maintain or hold together." Giving performances everywhere imaginable, from civilian recruitment events to military hospitals, from evening concerts for soldiers after battle to victory parades when the fighting ceased, the bands had just this effect—keeping fighters going. "Time hangs heavily," a Union soldier wrote in his diary in 1864, "and were it not for the bands, I should be almost homesick."[43]

Loud and boisterous, military-style bands had become a major phenomenon in American life in the decades leading up to the war. In the seventeenth and eighteenth centuries, woodwinds had dominated military bands in Europe. Now they were all brass and percussion. Drums and cymbals had been added around the turn of the nineteenth century, influenced by Janissary or "Turkish" bands. And technological and demographic changes led to brass instruments largely replacing woodwinds. Valved horns, which were easier to play and had greater tonal range than "natural" horns, became the norm after 1810. Then, in the 1840s and '50s, an influx of German immigrants brought an unusual number of skilled instrument makers into the United States. These craftsmen furnished bands with a wide range of metal horns—not just those common today like trumpets, trombones, and tubas but also many that have now disappeared: althorns, basstubas, bombardons, burdons, clavicors, cornophones, ebocornos, saxtubas, and sudrephones. Over these years, the proliferation of such instruments on a mass scale redefined military bands' instrumentation, repertoire, and timbre.[44] By the Civil War, woodwinds had largely disappeared. Shimmering brass and booming bass drums were now the bands' signature sound.

In the decades before the war, these bands appealed to both military and civilian audiences, performing everywhere from armory training grounds to private parties, hospitals to store openings, sporting events to club meetings, with a repertoire that included marches, patriotic anthems, arrangements of orchestral pieces, dance numbers, and even parlor songs. Some of these groups had no military connection, but many were state-funded military ensembles or civilian bands attached to state and local militias.[45] "It is the military," wrote the nation's leading music critic, John Sullivan Dwight, with some exaggeration, in 1856, "which creates and supports all our bands."[46] Indeed, military brass bands were prominent enough that Commodore Matthew Perry brought three of them when he sailed to "open" Japan in 1853, as tools of what would later be called "cultural diplomacy." At home and abroad, the quality of all these bands varied, but over the course of

BOSTON BRASS BAND.

Figure 1.4. In the antebellum decades, the bell (or opening) of some brass horns faced forward or straight up, but others, such as those of the Boston Brass Band, pictured here in 1851, projected backward, over the musicians' shoulders, reflecting their use in accompanying militias on the march.

the antebellum decades, a growing number distinguished themselves as highly accomplished ensembles. Indeed, by 1860, even Dwight, an erstwhile skeptic of the bands, extolled "the rapid advances in the *art militaire* by our citizen soldiery throughout the United States in the past few years."[47]

When state militias were mobilized starting in 1861, most were accompanied by bands. By the summer of 1862, the Union army had nearly 620 of them, each with sixteen to twenty-four members—some crack professionals, others barely above the amateur level—together numbering roughly fourteen thousand musicians.[48] This came at considerable expense. Although instruments were usually funded independently by a regiment's officers or a collection taken up by soldiers or hometown supporters (or a combination of these), the military paid for uniforms and the musicians' monthly wages: $17–$34 a month per bandsman. When added to the $12 or $13 a month that field musicians earned, the upshot by mid-1862 was that the War Department had spent some $4 million to $6 million on music.[49]

Some officials and politicians balked at this expenditure, especially as it became evident the war was not going to be short. The army's cost-conscious paymaster general, Benjamin Brice, considered the regimental bands "far more ornamental than useful" and favored eliminating them. Some public commentators agreed. A splenetic writer for the *New York Times*, for example, considered the bands "brazen monstrosities" which were unjustified and should be silenced to signal the government's commitment to financial restraint. Others, however, challenged this view, including Frederick Law Olmsted, then secretary-general of the United States Sanitary Commission, whose study of the Army of the Potomac concluded that the 143 bands in that unit were indispensable for morale. The soldiers themselves were "violently opposed to doing away with the regimental bands," reported the *Philadelphia Inquirer*, and at least some of their commanding officers concurred. "I am just now a good deal disturbed by the prospect of disbanding the bands," wrote Colonel Wilder Dwight, "A greater mistake could not be made."[50]

When Congress took up the matter, Alonzo Quint, chaplain of the Second Massachusetts Infantry, condemned the proposition of dissolving the regimental bands. "Those who advocate this cannot have an idea of their value among soldiers," he wrote. "If retrenchment must come, let it be somewhere else." Quint explained that he personally did not know much about music but "saw the effects of a good band, like ours, continually"—and that congressional representatives would too if they had experienced an evening of the band's "sweet stirring music" themselves. "Let the men have their music," he appealed.[51]

In the end, the pressure to trim expenses won out, and in July 1862 the War Department issued an order to eliminate the regimental bands and replace them with a smaller number of bands at the brigade level (each brigade was usually made up of four regiments).[52] Thus, brigade commanders kept the best musicians, and the new bands were of better, more consistent quality than the regimental bands had been. The majority of musicians, meanwhile, were mustered out of the service and sent home.

Yet orders notwithstanding, many regiments devised ways to keep their bands, a reflection of how much both soldiers and officers valued them. In some cases, discharged bandsmen promptly reenlisted in the army as privates and became de facto regimental musicians. Technically, they were soldiers first and bandsmen second, but most of the responsibilities they were assigned concerned band work. In other cases, new regimental bands were formed by having the field musicians—the drummers, buglers, and fifers—do double duty as bandsmen and drawing the rest of the players from the ranks of the various companies. Again, the soldier-musicians were relieved of other responsibilities as much as possible.[53] In this way, within six months many discharged bandsmen had returned to service and new bands had been constituted.

By the war's end, senior military officials often knew of these arrangements but looked the other way. When a Union inspector came across a band in a regiment of General William T. Sherman's army, for example, the regimental commanding officer claimed that, all appearances to the contrary, the bandsmen were merely field musicians and showed the inspector their names on the muster rolls, which the inspector accepted.[54] Thus, bands were less numerous after July 1862, but even after the order to eliminate them at the regimental level, many appear to have thrived and new ones were being formed as late as 1864.[55]

Moreover, in larger encampments soldiers could often hear and take pleasure in band music "floating and humming in the air" even if their own unit lacked a dedicated ensemble. "There is a fine brigade band not far off which we enjoy," a doctor in the Union army noted. Such comments remind us that music was not just an aural phenomenon but also a spatial one, its sound often traveling beyond the ears of its proximate audience. "Two or three of the neighboring regiments have fine brass bands, and so we have good music around us on some of the clear mornings," wrote George Grenville Benedict, a soldier in the Twelfth Vermont Infantry, in January 1862. A Union surgeon suggested the persistence of this experience even after the regimental bands were mustered out. "Our own band is not here, but the two other brigades have theirs," he wrote in 1863, "and as the camps adjoin we enjoy the benefit of both." Corporal George Allen of Rhode Island painted an even more tranquil picture: "The music from the brigade band floated sweetly out upon the still night air. We laid ourselves down under the shelter of the tall trees, and with the musical echoes floating through our brain, gently fell into a sweet and quiet slumber."[56]

The contributions of Black bands were valued at least as much as those of white ones. As James Monroe Trotter, a veteran of the Fifty-Fifth Massachusetts, one of the most famous of the African American regiments, wrote later, "In quite a number of the colored regiments, military bands were formed . . . under the instruction of sometimes a band teacher from the north, and at others under one of their own proficient fellow-soldiers." In Trotter's *Music and Some Highly Musical People* (1878), he highlighted the contributions of William H. Dupree and John Moore, manager and director, respectively, of the band of the Fifty-Fifth Massachusetts, which "often enlivened the dull hours and gave, by sweetest music, a certain refinement to what would have been without it but a life of much coarseness." Indeed, belief in music's power to refine could give special significance to Black bands, whose musical instruments, in some cases, were funded by Northern abolitionists who sought for these groups to be tools of uplift. Meanwhile, the soldiers themselves, who faced racism on many levels throughout the war, found that music was one means at their disposal to demonstrate their patriotism and discipline while also maintaining their own cultural identity.[57]

The Confederate military had fewer resources to commit to music, but 125 to 150 brass bands functioned similarly in its ranks, most with eight to sixteen players but some with as few as three or four. Although they varied in quality more than their Union counterparts, these bands had an impact no less striking. "I never heard or seen such a time before," recalled a South Carolina private of a military band concert in 1861. "I felt at the time that I could whip a whole brigade of the enemy myself."[58]

Some of the Confederate bands appear to have been quite talented, such as one an Alabama soldier described as providing "the best kind of martial music every morning and evening." Other groups, not so much. A soldier from Mississippi characterized his band as "a great institution

Figure 1.5. Of the 175 African American units that fought in the Civil War, many had their own bands. Pictured here is the band of the 107th Colored Infantry in 1865. Typically, Black regiments were commanded by white officers and, as here, Black bands by white bandmasters.

[that] labors with the greatest assiduity," but its music, he wrote in his diary, "is never the sweetest nor most harmonious." As for repertoire, the Confederate bands paralleled the Northern ensembles but with Southern anthems like "Dixie," "Maryland, My Maryland," and "The Bonnie Blue Flag" replacing "The Star-Spangled Banner," "Yankee Doodle," and "Hail, Columbia." Not surprisingly, these bands grew sparser in the Confederate army the longer the war went on, as the need for able-bodied soldiers increased and musical instruments became increasingly scarce. "Brass bands, at first quite numerous and good, became very rare and their music very poor in the latter years of the war," one Confederate veteran later recalled. Still, there were at least forty active bands in the Confederate army at the time of Lee's surrender—not a negligible number given the depletion of the Confederacy's resources.[59]

What Bandsmen Did

The responsibilities of bandsmen were considerably more complicated than those of the field musicians. In camp, bandsmen performed both during the day, for drills and dress parades, and in the evening, for entertainment. Often they were called on to serenade commanding officers and, occasionally, visiting dignitaries.[60] On the march, bands played for the rank and file trudging from one place to another—performing not for amusement but to energize the soldiers, to keep them going. In these environments, soldiers might variously sing along with the band, hum or whistle, sing sometimes and then fall silent, or simply move their bodies with renewed vigor as they listened. Or perhaps they did none of these things and simply took in the sound—particularly when overtaken by fatigue. "Toward the end of the day," one Union soldier recalled, "so tired were we all, that it was difficult to muster courage for [singing and whistling], then our only reliance for music would be the band."[61] Regardless, the bandsmen and the troops were entwined in a way that blurred the conventional line separating performers from audience members or distinguishing between active and passive participation. Everyone within earshot was, in a sense, involved in co-constituting the performance, for these were sounds that existed only for the sake of their effect on those who heard them. In some situations, like dress parades, the repertoire was determined by the military. In others, like evening concerts, it was dictated by tastes and reactions of the soldiers. Bands had to satisfy both requirements.

The duties of a bandsman did not end there. In some instances, bands were detached from their units to play at hospitals, to uplift the spirits of the wounded and dying (and of those caring for them). Other times,

they were called on to lend solemn accompaniment to funerals and executions. Depending on where they were stationed, the musicians might
also perform for the surrounding community, giving a concert or providing dance music—a reliable way to ingratiate the military with a local
civilian population.[62]

To meet these varied obligations, bandsmen needed to command a
broad and diverse repertoire. The musicians in the band of the Tenth
Vermont Infantry knew more than fifty pieces in January 1864, and later
that year, the band's industrious arranger Herbert George wrote to his
sister requesting additional material from his personal library at home,
including

> "*Viva La America*" "Wood up Quick Step" "Elfin Waltzes" "Glory
> Hallelujah" "Sontag Polka" "On to the field of Glory" and "Anvil
> Chorus," [as well as] Mocking Bird Quick Step. Blarney Medley.
> Brightest Eyes Q. S. Dirge By Ringold & one by Dodworth. Cicil-
> ien Vespers Quick Step. Cavatina from Lucia. Marksmens polka.
> "Ernani" or Introduction to Ernani. March du Sacre. Violet
> Medley. Grand Terzetto De La Duches from Lucretia Borgia. Grand
> March from Bellisario. We are growing Old quick step. Vailance
> Polka. Song of the Spring Waltz. and Gig Medley.[63]

As this eclectic inventory suggests, outside their official duties, bandleaders had considerable latitude in what they played, provided it amused
their audiences. (That said, commanding officers may have asked them
not to play songs that were particularly plaintive, like "When This Cruel
War Is Over," lest it undermine morale.[64])

In battle, bandsmen usually served as stretcher bearers for
the wounded or assisted medical personnel in other ways.[65] But
occasionally—as difficult as this is to imagine—bands were also ordered
to play during combat itself. At Petersburg, shortly before the war's end,
for example, "the bands were brought to the front," one soldier in the
125th New York Volunteers recalled, "and as we were now lying across the
path of the rebels, the air was made musical with 'Hail Columbia' and
kindred National airs." Brazen yet effective, this use of music worked: "It
was a saucy act, but it was inspiriting to the Union troops," the soldier
added. Similarly, according to Bruce Catton's Pulitzer Prize–winning *A
Stillness at Appomattox*, General Philip Sheridan ordered a band to the
front lines at the Battle of Dinwiddie Court House. At Gettysburg, it was
a Confederate band that played amid the vortex of violence. There, Colonel Arthur J. Fremantle, a British officer who was a guest of Lee's Army
of Northern Virginia, wrote in his diary after the second day of battle,

"When the cannonade was at its height, a Confederate band of music, between the cemetery and ourselves, began to play polkas and waltzes, which sounded very curious, accompanied by the hissing and bursting of the shells."[66]

Unlike music in battle, whose purpose was to embolden some fighters and intimidate others, there were instances, too, of music being used tactically as a feint, to give the false sense of the movement of troops or to create a diversion. To give the impression that his forces in Centreville, Virginia, in 1861 were larger than they were, Confederate General D. H. Hill had bands play for nonexistent audiences near empty tents and fires around which no one sat. And when Godfrey Weitzel, a Union general, sought to mask the redeployment of his troops outside Richmond, Virginia, in March 1865, he had field musicians perform reveille and the bugle call "tattoo" from different locations to suggest to enemies within earshot that more of his forces remained in place than was the case. Such stratagems did not always work, but the fact that they were attempted signals how deeply music was woven into military life and operations.[67]

When Union and Confederate troops were within earshot of one another, there were also instances when a spontaneous "battle of the bands" broke out, with one musical ensemble goading the other with patriotic song. "That [music] puts the fight right into me," a soldier in the Maine cavalry is reported to have exclaimed as he listened to two dueling bands just before the Battle of Dinwiddie Court House.[68] This was in March 1865, weeks before Lee's surrender, suggesting how much the power of bands to inspire remained undiminished through the end of the war. Other times, these exchanges marked moments of brief musical comity when feelings of mutual sympathy transcended wartime antipathy. General Thomas F. Toon, historian of the Twentieth North Carolina, recalled an evening when that regiment's band played "Dixie" at a dress parade; a nearby Union band repeated it; the band of the Twentieth responded with "Yankee Doodle"; and both bands played "Home, Sweet Home."[69] As with the attempts at musical subterfuge, exchanges such as these were certainly not part of a grand strategy. They indicate, however, how music could both excite and quell the passions of common enmity.

The Physical and Emotional Labor of Soldiering

Field musicians, bandsmen, and soldiers embodied musical activity in multiple ways: playing instruments, singing, and listening. Taken together, these activities enacted two different musical impulses. The first came from above and was highly structured, its intent being to affect soldiers' discipline and physical performance. The second came from below and was generally unstructured, its aim to enhance soldiers' psychic well-being and morale. The first was exemplified by field music, the second by singing. Bands fused the two.

Evident in many sources, this dialectical relationship was articulated with unusual clarity and force in the memoir of bandleader Frank Rauscher. "Experience has conclusively shown [that] the music of a band . . . is an important aid toward keeping up discipline and soldierly bearing of the men," he wrote. Band music, therefore, had material implications. "True, [bandsmen] do not go into battle and charge the enemy's strongholds with a flourish of trumpets and the clashing of cymbals," he conceded, "yet the precision and accentuation of step, as a preliminary to decisive action and unison of movement, owes much to the inspiriting strains of music in camp and on the march." On the other hand, he stressed the intangible importance of music beyond its power to instill martial discipline. "Nor does the value of regimental band music end here," he went on, "for its moral and elevating influence is actually beyond estimation." During drills and at night, music gave "a new life" to the men's "despondent spirits," while "on the march, their steps are lightened by the airs with which they have become familiar, and the concord of pleasing sounds proves a feast to their hearts, if not to their souls."[70]

To understand how music could touch soldiers in both body and spirit, it will be useful to approach music as an activity capable of exploring, asserting, and celebrating different kinds of relationships, both sonic and social, as the musicologist Christopher Small did.[71] That is, musical activity could test, strengthen, and reimagine the connections that each individual soldier had with the military, his comrades in arms, his loved ones at home, his enemy, and so on. And this was only possible because music was a phenomenon that could involve people in multiple ways at the same time—socially and individually, mentally, and corporeally.

Most broadly, musical activity built community—connecting people to one another through bodily motion.[72] Specifically, one way that group identity was forged in the Civil War was through the collective rhythmic practice of drills and marching—a process the historian (and World War II veteran) William H. McNeill called "muscular bonding." Whether in drill or dance, McNeill argued, keeping together in time is a means of intensifying group solidarity, capable of producing a "euphoric fellow feeling" experienced involuntarily by "nearly all participants." In coordinated corporeal movement, he maintained, people regularly experience what the dance historian Judith Hanna described as "boundary loss, the submergence of the self in the flow," the result of which is a heightened sense of group cohesion. Just as in agriculture, rowing, or religious dance rituals, this musically induced practice of falling into a groove together—called "entrainment" by musicologists and scholars in the social and natural sciences—can be recognized as a powerful social agent, which, in the context of waging war, has had concrete military implications.[73]

If few soldiers wrote about the relationship between rhythm and social bonding as such, many were explicit about how music affected their bodies. As troops on the march sang "with all 'their might and main,'" Union soldier John Whipple wrote to his sister, "every motion kept time with the music, changing whenever the time changed." Years later, soldier Levi Hemrick evoked the same experience in World War I: "As for keeping step, my feet and legs acted as if they were glued to the music and nothing could have separated them." Further, music did more than synchronize bodies; it also invigorated them. "By their inspiriting strains," wrote James Monroe Trotter, "[Civil War bands] did much to relieve the fatigue occasioned by long and tiresome marches."[74] Others put it more colorfully. Before bandleader Frank Rauscher's memoir was published, one veteran of his regiment wrote to him:

> Don't forget to put in the book how we boys used to yell at the band for music to cheer us up when we were tramping along so tired that we could hardly drag one foot after the other. Since the war I have often thought how cruel we were to do so; for, if we were tired, wasn't the band members equally so? And yet we wanted them to use up what little breath they had left to put spirit in us.

This anonymous correspondent was probably unusual in his empathy for the bandsmen, but his comments about the bodily effect of musical activity resembled many others'. Elsewhere, a private in the Fifth New Jersey Infantry noted "the boys had more rubber in their heels" when led by their band, while an officer in the Second Michigan Infantry remarked, "We have a good band . . . which puts new life into everyone."[75]

While offhand remarks like these could appear banal or trivial, in fact they point to an important and complex insight. Soldiers and officers alike recognized that nothing else in military life had the same capacity to fend off exhaustion that music did, for as one Union officer noted, musical activity not only *disposed* soldiers to bodily activity; it gave them *relief* as well. "A person can dance all night to the sound of instruments but will last only a quarter of an hour without music," he wrote, quoting the eighteenth-century military theorist Marshal Saxe.[76]

Indeed, even when the musicians lacked great talent or skill, music could still exert this power. As a Confederate veteran noted about the later years of the war when the bands declined in quality, "Poor as the music was, it helped the footsore and weary to make another mile, and encouraged a cheer and a brisker step from the lagging and tired column."[77]

Music did not work on the somatic level alone, just as effective fighting required more than physical conditioning. Soldiering was work, and in the course of this work, soldiers killed people. They risked their lives. They saw their friends and comrades maimed and killed. They endured boredom, homesickness, and the tedium of endless drilling. They lived in a "desert of discomfort and drudgery," as one World War II veteran described the soldier's life years later. In other words, the nature of the work placed heavy emotional demands on soldiers, forcing them to practice an extreme form of what the sociologist Arlie Hochschild has called "emotional management." That is, to do their work, soldiers had to actively shape their feelings to conform to norms about the type, and amount of, emotion appropriate to experience and express in a particular situation. As soldiers experienced feelings ranging from fear to courage, rage to longing, only a narrow span of outlets was available and acceptable, and the mandate of their jobs required managing those emotions in such a way that they were only expressed at appropriate times and in appropriate ways.[78]

This is where music came in, helping soldiers process and overcome the emotional, psychological, and existential challenges that were part and parcel of their work. By design, military life suppressed soldiers' individual identities, and the nature of their work was both dehumanizing—in the sense of destroying the humanity of others and jeopardizing one's own—and alienating—in the sense of becoming psychically detached from others, from oneself, from the object of one's labor, and even from humanity at large.[79] To the satisfaction of both officers and soldiers, musical activity helped mitigate these conditions, simultaneously supporting the apparatus of war-making and providing a safety valve to it. On the one hand, music was a social instrument. It united people, fostered esprit de corps, and strengthened identification with the group. On the other hand, because musical experience is highly individualized, soldiers could use music to express distance from, and perhaps resistance to, that same structure.[80] That is, not only did music enhance group cohesion and group morale, it also, at the same time, assuaged feelings of dehumanization and alienation.

Borrowing a concept from the history of emotions, we can say that musical activity helped soldiers form "emotional communities"—groups of people with common goals, values, or interests, who shared a common constellation of emotions.[81] That constellation of emotions, from bravery to fear, rage to boredom, came with the soldier's job. These emotional communities, moreover, did not simply *express* or *reflect* the individual members' shared values and emotions; they helped members *form* those emotions and to see themselves *as a group*. On the threshold between the inner and outer world, music offered members of these communities, in the words of sociologist Simon Frith, "a sense of both self and others, of the subjective in the collective."[82] Binding soldiers together and giving them an outlet for feelings of alienation, music functioned as a kind of catalyst for community formation. In turn, such communities enabled the emotional management that made the physical labor process possible. On a social basis, music bound people together; on an individual basis, it helped people manage emotions. Both contributed to music's military value.

Soldiers in the Civil War did not generally write about emotions in a way that we, in the twenty-first century, would immediately recognize or identify with (and indeed only in the nineteenth century did the word *emotion* come into common parlance).[83] But the bearing of music on soldiers' complex inner lives does come through. In some cases, the references are somewhat vague, such as an account of music "cheering our hearts." In others, the evocation of emotion is more vivid, as with the bugler who broke down weeping after sending his comrades into battle. Some soldiers lacked words for music's effect on their inner lives: "The music of the bands . . . just fills my soul. With what? Why, with the inexpressible." Others hinted at the turmoil throbbing beneath the often stolid language available to them, characterizing music simply as "a relief to the burdens and hardships of those whose lives are ever in peril."[84]

Music—with its affective and functional effects, linking social and individual identity, and embodying both the enactment of and resistance to military structure—was a component of soldiers' (mobile) workplace that helped them do their jobs better. What's crucial here is music's multiple effects: that it satisfied both officers *and* soldiers. From the perspective of officers, music enhanced discipline and morale and, by extension, effective military labor. From the perspective of the soldiers, music helped make military life bearable. Over and over, participants' accounts demonstrate how the playing and singing of patriotic songs, popular songs, songs about army life, and songs about home could bring amusement, comfort, and even joy. In this way, musical experience was at once highly social and highly individualized. On the social basis, music could be a means of strengthening the group, regulating physical behavior, and downplaying individual identity, while at the same time, on an individual basis, it could be a balm for alienation and a reaffirmation of the human.

·

Beginning on May 23, 1865, six weeks after Lee's surrender at Appomattox, the nation's capital celebrated the Union victory with a grand military pageant. Over two days with "propitious weather" and "cool and fragrant" air, the *New York Times* reported, nearly a hundred thousand soldiers paraded through Washington, DC, representing every major unit of the Union forces (except the Colored Troops, who were excluded). The sidewalks teemed with local citizens and hordes of visitors to the city, many of whom had arrived via specially scheduled trains, for a spectacle with "no equal in the history of our continent," wrote the *Philadelphia Inquirer*.[85] Hour after hour, throngs of spectators applauded and cheered. Women waved handkerchiefs. Bouquets were flung.

The soldiers in the Fourth Minnesota Infantry had marched long and hard to get to this parade—in this case, 350 miles from Raleigh, North Carolina. And it showed. After years of war, the buttons on their uniforms had long since lost their luster and their navy blue single-breasted jackets were stained, ripped, and ragged. Yet when the band marched past President Andrew Johnson, General Ulysses S. Grant, and other top officials standing in front of the White House, what was notable was that the shiny silver instruments the bandsmen played were new. As replacements for the horns and drums that had been damaged, destroyed, or worn out over four years of service, these instruments had been purchased only a month before, paid for by both the officers and soldiers of the Fourth Minnesota to show their appreciation for the bandsmen's service. This new set of instruments—the band's third since the war had begun—did more than pay tribute to the material contribution of the group. It also tacitly acknowledged the impact of music in general in the waging of four years of war.[86]

By the military conflict's end, the effect of bands like this one echoed through the service, having inflected the conflict in deep and divergent ways. Bands contributed to soldiers' physical and mental conditioning, on the one hand, and to the preservation of their mental and social autonomy, on the other. Along with field music and the soldiers' informal music-making, the bands had functioned both as instruments of order, discipline, and control and as vehicles for emotional management and self-care. They symbolized how musical activity both regulated soldiers' bodies and offered them cultural self-determination. It was here, in this combination, this synthesis of opposing forces—the formal and the informal, the top-down and the bottom-up—that the power and the significance of military music were located.

More broadly, as contemporaries understood, this musical activity also demonstrated a complex, sometimes uncomfortable relationship between aesthetics and war-making. By definition, Civil War soldiers had little power over the conditions in which they served, but through music and sound, they maintained (or regained) a limited but meaningful form of control over their environment. At the same time, from the institutional perspective of the military, music meant something else. It was a potent element in the complex chemistry of waging war, part of the chain reaction of forces through which armies were mobilized and battles were fought. Musical activity helped to build, strengthen, and direct military power, to honor one's soldiers, and, at times, intimidate one's opponents. Yet as with most aspects of military life, it did not develop or exist in isolation, cut off from the rest of society. Rather, it was entangled in a web of relationships which would only grow more complex in the years to come.

CHAPTER TWO

Music, Race, Empire

Around 1902, Albert E. Gardner, a private in the First Cavalry of the U.S. Army in the Philippine Islands, wrote a parody of "The Battle Cry of Freedom," the Civil War anthem composed by George F. Root to amplify Abraham Lincoln's call for military volunteers. In Gardner's adaptation, the song returned as a commentary on the Americans' practice of torturing suspected supporters of an independent Philippine republic. Retitled "The Water Cure in the P.I.," the updated version mocked the American soldiers' simulated execution of prisoners by forcing filthy water down their throats through a large syringe until they experienced the sensation of drowning—a practice known today as waterboarding. Gardner's new lyrics nearly jump off the page:

> Get the good old syringe boys and fill it to the brim.
> We've caught another n****r and we'll operate on him.
> Let someone take the handle who can work it with a vim,
> Shouting the battle cry of freedom.
>
> [*Chorus*:] Hurrah. Hurrah. We bring the Jubilee.
> Hurrah. Hurrah. The flag that makes him free.
> Shove in the nozzle deep and let him taste of liberty,
> Shouting the battle cry of freedom.

The second and third verses are, if anything, more harrowing:

> We've come across the bounding main to kindly spread around
> Sweet liberty whenever there are rebels to be found.
> So hurry with the syringe boys. We've got him down and bound,
> Shouting the battle cry of freedom.
>
> Oh pump it in him till he swells like a toy balloon.
> The fool pretends that liberty is not a precious boon.
> But we'll contrive to make him see the beauty of it soon,
> Shouting the battle cry of freedom.

The climax arrives in the fourth and final verse, urging the handiwork of "noble and brave" soldiers to continue until either the "squirt gun" or the captive ("the slave") expires, followed by a second, slightly modified chorus:

> Keep the piston going boys and let the banner wave,
> The banner that floats proudly o'er the noble and the brave.
> Keep on till the squirt gun breaks or he explodes the slave,
> Shouting the battle cry of freedom.

> [*Alternate chorus*:] Hurrah. Hurrah. We bring the Jubilee.
> Hurrah. Hurrah. The flag that makes him free.
> We've got him down and bound, so let's fill him full of liberty,
> Shouting the battle cry of freedom.

Reading these lyrics in the slim, leather-bound notebook in which Gardner recorded them, now in the collection of the U.S. Army War College, it is difficult to discern their author's intended tone. Did he compose this as a comic ditty or an acid critique of American foreign policy? Given other entries in the notebook, he probably wrote it as satire, but either way, the exuberance in the lyrics is arresting and discomfiting, recalling today the infamous photographs from Abu Ghraib prison from 2004 which showed smiling American soldiers next to Iraqi torture victims. To today's eyes, Gardner's words do more than bear witness to torture. They give it a soundtrack.[1]

Whether Gardner personally condoned torture or condemned it is lost to the years, but what remains is a remarkable artifact—for numerous reasons. Using "The Battle Cry of Freedom" as its inspiration, it evokes the echoes of the Civil War at the end of the nineteenth century. It also reflects a consciousness on the part of at least one soldier of the mordant irony in torturing people to whom the U.S. was putatively bringing "sweet liberty."[2] Further, disparaging the prisoners as "n****rs," it signals the process whereby the invading military not only racialized the Filipinos, whom the Americans had initially embraced, but did so in derogatory Americanized terms. And notable too was the song's craft. These were not just a few ungainly lines, casually tossed off in a spare minute. Gardner's four verses and two choruses required time and creative energy to compose, and he cared enough about them that he later transcribed them by hand into another notebook in which he collected selections of his wartime writings.[3]

In this respect, these words also illuminate the complex relationship between violence and amusement—indeed, between violence and art—collapsing the distance between making music and making war. They mark how, in at least some soldiers' imaginations, the enchantment of melody did not exist *apart* from brutality. It thrived *alongside* it. Making light of human degradation, the sound of song framed war's cruelty, commented on it, and may even have facilitated it. Culturally, this had great significance, for it challenged what had become in the nineteenth century a kind of orthodoxy. Was music not the condition to which all art aspires, as Walter Pater's much-quoted dictum put it in 1873? Was music not a force to "enrich, ennoble, purify, and perfect the powers and sensibilities of man," as John Sullivan Dwight, one of the most prominent American music critics of the nineteenth century, put it? In the Philippines, music was not war's opposite but its double.[4]

.

When the United States invaded Cuba and the Philippines at the end of the nineteenth century in what is generally referred to as the Spanish-American War, music coursed through military life in many of the same ways it had during the Civil War. Again, there were buglers and brass bands, concerts and informal singing. Again, music functioned as a top-down apparatus of the military and a bottom-up instrument of soldiers. Yet if the military actions in the Caribbean and the Pacific extended earlier practices in some respects, they also signaled a departure. For one thing, the scale and context had changed. The size of the mobilization was small compared to the Civil War—roughly four hundred thousand troops for Cuba and the Philippines combined, compared to the 2.7 million who had served in the Union army alone—but the military's actions had critical long-term consequences, politically, economically, and ideologically.[5] Music was now a resource not for the restoration of the republic but for the United States' overseas imperial expansion.

For another thing, a sea change had begun to take place in American musical culture, a transformation in where music came from, how it sounded, and what it meant. In part, this was visible in a kind of militarization of civilian popular culture, embodied by figures like John Philip Sousa, "The March King," the age's great popularizer of marches and brass bands. In sound and presentation, Sousa created a vogue for musical order and discipline, wedded to an unbridled nationalism. At the same time, the expansion of industrialized manufacturing of musical instruments and the rise of the popular song industry (which became known as Tin Pan Alley) led to music doing new kinds of cultural work, with changes in the political economy of music in New York and Chicago rippling through Havana, Manila, and other distant locales. Among soldiers and sailors, singing and songwriting took on increased ideological force, both continuing to be an important tool for soldiers' emotional management and now also used to articulate their emergent ideas and feelings about race and empire. Suffused with the legacies of blackface minstrelsy, popular music—some commercially produced, some written by soldiers; some old, some new—became a vehicle for formulating new, unapologetic, unabashed ideas about military aggression and national expansionism.

Strike Up the Band

At the time President William McKinley issued his first call for 125,000 volunteers to go to Cuba in April 1898, the music of military-style brass bands was heard widely both in and outside of the armed forces. As popular as such bands had been in the era of the Civil War, by the end of the nineteenth century they had become more spectacular and more deeply integrated into American national life than ever. Much of the credit for this was due to bandmaster Patrick Gilmore. A respected conductor as early as the 1850s, he earned a national reputation after he staged a pair of mega-concerts in Boston in 1869 and 1872 to celebrate domestic and international peace, featuring (somewhat ironically) the world's leading military bands, an orchestra of one thousand musicians and a chorus of ten thousand voices, performing in a specially constructed fifty-thousand-seat auditorium. Although he began as a civilian bandleader, Gilmore conducted a military band from Massachusetts during the Civil War and in 1873 took the lead of the band of the Twenty-Second Regiment of the New York National Guard, which, until his death in 1892, became his vehicle for raising the standards, repertoire, and reception of military-style bands in the United States. Under his leadership, a leading band historian has written, such groups became "unambiguously the most popular type of large-scale instrumental music in North America."[6]

Gilmore's heir, John Philip Sousa, was a figure of even greater renown and cultural authority, who elevated military-style bands further in the 1890s with his signature blend of highbrow and popular entertainment and left an indelible imprint on the musical culture of the American military. The head of the U.S. Marine Band from 1880 to 1892, he established a national reputation with a run of triumphant performances by his (civilian) band at the World's Columbian Exposition in Chicago in 1893. In the years that followed, a period marked by economic dislocation and widespread social unrest, Sousa emerged as one of the representative characters of the age. Wearing a military-style uniform bedecked with medals, he stood as a symbol of order, discipline, and intense nationalism, and he delighted audiences with his band's precision and range (figure 2.1). His musical programs popularized military marches, including his own celebrated compositions like "The Stars and Stripes Forever," and wind- and brass-band adaptations stretching from oratorios to popular airs. Every performance was a patriotic spectacle.[7]

Only a porous membrane separated military and civilian musical cultures. Not only did Gilmore and Sousa move in and out of the military domain, the two bandleaders both inspired and reflected a proliferation of musical activity on the community level. Although military bands were

Figure 2.1. Caricature of bandleader and composer John Philip Sousa, highlighting his penchant for wearing military-style medals.

well known in American life by the time the Civil War began, only in the last third of the nineteenth century did the "brass-band movement," as it was known, reach its apex. Indeed, a writer for *Harper's Magazine* estimated in 1889 that there were ten thousand brass bands active from coast to coast, everywhere from big cities to small towns. (No one seemed to mind that the designation "brass band" was slightly inaccurate, for such groups usually included some woodwind instruments as well.) By the turn of the century, such groups were often seen as emblems of civic identity or pride. Band concerts—offered either for free, in the growing number of park bandshells, or for a modest sum, at fairs, summer hotels, and industrial expositions—had become, in historian Neil Harris's words, "a ritual testifying to the unspoiled benevolence of national life."[8]

In turn, the pomp, pageantry, and popularity of bands in civilian life was echoed in the formal ranks of the military, where their varied performances elevated soldier morale from training camp to battlefield. Consequently, they enjoyed strong institutional support. Beginning as early as 1891, the army and navy had been contracting with J. W. Pepper, one of the leading manufacturers and merchants of band instruments and equipment, to outfit their bands.[9] These ensembles had around two dozen players each, made up of both professional musicians and amateurs recruited from within a regiment's ranks, playing a mix of piccolo, clarinet, cornet, trumpet, alto saxophone, tenor saxophone, trombone, tuba, euphonium, drums, cymbals, and others. (In some cases, a band member might play more than one instrument. Figure 2.3 shows J. H. Brandhorst, a bandsman in the Thirteenth Minnesota Volunteers, resting in bed below a trumpet, baritone saxophone, bassoon, and soprano saxophone, for example.[10]) This instrumentation would remain more or less fixed throughout the twentieth century and resembles what one still might find in a concert band in or outside of the military's ranks. At the turn of the twentieth century, moreover, the government's commitment to military music was also signaled by bandleaders being the highest-paid noncommissioned officers in the military and, on transport ships, by bandsmen generally getting berths on a deck below the officers but above the rank and file. (This was particularly notable because enlisted men's conditions could be quite foul—sleeping on bunks three or four tiers high, on moldy straw mattresses, in holds soiled with vomit and spoiled food waste, and so on.)[11]

Wherever they were, the regimental bands gave frequent concerts, whether for top brass, rank and file, civilians, or some combination. Their performances welcomed newly arrived soldiers in camp, bid farewell to others being shipped off, commemorated holidays and battle victories, and enlivened daily routines. In June 1898, the *Cleveland Press*

REGIMENTAL BAND.

Figure 2.2. The Forty-Ninth Iowa Volunteer Infantry Band, pictured here, was typical of the military brass bands that served in the Philippines, with twenty-four musicians plus a bandleader and assistant bandleader.

Figure 2.3. Some musicians played more than one instrument. Pictured here, bandsman J. H. Brandhorst of the Thirteenth Minnesota Volunteers kept his trumpet, baritone saxophone, bassoon, and soprano saxophone hanging on the wall next to his bed, amid his photographs from home, pinups, and other military gear.

described one of the nightly band concerts at a training camp in Mobile, Alabama, where the Fourth Army Corps was preparing to invade Cuba. With an audience comprised of army regulars, army volunteers who were training at a separate camp nearby, and townspeople, the program began with a patriotic melody, then moved "by degrees from classical selections to light opera, and finally to the tunes which everyone knows and all small boys can whistle." Although most in attendance seemed delighted by the music, one volunteer from Texas complained it made him homesick.[12]

Similar performances occurred wherever the military's forces amassed. In Cuba, band concerts accompanied preparations for the pivotal Battle of Santiago and then celebrated the American victory over the Spanish naval forces there on July 3. That same spring and summer, when thousands of troops arrived in San Francisco to be trained and equipped before departing for the Philippines, the city was awash with music to cheer them on. Bands played at the train station for incoming soldiers, marched with them through the streets, and bid them farewell from their point of embarkation—military marches setting nationalism to 2/4 time. (Intermittently, the city resounded with singing during training exercises and enjoyed wartime fundraising performances by vocal groups as well.)[13]

On the transport ships, morning and nightly concerts punctuated what one soldier called "the long hot days on a breathless sea," with different regimental bands alternating performances when more than one ensemble was aboard. During these trips across the Pacific, which generally lasted around a month, the bands tweaked their repertoires to match the new circumstances. According to a journalist who chronicled the exploits of the First California Volunteers, the open-air concerts on the deck of the *Charleston* included "songs of every description . . . , from the humble negro melody to the more ambitious sentimental ballad, with an occasional sprinkling of songs not altogether of the Sunday-school order."[14]

Commodore George Dewey, commander of the United States' Asiatic Squadron, had a special fondness for music, and the band aboard his ship, the *Olympia*, kept pace with all his activities. In Japan in the spring of 1898, before the outbreak of the war with Spain, he was known to enjoy concerts at lunchtime. His group gave regular evening performances in the lead-up to the Battle of Manila Bay (a.k.a. the Battle of Cavite) on May 1, the first major engagement of the Spanish-American War. And the night the city of Manila fell to the American forces, August 13, the band gave a special concert aboard Dewey's ship, the spectacle of which was deemed notable enough that the program was later reprinted in the

Figure 2.4. Dewey's band aboard the *Olympia*, 1899.

pages of *Frank Leslie's Popular Monthly*. That concert included mainly patriotic pieces such as "Victory of Manila," composed by bandleader Michele Valifuoco, and "The Star-Spangled Banner," but it also included Luciano Conterno's medley of "plantation songs" and a popular "coon" song titled "Ma Angeline."[15]

Then, in the interval between August 1898, when the Americans took control of the Philippine capital, and February 1899, when war broke out between the U.S. forces and the "Insurrectos" (fighters for an independent Philippine republic), American regimental bands delighted both military and civilian audiences with regular performances around Manila and elsewhere, including many from the bandstand in Manila's fashionable Luneta Park.[16] One extant photograph (figure 2.5) from October 1898 hints at the pomp and pageantry of the American musicians. It shows the band of the Thirteenth Minnesota Volunteers in formation, as they parade through the dirt streets of Manila in their impeccable white uniforms. At the right of the frame, three generations of Filipinos look in the direction of the photographer, perhaps warily, perhaps just curiously. Indeed, many locals enjoyed the band performances, but others may have seen them as distasteful exhibitions of martial extravagance.

Figure 2.5. The regimental band of the Thirteenth Minnesota Volunteers in formation in the streets of Manila, October 1898.

Complementing the concerts by American military musicians, which were widely attended by locals, skilled Filipino brass bands also performed frequently for American military personnel, many of whom were surprised by Filipinos' high level of musicianship. "Every place we go instruments are brought out," Lieutenant George F. Telfer of the Oregon Volunteers wrote in a letter home. "Some of them are really fine performers." In many cases, local elites threw elegant balls in honor of the Americans' arrival (a practice historian Paul Kramer has called "fiesta politics"). After one, naval cadet L. R. Sargent wrote in the *Outlook*, a popular magazine, "It was hard to realize that we were in the very heart of a country generally supposed to be given up to semi-savages." Then, on subsequent evenings in various different towns, he explained, "music was a leading feature" every time. Whatever the facilities, "the village band would be called into the building in which we were received, and would play tune after tune well into the night, while we conversed at our ease with the village fathers."[17] Similarly, a journalist for the *New York Sun* was deeply impressed by a group that serenaded high-ranking American military officials in Manila: the resident seventy-two-piece band of

Emilio Aguinaldo, the leader of the independence movement. "Such playing!" the journalist wrote. "It was recompense for every discomfort, every vexation, every disappointment, every hardship of seven thousand miles in a troop ship. You shut your eyes and you heard the orchestra of the Royal Opera at Vienna, the great Budapest Band, the famous military band in Berlin, the Boston Symphony at its best, . . . [comparable to] anything in the world."[18] Music, then, was crucial to where and how the Americans and the Filipinos came together socially, and at this stage in their relationship, it stood as evidence that at least some Filipinos had attained Western levels of "civilization" (see figure 2.6).

All this musical activity had consequences. With marches, classical selections, and popular songs ringing out wherever Americans and Filipinos came together, many Americans began to essentialize the musicality of the local population. Typical was Albert G. Robinson, correspondent for the New York *Evening Post*, who found Filipinos "a distinctly musical lot." In the United States by this time, tens of millions of homes were furnished with pianos or contained other musical instruments, but when Americans found the same conditions in the Philippines, they interpreted them as a mark of difference, not commonality.[19] "Next to his game-cock, the Filipino prizes his piano—for every well-to-do native possesses one of these instruments," noted the travel writer Marian M. George. George F. Telfer wrote, "They are very fond of music. Even the poorer class have pianos and play well. The lower class [also] play the harp, mandolin, violin, and guitar." Hearing their encounters with locals through what ethnomusicologist Mary Talusan has called "an imperial ear," these and other Americans concluded that the achievements of Filipino musicians were an effect of their "natural" endowments, attributing to them an unusual biological—that is, racial—gift for music and mimicry.[20] Or, put differently, music was a lens through which American military personnel, journalists, and others constructed ideas of racial difference.

Concerts attached to social events in moments of relative calm tell only part of the story of the American bands. Their performances also hailed victories in battle. An illustration from *Harper's Pictorial History of the War with Spain* (1899), for example, shows a band playing atop a gun turret on the battleship *Oregon* celebrating the American victory in the Battle of Santiago (figure 2.7). In other cases, the regimental bands may have played during combat too (as had occurred occasionally in the Civil War). According to one account of the Battle of Manila in August 1898, "As the Californians under Colonel [James S.] Smith came up the beach their band played the national air, accompanied by the whistling of Mauser bullets, and during the sharpshooting continued to encourage the men with inspiring music." Other times, bandsmen in Cuba and the Philippines

Figure 2.6. Posed under a thatched roof in San Roque (Cavite), Philippines, this group of American soldiers and bandsmen is entertained by a trio of Philippine musicians (two violinists and a piano player, pictured at rear).

served as stretcher bearers in battle or assisted in hospitals (again, as in the Civil War). A few lines from the diary of one bandsman, Tom Davis, a twenty-eight-year-old tuba player in the First Cavalry, demonstrate the interconnectedness of the bandsmen's musical and nonmusical duties. Beginning with the Battle of Santiago on July 3, 1898, the entries juxtapose concerts with sundry pedestrian details:

> Sunday [July] 3—Working in hospital all day. Tired out. White flag raised by Spaniards at 12 n[oon] and fleet captured. Plenty to eat. Am not very well. . . .

> Fri. [July] 8—Nothing new. Sent letters home. Plenty rations. Rec[eived], letters from home, Hattie and Bede. Played a concert in honor Cornell's victory.

> Sat. July 9th—Up early expecting fighting to commence, but it did not. Col. Woods made Brig Gen. Barron join us. Wilcox and I cooked dinner on river bank. Played concert as usual. . . .

Tues. 12th—Rained all night and till 1p.m. today. Every thing wet and muddy. Played concert.

Alongside matter-of-fact references to weather, health, and visits from dignitaries, concerts appear part of the daily grind.[21]

Elsewhere, even as the Americans dug into counterinsurgency beginning in February 1899, some of the bandsmen in the "colored" regiments found chances for paid commercial performances in Manila, doing minstrel shows. At a time when professional opportunities for Black musicians were narrowly constrained both in and outside of the military, these engagements marked ways African American performers could seize some control over how they were represented in popular culture.[22] Accordingly, the Black press in the United States tracked these endeavors, noting with approval their substantial financial rewards. Although a report in the *Colored American* (Washington, DC) that members of one such group, the Twenty-Fourth Infantry Band, were earning thousands

Figure 2.7. This illustration from *Harper's Pictorial History of the War with Spain* (1899) shows a band playing atop a gun turret on the battleship *Oregon* celebrating the American victory in the Battle of Santiago.

of dollars a day in 1902 was probably exaggerated, it is likely that Black performers who had professional stage experience were able to take lucrative advantage of these kinds of outside opportunities.[23]

•

For soldiers, band concerts offered temporary respite from military monotony. Meanwhile their days were regulated and punctuated by field music—the drumbeats and bugle calls that cued soldiers on where to go and what to do in camp, in battle, and on the march—much as they had been during the Civil War.[24] From the perspective of the military, field music was a powerful tool to instruct soldiers when to wake, when to assemble, and so on, throughout the day, but its effects were never purely functional. Rather, several writers suggest ways that these sounds affected soldiers emotionally as well. In 1911–12, Damon Runyon, later known as a popular Jazz Age fiction writer, published two volumes of verse he had written while serving in the Thirteenth Minnesota Volunteer Infantry in the Philippines, including several poems about bugle calls. One focused specifically on the call "to the color," whose "short, jerky notes," he wrote, produced what he characterized as "a fighty kind o' feelin'":

> Some strange sensation 'pears to lurk in them short jerky notes;
> A funny kind o' feelin' brings th' cheer inter yer throats;
> It's a fighty kind o' music an' we'd tackle all th' world
> When th' bugles give us notice that th' flag has been unfurled.

The call, he suggested, built up a well of martial feeling.

> When th' band has stopped a moment an' when everything is still
> Except th' sound o' scrapin' feet—then comes th' battle thrill—
> When th' bugles, soft beginnin'—but th' notes take up th' swell—
> A-singin' 'To th' colors!' an' it's then you wanter yell!

By implication, this welled-up emotion ("an' it's then you wanter yell") found release in violence ("th' battle thrill"), the impact of which he leaves unstated.[25]

Alongside Runyon's poems, the affective power of field music inspired verse by other writers too, with titles like "Bugles Calling" and "Three Calls" and, in at least one case, a song, "The Glorious Roll of the American Drum." It also left a mark on the regimental historian of the 161st Indiana Volunteers, who found a bugle call essential to the ritual enactment of the war. "When executed with such spirited precision," he wrote of the "guard mount" call, "the inspiring music, the inspection of guns, the entire ceremony . . . impressed thoughtful minds with a world of meaning." Indeed, he concluded, "In that ceremony one could see the whole history of a war."[26] With its signature bugle call, the guard mount performed pageantry and power, a symbolic encapsulation of military might itself.

What's in a Song

Bands and buglers did much to shape the musical soundscape of military life at the turn of the twentieth century, but they alone did not define soldiers' sonic worlds. In battle, warriors were immersed in an aural environment dominated by firearms and, to a lesser degree, artillery—a sonic setting characterized, as a member of the army's Gatling gun detachment in Cuba put it, the "music . . . of the Mauser bullets and the vicious popping of the Remingtons [rifles]."[27] Elsewhere, based on his experiences in the Philippines, Damon Runyon also sought to evoke this "music." In the poem "The Song of the Bullet," gunshots pierce an enchanting aural environment whose characteristic sounds otherwise were croaking lizards and water lapping in rice fields:

> Wot is that noise that breaks th' spell? Sh-h there! Hist!
>   *"Pang! Zing! Oo-oo-oo-zip!"*
>   *That's th' cry o' th' rifle ball,*
>   *That's th' song it sings ter all—*
>   *"Pang! Zing! Oo-oo-oo-zip!"*
>   *Hark to th' song o' th' bullet!*[28]

With his poetic interpretation of everyday oral utterances ("Sh-h there! Hist!"), Runyon not only conjures the sonic world of the battlefield but also aestheticizes its danger, the metaphor of the "song" romanticizing the real risks that soldiers faced. At the same time, his onomatopoetic transcription of gunfire (*"Pang! Zing! Oo-oo-oo-zip!"*), significant enough to be put in both italics *and* quotation marks, suggests the information value that such sounds would have had in the auditory regime of the Philippine battlefield.

With this "music" of combat in the wartime background, soldiers' singing often occupied the foreground. In some cases, the songs they belted out had been passed down orally, but in many cases, they were the latest popular-music hits of the day or lyrics the soldiers had penned themselves, often set to the tunes of recent best-sellers. This culture of song reflected the profound change that had occurred in the political economy of American music in the decades leading up to 1898, exemplified by the rise of the Tin Pan Alley popular song industry. While many of the airs sung in the years around the Civil War had been commercially published, that war predated the modern "hit" song as we know it. In the 1860s songs were still expected to "sell themselves," very few became known nationally, and little commercial apparatus existed to promote them. "Home, Sweet Home," for example, one of the most widely sung compositions of that war, had originally been published in 1823. Its popularity among soldiers in the Civil War reflected not only the appeal of its sentimental lyrics but also a musical culture not yet oriented around ephemerality and the never-ending production of new material.[29]

By contrast, the songs that soldiers sang around the turn of the twentieth century belonged to a different epoch. In the 1880s and '90s, a new song publishing industry began to emerge whose hallmarks were high volume and assertive marketing—turning out hundreds of titles per year and "plugging" them aggressively to generate sales. In this economy, the mode of production and distribution mattered more than musical style. Publishers were just as happy to push chaste parlor ballads (like Charles K. Harris's smash hit "After the Ball") as benign topical songs about bicycles or telephones or baseball. However, one popular song style central to Tin Pan Alley's success had particular implications for the soldiers in Cuba and the Philippines: "coon" songs. Written in so-called Negro dialect and featuring racist caricatures on the sheet music covers, this body of music mainstreamed the derisive tropes of blackface minstrelsy in 1890s.[30]

The subject matter of these songs ranged widely, from the nominally benign (love and courtship) to the grotesque (razor blades and watermelon stealing). Together they normalized the social dynamics of racial distortion, making blackface travesty the central figure of American popular music at a crucial moment in its development, when it was gaining a ubiquity and currency in daily life it had not had earlier. Commercially produced songs now had a visibility, a cultural presence, that altered their significance, including for soldiers. As Charles Post, a private in the Seventy-First New York Infantry put it in a posthumously published memoir about his military service in Cuba, "Not to know the popular songs of the day, whether one could sing or not, was the mark of an illiterate."[31]

Nothing exemplified this social penetration better than "A Hot Time in the Old Town" (also known as "There'll Be a Hot Time in the Old Town To-Night," the song's refrain) a leading anthem of the age and without question the signature song of the United States' imperial wars in Cuba and the Philippines. With music by Theodore Metz, first published in 1886 and most likely stolen from an African American night spot in St. Louis called the Castle Club, this ragtime march became one of the best-known, most inescapable songs of the era after it was republished in 1896 with lyrics in jaunty Negro "dialect," written by blackface stage performer Joe Hayden (whose other songs included "When the Black Folks Turn White"). Resounding from the stages of vaudeville and minstrel shows and belted out by brass bands in city streets and parks, "A Hot Time" seemed to be everywhere, resonating with many kinds of audiences. In 1897, for example, all three candidates for mayor of New York City adopted the song for their campaigns, each modifying the lyrics to suit his particular party and platform. Its mercurial character shifted according to crowd and context. As one scholar of the song has noted, "A Hot Time" was, by turns, "a sassy 'coon' shout, a minstrel march, a victory anthem, a battle song, and a patriotic air," its adaptability making it perfectly suited as a signifier of racial ideology.[32]

For years, the song's popularity and geographical reach grew, including to Cuba and the Philippines, where it was heard widely. Soldiers sang it, regimental bands blasted it. According to Benjamin E. Neal, one of five hundred teachers whom the U.S. government sent to the Philippines to establish a public school system, "Natives think it [the] national Air of America."[33] One soldier called it "the song by which we conquered the Spanish." According to the *Music Trades*, an industry journal, it was "the battle song of the entire Spanish War, sung in camp and field, and hospital and on shipboard. The soldiers sang it from one end of the Philippines to the other."[34]

The attraction of "A Hot Time" rested on several factors. Musically, the song was driven by a lively, undulating tune. It had a catchy melody, in a relatively narrow range, making it easy to sing. Its 2/4 meter made it just as easy to march to. At the same time, its lyrics gave the song an unusual versatility. In particular, its exhortatory chorus called for collective action, the aim of which was ambiguous:

> When you hear dem a bells go ding, ling, ling
> All join 'round and sweetly you must sing
> And when the verse am through
> In the chorus all join in
> There'll be a hot time in the old town tonight.

If "all join[ed] in," it was implied, there would be "a hot time . . . tonight," but here the specificity ended. Exactly what a "hot time" referred to was left unsaid—suggesting a range of possibilities, from revelry to carnage—and the future tense in the last line of the refrain ("There'll be . . .") could be a prediction, a promise, or a threat.[35]

More than just fresh, accessible, and open-ended, however, "A Hot Time" was also, in the words of one military officer in 1898, "defiant, full of hope, prophetic, American in its flippant, reckless, slangy dash, [and] so far as the music is concerned, . . . immeasurably superior to *The Star Spangled Banner* for the purposes of a national anthem." Such attributes made the song especially appealing in the context of war-making. Thus, in the spring of 1898, eager warriors whistled it as they waited to be shipped out to the Caribbean. Theodore Roosevelt's Rough Riders adopted it as their theme song. The Black soldiers of the Ninth and Tenth Cavalry who fought alongside the Rough Riders in the Battle of San Juan Hill sang it in combat, and the Tenth's band tooted it loudly when the battle ended. Elsewhere, the band of the Seventeenth Infantry played it while soldiers prepared for the Battle of Santiago, prompting two young officers to break into dance. In the Battle of Manila in August 1898, American troops were reported to have bellowed "A Hot Time" as they marched into the city, and one musical ensemble, that of the First Colorado Volunteers, became known as the "Hot Time in Old Town" Regimental Band for playing the song while bullets flew.[36]

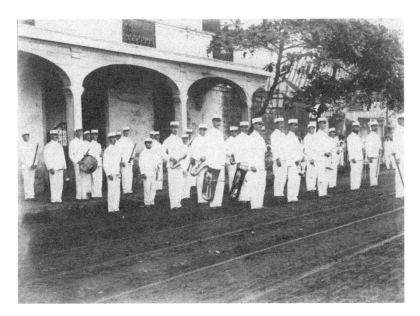

Figure 2.8. The First Colorado "Hot Time in Old Town" Regimental Band, pictured here, played "A Hot Time" during the Battle of Manila in 1898.

In at least one remarkable case, this exuberant song contributed to a mind-expanding experience for a racist white infantryman who was emboldened in battle hearing the Black soldiers of the Tenth Cavalry sing "A Hot Time" in the fog of war in Cuba. His account of the explicit effect of the song makes his powerful recollection worth quoting at length:

> I'm a Southerner by birth, and I never thought much of the colored man. But, somewhat, now I feel very different toward them, for I met them in camp, on the battlefield, and that's where a man gets to know a man. I never saw such fighting as those Tenth Cavalry men did. They didn't seem to know what fear was and their battle hymn was "There'll be a hot time in the old town to-night." That's not a thrilling hymn to hear on the concert stage, but when you are lying in a trench with the smell of powder in your nose and the crack of rifles almost deafening you and bullets tearing up the ground around you like huge hailstones beating down the dirt, and you see before you a blockhouse from which there belches forth the machine gun, pouring a torrent of leaden missiles, while from holes in the ground you see the leveled rifles of thousands of enemies that crack out death in ever increasing succession and then you see a body of men go up the hill as if it were in drill, so solid do they keep their formation, and those men are yelling, "There'll be a hot time in the old town to-night," singing as if they liked their work, why, there's an appropriateness in the tune that kind of makes your blood creep and your nerves to thrill and you want to get up and go ahead if you lose a limb in the attempt. And that's what those "n****rs" did."[37]

In the chaos of combat, he suggested, experiencing Black soldiers singing "A Hot Time" was transformative and inspiring, filling fighters like himself with vim and courage and a will to "get up and go ahead [even] if you lose a limb in the attempt." To be sure, soldiers sang and bands played many other songs as well—contemporary accounts mention by name "On the Banks of the Wabash," "Ta-Ra-Ra Boom-De-Ay," "Goodbye Dolly Gray," and others—but sources suggest "A Hot Time" was second only to "The Star-Spangled Banner" in the frequency with which it was performed, and no other song had this kind of impact.[38]

Meanwhile, soldiers' embrace of "A Hot Time" belonged to the broader popularity of coon songs in general at that time, both at home and overseas. Domestically, this included a number of compositions specifically *about* the Philippines. Charles K. Harris's "Ma Filipino Babe," for example, appeared in many newspapers around the country as a musical supplement and was published in multiple sheet music editions. The cover of one showed a caricature of the titular local maiden, superimposed over rough sketches of Commodore Dewey's ship *Olympia* and an imagined Philippine dwelling (figure 2.9). Other coon songs inspired by the war in the Philippines included "Ma Belle of de Philippines: A Cullud Ditty," "Hol' Dem Philuppines," and "Mister Sojer Man."[39]

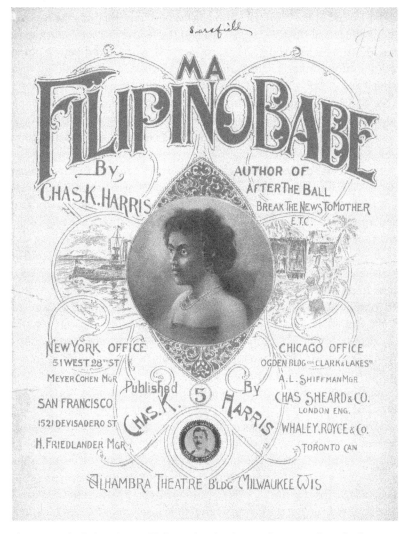

Figure 2.9. The lyrics of "Ma Filipino Babe," by the popular songwriter Charles K. Harris, appeared in many newspapers, and the sheet music was published in numerous different editions. This edition shows a caricature of a Filipina woman buttressed by Dewey's *Olympia* and a scene of village life.

Abroad, coon songs other than "A Hot Time" also found favor among the fighters. In some instances, white soldiers used them to insult or taunt Black soldiers, singing "All Coons Look Alike to Me" or "I Don't Like a N****r Nohow" as an act of aggression and provocation (which also occurred in civilian settings). In other cases, soldiers belted them out just for amusement, including, apparently, in combat. "A lot of the fellows were gagging and whistling and humming during the whole thing [i.e., the battle] not loud, but just loud enough to hear themselves," one soldier recalled of the Battle of Santiago. "When the firing was the hardest along the left of the line, a half dozen of the fellows, I heard afterwards, struck up the coon song, 'Get Your Money's Worth,' and kept it going until another bunch in the same outfit drowned 'em out with another coon song, 'I Don't Like No Cheap Man,' which they twisted into 'I Don't Like No Cheap Span [i.e., Spaniard].'"[40] Even if it is apocryphal that soldiers broke into song at the moment when "the firing was the hardest," this account still suggests that singing was common enough and coon songs popular enough for this soldier to believe it actually happened.

Moreover, the alleged changing of the lyrics "cheap man" to "cheap Span" calls our attention to an additional aspect of the soldiers' musical culture, beyond the vogue of coon songs: singers' transcendence of rote repetition of received material. The practice of soldiers crafting songs themselves reflected the enormous popularity that both songwriting and poetry enjoyed around the turn of the century. Indeed, one collection of verse about the Spanish-American War published in American newspapers in 1898 ran to more than nine hundred pages.[41] And people at that time wrote songs about every conceivable subject, including the wars in Cuba and the Philippines. A recent reference book on American popular music related to the Philippines lists twenty-two different compositions from 1898 whose titles began with "Admiral Dewey," published in ten different cities around the United States, from New Orleans to Boston— "The Admiral Dewey March," "Admiral Dewey's Triumphal March," "Admiral Dewey's Victory," and so on. And the famous naval commander was not the only muse: individual regiments inspired songs as well. The same reference book lists no fewer than seven published compositions about the Thirteenth Minnesota Volunteer Infantry alone, from "Hurrah for the 13th Minnesota, U.S.V." and "Soldier's Farewell" to the "Thirteenth Minnesota U.S.V. March and Two-Step" and "Thirteenth Minnesota Return." The volume even lists one song written in 1899 in honor of General Elwell S. Otis, probably the most unpopular and universally disparaged military commander in the U.S. armed forces in the Philippine Islands at the time, an instrumental titled "General Otis' Grand March."[42]

When soldiers wrote their own songs—some of which were humorous, others serious—generally they fell into several recognizable categories: patriotic airs, tales of heroism, elegies for fallen comrades, and plaints about food or other aspects of life in the military.[43] Many of these songs deliberately reused existing melodies, which made them easier to remember and to incorporate into a common repertoire. Typical was a song like "Dewey, King of the Seas," which celebrated the naval commander's leadership in the Battle of Manila Bay and his avenging the sinking of the *Maine*, to the tune of "Prodigal Son." Similarly, "Battle Song of Utah" glorified the exploits of the Utah Volunteers in the Battle of Manila, to the tune of Henry Clay Work's Civil War song "Marching through Georgia." An exemplary song about military life was "The Old Army Hardtack," a humorous denunciation of the hard biscuits that often made up soldiers' rations:

> There was hard-tack from wars of the past generation
> Which remained unconsumed till this late Spanish war
> 'Tis rumored that some which defied mastication
> Were marked "Civil War" or the stamp "B.C." bore!
> What a triumph this is for the skill of the baker,
> Indestructible product, defying time's tooth
> But it could not resist the assault of our grinders,
> The grinders we had in the days of our youth.

As in many songs, the grievance expressed here was serious but benign. It criticized the military but without actually challenging its authority. Indeed, "The Old Army Hardtack" was collected in the *Souvenir Song Book* of the Eighth Army Corps, privately printed in Manila in 1898 and one of numerous songbooks compiled by individual military units and published to facilitate soldiers joining together in song.[44]

There were also songs that had a keener edge. Among them was "The Governor-General or a Hobo," which mocked the leadership of the aforementioned general Elwell Otis. Written in 1900 shortly after Otis was relieved of his command (by General Arthur MacArthur, father of Douglas), the song ridiculed Otis's fecklessness in the face of Philippine resistance and jeered at his ability to command. "Oh, am I the boss or am I the tool?" its refrain asked:

> Am I the Governor-General or a hobo?
> For I'd like to know who's the boss of this show
> Is it me or Emilio Aguinaldo?

Sung to the tune of "Flanagan the Lodger," a college drinking song, "The Governor-General or a Hobo" expressed a pointed critique of military leadership in a way that probably felt transgressive but in practice functioned as a kind of safety valve, harmlessly voicing the soldiers' disapprobation of military leadership. Although the song did circulate widely enough to come to the attention of top brass, years of rumors that it was officially banned appear to have been false.[45]

The composer of "The Governor-General or a Hobo" was Lyman A. Cotten, a naval captain who had earlier participated in the blockade of Cuba and capture of Puerto Rico. Born to a North Carolina planter who had been a colonel in the Confederate army and a mother who was a writer and descendant of a signer of the Declaration of Independence, Cotten penned numerous songs that sailors and soldiers in the Philippines sang widely and continued to for years afterward. Besides "The Governor-General or a Hobo," another was "Philippinitis," a song which stands out for several reasons. The title and subject of the song referred to a public health concern the United States faced in the Philippines: a peculiar affliction that many American soldiers experienced, which contemporary sources characterized as "tropical neurasthenia" or, more generically, pathological "lassitude." The song opens by evoking what today we might call "brain fog":

> There's a malady terrific and it's very, very sad,
> For you can't think of anything.
> They call it Philippinitis and you have it very bad,
> When you can't think of anything.
> You start to write a letter and you try your best to think,
> You sit for half an hour and then overturn your ink.
> Then drop your pen and paper and go out and take a drink,
> For you can't think of anything, can you?

The chorus shifts the focus to short-term memory loss. It also slips in a word of Spanish, giving it a hint of local color:

> It's so easy to forget a little thing like a thought,
> When your mind is topsy turvy and your memory is short.
> I'd be a "savvy" hombre and I'd know a great lot,
> If I only could remember what I've quite forgot.

What gives the lyrics bite, however, is that two subsequent verses and a second chorus use the malady to critique U.S. policy:

> Oh, we have a civil governor; he does his very best—
> But he can't think of everything.
> He does what he is able, General Chaffee does the rest—
> For he can't think of everything.
> The Philippines are pacified, not tranquilized, said he;
> He overlooked a little thing as anyone may see—
> He forgot the Filipinos, and it's plain as plain can be
> That he can't think of everything—can he?

After feigning respect for military leadership, a second chorus amplifies this notion that the American operations have failed to take the Filipinos ("a little man in brown") into account:

> It's so easy to forget a little man in brown,
> When you start to put an insurrection down;
> He'd tranquilize the Philippines without a single shot,
> If he only could remember what he's quite forgot.

The final verse takes aim at the size of the U.S. contingent, suggesting it would take until the year 2010 for American objectives to be achieved.

> Now twenty thousand soldiers, oh, he said he thought would do
> But he didn't think of everything.
> If native troops are utilized, perhaps can spare a few
> But he didn't think of everything.
> We can occupy the Philippines with twenty thousand men;
> He overlooked a little thing—he didn't tell us when.
> He quite forgot the date of this, the year two thousand ten
> But he can't think of everything—can he?[46]

The mock sympathy ("But he can't think of everything—can he?") gives the song a wry twist, concealing its acid opprobrium.

Beyond the public health issue and the policy critique, this composition is revealing for another reason as well: its style as a song. Notable here is not just that soldiers channeled their concerns and protests into music but that they did so in a form so marked by the contemporary influence of Tin Pan Alley. The tone is light and playful ("There's a malady terrific [i.e., terrible] and it's very very sad"). The couplets are short and punchy ("He'd tranquilize the Philippines without a single shot / If he only could remember what he's quite forgot"). The rhymes are simple (*he/see/be/he*), the racism lighthearted ("little man in brown").

The refrain repeats over and over ("He can't think of everything"). In its tone, its arch cleverness, its formal construction, "Philippinitis" had all the hallmarks of the commercial popular song industry—a radical break from the relatively ornate earnestness typical of most Civil War songs. Admittedly, the sincerity of airs of the 1860s did persist in many other songs that soldiers in the Philippines kept in their repertoires, but at the turn of the twentieth century, such songs now coexisted with others of a more ironic posture, characteristic of the new musical era.

A different facet of Americans' lives in the Philippines was reflected in "The Jawbone of Lemery," a song about the U.S. soldiers running out on their bar tabs. Written in 1903 by the same composer as the song about waterboarding, Private Albert Gardner, it chronicled the abuse of credit ("jawbone" in military slang) extended by a local barmaid, Marie, in the "hospitable town" of Lemery. There, alcohol-guzzling soldiers "all made love to the ladies fair" and took advantage of the "unlimited jawbone." As the second verse recounted:

> Troop B of the 1st were honest men
> But their thirst for booze was strong
> They would sit and drink whiskey, beer, and rum
> In "Marie's" place all day long
> And they swore as homeward they went
> Life there was like a dream
> From which they never wanted to awake
> For many bottles of booze they'd take
> By asking Marie for jawbone

Fueled by their thirst for alcohol, these "honest men" ran up bar bills without a second thought, leading Gardner to explain how "jawbone" and its environment operated:

> Jawbone is a word for credit used
> And Marie the bar-maid so fair
> Was often very much amused
> By the soldiers who came in there
> "Que querie [sic] usted" to them she would say
> Cervasa [sic] they would all and one cry
> Bueno would be the reply
> They would then proceed to have a good time
> Drinking whiskey, beer, and rum
> And oh how Marie's eyes would shine
> As through the crowd she would skip and run.

Interestingly, the final verse both details and criticizes the soldiers' neglect of their debts, which leave Marie in financial ruin:

> But alas and alack the good times are over
> Troop B from Lemery has flown
> And Marie often sighs, I know she feels sore
> For none of them paid their jawbone
> Two thousand pesos won't pay the bill
> And I think it's a measly shame
> To take advantage of a maid's free will
> And drive her out in the rain
> For now Marie has got no home
> She's gone to Batanga to see
> If she can't collect part of the jawbone
> Owed to her by Troop "B."[47]

The disapproval is mild ("I think it's a measly shame"), echoing the ironic tone of Gardner's other lyrics.

"Jawbone" was far from the only song about soldiers' entanglements with local women. In others, singers waxed wistful about the female islanders' sultry charms, made light of Filipinas' refusals, and exulted in the fusion of military and sexual conquest. Airs like "At Naic" and "An International Affair" had special resonance among soldiers marked by the idealization of white male virulence around the turn of the twentieth century. As the writer Barbara Ehrenreich showed, the interconnectedness of war and masculine power has an ancient lineage, but it was particularly explicit at this historical moment, under the sign of what Theodore Roosevelt called the "strenuous life," exalting the combined forces of sexual, racial, and imperial domination. In these conditions, counterinsurgency in the Philippines was nothing less than a "fight for American manhood," as one historian put it, or, in the words of another, a battle over "manliness and civilization."[48] In a period when ideas about gender, race, and empire were all in flux, these songs expressed deep ideological positions, both putting into words and cementing a romanticized vision of American potency, seen through a peculiar imperial lens. That is, soldiers' musical activity did more than belittle sexual relationships with Filipinas or mock native people generally; it did these things in a manner that racialized them.

Singing contributed to a dynamic process whereby imperial intervention abroad both reinforced and expanded the prevailing racial discourse of home. In the Philippines, music belonged to a system in which domestic American ideas about race, identity, and social status were adapted to local conditions and inflected by the shifting circumstances of the U.S. occupation. The process of imagining Filipinos as a racially distinct and inferior people rested not simply on exporting and applying domestic racial thought and categories—for these were themselves unstable and changing. After William H. Taft, the civil governor of the Philippines from 1901 to 1904 (and future president of the United States), referred to Filipinos as Americans' "little brown brothers," for example, this became a catchphrase both in and beyond soldiers' musical practices, simultaneously reframing and taking strength from the landscape of racial violence in North America. As historian Paul Kramer has shown, Filipinos had not been described or seen by Americans in racially derogatory terms at the outset. Rather, this language and racial imaginary emerged in relation to the Filipinos' fight to establish a republic independent of the United States and to the increasingly incendiary American political rhetoric at home.[49]

In this imperial landscape, song was one discursive field in which Americans formulated and articulated ideas about Filipinos' racial difference and their supposed low (devious, duplicitous) character. "The Soldier's Song," another widely sung song by Lyman Cotten, expressed this unabashedly. Set to the tune of George F. Root's Civil War classic "Tramp, Tramp, Tramp," it cast the Filipinos as uncivilized racial Others:

> In that land of dopey dreams, happy, peaceful Philippines,
> Where the bolo-man is hiking night and day,
> Where Insurrectos steal and lie, where Americanos die,
> There you hear the soldiers sing this evening lay.

After painting the Filipinos as both innocuous ("happy, peaceful") and dangerous (carrying machete-like bolo knives; living "where Americanos die"), the chorus gave voice to the violence behind caricature:

> Damn, damn, damn the Insurrectos, cross-eyed kakiack ladrones,
> Underneath the starry flag, civilize 'em with a Krag,
> And return us to our own beloved homes.[50]

Those who put their lives on the line for Philippine independence ("Insurrectos"), in other words, were brown ("kakiack," i.e., khaki-colored), thieves ("ladrones"), physically compromised ("cross-eyed") savages who deserved—or would only respond to—violence ("civilize 'em with a Krag," i.e., a gun). Subsequent verses derided living conditions ("When I lay me down to sleep, slimy lizards o'er me creep") and local customs and food—returning with each chorus to the scornful message of violence.

Far from mere entertainment, songs like this one were a blunt ideological weapon in the war to snuff out the Philippine republic. Indeed, this composition was often known simply as "Damn, Damn, Damn the Filipino"; that is, it ceased to refer specifically to Insurrectos, eliding any difference between political behavior and the native population generally.[51]

As powerful as these lyrics are, the significance of "The Soldier's Song" rests not in its words alone but also in their circulation—in the extent to which these sentiments were rendered aloud, socially. The song was apparently known and sung by virtually every regiment, to the chagrin of military officials. By 1906, the navy had even taken steps to suppress it, although in 1913, in a book about the American occupation of the Philippines since 1898, it was still referred to it as "that old familiar song," suggesting that it had not gone away.[52] Around the same time, it appeared as the second of fifty-two titles in a collection of favorite songs of the Military Order of the Carabao, a group formed in Manila in 1900 to honor its members' military service in the occupation of the Philippines. Later, it was included in *Sound Off!*, a book of widely sung "army folk-songs" published in 1929 (with a second edition in 1942).[53] This song does not, then, represent some curious, antiquarian outlier. "The Soldier's Song" appears to have been *sung*—and not infrequently.

From 1899 on, U.S. soldiers increasingly referred to Filipinos in racialized terms both in conversation and in song. One enlisted man wrote to his parents, "Almost without exception, soldiers and many officers, refer to the natives as 'n****rs.'"[54] Among other soldiers, however, "gugu" and related slurs which were specifically Filipino were prevalent as well. (Sixty years later, "gugu" seems to have been the inspiration for a new epithet, "gook," in Vietnam.) In some cases, the two ideas of race appeared side by side, but often they were used interchangeably, in lyrics that might be addressed *to* Filipinos, be *about* Filipinos, or mention them only in passing. In some songs, the associations were explicitly violent, as in "A Rookie":

> When you go those black gugus to fight,
> There'll be blood flowing free.

Similarly, in "I Don't Know Why They Want You":

> I don't know why they want you, but they do-o-o
> There's lots of other n****rs just the same as you—
> But what Piang [a Filipino who appeared to be friendly but was
>   really on the fence and working both sides of the conflict] does
>   tell

Makes us hike and pike [i.e., kill] like 'ell—
I don't know why they want you but they do-o-o.

Another song, to the tune of "Everybody Works but Father," disparaged Filipinos' work ethic, as soldiers belted out,

Everybody works but a gugu
And he sits around all day
Smoking a large tobac—
Too strong to work for pay
Mujer takes in washing
To buy a good manuc [i.e., bird]
Nobody works in that land
So do not look.

Dotted with Spanish ("mujer") and Tagalog ("manuc"), the song wedded the jauntiness of Tin Pan Alley to specifics of the Philippine occupation.[55]

Elsewhere, the racial imaginary in which the foreign and domestic worlds merged was explicit. In "A Colored Sergeant's Wooing," a coon song written by a member of the Twenty-Eighth Volunteer Infantry, a jilted Black soldier strikes up a romance with a Filipina ("dis goo-goo gal"), who literally takes the place of his once-betrothed down in "Dixie":

I done left a gal in Georgia; she was to marry me,
But she hitched up to another man sens I kem o'er de sea.
But I kain't yet quite forget her and dem good ol' courtin' days
Dat dis goo-goo gal reminds me of, with all her winning ways.

Additional songs in the soldiers' repertoire delivered other insults, such as denigrating Filipino families ("A Filipino Family") and ridiculing local languages ("Explosions from Tropical Languages"). Another overtly rejected William H. Taft's suggestion of a fraternity between the Americans and Filipinos: "He may be a brother of Big Bill Taft, / But he ain't no brother of mine!" ("Little Brown Brothers").[56] Together, these songs belonged to a process of cultural invention, creating and defining Filipinos as a racial Other.

These ideas of racial difference and division developed in relation to a sense of national identity grounded in imperial expansion, based on a "template" established in the American West.[57] In the Philippines, most of the seasoned American military officers had begun their careers fighting Indians in North America, and at least some soldiers saw the efforts to suppress the Philippine insurrection as an extension of those campaigns. In 1898, a Nebraska regiment sang, "We've had many a scrap . . . with the Sioux and Comanches / We'll show . . . the Spanish . . . how we drove the reds off from our ranches."[58]

At the same time, this imperial national identity depended, too, on the postbellum reconciliation between the North and the South—a reunion which, as historian David Blight and others have shown, was itself predicated on the suppression of the political and civil rights of African Americans. Thus, at the turn of the twentieth century, U.S. imperialism depended on obscuring and rewriting the history of sectional division. As a new regime of legal and extralegal discrimination against African Americans became entrenched throughout the United States in the 1890s, underpinning it was a new narrative of the Civil War that stressed the parity of (white) Northern and Southern "honor" and sacrifice. In this spirit, when a soldier from Mississippi penned song lyrics about a harmonious Thanksgiving dinner, his words implicitly signaled an erasure of Black rights which dovetailed with the country's imperial ambitions:

> No matter what a man may be,
> A "Yank" or from the South,
> The thought of turkey baking brown
> Brings water to the mouth.[59]

By contrast, other songs voiced the spirit of imperial ambition outright. One, for example, reimagined the "recessional" hymn which soldiers were accustomed to at the conclusion of military ceremonies, as a paean to empire. The lyrics of "Accessional—A Victorious Ode" appealed both for divine restraint and assistance in the extension of American power abroad. In the first verse, soldiers humbly beseeched,

> Jehova, Lord, beneath whose smile
> Our fathers fought in Freedom's name,
> And wrested from the British Isle
> Our country, loved, and know to fame;
> Oh, gracious Lord, withhold thy hand
> While we expand—while we expand.

The next verse called for the U.S. to brush aside the long-standing Monroe Doctrine, which opposed European interference in the Americas alongside a U.S. pledge not to meddle in European colonial affairs elsewhere in the world. Unlike the first verse opposing divine intervention ("gracious Lord, withhold thy hand"), the second verse appealed for it directly:

> The doctrine taught by James Monroe,
> And maintained through a hundred years,
> Was but a bluff; it now must go,
> Since we've embraced both hemispheres.
> Oh, Lord, extend thy helping hand,
> While we expand—while we expand.[60]

Restraint, these lyrics contended, was obsolete, leaving in its place the logic of imperial growth that would have not only God's blessing but also assistance ("Oh, Lord, extend thy helping hand"). Another example, a drinking song of the Military Order of the Carabao, was addressed to comrades still in the Philippines by those who had returned to the U.S., extending support for those "bear[ing] the white man's burden" and waxing nostalgic for "the Empire days which we long to relive."[61] The idea of empire was not figurative in these songs. Imperial conquest was on the tip of every singer's tongue.

·

In response to political pressures at home, on July 4, 1901, the McKinley administration installed a civil government in the Philippines to replace the military regime, despite continued resistance to the American occupation. Two weeks later, in an effort to quell civil unrest with fewer American troops, the civil governor William H. Taft established an insular Filipino police force called the Philippine Constabulary, whose brass band, launched the following year to assist military ceremonies and official functions, became internationally renowned when the group performed at the St. Louis World's Fair in 1904. That fair, historian Paul Kramer has shown, was a showcase for the American imperial project, with outsized attention and resources lavished on the American exhibition dedicated to the Philippines. One outstanding component of that exhibition was the eighty-piece Constabulary Band, whose musicians were among more than one thousand Filipinos brought to St. Louis for the fair. There, the band's daily performances were recognized as a highlight and elicited one of the highest compliments imaginable. "The Philippine Constabulary band," wrote the *Milwaukee Journal*, "has furnished the musical sensation of the World's fair, being pronounced by John Philip Sousa the most wonderful military band he ever listened to."[62]

The Philippine Constabulary Band was organized and conducted by Lieutenant Walter H. Loving. One of the first Black bandleaders in the U.S. military, Loving was also the only African American among the American commanding officers of the constabulary. Under his direction, the Filipinos who made up the Constabulary Band comported themselves with exquisite military precision while delighting audiences with a repertoire spanning from light classical pieces to marches to popular songs. (Loving steered clear of coon songs and ragtime.) Eight thousand miles away from the Philippines, the Constabulary Band's concerts had more at stake than entertaining civilian audiences. President McKinley had declared the United States' goal in the Pacific was the "benevolent assimilation" of the Philippine people, and for fairgoers in St. Louis, the Constabulary Band stood as aural and visual proof of that mission's success. Two years after Albert Gardner had penned his tribute to waterboarding, these performances suggested the triumph of artistry over brutality, and discipline over savagery. Consequently, everything about the Filipino bandsmen was scrutinized and, in some cases, contrasted with the characteristics of other Filipinos who were part of the fair. In particular, as ethnomusicologist Mary Talusan has shown, newspaper reports juxtaposed the band's punctilious, Sousa-esque performances of American patriotic music (marches and anthems) with the "primitive" music and customs of unassimilated tribal peoples who were put on display elsewhere in the Philippine exhibition. With attendees thronging the Constabulary Band's daily performances, the concerts resounded as a testament to both the justness and the effectiveness of American imperial expansion through military conquest.[63]

If the Philippine Constabulary Band represented the spectacle of empire, a more subtle instrument of conquest was evident in the everyday musical activity of the American military. This activity varied widely, from field music to band performances to informal singing, and it touched the lives of every soldier. Of course, not all warriors experienced this music the same way or took from it the same meanings, but many apparently did, otherwise it would have failed to fulfill its function and would have been modified or abandoned. Although, in some respects, this musical activity resembled that of the Civil War, it also departed from that precedent, especially in the ideological work that songs and singing did. In the 1860s, the most widely sung songs actually said very little about the substance of the war. They tended to be silent about race, had little to say about slavery, and mentioned the enemy only infrequently and glancingly ("saucy rebels" in "Marching through Georgia" and "Down with the traitors / Up with the stars" in "Battle Cry of Freedom"). Even

"John Brown's Body," probably the most widely sung Union anthem, never specified the cause the eponymous Brown died for.

In Cuba and the Philippines, however, many of the lyrics soldiers belted out had a direct or explicit connection to the racial and imperial politics of the era in which they were sung, whether that meant a coon song produced by Tin Pan Alley or a self-styled parody of "Battle Cry of Freedom." Some of this music expressed deep, long-held commitments and convictions; some, thoughts that were still inchoate and not yet utterable. As in the past, it voiced fighters' feelings about their wartime circumstances, from confidence and pride to anxiety and resentment. Yet it did so in ways that were specific to the United States' efforts to enter the company of the world's recognized great powers. Imperial expansion depended on many factors, including making and maintaining the soldiers who embodied the violent imposition of American foreign policy on the ground in two hemispheres. No other force could mediate the welter of emotional and ideological impulses concomitant with soldiering as profoundly and effectively as music. No other instrument could approach its mutability, flexibility, and nuance, in terms and tones ranging from informal and generalized to highly structured and finely calibrated, serving both institutional and individual priorities. Drawing on the past and reordering the present, these forms also looked to the future, anticipating the revolutionary changes in making and listening to music then coming into view.

CHAPTER THREE

Music and Guns
Go Hand in Hand

A black-and-white photograph shows a group of men standing in a semicircle. Some hold guns. Some have musical instruments. Some are empty-handed. Most are looking toward the camera. It is July 1918, and the men are American and British soldiers. At center, a man with a saxophone appears ready to tootle a tune. The photograph is attached to a now-warped piece of cardstock in the United States National Archives. The image is credited to the commercial firm Underwood & Underwood, a pioneer of wartime news photography in World War I. The official caption reads, "MUSIC AND GUNS GO HAND IN HAND ON THE WESTERN FRONT IN FRANCE." The inscription explains that the men had just finished a rifle drill and were "preparing for a musical evening in their camp." It is one of dozens of images in a file of miscellaneous music-related photographs of the War Department from the First World War (figure 3.1).[1]

The photograph documents a casual intimacy between musical conviviality and wartime violence. As a material artifact, it reflects the government's self-conscious recognition of this intimate relationship as well as the aim to publicize it, for the purpose of such pictures was to be distributed to the press, usually by the Committee for Public Information, the government's wartime propaganda agency. In this respect, the photograph recalls another image, a vibrantly colored propaganda poster now at the Library of Congress: a triptych showing a soldier gripping a rifle and hurling a grenade, a bugler, and a trio of soldiers singing around a piano. The text above the center panel urges the purchase of war bonds. The text above the other two panels reads "Music Makes for Morale" and "A Singing Army Is a Fighting Army." Together, the photograph and the poster suggest that music and the violence of war were inextricably bound in two ways, both in the daily lives of soldiers and in the government's public-facing effort to mobilize people and resources on the home front. In the bloodiest, most destructive war the world had yet seen, the musicality of the military enjoyed unprecedented visibility (figure 3.2).[2]

Figure 3.1. "Music and Guns Go Hand in Hand on the Western Front in France," reads the caption of this photograph of American and British soldiers from July 1918.

Figure 3.2. A vibrantly colored propaganda poster, reproduced here in black and white, shows a grenade-hurling soldier buttressed by a bugler and soldiers singing around a piano.

Linked to efficiency, standardization, and Americanization—some of the watchwords of the era—music came to be recognized as a martial necessity in World War I, with innovative forms of musical activity integrated into the military infrastructure, promoted by government, laypeople, the music business, and rank-and-file soldiers in equal measure. Systematic attention to the production and consumption of music led to a host of new initiatives within the military, including the implementation of organized singing programs, the distribution of musical instruments (especially pianos and phonographs), and the staging of theatrical amusements. Fueled by the combined power of state, civic, and commercial institutions, these programs transformed what music meant for American fighters in World War I. In some cases, this promotion of musical activity grew out of a Progressive faith in music as a vehicle for moral uplift. And in some, it was driven by the private interests of the music business. Regardless, the upshot was that these programs gave soldiers novel opportunities to make and listen to music and the government new tools for waging war.

One of the great paradoxes of World War I was that it channeled the productive power of industrialization into mass destruction and carnage. Another was the zeal with which most Progressive reformers, erstwhile pacifists, came to embrace and promote American militarism, believing that out of the crucible of war could come widely shared social and political benefits.[3] Musical activity in the military embodied these contradictions—encompassing multiple agendas which often conflicted and competed. Individual soldiers, military officials, social reformers, religious welfare organizations, and the commercial music industries each had a stake in the ways music was used in the war but with different ends in mind. Together, they used old and new musical practices to pursue their different aims, the net effect of which was that musical activity was integrated into the large-scale machinery of waging war in ways and to a degree it never had been previously.

Managing Morale

"Why do psychologists who write on army morale never mention music, . . . one of its most important adjuvants?" asked G. Stanley Hall, the prominent American psychologist, in 1920. Calling music an "adjuvant," Hall likened it to a supplemental pharmacological ingredient that increased the efficacy of a principal ingredient. In Hall's view, music was what today's military strategists would call a "force multiplier": an asset amplifying the effect of another asset. Music "makes a good soldier better," Hall wrote, "and a trained soldier a more perfect one." Then, pushing the point further, he suggested that music's effect on morale had material implications for battlefield outcomes. Because of its "power to key up exhausted nerves and muscles," he continued, "music [was] no longer a luxury but a necessity for the soldier."[4]

If, as Hall suggested, psychologists did not see the value of music for military morale, many other contemporaries did. "What goes in through the eyes and ears will come out through the muscles," contended Captain Daniel La Rue. "Martial music will make a jaded column spring to life; the men are no less tired, but new nerve-forces have supervened and made them forget the fatigue," wrote Major General David Shanks.[5] One soldier recalled how a "long, weary hike to the trenches [was] counter-acted by spirited singing," another how breaking into song "seemed to shorten the monotonous miles" on the march. General Hugh L. Scott, commander of Camp Dix, one of the country's largest military bases, ob-served the same physiological phenomenon and explicitly recommended singing as a tool to reenergize the troops.[6] Two years after the war, Major Arthur H. Miller echoed this point in a book-length study of morale, management, and leadership.[7]

Probably no contemporary took the potential of music as a tool to influence troop morale as far as Brigadier General Edward L. Munson, head of the War Department's Morale Branch (established 1918).[8] In his eight-hundred-page treatise, *The Management of Men: A Handbook on the Systemic Development of Morale and the Control of Human Behavior* (1921), Munson discussed repeatedly the benefits music offered as a tool of man-agement. As others did, he noted how music could enliven soldiers who "believ[e] themselves fatigued," but he also went further. For example, he broke down how rhythm could be consciously controlled to coordi-nate and speed up work and described the musical characteristics that made this possible. "In these instances," he wrote, "it is not so much the musical sounds which produce the effect as the tempo in which they occur." Such qualities, he stressed, "[show] why music is a practical aid to efficiency . . . [and] should not be considered merely . . . a concession to entertainment." In his estimation, music was "a basic human craving" that could "be turned to the advantage of military efficiency." With this aim, based on observations from the war, he urged officials not only to permit but to encourage a range of official and informal musical activ-ities, from band concerts to impromptu singing sessions. In a chapter on the subject of recreation, he extolled what musical activity could do "for morale purposes," "influenc[ing] the psychological state" of partic-ipants, with the right musical selection preventing soldiers from being "swayed from the martial to the sentimental, from thoughts of war to those of home."[9]

"Morale," a loosely defined term that encompassed motivation, attitudes about the war, and mental health, was a complex subject without a single agreed-upon definition. It was also a delicate one that sometimes made people uncomfortable. Like digestion, noted Daniel La Rue, morale is "at its best . . . when nothing occurs to make us think of it at all." And this made music especially valuable as a management technique, for it affected morale without naming it. "It would be disgusting to a company of American stalwarts," he wrote, "to hear the announcement, 'Assemble, and I will subject you to influences designed to improve your morale.'" If it seemed to come from above, soldiers would resent it. The best way to enhance morale, La Rue maintained, was to try to manipulate it without explicitly appearing to do so—which music had the power to do seamlessly.[10]

•

Some of the work music was made to do as war matériel grew out of older practices, which reappeared in World War I in updated form, often with a particular twentieth-century emphasis on efficiency. Drums and bugles, for example, directed soldiers when and where to be in camp, on the march, and in battle as they had in the past, but soldiers now had to know a greater number of calls and signals than ever before.[11] Military bands performed much the same function as they had since the Civil War, playing for recruitment events, dress parades and funerals; serenading officers; and giving concerts for civilians and military personnel.[12] In World War I, however, there were proportionately fewer bands, and they were larger than in earlier major conflicts (now with as many as forty-eight musicians each).[13] In addition, bandmasters were now commissioned officers, and many underwent unprecedented formal training at the Army Music School, established in 1911 under the direction of conductor and music educator Frank Damrosch and Captain Arthur Clappé, a graduate of the eminent Royal Military School of Music outside London.

Then, in August 1918, General John J. Pershing, commander of the American forces in Europe, recruited the conductor Walter Damrosch (Frank's brother) to establish a school in Chaumont, France, where the best American bandleaders and musicians could learn from their better-trained French counterparts. "The whole thing is justified on the score of military efficiency," wrote the *New York Times*. "General Pershing recognizes the vital part of music in warfare; . . . French musicians are to teach the Americans for exactly the same reason that French artillery and aviation experts have been training American soldiers." (That school subsequently became the esteemed French Music School for Americans at Fontainebleau.)[14]

Setting the Great War apart from previous military conflicts, however, were numerous musical factors without precedent. One was the proliferation of pianos and phonographs. Both had existed at the time of the Spanish-American War, but only in 1917–18 were they integrated into the military. Pianos popped up here and there in the counterinsurgency in the Philippines, for example, but only in World War I were great pains taken to see that soldiers had access to them. For another thing, musical activity in the armed forces in World War I reflected an intensified commitment by the military to collaboration with civilian and commercial actors. In the course of supplying the bands, for example, the Quartermaster Corps placed the largest sheet music order in history up to that time, from twenty-seven different publishers.[15] Concurrently, partnerships with organizations like the Young Men's Christian Association (YMCA) and the Knights of Columbus made a variety of forms of musical activity available to soldiers far more widely than in the past.

In this context, many civilian and military authorities explained the wartime value of music in practical terms. Books like Shanks's *Management of the American Soldier* and Munson's *The Management of Men* represented the high-water mark for arguments about the power of music to enhance military efficiency. When it came to music, the authors of these books had no moral or aesthetic agenda. They embraced music purely for its potential to aid the military in the effective "control of human behavior" (as the subtitle of Munson's book put it). Along similar lines, the Progressive reformer Luther Gulick argued in *Morals and Morale*, "The use of the military band is not in order that the men may be pleased and entertained with excellent music; it is that the martial spirit may weld the men into a more perfect whole."[16]

Other officials attended not to music's social impact but to its individual effects. Captain Arthur Clappé, for example, cofounder of the Army Music School, agreed with Gulick that the value of music lay not in entertainment, but he was concerned with its ethical implications, arguing that music functioned as a "moral force" in military life.[17] Two generations earlier, in the age of the Civil War, music had been exalted by transcendentalists like John Sullivan Dwight for its capacity to elevate people spiritually, and traces of this argument continued to reverberate. Together, these twinned goals—management and morality, efficiency and uplift—shaped how the wartime military infrastructure came to thrum with musical activity.

Less than two weeks after the United States formally entered what was then known as "the European war," in April 1917, President Woodrow Wilson approved a proposal by his secretary of war Newton D. Baker, an erstwhile Progressive reformer, and Raymond B. Fosdick, a former settlement-house worker who became a well-connected urban reformer himself, to establish a new federal agency responsible for the social well-being of armed forces personnel. As Fosdick recalled in his autobiography, the Commission on Training Camp Activities (CTCA) was launched with the purpose "of rationalizing as far as it can be done the bewildering environments of a war camp."[18] He and Baker saw the camps as laboratories for social engineering and aimed for this new agency not only to enhance the production of spirited, disciplined soldiers and sailors but also to promote wholesome behavior among the troops when off duty. In other words, they sought to steer fighters away from behavior that might lead to venereal disease—a major concern of military authorities—and at the same time they aimed to foster a sense of community which would produce better citizens.[19]

Crucial to their work was a close partnership with social welfare organizations, particularly the YMCA but also, to a lesser degree, the Knights of Columbus, the Young Men's Hebrew Association, and the Jewish Welfare Board. The YMCA, for example, built hundreds of recreational facilities known as "huts" at military camps around the United States, a major purpose of which was to offer doughboys (as the U.S. soldiers were nicknamed) alternatives to drinking and seeking the company of prostitutes. The YMCA also built and operated huts on military bases overseas, where it collaborated directly with the American Expeditionary Forces in Europe, outside the remit of the CTCA. Domestically and abroad, the YMCA was essential to efforts to shape doughboys' character as well as training and supporting them as soldiers.[20]

The leaders of these welfare organizations saw great potential in music to help them realize their goals. Specifically, their aims produced three categories of musical innovation: mass singing; providing access to musical instruments, especially pianos and phonographs; and staging live entertainment. The first of these—mass singing—was the most audacious. Under the direction of Lee F. Hanmer of the Russell Sage Foundation (and earlier a cofounder of the Boy Scouts of America), the CTCA's Camp Music Division recruited (civilian) musicians from around the country to run a music program at each military camp.[21] Working with camp officials, these "song leaders" then directed large groups of soldiers- and sailors-in-training—sometimes an entire camp—in song together. The musical sessions were woven into the daily and weekly schedules at training camps around the United States.

In some instances, song leaders led entire camps in group "sings" fifteen minutes twice per day, once in the morning and again in the evening, involving thousands of troops at once. In others, song leaders might get only a half hour per week per regiment, or they might work with smaller groups to encourage singing at the company or battalion level. And by and large, commanding officers welcomed the song leaders, based on the belief that singing would enhance military morale, efficiency, and discipline. "There is no more potent force in developing unity in an army than that of song," claimed General J. Franklin Bell, commander of Camp Upton, Yaphank, Long Island. "Singing men are fighting men."[22] Most song leaders were male, but at least three women served in this capacity as well. And while most of the CTCA song leaders were white, two African Americans served as song leaders for African American units.[23]

The results could be stirring. "I wish you could hear that crowd sing," wrote Lieutenant Kenneth Gow in a letter to his father about the group sings at his training camp in McCallen, Texas. With attendance averaging from eight to ten thousand men, he wrote, "there is no use in trying to describe [the volume]. I will leave it to your imagination."[24] The photographs shown in figures 3.3 and 3.4 likewise suggest the impressive scale of the mass sings and the social power of coordinating all these bodies and voices at once.

Figure 3.3. This photograph, from Camp McClellan in Alabama, gives a good sense of the scale of the "mass sings."

Figure 3.4. A CTCA song leader in action at the Great Lakes Naval Training Station in Illinois.

In their history of the CTCA, *Keeping Our Fighters Fit for War and After*, Fosdick and coauthor Edward Frank Allen detailed the "distinct military value" of singing, which the War and Navy Departments already recognized as promoting "efficiency." If few military textbooks discussed singing explicitly, the authors noted, such books did "talk a good deal about morale and esprit de corps, on both of which singing has an immense influence." Major General David Shanks exemplified this tendency in his *Management of the American Soldier*. "The morale of armies is the most valuable asset they can have," he wrote, "and the morale of armies is found upon the esprit of individuals."[25]

Launched as early as June 1917, the CTCA built on what was then a widespread pastime around the United States—community singing— but its program stressed music's practical, not aesthetic, value.[26] "Mass Singing," the CTCA noted, "is to be considered primarily not from the musical point of view, which emphasizes a beautiful art product, but from the military . . . point of view, which emphasizes the disciplinary, character-forming, effect upon the men."[27] Such music-making was not to be confused with amusement. "Music is a necessary part of the soldier's equipment—not his entertainment," a writer for the *Chicago Tribune* explained in 1918. "It is more essential than that, although his entertainment is important enough." Elsewhere, the novelist and military music advocate Owen Wister took pains to distinguish the military benefit of singing from its amusement value. "These song leaders of army and navy camp music were . . . at first sometimes confused with the organizers of camp recreation," he wrote in the *New York Times*. "More and more clearly it is becoming understood that both activities . . . have their places. . . . One is for entertainment . . . , while the other is strictly a military measure, and its object to make the soldier a better fighter."[28]

To support such singing, in 1917 the CTCA distributed five hundred thousand copies of a pocket-sized songster, the *Army Song Book*, probably the first such songbook ever issued as a piece of military equipment.[29] With a mix of patriotic airs, hymns, anthems from wars past or related to the military, and a miscellany of popular songs, the purpose of the *Army Song Book* was not merely to promote singing but also to standardize soldiers' repertoire so that men from different camps would have, in the words of a manual for song leaders, a "nucleus of songs they could sing in common." At the same time, it was also to be an agent of Americanization for the nearly one-fifth of the U.S. troops who were foreign-born.[30] "Twice a week the men go to singing school and each patriotic or popular song sung by the men becomes also a lesson in English," noted Captain Bernard Lentz in his pamphlet "The Army as an Americanization Agency."[31]

Mostly, mass singing ended when soldiers left for Europe, but occasionally, it was revived spontaneously overseas, a reflection of the deep impression it made and its capacity to move soldiers emotionally. In a letter to his wife in Wisconsin in September 1918, a Major Lorenz detailed what he characterized as "the most impressive thing I ever experienced in all my life." It occurred as the Thirty-Second Division moved toward battle at the village of Juvigny, France. "That night, when all was settled and darkness was coming, my men camped about 50 yards from me, [and] began singing," he wrote. "I can't describe the sensation. . . . Here was an entire division of over 20,000 troops, camped on the floor of a big forest. In the gloom, one could see horses, mules, trucks, machine guns, artillery and what-not gathered in orderly groups, soldiers everywhere, first in subdued silence. Then groups of men starting to sing together— plaintive, then rollicking, and finally 'On, Wisconsin.' I believe it thrilled everybody within hearing." This impromptu rendition of Wisconsin's de facto state anthem and the whole experience "thrilled" those within earshot, Lorenz believed, its effect amplified for him (and no doubt many others) by the particularity of their circumstances. "Within a few more days many of those standing around would be no more, except in memory."[32]

TEN THOUSAND SINGING SOLDIERS

Figure 3.5. An illustration from the *Army Song Book*, probably the first songbook ever issued by a national government. The caption "TEN THOUSAND SINGING SOLDIERS" reinforces the idea of *mass* singing. The song leader appears in the distance standing above the throng.

Both the War Department and the YMCA had an interest in soldiers' discipline, recreation, and mental well-being, but the two institutions approached these concerns differently, Luther Gulick noted in his 1919 study *Morals and Morale*. The military sought to shape soldiers' behavior through compulsion and restriction, the YMCA through attraction and temptation—extending a carrot in contrast to the military's stick.[33] Making musical instruments—especially pianos and phonographs—widely available was a big part of this effort, and it represented a second major musical initiative of the war after mass singing.

Providing these instruments to soldiers took place through the system of huts that the YMCA built and operated within the military apparatus, both at home and overseas (as well as on ocean transports). Calling these facilities "huts" suggests they were small and ramshackle. In fact, they were fairly large purpose-built structures with multiple interior spaces serving numerous functions. One of their main purposes was providing a flexible space in which soldiers could unwind anytime, serving much as enlisted men's clubs did in World War II and later. In those spaces, YMCA agents provided soldiers with writing paper, books, periodicals, sporting equipment, and—invariably—material for making and listening to music.[34]

Figure 3.6. This picture of a typical "hut," in Angers, France, from exterior, shows that these were neither small nor ramshackle but substantial, purpose-built structures.

Figure 3.7. This photograph of the interior of YMCA Hut No. 7, at Camp Penhoët, St. Nazaire, France, shows a piano at left and phonograph at right.

To the YMCA, the presence of phonographs in these facilities was especially significant. Not only did the organization furnish its huts with these machines (which were, by this time, widely known but not yet ubiquitous in American life), it also took pains to publicize that it was doing so. In at least two instances, shown in figures 3.8 and 3.9, the YMCA issued color postcards depicting groups of doughboys actively enjoying phonographs in the context of their military service. One, showing a group of soldiers listening to a well-stocked pile of records, has the caption "Gathering Around the Phonograph" and features the seal of the YMCA superimposed in the top-left corner.

The other, with captions "LIFE IN THE U.S. ARMY CANTONMENT" and "SOCIAL ROOM, U.S. ARMY, Y.M.C.A.," shows a somewhat larger number of warriors singing (carols, presumably) along with the phonograph in a room adorned with Christmas decorations. The emphasis here is on the active music-making soldiers were involved in (that is, singing), not just on listening. The fact that these were *postcards*, intended for soldiers to send home, underscores their function of publicizing and promoting the musicality of military life.

In some instances, soldiers' hunger for musical equipment exceeded what the YMCA could supply, and other forces stepped in.

Figure 3.8. Postcard showing soldiers listening to a pile of phonograph records, with the caption "Gathering Around the Phonograph." The YMCA's logo appears in the top-left corner.

LIFE IN THE U. S. ARMY CANTONMENT.

SOCIAL ROOM, U. S. ARMY Y. M. C. A.

Figure 3.9. Showing soldiers singing around a phonograph, this postcard emphasizes the doughboys' active involvement in music, as opposed to merely listening.
Its captions read "LIFE IN THE U.S. ARMY CANTONMENT" and "SOCIAL ROOM,
U.S. ARMY, Y.M.C.A." The garlands are red and green, suggesting the soldiers were
probably singing Christmas carols.

For example, Helen Culver Kerr, a wealthy benefactor from New York
City, discreetly donated phonographs, records, pianos, player
pianos, and other musical instruments, as well as sporting goods
like boxing gloves and medicine balls, to nearly two hundred
individual ships of the navy, sixteen hospitals, and nine aviation centers.[35] In another case, the Phonograph Records Recruiting Corps, an
industry-led group masking itself as a citizens' program, launched an
appeal for donations of used records to be sent to the troops, which
resulted in the collection of several hundred thousand discs in the fall
of 1918.[36] The campaign was promoted by the Committee for Public
Information and even had an official Tin Pan Alley song, "When I Hear
That Phonograph Play," the sheet music of which depicted a doughboy's bayonet as a giant phonograph stylus (see figures 3.10 and 3.11).
And when all else failed, a unit of soldiers might take up a collection
and buy a phonograph or even a player piano themselves without any
external aid.[37]

Figure 3.10. With posters like this one, the Committee for Public Information, the government's wartime propaganda agency, supported the private-sector campaign for donations of used phonograph records for the troops. The term "slacker records" suggested that records not sent to soldiers were not "doing their part" in the war effort.

Along with mass singing and providing musical instruments, the third way that the War Department sought to influence doughboys with music was through the staging of live amusements. In close collaboration with the YMCA and numerous partners from the entertainment business, this effort was the forerunner of a similar but larger enterprise by the United Service Organizations (USO) in World War II. "Morale is a state of mind upheld by entertainment," John J. Pershing declared, and substantial resources were dedicated to ensuring suitable

Figure 3.11. "When I Hear That Phonograph Play," the official song of the Phonograph Records Recruiting Corps, published by a leading Tin Pan Alley publishing firm. The soldier is using his bayonet as a stylus.

entertainment was readily available for the troops.[38] This involved several interlocking initiatives. At training camps throughout the U.S., the CTCA established a network of forty-two performance venues called Liberty Theatres, which featured vaudeville acts seven nights a week scheduled by the major national booking agencies. At the insistence of co-organizer Marc Klaw, a theater industry heavyweight, the Liberty

Theatres employed seasoned professional managers, ticketing agents, and so on, and were run according to the same principles as the theaters' commercial counterparts. Ticket prices—between twenty-five and fifty cents—were well below the industry standard, however, in order to make them affordable to the soldiers (whose base monthly pay was around $36). In fact, military officials would have preferred free admission, but because the theater program did not receive congressional funding, it depended on paid tickets to survive. The CTCA also established a system whereby books of tickets could be prepurchased, enabling loved ones at home to buy them for their men in uniform, an arrangement that, over the course of the war, accounted for more than a quarter of the 8.5 million admissions sold.[39] The result was wholesome, high-caliber entertainment—from music to drama to novelty acts—at prices virtually any soldier could afford.

Abroad, live entertainment was furnished by the YMCA's overseas entertainment bureau working directly with the American Expeditionary Forces. This program was launched with great fanfare in the fall of 1917, endorsed by luminaries like Marc Klaw, composer George M. Cohan, and the theater owners and producers Lee, Sam, and Jacob Shubert. Although ultimately this program was less successful than the Liberty Theatres (in part because of bureaucratic impediments to obtaining the necessary visas for performers), the YMCA did present the talent of nearly 1,500 professional American and French entertainers to U.S. soldiers abroad. Thus, the YMCA was probably not exaggerating when it declared this work "the most extensive ever made for any army, in the history of the world."[40]

Another YMCA musical initiative involved mobilizing song leaders to facilitate recreational singing in the huts. Domestically, these YMCA song leaders operated in parallel to and sometimes overlapped with the song leaders of the CTCA, but unlike the latter, the YMCA's representatives also went overseas. In all, according to a postwar report, the YMCA instructed one thousand of its field agents in "the elementary principles of the art," sent two hundred "expert song leaders" to France, and trained more than thirty thousand other "soldier song leaders." Their impact may have been far-reaching, for the YMCA estimated thirty-seven million admissions at huts where "singing was the principal, often only attraction" in 1918 alone. In many cases, these facilities staged competitive "sings," which elevated the level of interest and excitement. "Singing," one field agent found, "is a good thing to get the boys in good spirits and to relieve the tension."[41]

Like the song leaders of the CTCA, those of the YMCA were bedeviled by the wide range of soldiers' backgrounds and were concerned about the implications of this heterogeneity for military effectiveness. This challenge led to a conference in February 1918 after which song leaders worked to standardize the song repertoire so that, in the words of the postwar report, "musical development would be uniform throughout the forces." And like the CTCA song leaders, they "emphatically affirmed the value of music as a factor in military efficiency," which could be maximized by stressing the same songs and methods.

To promote this standardization, the YMCA issued its own songbook, *Popular Songs of the A.E.F.* [American Expeditionary Forces], of which "millions of copies" were distributed gratis. With 142 selections, it was more extensive than the *Army Song Book* compiled by the CTCA, but in many ways, the two books resembled and complemented each other, each with a mix of patriotic airs, war songs, and evergreen ballads. The YMCA volume, though, had more hymns, quite a few current romantic ditties, and, most notably, a greater number of songs growing out of the blackface minstrel tradition. Both collections included "Dixie" and a clutch of Stephen Foster songs, but the YMCA book also included recent Tin Pan Alley compositions romanticizing the antebellum South (e.g., "Back Home in Tennessee": "Banjoes ringing, darkies singing / All this world seems bright") and several pieces by a British songwriter of minstrel songs, Alfred Scott-Gatty (e.g., "De Ringtail'd Coon").[42]

Although the YMCA ostensibly sought to serve all doughboys, its record with regard to the military's 350,000 African American soldiers was uneven. In some instances, YMCA secretaries and white soldiers accepted and included Black soldiers in their facilities and programs, but in many others, especially at training camps in the South, African Americans were relegated to separate facilities or excluded altogether. An investigation by Walter H. Loving, erstwhile leader of the Philippine Constabulary Band and by then a major in the Military Intelligence Division, found in 1918 that "colored soldiers have been stationed in this camp [Camp Humphreys, in Fairfax County, Virginia] since the first days of its opening, and so far, the YMCA has not given a single building for their use." By contrast, Black troops were welcomed at the facilities sponsored by the Knights of Columbus and the Young Men's Hebrew Association.[43] Other reports confirmed Loving's findings that the YMCA frequently disregarded the needs of Black soldiers or provided them with inferior facilities. A photograph in the YMCA archives suggests much the same, showing a segregated hut for African American soldiers in which a piano—a standard piece of equipment in the huts of white soldiers—is conspicuously absent (see figure 3.12).[44]

Figure 3.12. Unlike a typical hut for white troops, this hut for Black soldiers at Camp Travis, Texas, had a phonograph (barely visible in the rear) but not a piano.

Figure 3.13. The YMCA supported stage shows that soldiers put on, from musical theater to minstrel shows. Visible in the front row here is a troupe of performers in blackface in a YMCA facility.

Figure 3.14. This photograph of the "Company H Minstrels" from Camp Upton, Yaphank, Long Island, 1918, suggests that blackface minstrel shows were a regular part of soldiers' entertainment.

Although some restricted facilities in Europe were opened to Black troops after the armistice, by and large musical activity in the YMCA huts sent a different signal. When soldiers gathered at "the Y" on Sunday nights for an evening of song, minstrel tunes were likely part of the mix. They were in the songbook, and the YMCA regularly supplied doughboys with equipment to put on minstrel shows, including burnt cork, wigs, costumes, and props (see figure 3.13). Together, these suggest how commonplace racist caricature was in the YMCA's work. The YMCA was not particularly unusual in this way, but neither was its record better than those of most contemporary organizations.[45]

The Redemption of Listening

From the managerial perspective, what mattered most about musical activity was ends, not means. "Less attention is paid to the matter of what the men sing than to the more important consideration *that* they sing," noted the head of the CTCA, Raymond Fosdick.[46] But explaining musical activity in the American military only from the managerial perspective gives little idea of the social experience of music for soldiers themselves. Whether they were in the U.S. or overseas, doughboys sang, played instruments, and listened to music in relation to a broader field of wartime sounds, both military and civilian. In this respect, the war existed in, and as, sound everywhere from the battlefield to the home front, forming a backdrop for soldiers' musical activities.[47]

Domestically, the war was audible in the outpouring of martial and nationalistic songs across the United States leading up to and, especially, after the American entry into the war in April 1917. According to the chief bibliographer of the Library of Congress, more than three thousand such songs were penned and published in the two years the country fought in World War I, an output more than twice as large as those of all the other warring nations combined from 1914 to 1918.[48] The biggest songs—above all, George M. Cohan's "Over There"—were not only widely recorded and widely sung during the war; they also remained staples of the American vernacular repertoire long after. In a sense, the war was audible too in the considerable number of antiwar songs written and published in this era, but generally these were drowned out by the wave of prowar numbers that broke over the country, especially after the spring of 1917.

At many public gatherings, from sporting events to theatrical performances, it also became de rigueur to sing "The Star-Spangled Banner," sometimes with severe reprisals for nonconformity. At a Victory Loan pageant in Washington, DC, a man was shot in the back three times for refusing to stand when the anthem was played. The following day the *Washington Post* reported that "the crowd burst into cheering and hand-clapping" as the victim collapsed. On concert stages, German composers were scrubbed from the repertoire, and when the Boston Symphony Orchestra's renowned German-born conductor Karl Muck was (falsely) accused of refusing to include "The Star-Spangled Banner" on his program, he was arrested and jailed.[49] As millions of young men entered the military during the war, they would have known that, in various forms, music gave voice to the nation's martial spirit.

Once in the service, soldiers also learned that the war existed in the sounds of the battlefield, which was then undergoing epochal change. The sonic environment of combat had always been cacophonous, but no precedent existed for the aural violence produced by the weapons of the Great War. "The noise resolved itself into surf and tides of sound," one soldier recalled:

> It was impossible to pick out where it began or what [became] of it. One heard dimly the crack of one's own guns. For the rest there was an oppressive beating upon breast and ears, resolving itself now and then into a million coordinated echoes somewhat reminiscent of an express train plunging through a tunnel.[50]

In its most extreme forms, this surfeit of sound contributed to a new psychological disorder—shell shock, a condition comparable to what is today known as post-traumatic stress disorder (PTSD)—a form of trauma from which some soldiers never recovered. At these outer limits, sonic excess was not merely frightening but hazardous. Noise was invisible but could leave lasting scars.[51] Indeed, virtually every aspect of this conflict placed new emphasis on hearing and listening. While a great many writers had written about the noisiness of modernity—particularly in relation to urbanization and industrialization—the roaring, screeching, crashing sounds of the Great War were a thing apart.[52] These were the cultural and acoustic conditions within which doughboys' musical practices took shape.

•

The war changed listening: soldiers on the front lines were always on alert, "all ears" all the time, for better or worse.[53] Music, however, redeemed listening. At least for a moment. Musical activity reversed the valence of soldiers' acute auditory attentiveness from fear to pleasure, from dread to desire. It embodied sounds that belonged to a creative process, not a destructive one.

In this spirit, a group of soldiers in the 305th Infantry valued music so much that they went to extraordinary lengths in the trenches to procure their daily "ration." Cut off from the daily band concerts they had grown accustomed to at regimental headquarters, they listened instead by telephone. "However poor the [food] rations may have seemed at times, they didn't stop our daily music ration," the regiment's historian recalled:

> The boys in the trenches needed aesthetic enjoyment and Corporal Kosak of the Signal Platoon set out to provide it. Daily at three the band played at Regimental Headquarters in Hablainville. To relay this music forward to the trenches was a problem easily solved. At that particular hour the Corporal would call each Battalion Signal Detachment, and had them listen on the telephone while the band played. As the musicians were stationed directly beneath the room in which the switchboard was located, the melodies were audibly transmitted over the wire. For a long time, these sessions continued, and the lieutenant in charge wondered as to why and wherefore of all the connections on the switchboard.

With aural input from afar, these soldiers superseded their immediate sonic circumstances—if not displacing them altogether at least temporarily supplanting their totalizing dominance. Through the telephone lines, these doughboys accessed what the music scholar Josh Kun has called an "audiotopia," a utopia in which music is experienced not just as sound heard in the ears and felt in the body but also "as a space that we can enter into, encounter, move around in, inhabit, be safe in." For those doughboys, music was an idealized and unreachable space "to be safe in," far from the raw violence of the battlefield.[54]

Soldiers away from the front lines valued music at least as much as those in the trenches. "If you want to help win the war send me some phonograph records," wrote pilot Elliott White Springs to his father from London in 1918. Although he meant this remark playfully, its underlying message was serious. Music did important work to keep soldiers going, everywhere from huts to hospitals. A postwar report evokes the musicality of a typical YMCA facility so clearly that it warrants quoting at length:

> Through the haze of tobacco smoke came the sound of a piano, where perhaps a real musician might be playing Beethoven or Chopin, or with equal probability some one who called his playing "banging the box" would be pounding out the latest jazz success from Broadway. Perhaps a group would be lustily singing "The Long, Long Trail" or "Pull Your Shade Down, Mary Ann." Not always harmonizing, a phonograph in another corner would be grinding out records without intermission. Around the fireplace a group might be vociferously discussing the prospects of favorite teams in the professional baseball leagues or the last game in an inter-battalion series. By the big map of France on the wall, a soldier, newspaper in hand, would be locating the latest fluctuation of the battle-line in France, or sticking a flagged pin into the dot that represented his home on the map of the United States. Meanwhile, oblivious to the noise, men were writing letters at the tables, others reading the books and magazines liberally provided by the American Library Association and others intent upon the next move on a checker board.

Notable here is the variety of musical activity, the juxtaposition of piano playing, singing, and phonograph use, not to mention background listening. Even those who were "oblivious to the noise" were listeners too, practicing a variation on the subtle, discriminating listening practices that contributed to survival on the battlefield (see figure 3.15).[55]

Another place music was prized was hospitals, where bands occasionally played concerts but which more often had phonographs.[56] One nurse wrote, "We have a phonograph with a rasping voice that plays from morning to night. The soldiers . . . are so used to noise that they don't seem happy without it." Although this account comes from a Canadian nurse,

Figure 3.15. This "social room" in the YMCA hut at Camp Dix, New Jersey, had a grand piano, the playing of which may have been entertaining even to those troops who appeared not to be paying attention.

soldiers of all nationalities seem to have reacted similarly.[57] When an American nurse serving in a French army hospital in 1916 got her hands on a phonograph, she wrote, "We worked those records as they had never been worked before, and with such joyous results." The British poet Eva Dobell, who served as a nurse in the war, described this same phenomenon with particular vividness:

> Through the long ward the gramophone
>   Grinds out its nasal melodies:
> "Where did you get that girl?" it shrills.
>   The patients listen at their ease,
> Through clouds of strong tobacco-smoke:
>   The gramophone can always please.
>
> The Welsh boy has it by his bed,
>   (He's lame—one leg was blown away.)
> He'll lie propped up with pillows there,
>   And wind the handle half the day.
> His neighbour, with the shattered arm,
>   Picks out the records he must play.

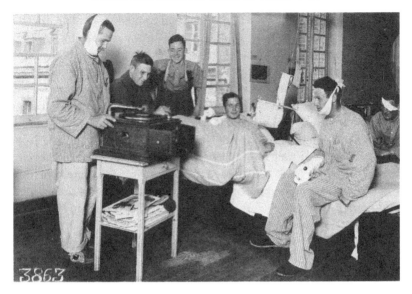

Figure 3.16. Whatever these wounded American and British soldiers are listening to in an army hospital in Évreux, France, in 1917 or 1918, it appears to be enlivening their spirits.

As if to illustrate the scene that Dobell described, a U.S. War Department photograph from an American army hospital in Évreux, France, shows American and British soldiers around a phonograph. The official caption gives no indication of what they are listening to, but whatever the music is, it appears to be enlivening their spirits (see figure 3.16).[58]

These effects of music in hospitals did not go unnoticed by contemporaries, but at that time, it was largely seen as a novelty. In *The Management of Men*, Brigadier General Edward Munson characterized its impact as "almost therapeutic." Little more than two decades later, the use of music in hospitals in World War II would become the basis for the modern field of music therapy.[59]

Repertoire

When listening to records, doughboys were at the mercy of what discs were available and intact. Supply was inconsistent, often dependent on donations from home, while the records (and machines) were fragile, liable both to breaking and wearing out. When it came to singing, however, soldiers had much greater control. Officials like Raymond Fosdick insisted that the act of singing mattered more than what soldiers sang, but from the doughboys' perspective, what the songs were mattered a great deal.

To some extent, the War Department attempted to standardize the doughboys' repertoire by providing them with songbooks, giving them a body of songs they all knew when a song leader stood before them for a session of organized singing. Away from official song leaders, however, which songs doughboys chose and how they sang them was up to their own discretion. Even when soldiers bristled at compulsory martial singing, as some did, many still sang for their own enjoyment, as in John Dos Passos's 1921 debut novel, *Three Soldiers*, based on his own wartime experiences. When they sang informally, their repertoire was mutable, as were the uses to which it was put. In such cases, soldiers valued and benefited from having a common pool of songs to draw on, but they also modified these songs, improvising as they saw fit. Sometimes this could mean silly parodies ("It's a Long Way to Tipperary" became "That's the Wrong Way to Tickle Mary," or "Over There" was remade as "Underwear").[60] Other times, however, they used songs to talk about and comment on their material and emotional circumstances.

Some insight into this practice comes from psychologist G. Stanley Hall, who analyzed the singing preferences of American soldiers according to a detailed questionnaire he sent to song leaders. For one thing, he noted, doughboys steered clear of patriotic and martial anthems. "Our soldiers are inclined to take patriotism for granted," he

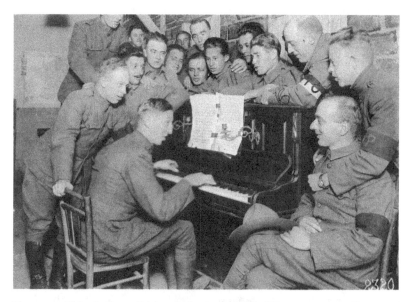

Figure 3.17. This photograph taken in the American Red Cross canteen at Chateauroux, France, evokes the popularity of informal singing.

found, "and are not especially fond of singing about it."[61] Instead, Hall found, they generally preferred recent or current popular songs; their repertoires varied from camp to camp, and they often took "great liberties" with music and words. American fighters embraced "songs . . . of all grades of merit and a wide range of sentiment dealing with every petty detail of the soldier's life," Hall wrote, "which our doughboys so love to see in a musical mirror." He then proceeded to break down the kind emotional work that he understood various oft-sung songs to be doing: "Where Do We Go from Here?" marked deeds accomplished, the pressure for greater heroics, and a spirit of subjection; "I Don't Care Where They Send Me" voiced a kind of fatalistic submission and obedience; and "Keep the Home Fires Burning" represented a souvenir of home, the defense of which became a fundamental war aim. Perhaps the most popular of all popular songs among the troops was "There's a Long, Long Trail," which he characterized as an expression of yearning, fate, and pathos.[62]

Hall's informants, the song leaders, may have obscured as much as they revealed, however. Soldiers expressed other feelings through singing as well, and used songs for other purposes, outside of song leaders' earshot. Modifying and rewriting lyrics as they wanted, doughboys also used music to air grievances and to perform a kind of ostentatious, hypersexualized masculinity, a long-standing feature of military culture. One grievance was dissatisfaction over wages. According to Elsie Janis, an entertainer who performed widely for American soldiers overseas, "a *strong favorite* in the A.E.F." was the "The Pay Roll," sung to the tune of "Battle Hymn of the Republic," with "Glory, glory, hallelujah / His truth is marching on" replaced by

> All we do is sign the pay roll,
> All we do is sign the pay roll,
> All we do is sign the pay roll,
> And we never get a G—d—— cent![63]

Not only did these lyrics critique an issue of individual concern, when sung aloud and in a group they also expressed solidarity.

A more candid sense of what soldiers sang was suggested by folklorist Ed Cray, who noted that many of the countless verses of "Mademoiselle from Armentières" (a.k.a. "Hinky Dinky Parlez-Vous?"), one of the doughboys' unofficial anthems, were risqué or pornographic but went unrecorded in favor of the more polite verses.[64] For the same reason, few sources acknowledged the popularity of "The Fucking Machine" (a.k.a. "The Big Wheel"), a song Cray characterized as having been "property of every man in uniform" by the war's end. To the tune of a hymn, "One Hundred," soldiers sang:

> A sailor told me before he died—
> I know not whether the bastard lied—
> He had a wife with a twat so wide
> That she could never be satisfied.
>
> So he fashioned out a big fucking wheel,
> Attached it to a big prick of steel.
> Made two balls and filled them with cream,
> And the whole fucking thing was run by steam.
>
> 'Round and 'round went the big fucking wheel,
> In and out went the big prick of steel.
> Till at last the maiden cried,
> "Enough, enough! I'm satisfied."
>
> But here is a case of the biter bit:
> There was no way of stopping it.
> The maiden was torn from twat to teat,
> And the whole fucking thing went up in shit.[65]

In this crude tale of female annihilation, doughboys celebrated a masculine identity indifferent to—indeed, finding humor in—mechanized sexual violence, perhaps an understandable posture for young men in the maelstrom of mechanized violence themselves.

A humorous anecdote recounted by Private Alfred "Red" Ettinger illustrates the tension between soldiers' vulgar repertoire and the conventions of propriety and patriotism. "Our regiment loved to sing on the march," he began. "To say our songs were risqué would be putting it mildly. They were as bawdy as the collective imaginations of 3,000 horny men could conceive." On the final day of their journey to Exermont, France, they broke into song "at the top of their lungs" as they marched into their staging positions. Then, he recalled, "I happened to look up, and there was Father Duffy standing on a bluff at the side of the road, giving his benediction to the troops as we were 'banging away on Lulu.' . . . He didn't care what we were singing, as long as we were alive and singing." The comic twist, however, was still to come:

> Some weeks later in the hospital at Allerey, I picked up an issue
> of the *Literary Gazette*, and there was a beautiful photograph of

Father Duffy with arms outstretched in benediction as the regiment filed below. The caption read: "Father Francis P. Duffy, regimental chaplain of the 165th New York Infantry, blesses his troops as they march into battle singing 'Onward Christian Soldiers.'"[66]

Few extant sources contrast the actual and the bowdlerized as pointedly. So great was the diversity and so rich the inventiveness of the soldiers' singing that John Jacob Niles, a veteran of the U.S. Army Air Service and later a well-known folklorist, singer, and composer, compiled two anthologies of songs which contrasted sharply with the songbooks of the CTCA and the YMCA. *Singing Soldiers* (1927) collected songs specifically of African American troops, while *The Songs My Mother Never Taught Me* (1929, coedited with composer Douglas S. Moore) sought to broaden Niles's remit and to correct the impression that the Black troops "were the only soldiers who sang anything original." Both books presented singing in generally jocular terms, but the thrust of the two anthologies was serious. According to the foreword of the latter volume, these songs "revealed thoughts that would otherwise have died unspoken . . . [and] told a tale the histories [would] try to untell for a good many years." That is, they showed the war not as an ideological crusade and a chance for adventure, as the official repertoire suggested, but rather as dirty, unpleasant, and rife with irony and contradiction.[67]

This came through with special clarity in the songs of Black soldiers. Notwithstanding Niles's own casual racism and the racist caricatures adorning many of the song entries (drawn by former *Stars and Stripes* cartoonist A. A. Wallgren), the anthologies demonstrated how Black fighters especially used song as an instrument of disapproval and critique:

> I don't know why I totes dis gun,
> Tell me, oh, tell me now.
> I don't know why I totes dis gun,
> 'Cause I ain't got nothin' 'gainst de Hun,
> Tell me now, oh, tell me now.

White troops, like Black ones, Niles noted, did not think much of the war, but in his experience they tended not to sing about it as much. For Black soldiers, songs constituted a persistent critical discourse on the war, military life, and what Niles called "embarrassing questions" for the War Department.[68]

Conversely, in at least one case, Black troops expressed their resentment by *not* singing. On Thanksgiving evening in 1918 near Metz, France, a month after the 369th Infantry Regiment was awarded the Croix de

Guerre by the French government for its valorous service in combat, the unit refused an order to sing "My Country, 'Tis of Thee." As journalist Roi Ottley recounted the incident, with the music of the band booming, the three thousand Black fighters who comprised the 369th "stood silent with grim and sober faces," having suffered continual indignities under the American command. "From all that great assemblage," Ottley noted, "rose only the voices of the regiment's six white officers!"[69]

The African American musical activity that generated the most discussion was not singing, however. It was the music of the bands of the segregated Black units, which introduced jazz to Europe. The most famous of these outfits, Lieutenant James Reese Europe's 369th Infantry Harlem Hellfighters Band, involved numerous musicians, including Europe himself, who had helped shape the music scene in pre–Jazz Age New York, accompanying the influential dance pioneers Vernon and Irene Castle, among other engagements. Playing everything from Negro spirituals to W. C. Handy's "Memphis Blues" to a jazzed-up arrangement of "La Marseillaise," the 369th Infantry Band dazzled both French audiences— fueled by a fascination with American popular culture and African primitivism and a hunger for a wartime emotional release—and American doughboys alike. To be sure, Black military bands had existed earlier,

Figure 3.18. James Reese Europe and the band of the 369th Infantry playing near a hospital in January 1919. The original caption reads: "Lieut. Europe's negro band entertaining convalescent American soldiers on the old race track at Auteuil. The negro musicians have been in great demand."

in the Civil War and the Spanish-American War, but not until 1909 did they perform under the supervision of Black bandleaders.[70] This had long-term consequences. Jim Europe was a bandleader par excellence as well as an outstanding manager and organizer, and his group's many public performances in France reverberated culturally long after the war had ended.[71]

Europe's band was, however, only one of more than two dozen Black army bands in World War I. Notable too was Will Vodery's 807th Pioneer Infantry Regiment Band, which was detached from its regiment and became the First Army Headquarters Battalion Post Band, a position secured by beating out four other (white) regimental bands. Vodery's group performed all over France, including once for French President Raymond Poincaré, who praised them lavishly. After the armistice, Vodery attended the military's bandmasters' school at Chaumont, where he was the only person of African descent among forty bandmasters, selected from 162 applicants.[72] Other important Black bandleaders included Egbert E. Thompson, who, like Europe, came out of the New York 15th National Guard; A. J. Thomas, who hailed from the Baltimore-Washington area; and J. Tim Brymn, whose band one contemporary described as "a military symphony engaged in a battle of jazz."[73] With one hundred musicians, Brymn's band was reportedly the largest musical unit of any of the belligerents in World War I. In an editorial in the *Crisis*, the monthly magazine of the NAACP, W. E. B. Du Bois, who sailed to Europe in February 1919 to observe the Paris Peace Conference, evoked a stirring performance by Brymn's band in a small town near Nancy:

> In France. . . . Tim Brimm [*sic*] was playing by the town pump. Tim Brimm and the bugles of Harlem blared in the little streets of Maron in far Lorraine. The tiny streets were seas of mud. Dank mist and rain sifted through the cold air above the blue Moselle. Soldiers—soldiers everywhere—black soldiers, boys of Washington, Alabama, Philadelphia, Mississippi. Wild and sweet and wooing leapt the strains upon the air. French children gazed in wonder—women left their washing. Up in the window stood a black Major, a Captain, a Teacher, and I—with tears behind our smiling eyes. Tim Brimm was playing by the town-pump.

In general, the best of these bands performed at military ceremonies; gave open-air concerts for civilians and private ones for top brass, politicians, and royalty; and played at hospitals and rest areas as well. Larger bands were frequently broken up into smaller groups to perform jazz or vaudeville shows too, often including comedy and song-and-dance numbers.[74] France's love affair with jazz began with these performances.

•

"The man who disparages music as a luxury and non-essential is doing the nation an injury," President Woodrow Wilson proclaimed during the war. "Music, now more than ever before, is a national need."[75] By the close of the war, music was recognized as having greater social importance than perhaps at any other time in the nation's history. The *Etude*, the leading magazine of music educators in the United States, wrote, "Never before has our art stood so high in the minds and hearts of the people." *Musical Quarterly* concurred, finding that "the war was the best thing which ever happened to music." Some of this elevated standing reflected the proliferation of musical activity on the home front—community singing, performances by phonograph stars at war bond rallies, public singing of "The Star-Spangled Banner," and so on. But the home front paralleled and complemented musical activity in the military, from group singing to recreational piano and phonograph playing. At times, the musical cultures of the military and the home front overlapped, as with the soldier show *Yip Yip Yaphank*, written by Sergeant Irving Berlin, which moved from Camp Upton on Long Island to Broadway.[76] Seen as an aid to morale, efficiency, and group cohesion, music became an explicit area of concern for the War Department in World War I, in a marked departure from the more informal music practices that had taken shape during the Civil War and the Spanish-American War.

Indeed, much had changed since those earlier conflicts, and many of those differences had far-reaching ramifications. There were new styles of music and new technologies for playing and listening, and by the 1910s, music constituted an essential component of an enormous emergent cultural apparatus.[77] At the same time, as an instrument of war, music continued to function dialectically, as it had before, a means by which the state trained and maintained citizens to kill enemy combatants and by which rank-and-file soldiers coped with the physical, psychological, and emotional stresses of military service. Whether they understood music as a tool of Progressive reform or purely on utilitarian grounds, many military officials embraced musical activity as a valuable management technique. For their part, doughboys used music time and again to reclaim some control over the conditions they found themselves in, from training camp to the trenches, even provisionally and momentarily.

The military did not achieve this by itself. Rather, it relied on partnerships with civilian social service organizations like the YMCA, the entertainment business, volunteer song leaders, and countless citizens who donated to phonograph and record drives. This convergence, however, rested on a delicate balance of factors, and if the value and utility of music for managing soldiers seemed self-evident by the time of the armistice, its status in the military was far from settled. In his pioneering 1921 treatise on military morale, Brigadier General Edward L. Munson wrote extensively about music and claimed that "mass singing [is] now recognized as a military measure."[78] Yet in the interwar years, a sea change took place in American popular culture brought about by the growth of the radio, film, and phonograph industries. By the time of the run-up to World War II, public singing had largely fallen out of favor. To be sure, musical activity among the troops would remain vitally important in World War II, but it assumed altogether new forms. And unlike in World War I, when music had been the responsibility of civilian groups working with the military, in World War II, as we shall see, this responsibility became centralized in the military itself.

CHAPTER FOUR

The Best-Entertained Soldier in the World

At the end of a grand luncheon at the Waldorf Astoria Hotel in New York in December 1945, Major General Joseph W. Byron stood up before the black-tie guests—a mix of "big men of affairs" (as one journalist put it) and pillars of the world of show business. "Today," Byron declared in his crisp, nasal voice, "the American soldier is the best entertained soldier of any army in the world." Much of the credit for this, he asserted, was due the event's guest of honor, Abe Lastfogel, a diminutive, cigar-chomping theatrical booking agent who was now president of USO–Camp Shows, Inc., an organization that had provided high-quality live entertainment to millions of military personnel in the recently ended war. On every continent but Antarctica, performances by stars great and small had buoyed the spirits of American G.I.s, keeping them going through fear, discomfort, boredom, and every other feeling that life in the military involved. So highly did the government value Lastfogel's contributions to the fight against the Axis that Byron then bestowed on him the Medal of Freedom "for meritorious achievement which aided the United States in the prosecution of the war against the enemy"—a newly minted honor created by President Harry Truman. Never before had national security and the popular entertainment industry been so intimately intertwined.[1]

Remarkably, however, the work of USO–Camp Shows, Inc., represented only one component of the public-private apparatus that made American soldiers "the best entertained . . . in the world." From stage shows to songbooks, pianos to kazoos, G.I.s had more access to music than the soldiers of any other belligerent in World War II—or any other army in history, for that matter. In retrospect, these initiatives marked the apex of efforts to mobilize music for purposes of waging war. In both scale and scope, what the War and Naval Departments did with music in World War II was unprecedented, and never again would so many resources and so much energy be put to this purpose. Certainly the governments of other countries took steps to entertain their soldiers in World War II and other conflicts, but no other nation had the cultural and economic capacity the United States did in the mid-twentieth century, encompassing both the vast commercial entertainment business churning out an endless stream of music, movies, and radio programs and the industrial infrastructure to manufacture everything from pianos to phonographs to radio sets for the troops.

This chapter concerns the extraordinary steps the U.S. military took to use music to advance the American war effort in the Second World War. It focuses on musical activity and entertainment put in place *for* soldiers, whereas the next chapter will turn to music and entertainment *by* soldiers. Expanding on arrangements from World War I, the government worked closely with private-sector partners and social welfare organizations to transform how, where, and to what end musical activity in the military occurred. The cultural and logistical landscape in which this happened differed sharply from that of 1917–18. Despite the popularity of mass singing in World War I, enthusiasm for it waned in the interwar period, when the United States increasingly became a nation of cultural *consumers*, accustomed to a steady diet of Hollywood films, network radio programs, and recorded music. Moreover, with sixteen million service personnel (including 350,000 women), the U.S. military was nearly four times the size it had been in World War I and represented a greater cross section of American society than in any previous conflict. When it came to recreation, these fighters had tastes and expectations more complex and diverse than ever before.[2]

Satisfying soldiers' needs and preferences was complicated by the immense size of the war, which was fought in theaters all around the globe, in countless different sonic environments. To accommodate these novel conditions, the military extended or modified older practices and invented new ones from whole cloth. The result was a host of music programs designed to meet these unique circumstances. Never before had a nation at war organized such a culturally rich and technologically sophisticated musical supply line, based on a global distribution network unprecedented in its speed, reach, and complexity. In World War II, the armed forces sought to use music to maintain soldiers' connections to home, including keeping them current on all the hit songs, no matter where in the world they were. As far as military officials were concerned, much was at stake in whether or not those efforts to connect life in the service to civilian life at home succeeded.

The Musical Apparatus

Music was not literally a weapon for the U.S. military in World War II. It did not directly inflict harm on the personnel or matériel of the nation's enemies. But American officials recognized that the musical life of the military could have profound implications for the strength of the armed forces, affecting the emotional, psychological, and physical readiness of the soldiery and the rehabilitation of warriors wounded and traumatized in the line of duty. Consequently, they threaded music into the fabric of military service in a wide variety of ways, which together made musical activity an extensive part of how the war was waged.

Responsibility for these musical initiatives fell under two newly created military entities. First, in 1940, the War Department established a Morale Division, which was renamed the Special Services Division (SSD) in 1943 as some military officials came to believe the term *morale* could be perceived as patronizing and should be avoided as much as possible. A major component of the Morale Division was the Music Section (later renamed the Music Branch), led by Lieutenant Colonel Howard C. Bronson, who came to the job with a robust skill set and extensive résumé.[3] A former army bandleader in World War I, Bronson had also been, as a civilian, a clarinetist in John Philip Sousa's band, an executive of a musical instrument company, a composer, and an arranger. Despite his personal penchant for traditional military music, Bronson oversaw the organization and administration of a diverse slate of programs, using every available resource and technology. (The navy, marines, and coast guard had their own equivalents of the army's Morale Division, but these were smaller and less influential, and they often followed the army's lead.)[4]

Second, in 1941, the Office of the Federal Security Administrator created a special body to coordinate and advise on programs of the army, navy, and other government and private agencies related to the welfare of the troops. Designated the Joint Army and Navy Committee on Welfare and Recreation, it was made up of seven subcommittees, one of which was dedicated to music and operated under the leadership of Harold Spivacke, chief of the Music Division of the Library of Congress. A respected and influential figure in the music world, Spivacke was a man of catholic musical interests eager to promote musical activity in as many forms as possible.[5] The nondescript, bureaucratic names of these two agencies obscures the rich and complex contributions they made to the war effort. Together, Bronson's Music Section and Spivacke's music subcommittee worked tirelessly to foster and advance formal and informal practices of music-making and listening, to the satisfaction of both top brass and rank-and-file warriors.

Despite their broad mandates, these two offices initially had to contend with what appeared to be a diminished commitment to music in the military compared to that of World War I. Some officials, for example, questioned the value of military bands. "You aren't going to win the war with piccolos," one scoffed.[6] Indeed, the Music Section had to make do with extremely limited supplies and staff at the outset, struggling even to get the use of a part-time typist. Eventually, the personnel shortage abated, but staffing was never commensurate to the group's myriad duties. Moreover, after the decline of the community singing movement in the 1920s, support for mass "sings" in training camps dried up, and some commanding officers now viewed singing while marching in training exercises as disruptive and distracting. Although Rear Admiral Chester Nimitz issued a circular encouraging large-scale group singing in the navy in the spring of 1941, after the U.S. entered the war later that year, such calls mostly disappeared.[7]

By numerous other measures, however, the military's enthusiasm for musical activity had grown stronger than ever. The steps it took to promote singing and instrumental music-making made this clear. In March 1941, before the United States formally entered the war, the War Department began publishing and distributing a revised edition of the *Army Song Book*, a copy of which was supposed to be issued to every new soldier. First published during World War I, it contained patriotic airs ("The Star-Spangled Banner," "America the Beautiful"), service songs ("The Caissons Go Rolling Along," "You're in the Army Now"), popular songs of earlier wars ("Dixie" and "The Battle Hymn of the Republic" from the Civil War, "The Monkeys Have No Tails" from the Philippines, "Pack up Your Troubles in Your Old Kit Bag" and "It's a Long Way to Tipperary" from World War I), and a miscellany of "old favorites" ("Auld Lang Syne," "Casey Jones"). In contrast with its World War I predecessor, whose cover showed only the title, in all capital letters without any adornment, the 1941 songbook featured a cartoon drawing of various figures (a soldier, a statesman, a frontiersman, etc.) joining together in song—a subtle but real indication of the military's greater efforts to keep soldiers amused when they were not fighting (see figures 4.1 and 4.2). This songbook was also published in two versions, one that was small enough to fit into a shirt pocket, with only words for singers; the other larger, with notated music for piano accompaniment. Ultimately, the goal of putting a copy in the hands of every soldier was never achieved, but millions of copies were distributed during the war. The *Army Song Book* also became a model for similar collections, such as the *Navy Song Book* and the *Women's Army Corps Song Book*.[8]

Efforts by the military to equip soldiers with songs did not end there. To scratch G.I.s' itch for popular music, the Music Section sent out a monthly circular called the *Army Hit Kit* from March 1943 on, with lyrics to six (later nine) new songs each month, usually a mix of current titles and older hits, and often including a featured song from one of America's allies that was printed in English translation, original language,

Figures 4.1 and 4.2. Covers of the 1918 and 1941 editions of the *Army Song Book*. The shift from a plain, nondescript cover to one featuring a cartoon illustration on it reflected the military's more self-conscious efforts to provide amusement for soldiers in World War II.

and phonetic transcription. Produced in collaboration with the commercial music publishers who waived their copyright fees, the *Hit Kit* had an initial distribution of 1 million lyrics-only editions and 25,000 music folios, with subsequent mailings swelling to 2.6 million lyrics-only editions, nearly 80,000 music folios, and 3,500 copies of orchestra and band arrangements by June 1944. By the war's end, the program had been extended to include the navy as well.[9]

The army also took steps to see that the songs were sung. To enhance the *Hit Kit*'s appeal, its cover featured a humorous cartoon drawing or, occasionally, a picture of a scantily clad woman (figure 4.3). Further, the actual singing of the songs was sometimes promoted by designated song leaders who were "planted" in military units to initiate singing spontaneously. Doing so, a Music Section report noted, "eliminates any thought or feeling of compulsion on the part of the men and when they join in (which they are sure to do, provided the song is of the right kind and in a good key) it will be done whole-heartedly and with real feeling."[10] The army's goal, in other words, was to seduce the G.I.s into singing, not coerce them.

The work of the Music Section went far beyond the *Army Song Book* and the *Hit Kit*, however. It also encompassed distributing musical instruments to soldiers. Some of these were small—harmonicas, ocarinas, ukuleles, and a kind of flute made of unbreakable plastic called a tonette—and were made available to soldiers, along with instruction guides for playing them, to the great satisfaction of some G.I.s and the annoyance of others (see figure 4.5). More complicated—though more popular—was getting G.I.s access to *large* musical instruments, including pianos. To make this happen, the Music Section worked with the nation's leading piano producer, Steinway & Sons, whose manufacturing operations were almost completely converted to making gliders for the military during the war but which managed to design, produce, and sell to the government a special type of piano suitable for use by soldiers and sailors in the field. This was the Steinway "Victory" model, known informally as the Olive Drab Government Issue (ODGI) field piano because each instrument for the army was painted green to match the color of all other government-issued equipment, from underwear to tanks. Instruments sold to the navy were painted gray or blue.[11]

The distinctiveness of these pianos did not end with their color. These were forty-inch-tall uprights without legs, looking like a big box with a shelf sticking out, outfitted with keys made of celluloid instead of ivory (which often peeled off in tropical conditions), inside of which the steel bass strings were wrapped with soft iron in lieu of copper, a restricted

Figure 4.3. Most *Army Hit Kit* covers had cartoons on them, but occasionally there were other designs, like this one, from March 1944, featuring the image of an ornamental, ditzy ("GEE, IF I COULD ONLY SING!" she says), scantily clad woman. The lower left-hand corner also indicates it was "for use by the U.S. Armed Forces only" and "NOT FOR SALE."

Figures 4.4 and 4.5. Military publicity photographs showing soldiers singing and learning to play small musical instruments.

material. Each instrument weighed some five hundred pounds and was transported in a custom-designed olive-green packing case with four handles for carrying and also containing a set of tuning tools, spare parts, a book of instructions, and some sheet music that ranged from simple Protestant hymns to advanced boogie-woogie. By the time the war ended, Steinway had sold approximately 2,500 of these pianos to the U.S. armed forces, which deployed them around the world. In some instances, the navy even installed them on submarines while the ships were being constructed—a clear indication that providing music for the crew was no mere afterthought—and the army brought them along with its other equipment, including, according to some reports, airdropping them in by parachute when necessary (see figures 4.7 and 4.8).[12]

Songbooks, *Hit Kits*, musical instruments—these were only a few of the dizzying array of musical initiatives of the Special Services Division. Some military units received printed materials for choral singing. Many got sheet music and folios, whose contents ranged from ballads and art songs to minstrel and comedy numbers. The Special Services Division

Figure 4.6. Soldiers in the Special Service Unit at Fort Meade, Maryland, give a demonstration of the Steinway & Sons "Victory" piano in 1943.

Figure 4.7. The boxy, no-frills "Victory" piano in the field. (The singer is baritone Benjamin DeLoache, later a longtime instructor at the Yale School of Music.)

sent out "blueprints" for entire shows, including not only musical scores and scripts but also instructions for costumes and set design. It distributed short musical films with follow-the-bouncing-ball lyrics to encourage participatory singing. And in collaboration with the Army Corps of Chaplains, the Special Services Division gave out millions of copies of *Hymns from Home*, a nondenominational collection of sacred songs and the twenty-third psalm.[13]

At the same time, the military did more than outfit soldiers to make music themselves. It also *supplied* musicians. The armed forces supported more than eight hundred military bands, which played not only for ceremonial functions but for social occasions too, both continuing and departing from practices of earlier wars.[14] One such band, typical in some respects but exceptional in others, was the B-1 Band, organized at the Navy Pre-Flight School at the University of North Carolina in May 1942. Authorized at a time when tensions over African American participation in the war effort were running high, the band's members comprised the first African Americans to serve in the navy in other than galley positions. The ensemble consisted of forty-five exceptionally talented musicians who had had to score higher on the military intelligence exam than whites in order be accepted into the service. One of them, James B. Parsons, the band's leader, went on to become the chief judge of the U.S. District Court in Chicago (the first African American appointed to such a position). Another, William Skinner, later worked as a mathematician for NASA. Forced to billet in what bandsman Thomas Gavin described as a "hotel in Raleigh . . . on a back street in a blighted part of the city, segregated," they served for twenty-one months, mostly in Chapel Hill, where they initially faced substantial racist hostility but were eventually embraced in the local community, playing everywhere from regimental reviews and flag-raising ceremonies on campus to war bond rallies and sporting events in the surrounding area.[15]

Also included among the military's official music groups were at least eight all-women bands attached to the female branches of the service—five in the Women's Army Corps (WAC), including one segregated band of African American women, and one band each in the Navy WAVES, the Coast Guard SPAR, and the Marine Corps Women's Reserve. Generally, these bands performed in their military uniforms, as their male counterparts invariably did, but a member of the band of the Marine Corps Women's Reserve remembered that at the weekly performances at Camp Lejeune, North Carolina, "the clothes for the show were lovely evening dresses, which were provided." Regardless of costume, however, both the military and the public tended to treat these highly skilled all-women bands as novelties, and consequently, as band historian Jill Sullivan has noted, they were deployed as widely and often as possible in stateside campaigns to sell war bonds, with profiles of the bands featured in the pages of *Life*, *Look*, *National Geographic*, *Collier's*, and *Downbeat*, and in numerous national radio broadcasts. In one typical instance, in 1945, the 404th Army Service Forces Band, the segregated all–African American band of the WAC, traveled to Chicago. They were dispatched to play throughout the city's Black neighborhoods to sell war bonds; they also performed at the Savoy Ballroom, on a makeshift platform outdoors downtown, and, finally, on a stage with Humphrey Bogart and Lauren Bacall at Soldier Field.[16]

Overseas, some military bands had primarily ceremonial responsibilities, while others played principally for entertainment purposes, either as a full ensemble or in smaller spin-off groups. Some of the players were erstwhile professional musicians, including from Hollywood and the recording industry, while others' musical backgrounds were only as amateurs. Regardless, their performances to entertain soldiers abroad ranged from outdoor gigs near the front lines to indoor concerts far from the actual fighting. Richard Burt, a trumpeter in the 746th Far East Air Force Band, recalled performing in the Philippines in improvised accommodations, where "G.I.s [climbed] up . . . half-blown-up palm trees to attach spotlights that could be used by the show people, . . . the

Figure 4.8. This photograph of "35 tons of band music" collected for the U.S. Naval School of Music by the music supply company J. W. Pepper & Son suggests the scale of the material investment in music made by the navy.

men who came to see the show came with their ponchos and helmets on and their rifles sticking out," and there was audible automatic weapon fire and visible flashes from shooting across the nearby ravine while the band played. A rare surviving recording of this group suggests a repertoire that featured numerous current jazz and popular hits, reflecting the G.I.s' ongoing involvement with contemporary popular music despite being thousands of miles from American shores. Current hits included "I'll Remember April" (1942), "Perdido" (1942), "Sentimental Journey" (1944), "If You Are but a Dream" (1944), and "Long Ago (and Far Away)" (1944), which the band featured alongside standards like "Moonglow," "Tea for Two," and "East of the Sun (West of the Moon)." Such bands often played concerts for nonmilitary audiences too, an effective way of cultivating positive relations with local populations. In the spring of 1945, for example, the band of the 106th Infantry Division played for the people of Saint Quentin, France; their performance was all the more poignant, the band's historians noted, for being "perform[ed] from the bandstand which the Germans had used during their occupation of the city."[17] At home and overseas, bands such as these embodied the military commitment to use its own personnel to provide musical entertainment for the troops. Figure 4.8 shows the scale of this supply chain.

Figure 4.9. The government's official caption for this photograph from December 1944 made the military sound like a hotbed of musical excitement: "Somewhere in England one of the hottest bands in the European Theater of Operations belongs to a Special United States Naval Construction Battalion."

The USO

In World War I, looking after the moral and emotional well-being of America's fighters had fallen largely to the YMCA, which, according to government figures, had conducted 90 percent of the welfare work for the American Expeditionary Forces in Europe (not including the ministrations of the Red Cross). In World War II, this arrangement was superseded by the work of two new entities: the United Service Organizations (USO) and its subsidiary USO–Camp Shows, Inc. The USO was established in 1941 as a joint effort by six national organizations—the YMCA, the Young Women's Christian Association, the Salvation Army, the National Catholic Community Service, the National Jewish Welfare Board, and the National Travelers Aid Association—to provide civilian support for troop morale, working so closely with the military that one historian characterized the USO as a "quasi-state agency."[18] Nominally, the USO remained in civilian hands, but the government was responsible for constructing USO facilities, directing its programs, and managing its budget.

Most of its work revolved around operating more than three thousand clubs and canteens around the U.S. and, to a limited extent, abroad.[19] These facilities provided G.I.s with a place for various forms of recreation, including listening to a radio or phonograph, singing, or, most famously, dancing with young women known as "hostesses." According to a 1944 poll of more than eight thousand white and Black G.I.s conducted by the National Opinion Research Center, a quarter of the visitors to the clubs enjoyed playing records at the USO facilities and a third liked listening to the radio, while the sociality of singing and dancing with hostesses ranked as the greatest attraction. In the national memory, these facilities have been celebrated as wholesome and egalitarian spaces emblematic of a particular American ethos, where "a big shot" was friendly to "little shots" (as a soldier in the 1944 film *Hollywood Canteen* puts it). In practice, the USO canteens often departed from this democratic ideal. As historian Sherrie Tucker has detailed, many were in fact racially segregated, and behavior that deviated from racial and gender norms was assiduously policed.[20]

Figure 4.10. Although USO clubs and canteens were best known as places where G.I.s could dance with young women, they also afforded opportunities for other musical activity, including listening to the radio or a phonograph or, quite often, informal singing. Pictured here, G.I.s sing with a young woman at a USO club in Alabama.

As much as the USO was known for providing spaces where lonely G.I.s could dance the jitterbug with attractive young women, it was famous equally for the work of its subsidiary organization, USO–Camp Shows, Inc., whose mission was to provide live entertainment for military personnel across the United States and around the world. The YMCA (in collaboration with the military) had attempted something like this in World War I but to a much smaller extent and to limited effect. World War II was another story.

Operating on an unprecedented scale and with a level of show-business panache and management expertise unlike anything the military had been connected with previously, the Camp Shows enterprise was funded by the USO but had its own board of directors, which, unlike the USO, consisted mostly of executives from the entertainment industry. From 1941 to 1948, the organization presented 428,521 performances by stars of all stature in forty-two countries from Iceland to the southwest Pacific, to an aggregate audience of more than 212 million military personnel. Performances took place in virtually every setting imaginable, from cow pastures, railroad yards, and bowling alleys to castles, churches, attics, and cellars. Sometimes they even occurred in theaters.[21]

The Camp Shows organization was a child not only of the entertainment industry but also of the business community. Its president was the cigar-chomping booking agent Abe Lastfogel, whom we met at the start of this chapter, but it grew out of an earlier philanthropic initiative to arrange amusements for soldiers and sailors that was led by Thomas J. Watson, president of the International Business Machines Corporation (IBM), beginning in 1940. After the USO was founded in 1941, Watson worked with Frederick Osborn, head of the Joint Army and Navy Committee on Welfare and Recreation, who came out of the business world as well, to secure funding for an entertainment program for G.I.s on an ongoing basis. Out of this effort grew USO–Camp Shows, Inc., then designated the military's sole agent for procuring civilian entertainment. Another businessman with no background in commercial entertainment, Lawrence Phillips, served as the executive vice president of the Camp Shows organization. Phillips, wrote journalist E. J. Kahn Jr., "looks and talks like a man of distinction," with the disposition of someone who had once spoken of soldiers "as 'human pawns that move across the chessboard of the world.'"[22] Both entertainment and business sensibilities shaped the enterprise.

Operationally, Camp Shows was organized like the vaudeville business, with different tiers of performers traveling along different geographic circuits. In this case, the equivalent of vaudeville's "big time" was the Victory Circuit, which involved stops at military installations with 1,500 troops or more, while the Blue Circuit visited smaller facilities. A third route was the Hospital Circuit, and those artists who performed overseas moved along what was known as the Foxhole Circuit (figure 4.11). This schema maximized efficiency for the greatest number of performances by the most acts at the lowest cost. This mattered immensely because the Camp Shows were costly to produce, with expenses of some $40 million between 1941 and 1946, the greatest portion of which went to artist salaries. The biggest performers donated their star power for free, but they were far outnumbered by the low- and medium-level artists who were dependent on weekly compensation to get by. With the assent of Actors' Equity, the American Federation of Musicians, and other unions, performers generally received around 60 percent of regular vaudeville rates. (In a gesture to make performing on these circuits financially tenable for artists, Lastfogel insisted that when Camp Shows, Inc., booked any of his

Figure 4.11. On the Foxhole Circuit, ten thousand G.I.s are on hand to listen to a female trio sing as part of the Copacabana All Girl Review, near Marseilles, France, in August 1945. Music, of course, was not the only attraction for G.I.s, but it was an inextricable part of the spectacle.

own clients, his firm, the William Morris Agency, would waive its regular 10 percent commission. Other large agencies soon followed suit.)[23]

Many of the more than five thousand Camp Shows performers were singers or musicians, but the vaudeville model meant that they shared the stage with a dazzling variety of other kinds of acts too, including a trick golfer, a champion bowler, a high diver, a Russian dagger dancer, a one-armed billiard player, a roller skater, a baton twirler, and a fishing and hunting expert. Because the military's aim was to assuage G.I.s' boredom, uplift their morale, and steer them away from alcohol abuse, the company of prostitutes, and other forms of moral turpitude, the only thing that mattered was that the acts brought light, unobjectionable amusement to the restless, entertainment-starved, captive audience.[24]

To ensure the suitability of their material, all performers had to satisfy stringent censorship requirements, imposed by an office of the Special Services Division in New York. Before they went on the road, performers were required to write out every line of their act and sign a notarized statement attesting they would not deviate from it without official approval. These regulations left room only for the most anodyne content. A breakdown of these policies by historian Sam Lebovic merits quoting in full:

> [The Camp Shows'] censorship policy considered a wide range of words to be taboo, [including] "God, gawd, Jesus, jeez, Christ, hell, damn or any contractions or combinations thereof, regardless of spelling; bitch, bastard; references to prostitution, white slavery, sexual intercourse, dope or those associated with such things regardless whether the word is weak or mild because of colloquialism and general usage elsewhere today." Similarly, a number of situations were to be avoided, such as "a man and a woman about to enter into a seduction, regardless of the outcome," "allusions by word or gesture of homosexuality," making gambling or intoxication "appear attractive" and "double entendres, where the meaning can only be the one in poor taste."

These restrictions, however, were not limited to profanity and sexual references and innuendo. They covered political content in much the same way. As Lebovic explains, Camp Shows also

> banned all references to the President and his family, members of the Congress or Cabinet, allied or neutral statesmen, "persons connected with political parties," "political issues, domestic or foreign," and "voting and political issues." Disparaging jokes

about "American heroes, battles or general history" were to be avoided, as were the following situations: "an officer 'having it better' than an enlisted man," "favoritism by draft boards and government agencies," and "present or post war labor problems affecting members of the army, before leaving or returning to civilian life."

Indeed, such constraints were most certainly at odds with G.I.s' actual behavior and tastes, but for these audiences with few other options, even material that was stripped of topicality, politics, and sexuality was generally welcome.[25]

The Camp Shows enterprise was not immune to criticism, however, or capable of satisfying all audiences all the time, regardless of its many successes. For one thing, there was at least occasional off-color ad-libbing, despite the censorship rules, leading one chaplain to write, "Sodom and Gomorrah would blush with shame if they were forced to sit and listen to such obscenity." Camp Shows also ran into a supply problem. The organization sought talent from all over the country, holding auditions in two dozen cities, but it was not possible for Camp Shows to recruit enough high-quality acts to satisfy the military's demand. This led to complaints from soldiers, who could be a tough and critical audience, that many acts were simply not that good. To this, Lastfogel, the organization's president, could only reply that it was sending out the best talent it could get. With a finite pool of artists to draw from, he allowed, "we've had to scrape the bottom of the barrel."[26] Under the exigencies of war, this "quasi-government agency" operated within serious restrictions, but it managed to fill the seats at hundreds of thousands of performances.

"We're Making These V-Discs Just for You"

When it came to providing professional entertainment for the troops, the USO was not the only arrow in the military's quiver. Another initiative of the Music Section of the Special Services Division was a program to produce and distribute millions of specially recorded phonograph records for G.I.s, wherever in the world they were. The program was the brainchild of a remarkable sound technician, Lieutenant George Robert ("Bob") Vincent, who went on to become chief sound engineer at the Nuremberg trials and then at the fledgling United Nations. Early in the war, when he was assigned to the Radio Section, the intense and indefatigable Vincent dreamed up a plan to send records to the troops. In the summer of 1943, he walked into the Pentagon seeking approval and funding for a recording program. He walked out with the War Department's authorization and a commitment for a million dollars. Within a short time, he also secured a transfer to the Music Section, which was to administer the program, a promotion to captain, and appointment as the head of the division that would oversee the records, which were to be called V-Discs (for "Victory Discs").[27]

Working out of three cubbyhole offices on the thirteenth floor of an office building on Forty-Second Street in New York, the V-Disc group was comprised mostly of seasoned music-industry veterans from RCA Victor, Columbia, and other companies. Steve Sholes had been an artists-and-repertoire executive at RCA Victor with many contacts in both the popular and classical music fields (and who went on to become an influential producer for RCA Victor in the postwar period, known for bringing both Chet Atkins and Elvis Presley to the label). Walt Heebner came from RCA Victor's sales department. Morty Palitz (a.k.a. "Perfect Pitch Palitz") had worked at Decca, Brunswick, and Columbia and was likewise well connected. Other personnel included recording engineer Tony Janak, who came from Columbia, and George Simon, who had played in Glenn Miller's band. Also crucial was assistance by Frank Walker, vice president of RCA Victor.[28] The program's success grew out of these close ties between the military and the commercial record industry.

The first V-Disc records were shipped out to G.I.s in October 1943, a modest dispatch of fifty-four thousand discs pressed by all the record companies with plants on the East Coast. The shipment came a mere three months after the program was approved. By the time it was discontinued, in 1949, the program had sent out some eight million records, featuring a who's who of leading popular-music artists, including Benny Goodman, Bing Crosby, the Andrews Sisters, Gene Autry, and others, plus a variety of symphony orchestras, concert bands, string ensembles, and military bands. According to the Music Section's allocation, 70 percent were popular music; 15 percent were "classical and semi-classical"; and another 15 percent were marching bands and military music (favored by Music Section chief Howard Bronson, the former bandsman). To heighten their morale-raising effect, many records had spoken introductions, directly addressing the troops. For example, one opened, "Hello, all you fellows, all over the world. Greetings from the Andrews Sisters. . . . We're making these V-Discs just for you, and along with them we want to send all our love and kisses." Other discs featured not bespoke recordings but rather whatever material the V-Disc group could get its hands on, including selections from radio shows and broadcast dress rehearsals; commercial recordings (some previously issued, others not) loaned from the record companies; and excerpts from film soundtracks.[29]

To appeal to the greatest number of troops, Vincent solicited feedback by enclosing a letter with each record shipment, inviting comments on selections and suggestions for future recordings. Whether Vincent and his team responded appropriately, however, is questionable. In response to Mexican American troops who said their tastes were not being met, for example, the V-Disc group sent out a number of records by Xavier Cugat, the Spanish-born, Cuban-trained New York bandleader who, with his Waldorf-Astoria Orchestra, dabbled in Mexican music. Still, generally speaking, the program was a runaway success, and by late 1944, the navy, marines, and coast guard were distributing V-Discs as well. In February 1945, bandleader Spike Jones expanded on this popularity in a letter to Vincent after Jones returned from a USO–Camp Shows tour overseas. "Everywhere we went, we saw the men playing V-Discs," he wrote, "on the boat going over and on the boat coming home; . . . everywhere in France, including foxholes! I can state definitely . . . that of all the music morale builders, . . . V-Discs are easily the most popular and most effective medium for giving our men the music they want and need to keep going."[30]

This success was all the more impressive for the number of pieces that had to be put in place to make it happen. For one thing, the V-Disc program would have made no sense without any equipment on which to play the records, but by the time the record program got off the ground, the army had already begun to distribute specially designed phonographs for G.I. use (figure 4.12). These machines, painted olive green, were shipped to individual military units in what were known as B-Kits (or "Buddy Kits"), bundled with a stock of records, a radio receiver, some songbooks, some novels, and miscellaneous supplies. The machines were powered by a spring-wound motor that soldiers cranked up by hand, with two speed settings: 78 rpm and 33⅓ rpm (The latter was not yet a standard setting on consumer equipment but was included to play recordings of radio programs—known as transcriptions—which used a slower speed in order to be able to play continuously for fifteen minutes at a time). Development of the B-Kit began as early as the fall of 1941 under the direction of Major Gordon Hittenmark of the Morale Division and civilian consultant Irving Fogel, a Hollywood recording specialist. They were aided in early 1942 by a $100,000 grant from the Carnegie Corporation. In other words, the importance of these sound technologies for soldier morale was recognized even from the outset of the war. Eventually, an enhanced version of the package, the B-1 Kit, was developed as well, including an electrically powered phonograph, an amplifier, microphones, and speakers; it could also function as a small public-address system.[31]

Figure 4.12. G.I.s listen to an army phonograph sitting atop artillery munitions during the Vosges campaign in France in 1944.

The V-Disc program faced several legal hurdles. Vincent had the support of the military and was confident musicians would participate, but in 1942, a labor dispute between the American Federation of Musicians (AFM) and the record industry led the union to impose a ban on all recording by its members. Moreover, the military needed the cooperation of the record companies to let musicians out of exclusive contracts, and the consent of the music publishing industry to bypass costly licensing requirements. Vincent and his staff were undeterred. They appealed to the union's and the industry's sense of patriotism and civic duty, and in short stead, they had agreements in hand with the AFM, the Music Publishers Protective Association, and the American Federation of Radio Artists to allow recording to proceed and to waive the fees and royalties (for musicians) and copyright payments (for publishers), under the condition that the recordings would be distributed only to military personnel and not commercially exploited in any way.[32]

Another obstacle was distribution: how to ship records to avoid damage or breakage. For this, the group came to rely on specially designed cardboard boxes, each coated with wax and sealed with waterproof glues, impervious to varying climatic conditions and strong enough, it was said, to withstand the weight of a horse. When they were shipped, every water- and shock-proof box included not just records and the letter from Vincent soliciting feedback but also replacement phonograph needles, a *Hit Kit* songbook (usually featuring lyrics to songs on some of the enclosed records), and a list of the releases in the box. By January 1945, the program was sending out more than three hundred thousand discs a month.[33]

The program also faced problems involving the materials from which the records were produced. Until this time, phonograph records had been made out of shellac, a substance that was heavy, breakable, and in short supply during the war. As a result, the V-Disc group found a new, lighter, "unbreakable" material called Vinylite, which proved an excellent replacement—they thus produced the first vinyl records. For a while, Vinylite was the material of choice for V-Discs, but Vinylite was also used to make life rafts, medical gloves, and other materials of war, and soon its use was prohibited for anything but urgent military needs (a classification the V-Disc group failed to get). As a result, Vinylite was replaced by another new, similar material called Formvar, produced by a Canadian subsidiary of the Monsanto Chemical Company.[34] Vincent and his team proved to be virtuosos of flexibility and ingenuity with a deft command of the latest technology.

Ultimately, as in World War I, recorded music in World War II connected American soldiers to a different world—a somewhere else. Often this meant that V-Discs reduced the cultural and psychological distance between G.I.s' immediate circumstances and the civilian lives they left behind. For many fighters, serving in the military meant enduring environments in which their senses were under assault. Other soldiers passed the war in conditions that were relatively calm and secure, far from the front lines. Either way, listening to records reclaimed the space around them (figure 4.13). Often, the phonograph conjured powerful associations with the domestic sphere, the primary environment in which most soldiers had experienced recorded music before the war.[35] For many, the sounds emitting from the grooves of the records reinforced (and perhaps amplified) those domestic associations. With the V-Discs' high-caliber musical selections and general technical quality, a historian of the program has written, "the [records] were a tie to home and presented an almost instantaneous projection of what was transpiring across the total musical spectrum in our country." Relocating American popular culture to overseas outposts, phonographs and V-Discs could make war seem less like war (see figure 4.13).[36]

Figure 4.13. Corporal Robert Umholz and Sergeant Jerry O'Neal from the Thirteenth Air Force relax with some Strauss waltzes on the phonograph in the South Pacific, March 1944. While this scene looks domestic, the two are sitting on homemade furniture made from scrap lumber, and the sandals O'Neal is wearing were made from discarded G.I. field shoes.

Armed Forces Radio: "The Shimmy Dancer"

If V-Discs represented one direct connection to home, radio represented another. In the course of only a few years, the U.S. military built the world's first truly global radio network, the Armed Forces Radio Service (AFRS), whose goal, explained its head, Colonel Thomas "Tom" H. A. Lewis, was to make home seem as close as possible for "a boy from Grand Rapids [getting used] to military life in Persia." Gone was the military's fear about making soldiers homesick. The aim now was to bring home to the military. This seemed possible because the war coincided with what is now known as the Golden Age of Radio—an era before the internet and television, when radio was America's primary medium for both entertainment and information, and a means by which listeners came to feel that they belonged to a single national community. In fact, it was radio-starved army technicians stationed in remote locations who constructed the first radio network specifically for military personnel, initially in the Philippines in 1939, then in the Panama Canal Zone (1940) and Alaska (1941).[37] For their part, government officials recognized that the emotional attachment people felt to radio made it a valuable component of troop morale, leading them in 1941 to establish a Radio Section parallel to the Music Section in the War Department's Morale Division.

Buoying morale, however, was not the government's sole motivation. Having seen the powerful effects of radio on advertising (in the United States) and political mobilization (in Europe) in the interwar years, officials were also concerned with the potential of radio broadcasting as a tool of motivation and persuasion. Among the leadership class, the *War of the Worlds* scare in 1938—when a popular radio drama series allegedly convinced many listeners that the country (or rather, planet Earth) was being invaded by Martians—triggered a wave of anxiety about audiences' susceptibility to misinformation.[38] Armed forces radio, then, was organized with all of these conditions in mind, aiming to amuse and inform soldiers, to motivate them, and to divert them from listening to enemy propaganda.

For these ends, music was key. Modeled on domestic network broadcasting, AFRS featured many kinds of programs, including variety shows, comedies, dramas, news and information programs, religious segments, and more. Music programming, however, was preferred above all others. According to a 1944 listener survey, more G.I.s (90 percent) liked American popular-music programs than any other category. (Comedy shows and sports broadcasts ranked second and third.) The most popular style, by a wide margin, was swing music, but classical, hillbilly/Western, and religious music had their partisans as well.[39] Music was certainly not the only reason that soldiers the world over tuned in, but it was a big one.

The machinery that created the AFRS was set in motion in late 1940 by the head of the Radio Branch of the Morale Division, then-Captain Gordon Hittenmark, erstwhile a Washington-area disc jockey who had developed the aforementioned Buddy Kit. When it came to building a worldwide radio network from scratch, however, Hittenmark had neither the organizational nor the management skills needed for the job at hand. In May 1942, Hittenmark was replaced by then-Major Tom Lewis, under whose leadership armed forces radio took off. By that time, the head of the government's *domestic* radio agency in the Office of Facts and Figures, a former vice president at CBS named William B. Lewis (no relation to Tom), had articulated a position anticipating the work of the Armed Forces Network. He believed that the best way to take advantage of radio in wartime was to build on what the radio industry already did well: provide amusement. "Let's not forget that radio is primarily an entertainment medium and must continue to be if it is . . . to deliver the large audiences we want to reach," William Lewis said. The best government messaging was that which most conformed to existing habits and schedules. "Radio propaganda," as he put it, "must be painless."[40] These were precepts that Tom Lewis acted on as well.

Unlike Hittenmark, who came from the nation's capital, Tom Lewis was well connected in the epicenter of the entertainment industry—Hollywood—and had the ideal professional background for getting AFRS off the ground—radio advertising. Lewis came to the Radio Section (as it was now called) from a position as vice president of Young & Rubicam, one of the world's leading advertising agencies, where he had developed programs such as *The Abbott and Costello Show* and *The Kate Smith Show*. He attributed the success of these shows to careful audience research, a deep interest of his which led him in 1939 to form the Audience Research Institute (later Audience Research, Inc.) with his Y&R coworker George Gallup, the pioneering pollster and market researcher, to analyze the movie industry and its audiences. Through both his work and his wife, the Hollywood actress Loretta Young, Lewis enjoyed a robust network of connections in the entertainment world, including a close relationship with the Hollywood Victory Committee, a group founded immediately after Pearl Harbor to supply stage, screen, and radio performers to the war bond effort.[41]

Crucial, then, was Lewis's background in advertising and market research. Not only did he recruit personnel from the advertising industry, but he made one of his first priorities as head of the Radio Section to analyze the peculiar character of the military listening audience, which was, in the words of AFRS staffer (and future radio historian) Erik Barnouw, made up "of American Civilians-in-uniform [but] is not a civilian audience."[42] At Lewis's request, the Research Branch of the Special Services Division conducted a survey of a cross section of white ground soldiers in fifteen military camps across the United States in the summer of 1942. The result was a classified report, "Radio Habits of Enlisted Men": a compilation of data about the density of the soldier audience, when and where they listened, and the specific kinds of programs they liked and disliked.[43]

This information then shaped broadcasting strategies whose ultimate goal was not just to entertain the armed forces but to strengthen them. In Lewis's estimation, the most effective way to achieve this was by using the techniques of commercial advertising. In this adapted context, though, the "commercial" message that AFRS was "selling" to troops, he said in a postwar interview, was "morale, Americanism, security, things are going 'OK' at home, we are sending you the needed materials, we are doing all we can to help you, this is your country—America, you are the best soldier there is, the 'why' of things, and finally *you will win*."[44] More specifically, radio was valued by military officials not only because music (and other programming) elevated morale but also because it *attracted* listeners to the radio, a uniquely useful means by which the military could communicate with soldiers en masse. Thus, in lieu of advertisements for consumer goods, which tended to make G.I.s homesick, the military inserted into its programming "morale commercials" to encourage soldiers to do things like buy war bonds, avoid venereal disease, and take precautions to prevent trenchfoot, a condition caused by prolonged exposure to wet or unsanitary conditions.[45] As Lewis knew from his work at Y&R, the most persuasive means to convey these messages was entertainment, which often meant music.

To officials who oversaw radio operations, the idea of seducing G.I.s with music in order to influence their behavior was not abstract or vague. A letter written to Lewis in 1944 by Ted Sherdeman, General Douglas MacArthur's troop radio officer, laid this out in an exceptionally candid manner, likening the music on AFRS to a sexually alluring "shimmy dancer" at an old-time medicine show. "Radio entertainment as provided by you," he wrote to Lewis,

> serves as the shimmy dancer in front of our medicine tent, and when the dancer is through, we sell the health medicine of the day to the crowd that's gathered, just as we sold soap when the last joke was told at home. . . . We gather them in with Bing Crosby and then sell them their atabrine [i.e., antimalarial medication].[46]

Lewis and his associates, that is, understood entertainment strategically, as a means to an end, rather than as an end in itself. Calibrated to the tastes and habits of enlisted men (not officers), the tantalizing gyrations of the "shimmy dancer" were on display to produce a transactional outcome.[47]

An advertising true believer, Lewis scorned browbeating in favor of enticement, of seduction. When it came to persuasion, his philosophy (and therefore AFRS's) contrasted sharply with that of U.S. wartime radio operations aimed at foreign listeners, which were more heavy-handed in their approach to propaganda. As the "shimmy dancer" evoked modern advertising's primordial roots, it distinguished AFRS from what listeners heard on Voice of America (established 1942) at this time or later on Radio Free Europe (established 1949).[48] And although some American officials expressed deep concern about G.I.s falling under the sway of enemy broadcasting (especially that of propagandists Lord Haw Haw, Tokyo Rose, and Axis Sally), Lewis had complete faith in his product and paid little attention to the competition. If AFRS provided American fighters with programs they missed and had confidence in, he believed, they would not tune in elsewhere. It appears he was right.[49]

From a technical standpoint, armed forces radio was a titanic achievement, an enterprise of immense size and complexity, concerned with all aspects of radio—from production to distribution to consumption. What this encompassed becomes manifest when we recognize that the meaning of "worldwide network" was (and is) not self-evident. AFRS was not simply broadcasting a single signal globally from one giant, super-powerful, central transmitter in the United States. Rather, most AFRS programming consisted of playing transcriptions (that is, material pre-recorded for the radio) asynchronously around the world. At the time, broadcasting transcriptions was an unusual practice in commercial radio, most of which was live. Yet, aside from news reports, nearly all AFRS programs were prerecorded in the United States and played back on different schedules through a variety of means and systems—including longwave, shortwave, and wired networks—some reaching across thousands of miles, others functioning only within a single building. (After the war the practice of playing transcriptions over the air became more common, in part because AFRS had normalized the practice.)[50]

This coordinated system required AFRS to produce, manufacture, and distribute transcription discs quickly, which led to some of the first major changes in the record-pressing process in more than a quarter century. The result was that transcription discs could be manufactured within a few hours' time—particularly important for time-sensitive broadcasts like President Harry Truman's address to the armed forces after Franklin Roosevelt's death in April 1945. To create a semblance of synchronicity within the "network," each week AFRS headquarters in Los Angeles sent out a shipment of transcription discs known as "the package" to battle and supply areas all around the world, including by 1944 to submarines and service ships. At its peak, AFRS was shipping more than twenty thousand records a week to hundreds of stations, from the Caribbean and North Africa to the South Pacific and the China-Burma-India theater.[51]

Broadcasting these transcription discs depended on a vast web of im-provised radio stations which the military set up either in local facilities (commandeered or borrowed) or using small, portable transmitters which G.I.s carried with them. As the U.S. forces moved across Europe in 1944, for example, nearly all the armies included their own portable radio stations. Generally, these transmitters functioned primarily as relay stations, with little original programming, but as the troops moved on, fixed stations were often established in their wake. After VE Day, the Armed Forces Network (the AFRS's network in Europe) set up permanent broadcasting facilities in Munich, Stuttgart, Bremen, and Berlin, as well as in Frankfurt, where the walls were allegedly soundproofed with cloth from Wehrmacht uniforms. The situation was similar across the globe, where the stations that made up the so-called Jungle Network in the central Pacific (Hawaii and the Philippines) and the Mosquito Network in the southwest Pacific provided radio for millions of G.I.s who were serving in those theaters while spread out across thousands of miles, separated by water.[52]

When it came to tuning in to these broadcasts, G.I.s often used special radio receivers that the military obtained and distributed in the Buddy Kit sent out to each unit (along with the phonograph, records, and other items). In practice, though, demand outstripped supply, and soldiers listened by any means they could. Indeed, the scarcity of radio receivers became one of biggest problems AFRS contended with.[53] By July 1945, 40 percent of respondents to a survey of radio habits of G.I.s stationed in Europe reported it was "pretty hard" or "very hard" to find a radio when they wanted to listen, and 80 percent said that the soldiers needed more radio sets. Air force men, it was reported, flew five hundred miles from southern Italy to Bucharest to buy radios at their own expense at "fantastic figures."[54] The problem was especially acute in the Pacific, where excessive humidity rendered most radio receivers inoperable after a few months, a problem not fully resolved until late in the war with the distribution of plastic-coated receivers. Ultimately, though, G.I.s found ways to listen. Official figures indicate that the army and navy distributed some 206,000 radio receivers overseas during the war, but the true number of sets in circulation was significantly higher, including commandeered receivers, radios obtained overseas, and not a small number of improvised, Rube Goldberg–style inventions.[55]

The programming on AFRS involved a mix of commercial network shows adapted for the military audience, original content produced specifically for the G.I.s, and local programs unique to a region or military base. Throughout the schedule, music figured prominently—sometimes as a show's main focus, and other times mixed in with other kinds of performances. The network's signature program, for example, was a weekly half-hour variety show called *Command Performance*, featuring music, comedy, and particular sounds that G.I.s requested by mail. In one instance, sultry actress Carole Landis simply *sighed* for a soldier stationed somewhere in the Pacific. In others, listeners were treated to the sizzle of Lana Turner frying a steak or Jascha Heifetz and Jack Benny in a violin duet. Produced in collaboration with CBS, the show boasted a wealth of A-list musical talent. Bing Crosby alone performed on more than two dozen occasions, while Frank Sinatra, the Andrews Sisters, Dinah Shore, and others also appeared many times.[56]

Another show which featured prominently in the AFRS lineup was *G.I. Jive*, hosted by "G.I. Jill," probably the troops' favorite radio personality. Conceived as a show in which a female disc jockey would answer requests from servicemen, *G.I. Jive* was broadcast six days a week beginning in January 1944 and proved so popular that it spawned a weekly spin-off program, *Jill's All-Time Juke Box*, launched nine months later. Indeed, no other AFRS program brought in as much fan mail as *G.I. Jive*, and by the summer of 1945, "Jill" (Martha Wilkerson, wife of radio producer Robert "Mort" Werner) was receiving more than a thousand letters a week, each of which she attempted to answer with a personal reply and a photograph. While heterosexual male desire no doubt contributed to her popularity, Jill departed from the eroticized personas of Axis Sally and Tokyo Rose. Rather, Jill was imagined, in Lewis's words, as "the kid sister, the girl next door" to every G.I. She was, in this sense, an aural counterpart of Betty Grable, the Hollywood pinup known for her wholesome values, whose image, historian Robert Westbrook has argued, personalized the war for many soldiers. Aside from *G.I. Jive*, other shows that were specifically music themed, in a variety of styles, included *Yank Bandstand*, *Melody Round Up*, *NBC Symphony*, *Music for Sunday*, *Downbeat*, *Yank Swing Session*, *Music by Kostelanetz*, and *Hymns from Home*.[57]

Although AFRS programming was overwhelmingly white, one show did foreground African American performers. *Jubilee* premiered in October 1942, conceived as a show that might alleviate the racial tension then mounting over the mistreatment of Black G.I.s and other forms of wartime discrimination. A variety show in the vein of *Command Performance*, it studiously avoided mention of racial policies or any issues of particular interest to African Americans (soldiers or otherwise), with the intention of placating Black soldiers while still making the show palatable to an interracial audience. Its debut episode featured Black artists including Duke Ellington, Ethel Waters, and Rex Ingram, among other top talent, and from there, *Jubilee* went on to become another of AFRS's most popular offerings. The result was that *Jubilee* (along with V-Discs and USO–Camp Shows) helped effect what one scholar has called the "militarization" of swing—the wartime promotion of swing, at home and overseas, not just as a style of music but as an ideology based on liberty, democracy, equality, and tolerance, regardless of the ways that these ideals departed from reality. Although eventually some white artists did appear on *Jubilee* and some Black artists on *Command Performance*, for the most part AFRS programming and the bands it featured both remained as segregated as the rest of the armed forces. Historian Lauren Sklaroff has shown that numerous Black performers succeeded in politicizing *Jubilee*, despite the show's design and operational protocols, but they did so without upsetting its underlying function.[58]

The exact effects of AFRS are difficult to pinpoint, but numerous high-ranking overseas commanders attested to its significance as the war drew to a close. "You have rendered an important service" to the war effort, Major General Mark W. Clark wrote to Tom Lewis. General Dwight D. Eisenhower sent this message: "I believe your station has made a substantial contribution to the high morale of our fighting forces." Generals Lucian K. Truscott, William C. Chase, and Donald H. Connolly likewise sent commendatory comments. The willingness of high-ranking officers up and down the chain of command to cooperate with AFRS (e.g., transporting and operating mobile transmitters) stands as another reflection of radio's perceived value during the war, as does Congress's consistent largesse in funding troop broadcasting activities.[59] Meanwhile, AFRS left an indelible imprint on American commercial broadcasting, introducing influential editing practices and other technical innovations, training a generation of postwar broadcast engineers and other industry professionals, and helping to demonstrate the viability and value of broadcasting based primarily on prerecorded programs, which was soon to become the norm on domestic American airwaves.[60]

Music in Hospitals

One other manifestation of the military's commitment to musical activity in World War II was found in hospitals and rehabilitation facilities, where innovative uses of music among the war's wounded and traumatized gave rise to the professional field now known as music therapy. Although its practical roots were far older, the term *music therapy* emerged in the interwar years, growing out of experimental treatments of soldiers who had fought in World War I. At the time the United States entered the Second World War, however, few in the medical community took it seriously. This changed rapidly over the course of the war. By 1945, music was being used widely in a variety of modalities in hospitals and rehabilitation facilities for soldiers, leading to a vast expansion of its use in the care of veterans in the immediate postwar years. By the end of 1946, some 875,000 veterans had attended concerts and participated in music-listening programs at veterans' hospitals or centers. The following year, more than 130,000 participated in organized music-making activities of one kind or another, ranging from group singing to band performance to songwriting and arranging.[61] By the late 1940s, the field was growing so quickly (and haphazardly) that in 1950 a group of its practitioners established a national professional body, the National Association for

Music Therapy, whose successor organization, the American Music Therapy Association, today treats hundreds of thousands of people annually.

Music therapy, however, was divisive, promoted ardently by some (often women) and scorned by others (often men). Theories of the healing powers of music go back millennia and stretch across many cultures, but in the wake of the scientific revolution in medicine in the West in the eighteenth and nineteenth centuries, such theories were generally dismissed out of hand for being empirically unverifiable. In the United States, a smattering of physicians, musicians, social reformers, and others did explore the use of music in the treatment of various medical conditions in the nineteenth century, but their work never cohered as a formal practice. To the extent that music was involved in patient care of any kind, its benefits were recognized only anecdotally. Military bands played in field hospitals in the Civil War, for example, and there was general consensus that they elevated the morale of the sick and wounded. Whether such activity had *medical* benefits, however, remained an open question.[62]

In the twentieth century, numerous professional caregivers, most of whom were women, returned to the issue, particularly in relation to the treatment of soldiers during and after World War I. In the interwar years, however, these innovators faced an uphill battle. Most doctors and hospital administrators wanted no truck with musical interlopers and the programs they advocated, and none of the early innovators succeeded in establishing a permanent foothold in an established medical institution. After Pearl Harbor, though, the wartime surge in casualties led to a sea change in support for therapeutic approaches to music. Doctors and administrators who had formerly shunned music in hospitals faced unprecedented numbers of wounded warriors. The result was an openness to new initiatives just as advocates for music in hospitals were proposing new treatment ideas, and organizations like the Red Cross, the Musicians Emergency Fund, and the Hospitalized Veterans Music Service were offering hospitals legions of eager volunteers. Under the aegis of both the surgeon general and the Music Section of the Special Services Division, programs in rehabilitation hospitals around the United States proliferated, using both music-making and listening to music as part of treatments for a wide range of conditions.[63]

Essential in this development was Lieutenant Guy V. R. Marriner, an erstwhile concert pianist who was both chief of the Hospital Section within the Music Section and the liaison between the Special Services Division and the Office of the Surgeon General. Under his direction, the Hospital Section worked with hospital and rehabilitation facilities to integrate music in numerous modalities both for entertainment and to encourage soldier participation. As figure 4.14 shows, this work took many forms, implementing programs that organized performances for patients, led them in group sings, assisted them in forming glee clubs and barbershop quartets, supplied small instruments and instruction, conducted phonograph-listening sessions, integrated music into calisthenics, and so on.[64] Meanwhile, armed forces radio set up its own hospital distribution network, much of which involved music programming, and music was a feature, too, of hospital ships, which had singing, performances by live bands, and playback of musical recordings over public-address loudspeakers. With a focus specifically on the morale benefit of music, a War Department statement from October 1944 made the hospital ship sound like a veritable juke joint. "It's not listed in the Army's pharmacopoeia," it read, "but American 'jive' dished out by G.I. musicians is good 'medicine' for bolstering the morale of wounded men returning home aboard the United States Hospital Ship *Marigold*."[65]

This is not to say, however, that the matter of music in hospitals was settled. Numerous officials recoiled at the appeals made by music-therapy advocates to the healing powers of emotion brought on by music. They fulminated against what they believed were exaggerated claims for

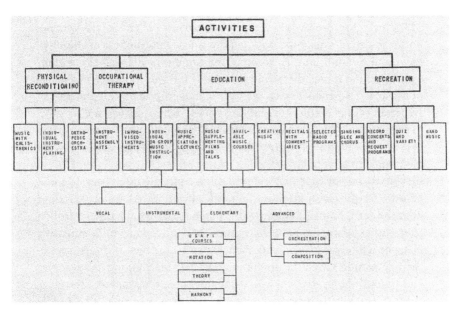

Figure 4.14. This extensive organizational chart illustrates the diversity of musical initiatives of the Hospital Section. It originally appeared in a bulletin issued by the War Department.

music's salutary effects, and they strenuously objected to initiatives that were not based on formal clinical studies (such initiatives, incidentally, were led mostly by women). Harold Spivacke, head of the Music Division at the Library of Congress and chair of the subcommittee on music of the Joint Army and Navy Committee on Welfare and Recreation, railed against Harriet Ayer Seymour's 1943 pamphlet *Music Answers the Call* in a letter to another member of the joint committee, Raymond Fosdick. "Following our recent conversation on the subject of the possibility of organizing a study on musical therapy, I am taking the liberty of sending you the enclosed three booklets," Spivacke wrote. "I do not expect you to read all of these, but I do hope you will read the first paragraph of *Music Answers the Call*. If I see much more of this kind of stuff, I fear that I shall become violent even before my admission into one of the mental hospitals." Two years later, he remained as vexed about this issue as ever. In response to an article by another female advocate for music therapy, Esther Goetz Gilliland, in the *Music Educators Journal*, he threatened to resign from the journal's editorial board. "To say that I was shocked by this article, would be putting it very mildly," he wrote. "It would be much more accurate to say that I am incensed." He went on to liken part of the text to "the old snake oil advertisements," known for their fraudulent claims. "I feel sure that if you had printed this as an advertisement for a patent medicine you would have run afoul of the law."[66]

Tellingly, however, while the skeptics warned of "charlatans who are doing so-called music therapy" (as the music coordinator of the USO, Raymond Kendall, put it), some of the same officials also threw their weight behind music therapy in practice.[67] Indeed, the surgeon general of the army, Norman T. Kirk, sought to make music an integral part of "reconditioning" soldiers to return to duty or, when that was not feasible, to prepare them for war-related work on the home front.[68] To this end, in 1943 he commissioned a survey of music-related activities then being implemented in hospitals around the United States. Although the result of the survey, in Guy Marriner's summation, confirmed that "music could be utilized [for reconditioning] in many advantageous ways," Marriner kept the term "music therapy" at arm's length. "Medically controlled tests and experiments have not proven 'Music Therapy' to be scientific fact," he wrote, yet he also endorsed what was, in effect, a robust music-therapy agenda. Given the predominance of women among its advocates and practitioners, musicologist Annegret Fauser has noted, "the clear subtext was that [music-therapy activities] needed to be put in male hands."[69]

By the end of the war, such activities were being widely institutionalized, as reflected by a ten-page bulletin issued by the War Department in

July 1945 that broke down why and how to implement music programs in "reconditioning" soldiers, encompassing everything from physical rehabilitation and occupational therapy to education and recreation. Yet the bulletin also included a notable caveat in a footnote on the first page: "The Office of the Surgeon General cannot consider music a therapeutic agent until further scientifically controlled tests have proved its value as therapy." Thus, officials walked a fine line between promoting the evident benefits that music yielded and pushing for policies based on quantitative data. Misogynistic dismissal of women's expertise notwithstanding, there was strong support for the position that music could be a "dynamic agent" in the care and rehabilitation of the traumatized and wounded, as Marriner put it, "if guided, controlled, and applied under rightly established conditions."[70]

·

Some officials may have felt uneasy about female-led innovations or about exaggerated claims for music's healing power, but most accepted and endorsed the strong role the government took in promoting musical activity among soldiers generally. They believed music had a valuable place in the war effort and warranted the broad range of resources the government directed toward providing it. More than any conflict before or since, the American war effort in World War II involved mobilizing music on a mass scale, using every available technology, drawing on every possible connection to the nation's rich musical culture, both amateur and professional.

Much of this work depended on the expertise of dollar-a-year businessmen and a broad swath of the entertainment industry as well as partnerships with social welfare organizations, as represented by the USO. In his study of the relationship between the military and big business in World War II, historian Mark Wilson has detailed the deep antagonisms that existed between government and its suppliers of munitions and heavy equipment.[71] The relationships involved in the music supply line appear to have been substantially less fraught. Radio broadcasters like NBC and CBS sought to avoid excess regulation, and producers like Steinway and RCA Victor yearned for a postwar return to regular manufacturing operations, but by and large, providing musical activity for G.I.s generated relatively little ideological friction.

The United States was not the only belligerent in World War II to mobilize its domestic media and entertainment infrastructure for war. In important ways, Germany, Japan, Great Britain, France, and the Soviet Union all did as well.[72] But the juggernaut of the American culture industries set the United States apart. While other countries had strong musical cultures, no other had the same technological and organizational assets to draw on or could systematically furnish its fighters with so many forms of musical activity. This was possible because of the peculiar historical conjuncture of World War II when American record companies, radio broadcasters, musical instrument manufacturers, and music publishers, along with the Hollywood entertainment community, made up a unique web of industrial forces that could be marshaled for military ends. This capacity dovetailed with unalloyed confidence in the use of music as an instrument of war, as strong a belief as ever that making and listening to music could bolster the American soldiery and contribute to military victory. In retrospect, this was the high-water mark for such thinking. Never again has the U.S. government taken such pains to shape the musical lives of its warriors, who, for their part, often had their own ideas about what music was for. What these ideas involved and what their implications were is the subject of the next chapter.

CHAPTER FIVE

The Powers of Song

"Each month the Army's hard-working Special Services Division distributes 2,000,000 *Hit Kits* to encourage soldiers to sing at home and overseas," *Life* magazine's Lilian Rixey reported in 1943. "These gay little brochures contain words and music to the Army's latest selection of popular songs, including 'Blue Skies,' 'Dinah,' 'For Me and My God,' 'Sweet Sue' and 'Margie.' Soldiers don't sing them."

"Tin Pan Alley has worked itself into a lather," the article continued, "trying to produce a song that will strike the soldier's fancy. They brought forth 'Goodbye, Mama, I'm Off to Yokohama,' 'You're a Sap, Mr. Jap,' 'We'll Be Singing Hallelujah Marching Thru Berlin' and 'Let's Put the Axe to the Axis.' Soldiers don't sing these either."

What soldiers did sing, Rixey explained, was bawdy songs. Soldiers belted them out "with . . . gusto." The lyrics were "unprintable." Soldiers sang them everywhere. Despite the elaborate measures the military took to provide music for G.I.s (as we saw in chapter 4), American fighters had their own ideas about what to sing, when, and for what ends. That is, military officials had certain goals and expectations for music in the ranks, but G.I.s embraced music on their own terms, for their own reasons, without regard for those of the institution. Certainly, millions of soldiers did enjoy the USO shows, V-Disc records, and music programs on armed forces radio, but music did not come only from "above." It also sprang upward, from below. If G.I.s were the best-entertained soldiers in the world, they were also entertainers themselves—singers, instrumentalists, and, in some cases, stage performers. To better understand their musical habits, this chapter analyzes and interprets musical activity among soldiers from the bottom up. It shows that soldiers maintained their own musical culture, distinct from the practices and values of the military. Although G.I.s could not escape the bounds of the institution, they were able to use music in numerous meaningful ways, not simply for fun but also to articulate and express their multiple, sometimes competing wartime identities, including "American," "soldier," "consumer," and "horny postadolescent." In many cases, these uses were at cross-purposes with

military life, reaching for experiences and feelings far removed from soldiers' immediate circumstances.[1]

Like a prison or a hospital, the military was what sociologists after
the war would call a "total institution," meaning that it had power over
almost every aspect of the lives of the people contained within it.[2] An
important consequence of this was that G.I.s had few means of pushing
back against the systematic dehumanization of military service, which
spanned from being identified by a service number (i.e., "serial" number)
to putting their lives at risk on the battlefield. As soldiers learned on
the first day of boot camp, the military brooked no deviation, and any
resistance or overt insubordination could bring severe reprisals and punishment. For those subject to this absolute institutional authority, singing and other forms of music offered opportunities to collectively assert
control over their mental lives and identities as individuals.

In this way, vernacular musical activity in the military constituted a
kind of "hidden transcript," as anthropologist James C. Scott would call
it, or fugitive culture through which a subordinate group could challenge
a superior power by a means safer than open defiance.[3] Where outright
confrontation was impossible, other, transient practices, hidden from
public view, could provide meaningful forms of dissent and, in some
cases, opposition. By definition, the hidden transcript is elusive, but by
mining published and unpublished songbooks, photographs and draw-
ings, soldier memoirs, and numerous folklore collections, we can make
out its contours, attending to the roles that music played in soldiers'
actual lives, rather than the script written for them by the institution.

More than sixteen million Americans served in the military in World
War II, including over a million African Americans; 500,000 Mexican
Americans; 44,000 Native Americans; and 33,000 Japanese Americans.[4]
Some 350,000 were women. Together, they made up a force of unprecedented scale and diversity, and consequently, there was no "typical"
soldier experience. As Studs Terkel showed in *"The Good War": An Oral
History of World War II*, a few entered the service for idealistic reasons, out
of a sense of duty or obligation, and some sought adventure or to prove
their mettle in combat. Many others, however, joined up for the sake of
economic opportunity after years of suffering through the Great Depression. And those who enlisted voluntarily made up only around 40 percent
of those who served; roughly six out of ten who served did so because they
were drafted.[5] But regardless of why G.I.s were there, in which branch
of the military they served, or where they were stationed, music touched
virtually all of them. For an untold number of soldiers, informal musical
practices functioned as a medium for formulating feelings and a means

of exploring, claiming, or reclaiming a variety of subjectivities. Bawdy songs mattered—a lot—but the story does not end there.

The Elusive Hidden Transcript

Interpreting the musicality of military life from the bottom up presents several challenges. The greatest comes from the accretion of associations that Americans have with World War II generally, tending to bury historical complexity and nuance beneath layers of myth. Few subjects are as romanticized in the popular imagination as World War II, and the layering of myth has produced something akin to a national catechism. The tenets of this belief, according to writer Elizabeth Samet, hold that Americans fought in order to rid the world of fascism and tyranny; that they were united in this fight; that they fought decently and only reluctantly; that the war was a "foreign tragedy with a happy American ending"; and that these precepts have always been universally agreed upon. Powerful works by Samet, Paul Fussell, Michael C. C. Adams, Matthew Delmont, and others have attempted to dislodge the World War II mythology, but they and the legions of memoirists and scholars who have complicated one or more of these positions have barely moved the needle.[6]

Historicizing G.I.s' musical activity without giving oxygen to mythical clichés is especially difficult because of the part that emotion plays in musical practice. Singing and enjoying music are inherently affective acts and were frequently sentimentalized, even in the moment by soldiers themselves. Consequently, a sober assessment of the work that singing and other forms of musical practice did in G.I.s' lives during World War II requires that we differentiate between their own sentimentalization and the feelings that others projected onto them. On the one hand, music communicated through affect, and soldiers valued musical activity because of what it did for them emotionally. At times, romanticizing the military helped keep soldiers going day after day, whether that meant enduring tedium and boredom, preparing for the battlefield, or coping with the aftershocks of combat. And homesick as they were, many of their songs reveled in nostalgia, a source of comfort and distraction. On the other hand, G.I.s understood music as a resource they could draw on for numerous different ends, and the forms it took could be, in today's argot, demonstrably NSFW—not safe for work. That is, if music was a medium for feeling emotion in an environment that might otherwise render soldiers numb, some of the uses to which it was put were decidedly unsentimental.

For that reason, the extant sources tend to be heavily expurgated, which poses a second obstacle to understanding music in the military from the bottom up. This challenge is epistemological and evidentiary—is it really possible to know what G.I.s sang?—and it makes gaining access to rank-and-file musical culture far from straightforward. "The songs which soldiers and sailors sing," folklorists Gustave Arlt and Chandler Harris stressed in 1944, "are rarely those printed in their official song books or those inspired by morale officers or song leaders."[7] By the mid-twentieth century, folklore and song collecting were well-defined pursuits, and numerous practitioners recognized the distinctiveness of music among soldiers, but folklorists operated within conscious social conventions which restricted what they collected and how they presented their findings—steering clear of indelicate language and never straying from a patriotic script.

Indeed, song collectors were generally quite candid about these constraints, explaining regularly that they omitted crude content, that much of the material they encountered was too vulgar to be published, or that they bowdlerized lyrics for publication. Eric Posselt, editor of the collection *Give Out! Songs of, by, and for the Men in Service* (1943), explained that he left out material that "might have to be 'cleaned up'"—though he claimed he did so only because he lacked "complete and authentic versions" by the time of publication. A year later, under a pseudonym, Posselt published another compilation, *G.I. Songs: Written, Composed and/or Collected by the Men in the Service* (1944). In the introduction, he noted the large volume of material he had encountered which fell outside the bounds of propriety and openly acknowledged that he had replaced offensive terms with "weasel-words" in order to avoid running afoul of obscenity laws.[8]

Likewise, collector Austin Fife was explicit about the limits of his inclusiveness. After serving two years in the South Pacific, he compiled a report, "Anthology of Folk Literature of Soldiers of the Pacific Theater," in the foreword of which he wrote, "I have consciously excluded only those items—ever present though they were—which were of such vivid pornographic suggestiveness that present day mores will not tolerate their circulation." *Ever present though they were.* In other words, objectionable songs were far from exceptional. In fact, he did collect obscene material but excluded it from his final document, and in the archive of his papers at the Library of Congress, this material is relegated to a separate folder appended to the other files, marked "Extra Songs and Poetry (Pornographic)."[9]

In other cases, censorship was not limited to collectors. Informants held back too. "My research has been handicapped by my sex," wrote Agnes Nolan Underwood, a folklorist and English instructor who taught army, navy, and marine veterans after the war. "All the songs, my students had assured me, are not fit for my ears," she explained. "Many . . . expressions used in the services . . . are so unprintable that my students couldn't tell them to me; and if they did, I could never repeat them. So I have had to struggle along as best I could, handicapped as I am by decency."[10] The elusiveness of G.I.s' musical culture, therefore, is more than a function of the transience and mutability of singing. It is a product too of what could be recorded and revealed publicly.

Men Who Sang

Listening for soldiers' fugitive musical activity must also take into account how the place of singing had changed in American life in the decades leading up to World War II, beginning a deep, long-term shift away from making music and toward only listening to it (that is, from production to consumption). One facet of this shift involved the development of electric microphones in the latter half of the 1920s, which reduced distortion, enabled a greater dynamic range, and generally made records and broadcasting sound more immediate and intimate. Out of this technological innovation grew a new breathy, soft-voiced style of singing—"crooning"—which enjoyed enormous popularity among women but whose emotionality was assailed by many male critics as "unmanly." Although some aspects of music had long been derided as "feminine," modern sound technology presented a novel problem. As scholar Alison McCracken has shown, this clash made crooning the subject of intense debate in the late 1920s and early '30s, and only with the rise of Bing Crosby in the mid-1930s did a crooner emerge whom critics found sufficiently "masculine." By and large, the nation's moral panic over crooning had been resolved by the time of World War II, yet some officials and G.I.s remained on guard. Certain musical forms and practices seemed at least potentially "sissy."[11]

While this concern about singing and sexuality seems to have receded by World War II, musical activity could still be suspect. In the 1940s, the armed forces went to great lengths to police and punish homosexuality, one sign of which, military psychiatrists believed, was a pronounced affinity for music. In his landmark study *Coming Out under Fire*, historian Allan Bérubé described one gay sailor whose case history noted specifically that he "displayed a fervent interest in music" and had put himself through college by working as a church organist and choir director. This, navy researchers concluded, was a typical attribute. It was unusual, they found, "for a homosexual not to like music," and many gay men "had their own pianos, whether or not they could play, and they frequently owned albums of fine recordings." Experts did not always speak in one voice, however. A handbook for military trainees written by civilian psychiatrists and psychologists actually *recommended* musical activity for men trying to control homosexual impulses. Rather than succumbing to their same-sex urges, it encouraged them to find other outlets for their libidinal drive—such as dancing, band concerts, and mass singing (as well as athletics and religion). Confusing matters further, the manual included a disclaimer that its authors' views did not represent those of the army or navy, although it was copublished by the *Infantry Journal*, an army publication. (The association between music and homosexuality, it should be noted, was not entirely wrong. According to Bérubé, in some cases, the piano and music rooms at service clubs were used to create "a gay 'cocktail party' ambiance" where like-minded men might meet.[12])

By contrast, numerous contemporaries worried not about the association with homosexuality but that the military's musical initiatives might be falling on deaf ears. "The average American does very little singing in civilian life," noted a memorandum of the Joint Army and Navy Committee on Welfare and Recreation. "Twenty years of radio and fifteen of sound pictures have made him quite passive in his musical habits."[13] Speaking at a public symposium on music in the armed forces held at New York's Town Hall, Lawrence Tibbett, a prominent opera singer and World War I veteran who performed for soldiers throughout the United States and Canada in 1942, reached a similar conclusion. Although he had a favorable impression of soldiers' musical tastes overall, he was "disturb[ed] . . . that men in the service don't sing as much as they did in the last war." Others who had direct experience in the military concurred. "Our Army is definitely not a 'singing soldiery,' and, except for isolated instances, the men will not wholeheartedly join in this type of expression," wrote Private Joseph W. Landon, a former school music supervisor, to the *Music Educators Journal* after three years in the service. Another soldier, Sergeant Robert E. Nye, reported to the same publication after his own three years in the military, "At no time have I observed spontaneous singing in any of the various units of which I have been a member."[14]

Other evidence pointed to the opposite conclusion, including other letters to the *Music Educators Journal* which described a rich musical life in the military. Notably, a survey of the morale of 1,113 white enlisted men conducted by the Research Branch of the Special Services Division in 1943 suggested a great deal of enthusiasm for musical activity. Only 13 percent said they disliked singing, and nearly 90 percent indicated they liked to sing when they gathered with "a few fellows." These numbers varied only slightly when broken down by age, rank, and geographic region. While respondents showed less interest in organized singing such as in glee clubs, more than two-thirds felt it was "personally important" to have singing in the army, and more than a third (36 percent) stated that the army should try harder to get soldiers to sing. Such figures about the popularity of singing may have been inflated by respondents telling interviewers what they thought the interviewers wanted to hear, but even half these numbers would represent a very substantial minority. It also bears emphasizing that these views had little to do with the singing materials that the military provided. Nearly half of respondents said they had never received the *Army Song Book* and another 15 percent did not know whether they had gotten one or had misplaced it if they had. The results pertaining to the monthly song circular, the *Army Hit Kit*, were even less encouraging, with 76 percent answering they had never seen one.[15]

As for *where* they sang, this varied widely. Occasionally, it occurred unbidden, in unexpected places. The journalist and novelist John Hersey, for example, recounted an impromptu performance of "Oh, What a Beautiful Mornin'" among G.I.s in Sicily in 1943 in a letter to one of the song's composers, Richard Rodgers, in 1979:

> I'd had a pretty crummy night, sleeping on the ground, muddy and damp, nothing to look forward to but cold C-rations for breakfast. A G.I. who might perfectly well get killed that day . . . got up and stripped to the waist and poured some cold water in his helmet and began to shave. The sun hit us. Everyone was grumbling as usual. Suddenly the soldier stood up and began singing, "Oh, what a beautiful morning." A pretty good voice. There was a fair amount of irony in his singing, and his pals laughed.[16]

Hersey's recollection of this incident is revealing, for it suggests G.I.s remained up to date on the latest hits in popular music, despite their circumstances. (Bing Crosby and Frank Sinatra both released best-selling recordings of "Oh, What a Beautiful Mornin'" in the fall of 1943, and *Oklahoma!*, the Broadway musical for which the song was written, had opened only six months earlier.)

Hersey's anecdote stands out as both poignant and pedestrian, suggestive of the ways singing was seamlessly integrated into the rhythms of soldiers' daily lives. Just over half of survey respondents said they enjoyed singing when marching, roughly the same proportion as liked singing in the barracks. It was also common for soldiers to sing when drinking, as suggested by a drawing on the envelope of a letter from Sergeant Gerald W. Duquette to his wife in 1944. This cartoonlike illustration shows five soldiers in their cups, three of whom are belting out a song in comradely fashion (see figure 5.1).[17]

Figure 5.1. The illustration drawn on this air mail envelope suggests soldiers' propensity to sing during a night of drinking. The letter was sent by Sergeant Gerald W. Duquette to his wife in 1944. The illustration was drawn by Duquette's friend, Sergeant Samuel Boylston.

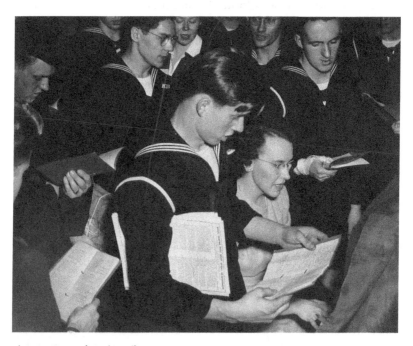

Figures 5.2–5.4. (continued)

Figures 5.2–5.4. These photographs from USO clubs in Oregon and Mississippi suggest that social singing was a commonplace occurrence. As shown here, sometimes male G.I.s sat behind the piano; other times local "hostesses" did; and occasionally they played together.

Other times soldiers sang at USO clubs and canteens, where groups of G.I.s gathered around a piano with local USO "hostesses," with either a soldier or one of the women (or occasionally both) seated at the keyboard. In some extant photographs, soldiers hold lyric sheets or songbooks, but in most they sing from memory. Although the allure of socializing with attractive young women may have been an underlying motivation for these sessions, the role of music was far from incidental, offering both a framework for their interaction and an opportunity for shared emotional expression. If social singing of this kind was less ubiquitous than it had been a generation earlier, it still remained widespread (see figures 5.2–5.4).

Soldier Shows

Everywhere from the American Midwest to Guadalcanal, shows performed by soldiers for soldiers represented another form of vernacular musical activity. In many cases, these were supported by the Special Services Division, which sponsored troupes of military personnel who traveled around the United States and abroad as touring entertainers, including both musicians and thespians who could act in either musical or dramatic productions. Meanwhile, Special Services also sent out supplies and guidebooks known as "blueprints" for entire productions, including scripts, stage directions, musical scores, patterns and tips for costumes, and instructions on lighting and set design, so that individual units could organize and stage their own spectacles. To today's eye, the printed material that the Special Services Division distributed can have a surreal quality, such as the War Department Pamphlet No. 28-12A, titled *OK, USA: A Soldier Shows "Blueprint" Special*, whose cover, with a Disneyesque cartoon, jarringly claims music and comedy as a province of the military (see figure 5.5). Similarly, the Special Services Division also distributed a booklet titled *Comedy Acts and Minstrel Show Material*, published by the *Infantry Journal*, whose cover underscored the military's proprietary claim with the injunction "For use exclusively in military and naval establishments by personnel of the armed forces of the United States."[18]

The most famous of the Special Services theatrical productions was the musical *This Is the Army*, written by civilian Irving Berlin. It was a follow-up to his World War I success, *Yip Yip Yaphank*, which he had written while he served in the army and was stationed at Camp Upton, New York. Opening on the Fourth of July, 1942, at the Broadway Theatre in New York as a fundraiser for the Army Emergency Relief Fund, *This Is the Army* was a lavish spectacle with a cast of three hundred actors. An instant hit,

Figure 5.5. This War Department pamphlet, No. 28-12A, titled *OK, USA: A Soldier Shows "Blueprint" Special*, was billed as a "guide book in music and comedy."

the show quickly spawned a Hollywood film of the same name, directed by Michael Curtiz (hot on the heels of *Casablanca*) and starring Ronald Reagan and George Murphy. The stage version, meanwhile, toured the United States, Europe, and the Pacific.[19] Alongside these efforts were countless other soldier shows organized at the level of individual units and staged in USO clubs, in whatever local facilities may have been available, or on military bases themselves. In some cases, they followed the instructions and specifications contained in the "blueprints" included in the shipments from Special Services. In many others, soldiers simply put on plays and talent, variety, and minstrel shows as they pleased. They ranged in quality from shambolic and amateurish to well organized and polished.

Nearly all of these productions, from the elaborate *This Is the Army* to far-flung, makeshift shows on small bases around the world, featured a great deal of female impersonation. According to historian Allan Bérubé, this theatrical practice worked on two distinct levels, like complementary vocal registers in a choir. First, for military officials, men dressing up as women boosted troop morale, "allowing soldiers without women to entertain each other and affirm their heterosexuality." Having established their masculinity by becoming soldiers, Bérubé explains, men in these shows could play around with gender roles without unsettling their "straight" sexual identities. They were aided by both public-relations officers and reviewers in the press who distanced military drag performers from the stigma of female impersonation as immoral or sexually deviant. Concurrently, the shows offered a refuge for gay male G.I.s who took full advantage of opportunities for witty repartee and double entendre to "queer" military theatrics at a time when the army, navy, and marines were beginning to crack down on effeminacy and homosexuality. However coded or unspoken this language was, it helped gay men in the military not to feel so alone and, at times, to find one another. "The joke was on the unaware members of the audience," Bérubé writes; "a subplot about homosexuality was being created right before their eyes and they didn't even know it."[20]

A staple of these shows was impersonations of the Andrews Sisters—the war years' most popular musical trio. When performed by three male G.I.s in drag, for example, that group's song "Three Little Sisters" from the 1942 film *Private Buckaroo* crackled with innuendo:

> There were three little sisters, three little sisters,
> And each one only in her teens,
> One loved a soldier, one loved a sailor,
> And one loved a lad from the Marines.

Along these lines, three soldiers at Hunter Field, Georgia, in 1943 gave their own original take on the "female" trio. On the one hand, their costumes of evening dresses, comic makeup, mop wigs, and G.I. boots hammed up the female burlesque rather than putting on serious impersonation. On the other, the lyrics of a song they wrote represented a master class in gay double entendre. Playing ostentatiously with the word *camp*, a piece of gay lexicon not yet known to outsiders, they sang:

> Here you see three lovely "girls"
> With their plastic shapes and curls.
> Isn't it campy? Isn't it campy?
> We've got glamor and that's no lie;

Can you tell when we swish by?
Isn't it campy? Isn't it campy?
Those GIs all stop and stare,
And we don't even bat an eye.
You'd think that we were shy.
Now isn't that campy? Now isn't that campy?
So now drink a toast to these lovely "girls,"
Doing their utmost to upset you most.
Now who do you think is campy?

Although the lyrics all but taunted the crowd, spectators appear to have remained oblivious—to the performers' great amusement, no doubt. The day after the show, a journalist for the *Savannah Morning News*, who either missed the joke or covered it up, reported that "the 'female trio,' who almost stopped the show on opening night, were again received by a roar of ovation." In some situations, homosexual insinuation could get soldiers into trouble, but here it seems to have skated by unnoticed. Indeed, that obtuseness itself may have been the point as far as the performers were concerned. As Allan Bérubé put it, "the song's ending suggested that the three men thought the audience's naïveté was even campier than the gay drag itself."[21]

Wherever they were stationed, then, male G.I.s wrote musical shows that were performed for military audiences, almost invariably involving the spectacle of female impersonation. Apart from the special meaning such shows had for gay servicemen, both senior officials and rank-and-file warriors welcomed these shows for their beneficial effect on morale, particularly in basic training camps, remote outposts abroad without accessible local entertainment, and occupied zones where military personnel were barred from socializing with locals. "You are not fighting with machine guns," General Dwight D. Eisenhower, the Allied commander in chief, told a troupe of performers in Algiers in 1943, "but your job is just as important. As long as you are doing your job well—and you are doing it extremely well—you will be rendering a service, and a great one, to your fellow soldiers and your country." Whether they were on stage or in the audience, many soldiers saw female impersonation in this context as affirming their heterosexual identities, as boy-girl couples were performed by men who had demonstrated their manhood by becoming soldiers. For others, the same performances buzzed with homosexual undertones, opening up a secret cultural space—or hidden transcript—within the increasingly hostile environment of the military.[22]

What They Sang—and Why

As this dual interpretation of female impersonation suggests, singing had different meanings and did different things for different G.I.s in different situations. For example, soldiers may have disdained the *Army Hit Kit* (which few appear to have gotten anyway), but belting out the popular hits of the day may have been exactly what was called for in USO clubs when gathering around a piano with a few attractive young women. The same repertoire, however, may not have suited soldiers singing on the march or out for a night of drinking. In homosocial environments such as those, soldiers typically favored other types of songs, some pertaining to their lives in the military, some not. By turns, when they were in the company only of their comrades in arms, G.I.s might opt for a ballad lionizing their service, a fatalistic air bemoaning the twisted logic of military decision-making, or an obscene ditty about sexual conquest. The War Department sent them Tin Pan Alley, but soldiers themselves controlled the songs they sang and the uses to which singing was put.

Taken together, the body of music that soldiers sang appears to have fallen into four loosely defined, mutually reinforcing categories, which fell on a spectrum from innocuous to grossly offensive. First, the most anodyne repertoire consisted of commercial popular music of recent vintage and traditional songs. Usually these were secular, but some religiously themed music fell into this category too, like Christmas carols and well-known hymns like "Swing Low, Sweet Chariot." These popular and traditional songs were heard in places like USO canteens when soldiers socialized with a few "hostesses" or participated in a "sing" led by a designated song leader (figure 5.6). Under these circumstances, popular and traditional songs functioned as a convenient, practical archive from which to draw in polite company. It may have been in this spirit that Sergeant Dominick Salerno of the 839th Anti-aircraft Artillery Battalion wrote out the lyrics to numerous popular songs in a small notebook he carried in his pocket, which is now in the collections of the Library of Congress.[23] Even Tin Pan Alley songs could do valuable social and emotional work.

This first repertoire of commercial popular-music and traditional songs varied widely, but particularly popular among overseas troops was "Lili Marlene," a wistful German ballad that enchanted soldiers of both the Allied and Axis powers. Sung from the point of view of a soldier missing his sweetheart, it was first recorded in German in 1939 and popularized in English by Vera Lynn and Marlene Dietrich starting in 1944:

> Resting in a billet, just behind the line
> Even tho' we're parted, your lips are close to mine;

You wait where the lantern softly gleams,
Your sweet face seems to haunt my dreams,
My Lili of the lamplight,
My own Lili Marlene.[24]

According to folklorist Alan Lomax, who spoke extensively with G.I.s returning from the European Theater of Operations, "Lili Marlene" ranked
"without question" as one of the two most popular songs among the
soldiery, along with the ribald "Roll Me Over (in the Clover)."[25] Again,
under some circumstances, commercial popular music served valuable
personal needs.

A second category of song consisted of the kind of earnest material
that G.I.s might find in an official military song collection. Ranging from
the *Army Song Book* to small compendiums issued on individual military
bases, such collections generally featured a mix of patriotic airs, military-
related songs, and sundry other material. Functionally, they offered G.I.s
a resource to help them endure the tedium and strain of marching, especially during basic training or similar circumstances where singing
represented a sanctioned form of diversion over which they had some
autonomy. In some cases they might have been enjoined to sing during

Figure 5.6. Soldiers participating in a "sing" at a USO club in Galveston, Texas. Both
the discretion of the song leader and the presence of a few women would have
ensured that they steered clear of any indelicate material.

basic training by a drill sergeant, but in many others, the initiative to sing percolated up from below.

This category of song included the anthems of the different branches of the service ("The Caissons Go Rolling Along," "The Army Air Corps Song," "Anchors Aweigh," "The Marine Hymn"); several current popular war songs ("Praise the Lord and Pass the Ammunition," "Der Fuehrer's Face"); and a few jocular, lighthearted songs of complaint ("You're in the Army Now," "G.I. Song"). It also involved the unofficial original anthems that some individual military units adopted (though these were rarer in World War II than in the First World War and the Philippine Insurrection). The Chemical Warfare Service, for example, had "The Gas House Gang," a song catchy and novel enough to be copyrighted by a prominent Tin Pan Alley music publisher, Shapiro, Bernstein & Co. ("When the infantry, artillery / And all the engineers / See they can't pass / They call for gas").[26] These service-friendly songs encompassed numerous compositions from wars past, too, which likely encouraged at least some G.I.s to feel part of a longer martial tradition. Most of these older songs came from World War I ("Over There," "You're a Grand Old Flag," "It's a Long Way to Tipperary," "Oh! How I Hate to Get Up in the Morning," "Pack Up Your Troubles in Your Old Kit Bag," "There's a Long Trail A-Winding"), but a few dated back to earlier conflicts ("When Johnny Comes Marching Home," "Dixie"). Additionally, these songbooks always provided the lyrics to a handful of popular hits from the World War I era as well ("K-K-K-Katy," "Li'l Liza Jane," "Daisy Bell [Bicycle Built for Two]"), and sometimes songs that dated back to the Philippines ("The Monkeys Have No Tails in Zamboanga").

To be sure, the appearance of a song in a published collection does not prove it was sung, but some evidence suggests that the lyrics published in such songbooks were indeed put to use. For example, one extant copy of a pocket-sized songbook issued by the army's Basic Training Center No. 4 in Miami Beach, Florida, belonged to a soldier named Richard Hoppe, and written in pencil on the cover are Hoppe's name and serial number and an annotation in one corner: "These are some of the songs we sing." While it is unclear whom this remark was addressed to, the comment suggests that songbooks such as this were more than mute surplus accessories.[27]

These songs of the service had special meaning for female personnel: the 350,000 women who filled the ranks of the women's corps for the various military branches (the WAC/WAAC, WAVES, WASP, Women's Reserve, and SPAR for the army, navy, air force, marines, and coast guard, respectively), for whom the stakes of serving in the military were quite different than they were for men. In short, these women had a lot to prove. They faced widely held beliefs that women had no place in the military, and consequently everything about their service was scrutinized, from appearance to performance. Unlike most of the men in the military, all of the female service personnel enlisted voluntarily, eager to show that they were qualified to perform a wide range of duties. As a group, they yearned to aid the war effort in whatever capacity the military saw fit, which ultimately ranged from intelligence analysis to flying supply planes.[28]

For female military personnel, singing represented one way to express the pride they felt in serving their country. With this in mind, in 1944, the War Department issued the *Women's Army Corps Song Book*, which reproduced lyrics for many of the same songs as the men's edition but included a variety of WAC-specific numbers as well—"The WAC Is a Soldier Too," "The U.S. Army WAC," "When You See a Girl in Khaki," "Salute to the WAC," "We'll Be Good Soldiers," and so on. That same year, the military also published another WAC songbook, *Songs for the Women's Army Corps*.[29] These compendiums were not merely prescriptive, bringing together a group of songs that WACs *should* sing. Rather, they represented efforts to circulate a body of material that WACs actually sang already. Likewise, another collection, *W.A.C. Songs* (1943), was *compiled* by a WAC, Private Hazel Meyers, perhaps for folkloric purposes. It does not appear to have been intended for circulation. Along the same lines, *Camp Monticello 43 Song Book* identifies numerous WACs by name as songwriters. A WAVES songbook, *Marching to Victory*, went through at least two editions and thirteen printings. Other compilations of women's military songs, often printed informally, also seem to represent songs already widely sung.[30]

The messages conveyed by the songs which these women sang were complex and sometimes contradictory. Some numbers were the same as those sung by their male counterparts, perhaps with a few details modified. Both male and female soldiers sang the "Beer Barrel Polka" and the World War I hit "K-K-K-Katy," the latter sometimes parodied as "KP" (slang for "kitchen patrol," or menial cooking duties like peeling potatoes)—

> K-K-K-KP, beautiful KP
> You're the only army job that I abhor
> When the m-m-m-moon shines over the mess hall
> I'll be mopping up the k-k-k-kitchen floor.[31]

Numerous other songs spoke directly to the significance of the singers' status as *women*. Of these, many proclaimed the singers' pride in, and dedication to, the service. In this parody of "Praise the Lord (and Pass the Ammunition)," they sang:

> Praise the Lord
> We're full of high ambition,
> Basic's given us the ammunition,
> The WAACs are off to fill another mission
> Minus old KP
> We're soldiers, you said it
> You've gotta give us credit,
> For the arm of the arm of the Army we are.[32]

This same spirit of demanding respect and showing off their new social position runs through this parody of "Goodbye to Broadway," which notes the satisfaction gained from learning novel skills, punctuated at the end by martial cheerleading:

> We said good-bye to Broadway
> And the dimout in old Times Square,
> Now we're in the __ company,
> A brand new life to share.
> We like the things we're learning
> And the work we're doing in the corps,
> We're proud to back up our Army
> And we're going to win this war.

Other songs in this vein expressed exuberant defiance. Unbowed by inclement weather, WACs sang:

> We don't care if it's ten below,
> Cold gives our faces a healthy glow,
> We don't care if it rains or freezes,
> We'll march along to the cadence of sneezes.
>   . . .
> We don't care—we'll show them how—
> We're in the Army now![33]

With this resounding punch, these kinds of songs lay claim to a new, elevated status.

Celebratory affirmation was not the only note these songs struck, however. The lyrics of other WAC songs took pains not to upset gender norms. As scholar Carol Burke has noted, the women who served in these branches of the military were exceptionally competent and well educated compared to the general population—99 percent had held a job before joining the military and 95 percent had had some college education—yet numerous songs depicted women instead as scatterbrained or inept.[34] In a parody of "Over There," the smash hit of World War I, they sang:

> Over there, over there
> Send the word to the boys over there
> That the WACs are coming, the WACs are coming
> To get in everybody's hair.[35]

Other songs downplayed women's assertiveness, affirmed their status as auxiliaries to men, and emphasized the modesty of the change they brought to the military:

> I don't wanna march in the Infantry,
> Ride in the Cavalry, shoot in the Artillery.
> I don't wanna fly over Germany.
> I just wanna be a WAAC.[36]

Furthermore, Burke observed, even when songs began by playing up women's professionalism, they still might conclude by portraying them as zany or ineffectual. "Petticoat Soldiers," for example, began by celebrating women's service, "defending life and liberty . . . in step to victory," but ended by making light of their seriousness as soldiers:

> We'll always serve our country
> In every cause it backs.
> We don't tote guns or bayonets,
> Our powder comes in compact sets.
> We're petticoat soldiers,
> Wacky WAACs![37]

Although they were proud to "do our part for Uncle Sam," calling themselves "wacky WAACs" trivialized or belittled their service.

Self-denigrating songs appear less often in the songbooks of the WAVES, WASP, SPAR, and Marine Corps Women's Reserve (all groups much smaller than the WAC), but even there, a few pop up. One was "A Guy to Tie My Tie," which was sung by both WAVES and the Marine Corps Women's Reserve. The WAVES version began:

> Men wanted—to fly our planes
> Men wanted—to rack their brains
> We gotta keep 'em flying

Gotta keep 'em buyin'
Liberty from dyin'
And we gotta keep 'em safe
For tyin' our ties.[38]

No song by men voiced such dependency. By contrast, the pilots of the WASP, the most exclusive of the women's forces—there were only around a thousand of them—were probably the most rebellious of the women's corps. They belted out, to the tune of "The Battle Hymn of the Republic" (one of many parodies of this song):

When the war is over, we will be instructors' wives
When the war is over, we will be instructors' wives
When the war is over, we will be instructors' wives
Like hell we will, like hell![39]

Notwithstanding the songs that undercut or contradicted this confident, unapologetic assertiveness, a far greater number represented a heartfelt declaration of independence and emphasized women's pride in their service.

•

Unlike the mild, good-natured songs of complaint like "You're in the Army Now" and "KP," which could be published in songbooks, a third category of songs came from a far darker place. These were grievance songs of another order, bitter and cynical, voicing unalloyed anger and frustration at the situation in which G.I.s were enmeshed. Often sung when drinking, in transit, or to pass the time during work detail, they belonged to a tradition of folk song associated with workers like miners and sailors, who forged an unusual solidarity in the course of doing their dangerous jobs. "They were a genuine oral tradition, like folk ballads," recalled marine aviator Samuel Hynes about their drinking songs. "Most of them were about sex or death, though a few were devoted to despising senior officers and the military life." As for tone, "all were comic, or were intended to be." In effect, such songs never challenged the supreme power of the military, but through humor, they enabled those in the ranks to criticize the institution and the circumstances it placed them in. As Les Cleveland, a folklorist and World War II veteran, noted, within the bounds of a "total institution" like the military, singing represented one of the few accessible channels of protest—an invaluable way that soldiers could push back, at least rhetorically, against their conditions.[40] While the ephemerality of songs belted out while drinking limited the reach of their critique, this transience was exactly what made the critique possible and thus was the key to the songs' utility.

This large body of song covered an impressive range of perspectives and was continually being modified and expanded. For example, "I Wanted Wings," said to be "by far" all airmen's favorite song, expounded on aviators' disillusionment:

> I wanted wings 'til I got those goddamn things
> Now I don't want 'em anymore.
> They taught me how to fly
> And they sent me here to die.
> I've had a bellyful of war.

Subsequent verses highlighted airmen's indifference to martial glory and preference for sex and drink over flying various types of aircraft:

> I will leave all Zeroes [Japanese planes] to those goddamn heroes,
> For Distinguished Flying Crosses do not compensate for losses.
> I'd rather *fuck* [emphasis in original] than to fly a Grumman Duck.
> No, I don't want 'em anymore. . . .

> Now I'd rather be a bellhop than a flyer on a flat top [aircraft
>   carrier],
> With my hands around a bottle than to nurse a fucking throttle.
> I'd rather screw than to fly an F4U.
> No, I don't want 'em anymore.

With spiteful (and racist) disregard for the enemy, the singer returned to the theme of favoring fucking over flying:

> You can take those Mitsubishis and those yellow sons of bitches,
> But I'd rather lay a woman than to gun a goddamn Grumman.
> I will take the dames while the rest go down in flames.
> No, I don't want 'em anymore.[41]

This was a far cry from the earnest militarism and patriotism found in the official songbooks.

Cynicism and caustic humor were staples of G.I.s' singing, and such grievance songs made up as important a part of soldiers' repertoire as the sweet confection of recent Tin Pan Alley hits or the lighthearted diversion of "service songs." Alongside the seething bitterness of "I Wanted Wings," other numbers in this vein expressed their contempt with an ironic matter-of-factness. One of Alan Lomax's informants reported that paratroopers training at Fort Benning, Georgia, sang these lyrics about fatal accidents in training camp, to the tune of "The Battle Hymn of the Republic":

> There was blood upon his risers, and blood upon his 'chute,
> There was blood that came a trickling down the paratrooper's boot,
> As he laid there rolled in the welter of his bloody gore—
> And he ain't gonna jump no more.

> [*Chorus:*] Gory, gory, what a helluva way to die
> Gory, gory, what a helluva way to die
> Gory, gory, what a helluva way to die
> And he ain't gonna jump no more.

At least six more verses followed, ghoulish in their detail of the consequences and context of training accidents:

> The lines were twisted round his neck, the connectors broke his
>   dome,
> The risers tied themselves in knots around his skinny bones,
> The canopy became his shroud as he hurled to the ground,
> And he ain't gonna jump no more. . . .

> The ambulance was on the spot, the jeeps were running wild—
> The medics jumped and screamed with glee, and rolled their
>   sleeves and smiled,
> For it had been a week or more since a parachute had failed—
> And he ain't gonna jump no more.[42]

Both comic and splenetic, these lyrics inverted the righteousness of the original song ("The Battle Hymn"), transforming it into a mordant indictment of the indifference the military showed to G.I.s' lives.

G.I.s' disaffection came through clearly in one account of drunken aviators joining in on a parody of "Casey Jones," the traditional ballad about an ill-fated railroad engineer. This version of the song focused on soldiers' $10,000 government life-insurance policy. First, one pilot sang of an airman annihilated in a crash:

> He was found in the wreck with his hand on the throttle,
> And his airspeed reading forty knots.

They searched all day for the poor pilot's body,
But all they could find were spots.
Hundreds and hundreds of spots.

Then, all joined in on the chorus, celebrating the insurance payout:

[*Chorus*:] Ten thousand dollars going home to the folks.
Ten thousand dollars going home to the folks.
Oh won't they be delighted!
Oh won't they be excited!
Think of all the things they can buy![43]

Taking aim at both militarism and consumerism, this satire captured a sardonic sensibility sharply at odds with the breezy sincerity of Tin Pan Alley fare and military songbooks.

Among the most beloved grievance songs was the trenchant "Bless 'Em All." Originating in the ranks of the British military, probably in the 1890s, it was embraced widely by American soldiers in all branches of the armed forces in World War II, among whom it was frequently refashioned "Fuck 'Em All," replacing sarcasm ("Bless 'em") with unconcealed, in-your-face scorn and disgust ("Fuck 'em").[44] As "Bless 'Em All," the song had a higher public profile than many others in the protest vein. Cleaned up, it appeared in songbooks, numerous wartime movies, and on record in versions by Vera Lynn, Bing Crosby, and others. The version published in the *Women's Army Corps Song Book*, for example, was completely innocuous:

Bless 'em all, Bless 'em all,
The long and the short and the tall;
Bless all the blondes and all the brunettes,
Each lad is happy to take what he gets
'Cause we're giving the eye to them all,
The ones that attract or appall;
Maud, Maggie or Susie, you can't be too choosey,
When you're in camp, Bless 'em all!
Heavyweight, underweight, big or small,
When you're in camp, Bless 'Em All![45]

By contrast, in its unvarnished form "Bless 'Em All" seethed. With a countless and ever-growing number of verses, the song was an all-purpose vehicle for lashing out but especially for lacerating senior officials and deskbound decision-makers. According to singer and folklorist Pete Seeger, who served in the Pacific, G.I.s there sang:

> They sent for the Army
> To come from Tulagi
> But General MacArthur said "No"
> And this is the reason
> It isn't the season
> Besides, there is no USO.

> [*Chorus*:] Bless 'em all, bless 'em all
> The long and the short and the tall
> Bless all the admirals in ComSoPac [office of the Commander of
>   the South Pacific]
> They don't give a shit
> If we never get back
> So we're saying goodbye to them all.[46]

Beyond indifference to their lives ("They don't give a shit / If we never get back"), soldiers particularly resented what they saw as the aloofness of military commanders who were far from the actual fighting. In another—notably well-crafted—verse, marines inveighed against MacArthur's communiqués:

> Now the greatest of generals is Douglas the Proud,
> Writer of fine flowing prose,
> He paces the floor as his orders ring out,
> Down through his aquiline nose.
> Now he writes his dispatches in bundles and batches,
> And each in a style so sublime.
> The gyrenes [marines] are doing my fighting again,
> So give 'em a fucking this time![47]

Not every verse took aim at officials, however. Some commented on the hardship of G.I.s' living conditions. According to Alan Lomax, for example, a verse sung by G.I.s in Germany went:

> Just think of the boys at the front
> No beer, no whiskey, no cunt,
> They sit in their trenches
> And think of their wenches
> So cheer up, my boys, and etc. . . ."[48]

However popular "Bless 'Em All" was in bowdlerized form, lyrics like these suggest the intensity of the alienation that many G.I.s felt, and the song's popularity among soldiers in the field points to how widely those feelings were shared.

To Paul Fussell, author of *Wartime* ("the best book I know of about the Second World War," according to novelist Joseph Heller, author of *Catch-22*), G.I.s' bitterness was compounded by the sense that the reality of their experiences was being erased from the historical record—obscured by propaganda, obfuscated by military euphemisms, and buried beneath petty bureaucratic "chickenshit." The war that civilians knew was the "Norman Rockwellized" one, as Fussell put it, sanitized, sentimentalized, gutted of nuance, complexity, and honesty.[49] By contrast, singing represented a rare form of control and uncensored expression of sincere emotion, which the indelicacy of the soldiers' repertoire underscored. "The vulgarity opened up an avenue for the pent-up hostility each airman harbored against [a military] service that had stationed him in some ghastly hole, halfway round the world," a former Canadian aviator explained. "Why did we sing? Helpless to control our lives, we turned to song to express the insanities of the moment. We were lonely, homesick, frightened, powerless, and as one of the songs so aptly caught it, 'There's fuck all else to do.'"[50] Few other summations capture the appeal of singing so concisely.

This congeries of feelings (rage, fear, homesickness, impotence, etc.) coursed through what were known as "bawdy" songs—the fourth category of songs that G.I.s sang, after commercial popular songs, official military songbook songs, and grievance songs. The term *bawdy*, however, hardly captures how crudely misogynistic, and sometimes racist, this repertoire could be. In fact, none of the adjectives commonly used to describe this material—*ribald*, *risqué*, *blue*, *unprintable*—evokes much about its actual range and character.[51] The result has been to mystify, not clarify, what "bawdy" songs encompassed and how they functioned. For this reason, the category of music it refers to invites closer analysis. Even if the ephemerality and elusiveness of these fugitive songs make a comprehensive study impossible, enough examples survive for us to glean something of this category's attributes. In light of what we know about earlier wars, the sexual nature of soldiers' songs in World War II should hardly come as a surprise, but this does not make their content or meaning less distinct. Indeed, given the degree to which Norman-Rockwellized clichés still dominate our national memory of World War II, the crudity of this body of material warrants some attention.[52]

According to Fussell, G.I.s' wartime service was rarely motivated by a drive to defeat fascism, to exact revenge for the attack on Pearl Harbor, or any other abstract political goal—a conclusion the historian Robert Westbrook and others have also reached.[53] Instead, Westbrook maintained, American soldiers primarily went to war "to defend *private* interests and discharge *private* obligations," particularly as these were filtered through ideas about American sexuality and womanhood.[54] "We are not only fighting for the Four Freedoms," one soldier remarked, "we are fighting also for the priceless privilege of making love to American women." The woman which heterosexual male G.I.s like this one had in mind, Westbrook posited, was an idealized girlfriend, sister, or mother—more like the wholesome Betty Grable than the racier Rita Hayworth, judging by the soldiers' preference for pinups. Used to decorate the walls of barracks, the bulkheads of ships, and the fuselages of airplanes, images of Grable and other exemplars of Hollywood female pulchritude symbolized what G.I.s were fighting for. Such women were not (only) masturbatory fantasies, Westbrook argued, but (also) stand-ins for wives and girlfriends on the home front. Like Grable's carefully tailored public image, crafted by the publicity machinery of 20th Century Fox, the women G.I.s were thinking of were decent, accessible, and straightforward—erotic, but not exotic. Indeed, "[Grable's] popularity *increased* after she married bandleader Harry James in 1943 and had a child later that year," Westbrook noted. That is, she and other "icons of obligation" represented a particular set of values, both prescribed and felt, grounded in conventional, white, heterosexual monogamy.[55]

The widespread popularity of graphic songs about sex complicates this interpretation, however, suggesting the existence of another less family-friendly story alongside the first. In 1943, *Life* magazine suggested that the most popular song among soldiers was "Dirty Gertie from Bizerte," a sort of successor to World War I's "Mademoiselle from Armentières" (which G.I.s still sang occasionally as well). The writer and song collector Eric Posselt concurred, calling "Dirty Gertie" "the 'great' song of this war—sung everywhere and anywhere." Written by Private William L. Russell, who was inspired by the military's North African campaign, the first verse of "Dirty Gertie" was mildly off-color but not so much that it ran afoul of the censors of *Yank* magazine, where it was first published in December 1942:

> Dirty Gertie from Bizerte
> Hid a mouse trap 'neath her skirtie
> Strapped it on her kneecap purty
> Baited it with Fleur de Flirte
> Made her boy friends' fingers hurty
> Made her boy friends most alerte

She was voted in Bizerte
"Miss Latrine" for 1930.

Countless other soldiers, however, supplemented the original lyrics with reportedly hundreds of other verses which were deemed "unprintable" by song collectors. "Dirty Gertie" also inspired numerous takeoffs, such as "Filthy Fannie from Trepani" and "Venal Vera from Ghiziera."[56]

Other songs were explicitly racialized, with white G.I.s in Africa, India, and the Pacific singing songs like "I'm Dreaming of Jeannie with the Light Brown Skin" (to the tune of Stephen Foster's "Jeannie with the Light Brown Hair") and "White Mistress" (to the tune of Irving Berlin's "White Christmas"):

> I'm dreaming of a white mistress,
> Just like the ones I used to know,
> With lips empassioned and charms unrationed,
> And thighs that glisten like the snow.
> I'm dreaming of a white mistress,
> The kind that the Arabs do not know.
> For though colors may change at night,
> Yet may all my mistresses be white.[57]

If Betty Grable's obvious whiteness was part of her appeal (as Westbrook suggested), lines like "may all my mistresses be white" eliminated any trace of subtlety or ambiguity. From "Dirty Gertie" (especially its unprintable verses) to "White Mistress," these songs articulated less guarded ideas about race and sexuality than those Westbrook associated with the "icons of obligation."

Of course, singing was an activity soldiers did to amuse themselves, and part of the pleasure G.I.s derived from songs such as these came from the feeling that singing them was an act of transgression in an environment of otherwise near total control over soldiers' lives. This feeling of transgression may have increased in proportion to the songs' rudeness. Only a small number of grossly obscene lyrics have survived, but folklore collectors' notes and several unpublished songbooks hint at the flavor of this portion of G.I.s' repertoire. "My Sweet Evalina," for example, began:

> 'Twas down in Cunt Valley where the maidenheads grow.
> On Cocksucker's Levy where the Piss River flows.
> 'Twas there that I met her, the girl I adore—My Sweet Evalina
> My Cow Cunted Whore.

This animalistic objectification of the eponymous Evalina ("cow cunted whore") was not just degrading. It was dehumanizing. And sung for fun, it appears to have coexisted easily with soldiers' erstwhile commitment to more "wholesome" values.

Other songs bring this contradiction into still sharper focus, including relatively benign lyrics which take on an air of menace when read in relation to other sources. This occurs with "The Wolf," a song describing a predator interested only in sexual conquest. On its face, it resembles countless other songs about no-good men with one thing on their mind:

> If he parks his little flivver [i.e., car]
> Down beside the moonlit river
> And you feel him all a-quiver
> Baby, he's a Wolf.
> If he says you're gorgeous lookin'
> And your dark eyes set him cookin'
> But your eyes ain't where he's lookin'
> Baby, he's a Wolf.

By themselves, these lyrics are not alarming, but they seem unusually charged in the notes of an unidentified folklore collector printed below what appears to be an aphorism of one of the collector's informants:

> *To avoid being raped, relax and enjoy it.*[58]

While this adage is not a song lyric, the fact that it appears adjacent to "The Wolf" offers insight into the environment in which the song was sung.

Along these lines, some songs in soldiers' repertoire were far less subtle than "The Wolf," like "Violate Me": "Violate me, in violet time / In the vilest way you know."[59] Another was "Bell-Bottom Trousers," a song learned from the British navy glorifying what was, in effect, a tale of rape ending in pregnancy. The first verse introduces an innocent barmaid and a happy-go-lucky sailor who ends up "the cause of all her misery." In the second verse, the barmaid innocently crawls into bed with the sailor "just to keep [him] warm." The third verse jumps to the following morning, by which time the sailor has raped the barmaid in the night, after which he leaves her some money and speculates about whether she may give birth to a boy or girl:

> Early in the morning at the break of day,
> He handed me a five-pound note and then to me did say:

"If you have a daughter bounce her on your knee,
And if you have a son send the bastard out to sea."

The final verse, in which the barmaid warns other maidens to beware of sailors, frames the story as a cautionary tale, but repeated after each verse, the rousing chorus appears to celebrate the whole incident:

Singin' of bell-bottom trousers, coats of navy blue,
He'll fuck the women like his daddy used to do.[60]

G.I.s in other branches of the American forces had their own versions of "Bell-Bottom Trousers," including the WASP, among whom it was presumably not a mock-cautionary tale but a real one.[61]

G.I.s themselves recognized that obscene songs functioned, in part, to challenge obfuscation and hypocrisy. In fact, they even had a song specifically about this, "Ode to the Four Letter Words." In the first of its six verses, they exhorted:

Banish the use of the four letter words,
Whose meanings are never obscure.
The Anglos and Saxons, those bawdy old birds
Were vulgar, obscene, and impure.
But cherish the use of the weaseling phrase
That never quite says what it means.
You'd better be known for your hypocrite ways
Than as vulgar, impure, and obscene.[62]

Mocking the hypocrisy of avoiding "vulgar, impure, and obscene" language, the song was a wry reminder of the silencing that G.I.s were generally subjected to and were railing against. According to one British collector of soldiers' songs, a virtual "conspiracy of silence" had kept most people unaware of the real songs of wartime.[63] Few G.I.s, it seems, would have disagreed.

"The Men Discipline Themselves" (or, The Musicalization of Military Training)

All this singing mattered. In World War II, the U.S. government went to extraordinary lengths to provide music for soldiers' amusement, from USO shows to armed forces radio, but soldiers had their own ideas about the roles music should play in their lives. The results were varied and complex. From Tin Pan Alley hits sung from memory to "service" songs learned from official songbooks to grievance and obscene songs made up on the spot, singing did different kinds of work in vernacular military culture depending on the location and circumstances. Taken together, the various categories of song that soldiers embraced helped them withstand soul-crushing homesickness and boredom. Songs helped them face the fear and trauma of combat. And they helped G.I.s speak back to the Norman Rockwellization of the war which was rendering their experiences invisible and inaudible to others. For these reasons, many soldiers remembered those songs with fondness years later.

At the same time, if singing benefited soldiers *as people*, this musical activity aided the military, too, as a release for G.I.s' frustration and hostility. While singing could be a form of protest, it also kept G.I.s going *as soldiers*. Sustaining combat troops and rear-echelon personnel alike, it kept the gears of the war machine turning. Recognizing this fact, military officials took no steps to police or tamp down even the lewdest material—the existence of which was an open secret. As early as 1943, journalist Lilian Rixey explained this to readers of *Life* magazine in her article about G.I.s' fondness for "bawdy" songs. Believing that singing such songs signaled healthy (i.e., heterosexual) male desire, officials had no problem looking the other way. "Whatever the tone of the songs the soldiers sing, [morale officers] do not jump to the conclusion that the whole Army is about to go A.W.O.L.," Rixey concluded. "On the contrary, morale officers in the Southwest Pacific teach their men every new song they pick up. They maintain that such mass singing is a safety valve which helps ease the tension of war."[64] Given the effectiveness of singing as a "safety valve," in other words, all songs were good songs, as far as military officials were concerned.

Perhaps no activity exemplified the dialectical function of music as clearly as the novel practice of chanting "cadences" during military training drills—call-and-response singing whose purpose was to keep time and synchronize bodies. The most famous chorus:

Sound off!
  One, two
Sound off!
  Three, four
Cadence count!
  One, two, three, four
  One, two . . . three-four!

Ain't no use in goin' home
  You're right
Jody's got your gal and gone

You're right
Ain't no use in feelin' blue
You're right
Jody's got your sister, too
You're right.[65]

Credited to Private Willie Lee Duckworth, a trainee at Fort Slocum in New Rochelle, New York, in 1944, these lines became known as the "Duckworth Chant" or, later, "Sound Off." Because "Jody" was a recurring character in the verses, such cadences were dubbed generically "Jody calls" or "Jodies."

As a practice, Jody calls represent the war's greatest innovation in music: the introduction of call-and-response chanting during drills and marching—that is, the *musicalization* of military training. To be sure, soldiers for centuries had sung when marching, and since World War I, they had shouted responses to drill instructors, but only in the later years of World War II did a fusion of these practices emerge as a new, distinct idiom, both a bottom-up oral tradition—a kind of organic folk culture— and a top-down tool for conditioning soldiers' minds and bodies.[66]

According to the official history, the singing of cadence chants was invented spontaneously in May 1944 by Private Duckworth, who belonged to a segregated African American unit. In fact, it is unlikely that he initiated it without some official sanction, given that spontaneous singing during exercises would have been a punishable breach of military conduct. In any event, when Colonel Bernard Lentz, the commanding officer, overheard Duckworth's call-and-response chanting and observed its enlivening effect on the soldiers, he directed Duckworth to work with several training instructors to transcribe what he had been singing and to work out some additional verses and choruses. Lentz then made call-and-response singing a regular part of training at Fort Slocum, and its popularity there among both trainees and drill instructors soared. This led to the War Department making a V-Disc recording of the "Duckworth Chant," which was distributed to other military camps throughout the armed forces and triggered a transformation of military drilling.[67] A mere four months after Lentz first heard Duckworth leading his unit in chanting, Alan Lomax was writing to the Library of Congress's Harold Spivacke from Camp Crowder, Missouri, "Have you ever got the record of the Negro cadence? They played it over the loudspeaker system here the other day and the boys have been humming it ever since."[68] (Lomax would later include "Sound Off" in his collection *The Folk Songs of North America*, noting that "in many variants this song was sung by all Negro outfits in World War II."[69])

Bernard Lentz was not just any commanding officer. In World War I, he had authored a pamphlet about the army as an agent of

Americanization—a process facilitated by song, he argued. He also wrote an influential manual, *The Cadence System for Teaching Close Order Drill*, published in eight editions from 1918 to 1957, which trained an entire generation of drill instructors on the fine points of conditioning troops to move their bodies in a systematic, coordinated manner. Instructors had long counted off ("One, two, three, four!") to preserve the step of soldiers on the march, the importance of which military manuals had insisted on for thousands of years, but Lentz shifted the burden of discipline from the instructor to the troops themselves.[70] The key, wrote Lentz, was call and response. His innovation was to have the company respond, in the same rhythm, with the left foot hitting ground on the beat, the result of which was that they learned to march in time by repeating the instructor's cadence. "In this way, the men discipline themselves," Lentz explained. "Each man becomes his own drill master." (It is doubtful that philosopher Michel Foucault read Lentz's manual, but fifty years later, he famously theorized what was essentially same phenomenon in his book *Discipline and Punish*.)[71]

The advent of call-and-response cadence chants, then, marked a subtle revolution in the form and content of military training. In form, the introduction of singing enhanced the effectiveness of the "Lentz system" by sugarcoating the call-and-response process for inculcating military discipline. This was not music for entertainment. It was music for the sake of rhythmic regularity and distraction during arduous, repetitious physical exertion. It was music in the service of conditioning minds and bodies for military use. In content, it marked the birth of a dynamic new tradition of vernacular singing in the military whose roots stretched back to African American prison songs. In the years after World War II, cadence singing was institutionalized as part of the mass production of soldiers (as we shall see in chapter 6). It also entered popular culture, becoming a shorthand for military training itself. In 1949, the "Duckworth Chant" appeared in the popular Hollywood film *Battleground*. Two years later, Vaughn Monroe scored a hit during the Korean War with a big-band arrangement of "Sound Off," which also became the title of a Mickey Rooney movie about an entertainer who gets drafted. By the time the United States sent hundreds of thousands of troops to Vietnam, cadence chants were a basic part of basic training, integral to how the military prepared young men to fight America's wars. In the "consumers' republic" of the postwar years, as historian Lizabeth Cohen has called it, recreational singing grew less common, but this hardly meant musical activity ceased to be part of the military apparatus.[72]

CHAPTER SIX

Demythologizing the Rock-and-Roll War

Today, more than any other American conflict, the military action popularly known as "Vietnam" (though it eventually involved Cambodia and Laos as well) has a soundtrack in the popular imagination. Thanks to Hollywood and documentarians like Ken Burns, we think we know the characteristic sounds of that war and what they meant for how it was fought. Cue up the Jefferson Airplane, the Doors, and Jimi Hendrix, with Grace Slick's shimmering vocals catapulting us into the underground in "White Rabbit," Jim Morrison's baritone intoning the epic psychodrama of "The End," and Hendrix's wailing Stratocaster reinventing "The Star-Spangled Banner" as *cri de coeur*. In the exposition sequence of *Apocalypse Now*, Captain Willard (played by Martin Sheen) grouses about young soldiers he characterizes as "kids, rock and rollers with one foot in their graves." That film, like *Platoon*, *Born on the Fourth of July*, *Full Metal Jacket*, and others, features music so prominently that the significance of music for American war-making in the 1960s now seems well understood and self-evident—if not a cliché. The defining, iconic music of the era—with its jangly guitars, deep reverb, and howling feedback—is heard as voicing the psychic lives of both American soldiers and the nation at large. In a 1977 review of Michael Herr's landmark book *Dispatches*, critic John Leonard called Vietnam "our first rock-and-roll war," and since then, many have come to see it that way.[1]

While not entirely wrong, the Hollywood version is too loud. It drowns out a history that was more complicated—and more important—than Hollywood and Ken Burns have led us to believe. Sounds of Jefferson Airplane, the Doors, et al. did resonate among many soldiers, yet the real story of music in the war in Vietnam neither begins nor ends there. Rock and roll was not the only music that mattered, and it may not have mattered in the ways that many people think. More often than not, music in the ranks in Vietnam extended—rather than departed from—older conventions of war-making. Moreover, what *was* new wasn't necessarily what today's popular memory of the war usually calls to mind, which is protest music. Antiwar songs "weren't appropriate," one veteran remembered; "even though 90 percent of the troops were against the war,

. . . it just didn't come up." In another veteran's estimation, "an antiwar song may have been right, but it had nothing to do with our situation." In Vietnam, the phrase "rock and roll" was not a harbinger of rebellion. It was G.I. slang for switching an M16 rifle into automatic firing mode.[2]

Simply put, whatever music meant for the counterculture and the antiwar movement, it did not mean the same thing in Vietnam. There, music was part of the machinery of waging war. Rock and roll did not disrupt how the war was prosecuted as much as it stood in for actual dissent, the opportunities for which were quite limited within the constraints of the military. If anything, from the military's point of view, it was soul music—not rock—that threatened the status quo. Paradoxically, an account of the war attuned only to rock as a revolutionary force may unwittingly serve the interests of the war machine, for such a narrative diverts attention away from what music was actually made to do in Vietnam, obscuring the ways music affirmatively kept the war going.

This chapter proposes a new way to hear the music of the war in Vietnam. Beginning with the sounds of basic training, it reveals the multiple, sometimes contradictory meanings of the diverse musical practices accompanying, underpinning, structuring, and critiquing the U.S. war effort. It shows how those practices galvanized the prosecution of the war. This is not to say that music had nothing to do with how soldiers expressed opposition to their circumstances. It did. But musical activity was also part of conditioning the American fighting forces and preparing them for battle, and it was part of sustaining them once they were overseas. In basic training, making music was literally part of making soldiers. In Southeast Asia, the military made it possible for musical sounds to course through G.I.s' lives in a variety of ways. Some music cultivated camaraderie. Some drove racial division. When tension between white and Black soldiers led to outright violence, what was on the jukebox mattered.

In the Vietnam War G.I.s listened to music that was broadcast, purchased, traded, smuggled in, and experienced through live performance. At times, they also made music themselves, from boot camp in the U.S. to their billets in Southeast Asia, especially when one of them was armed with an acoustic guitar. When a group of marines was asked by a CBS News reporter how they were keeping their spirits up while under siege during the Tet Offensive of 1968, one explained, "I guess we play cards and sing at night."[3] For all that was new about the circumstances of Vietnam, the musical activity of the war rested on extensive historical foundations. Singing Jody calls in boot camp, listening to armed forces radio and phonographs, participating in soldier shows, attending USO performances and concerts by military bands—these could be traced back to the Korean War, World War II, and earlier.

Recognizing these continuities can help us appreciate what was significant—and what wasn't—about the music in soldiers' lives in Vietnam, which included not only rock but also generous amounts of anodyne Top 40 pop, easy listening, and Nashville-style country music in addition to cadence chants and drinking songs about sexual conquest and the joys of dropping napalm. Some soldiers in Southeast Asia were avidly attuned to the latest psychedelic releases in the U.S., but most were not. To the extent that G.I.s did listen to rock, it was always within a broader field of musical activity, much of which bore the hallmarks of historical persistence, not rupture. In this soundscape, what mattered most was not critique or rebellion but enduring the war as best as one could. Ultimately, Andy Williams's easy-listening hit "Music to Watch Girls By" might tell us as much about music in the American war in Vietnam as anything by Bob Dylan or Credence Clearwater Revival, and a synoptic view of the *longue durée* may reveal more about how music helped the war machine in the 1960s and '70s at least as much as it hindered it.

Sounding Off

Postwar American youth culture thrummed with music. For a generation of young people, songs were not mere entertainment but a social force reflecting and shaping how they understood and confronted the world they were becoming part of. Popular music was, by turns, urgent, earnest, euphoric, and mind-expanding. It liberated, and it spoke truth to power.

Facing this juggernaut, the military did not blink, and by 1960, the army had humbled the king of rock and roll. Drafted in 1957, Elvis Presley entered the service as the paragon of youth rebellion, served dutifully for three years, and left the military as a respectable, upstanding young man. In his first press conference after being discharged, his advice to other young men facing the draft said it all: "Play it straight and do your best because you can't fight them. They never lost yet, you know. You can't fight them, so you can make it easy or you can make it hard for yourself. If you play it straight and get the people on your side, let them know you're trying, the Army would say you got it made. If you are going to be an individual or try to be different you are going to go through two years of misery."[4] Elvis's transformation spoke volumes. In the military, rebellious popular music was not the only sound that mattered.

Nowhere was this more evident than boot camp. For the men who would fight in Southeast Asia in the 1960s, the eight or nine weeks spent in basic training imposed a radical break in their lives, detaching them from the world they had known previously.[5] Music helped produce this break. "We'd sing all the time," army specialist Joseph Pessenda recalled about his time in basic training. "We'd sing from morning 'til night."[6] No mere diversion, this music-making was integral to transforming millions of young civilian men into warriors, and it lay the foundation for music's role in the war generally.

Introduced in World War I, basic training was a system for the mass production of soldiers—a means of turning out large numbers of standardized, compliant, and battle-ready fighters. By the 1960s, the military sought to achieve this goal by destroying recruits' sense of individuality, breaking down their private selfhood, and replacing their civilian culture with a new set of martial values and practices. In the Marine Corps, for example, the military sought control over every aspect of trainees' lives, regulating and restricting everything from their physical movements as they ate to the times when they were permitted to defecate. Recruits were also required to refer to themselves in the third person when addressing a drill instructor, denying them even a personal *I* of their own. "They tore you down," onetime marine Gene Holiday recalled. "They tore everything civilian out of your entire existence—your speech, your thoughts, your sights, your memory—anything that was civilian they tore out of you and then they re-built you and made you over."[7]

Army boot camp was said to be less severe than the training marines went through, but Stan Bodner, an army veteran, also described the experience as a psychic makeover:

> [The trainee] is ingrained with the spirit of the corps, but his own personal self is sacrificed. His personal identity is put on ice. I mean he forgets totally about himself, he becomes . . . a person who is totally acquiesced to a system. . . . What's taught in basic training is a whole unquestionable obedience.[8]

Based on self-loss ("he totally forgets about himself"), the system inculcated absolute acceptance and conformity. Getting trainees to internalize a split from the world they had known was deliberate and strategic. As Fred Fagan, a former head of Marine Corps drill instructors, explained, "Training was designed . . . to break the umbilical cord between military and civilian life, designed to break [a trainee] down to his fundamental self, take away all that he possesses and get him started out in the way that you want him to be." Such an experience denuded a trainee of what he had, debased him, and then offered redemption. While the military would "issue him all new clothes, cut his hair, [and] send his possessions home," Fagan explained, a drill instructor's role was to "tell him he doesn't know a damn thing, that he's the sorriest thing you've ever seen, but with my help you're going to be worthwhile again."[9]

Central to this process of transforming civilians into soldiers was hours of drilling and marching, the effect of which was more than physical conditioning. According to historian and World War II army veteran William McNeill, the rhythmic physicality of these exercises produced an experience of "muscular bonding"—the falling away of ego and the surge of feeling of belonging to a group. A counterpoint to the debasement of boot camp, "keeping together in time" could trigger a transcendent, almost spiritual feeling, he noted. Although not particularly militaristic himself, he recalled many years later that he experienced an emotional and psychological charge during those exercises. "What I remember now," McNeill wrote,

> is that I rather liked strutting around, and so, I feel sure, did most of my fellows. Marching aimlessly about on the drill field, swaggering in conformity with prescribed military postures, conscious only of keeping in step so as to make the next move correctly and in time somehow felt good.

Not only did "keeping in step . . . [feel] good," it changed him in an ineffable way:

> Words are inadequate to describe the emotion aroused by the prolonged movement in unison that drilling involved. A sense of pervasive well-being is what I recall; more specifically, a strange sense of personal enlargement; a sort of swelling out, becoming bigger than life, thanks to participation in collective ritual.[10]

If McNeill was correct that others felt similarly to him, his "strange sense of personal enlargement" helps us understand the connection between the military's goal of producing soldiers and the granular experience of individual transformation.

The music came in with the chanting of cadence calls: "Sound off! / One, two / Sound off! / Three, four," and so on. Having gone through basic training in World War II before call-and-response chanting was incorporated into it, McNeill did not detail the effect of this singing, but by the Korean War, cadences (a.k.a. Jody calls or Jodies) had become integral to the incessant drilling and marching soldiers were enjoined to do. Like the work songs of rowing or chopping wood, they were sung both to synchronize rhythmic bodily movements and to divert the singers' attention from fatigue, pain, and the monotony of the labor at hand.[11] In other words, they made drilling and marching easier for trainees to tolerate, enlivening soldiers physically and mentally. Although this musical practice went unmentioned in the official military training manuals, cadences were unquestionably part of the warp and weft of G.I.s' structured transformation from civilian to soldier.[12]

The military has seldom recognized chanting cadences as a *musical* practice—perhaps because of a long-standing association in American culture between music and effeminacy. But cadences were musical. Like the soldier Joseph Pessenda, quoted above, who recalled, "We'd sing from morning 'til night," military personnel frequently used the language of "singing" to refer to performance of cadences, and the best-known published collection of cadence texts (a heavily bowdlerized two-volume handbook compiled in the 1980s by an army librarian) employed musical terms—*chorus, refrain, song,* etc.—to discuss them.[13] Admittedly, they were not usually vocalized in a particular key and had only a limited melodic range (generally a perfect fifth), but these qualities made them easy for untrained singers to sing. Indeed, their most important musical characteristic was rhythm, always in 2/4 time, with the attack on every downbeat, set by soldiers' footfalls as they learned to march or run at 120 or 180 steps per minute.[14]

The singing itself involved a caller—the drill instructor or a surrogate—who would cue the trainees, line by line, and they would either repeat or respond. The lyrics they sang did more than take soldiers' minds off the rigors of physically demanding and endlessly repetitive drilling, however. They did so in a way that, by turns, promoted a particular set of militaristic values, detached from civilian life and emphasizing loyalty to unit, branch of service, and nation. On a personal level, they also provided soldiers with a means to process at least some of the emotional and psychological challenges involved in adapting to their new life. As the musician Henry Threadgill later recalled, "the jodies were the rhythm we stepped to—they synchronized our anxieties and kept our feet moving."[15] Cadences may have been only a small gear in the war machine in the Vietnam era, but they were an essential one, as both the lyrics of the cadences and the physical act of singing them harmonized the institution and the individual.

Transmitted orally, Jody calls represented an organic folk idiom, decentralized and never performed the same way twice. For this reason, our knowledge of the lyrics that soldiers sang is necessarily fragmentary, but based on interviews, written submissions by veterans in response to published solicitations, and the occasional folklorist running alongside trainees with a handheld tape recorder, we can discern certain patterns and a compass of subjects and identifiable themes.[16] Some cadences were based on nursery rhymes or wordless vocalizing, while many aired complaints about the daily discomforts of military life (e.g., "Coffee in the army / They say is mighty fine. / It's good for cuts and bruises / And tastes like iodine"). Others celebrated the military or some aspect of it, often extolling one's own unit or branch of the service, generally with a flair of insouciance and bravado.[17]

But what "drove" the cadences—what gave them their greatest appeal and power—was their intentional offensiveness. In some cases, folklorist Carol Burke noted, this meant jeers and insults aimed at officers, while in others, it involved a kind of "playful" sexism or the "ghoulish celebration of the slaughter of innocents."[18]

The misogyny took many forms. Sometimes, it involved the sexualization of violence, juxtaposing firearms and phallus ("This is my rifle, / This is my gun. / One is for fighting, / One is for fun"[19]). Other times, cadences boasted of disregard for parental responsibility ("I've got a girl in every port / Suing me for non-support"[20]) or featured extended metaphors for a trainee's voracious sexual appetite and limitless potency:

> I wish all the girls were bricks in a pile,
> And I was a mason; I'd lay 'em all in style.

> I wish all the girls were pies on a shelf
> And I was a baker; I'd eat 'em all myself.

Subsequent verses, of which there were many, compared women to holes in the road, hammers in the shed, hoops in the gym, nails in a board, and so on.[21] Under these circumstances, what William McNeill called "muscular bonding" was not just about the physicality of drilling but also learning a shared language of masculinity and a particular set of values associated with manhood. Moreover, these boasts may have been especially titillating to soldiers who were, in fact, young and, in many cases, sexually inexperienced. The average age of enlisted men in Vietnam was only nineteen (compared to twenty-six in World War II). These soldiers were also less worldly than those of past wars, coming disproportionately from small towns and in-between places.[22]

Other cadences delighted in violence rained down upon civilians—especially the harm caused by napalm, particularly to the most vulnerable populations (children, the infirm). Recalled in a 2014 Reddit thread on the subject of "'dirty' cadence calls," this cadence was sung to the tune of a Sunday-school standard, "Jesus Loves the Little Children" (itself derived from the Civil War marching song "Tramp, Tramp, Tramp"):

> Napalm sticks to all the children,
> All the children of the world.

Red and yellow, black and white,
They all scream when it ignites,
Napalm sticks to all the children of the world![23]

Other napalm cadences, collected by Carol Burke, included:

See the family beside the stream,
Flyin' high and feelin' mean.
Pick one out and watch 'em scream,
Yo, Oh! Napalm, it sticks to kids. . . .

See the orphans in the school,
Don't they know that they're all fools
Burnin' flesh, it smells so cool.
Yo, Oh! Napalm, it sticks to kids.

and

Children in a school house trying to learn.
Drop that napalm; watch 'em burn.

People in a hospital trying to get well.
Drop that napalm; send 'em to hell.[24]

For many G.I.s, this fascination with the violence of napalm did not end with basic training. As we shall see, it reappeared in songs sung in Southeast Asia.

Lyrics such as these were not offensive by accident. A big part of the appeal of cadences—what made them fun to sing—was that they felt transgressive, despite being sung in an environment defined by conformity and discipline. At the same time, what is particularly important for our purposes is that this sadistic, macabre humor prefigured the real acts of violence that trainees might soon be responsible for. After World War II, the U.S. military made a concerted effort to reverse what were reported to be high rates of soldiers who could not, or would not, fire their weapons in battle, even at the risk of their own lives. Although the data and methodology of such reports have since been disputed, military officials in the postwar decades took these claims very seriously and consequently took deliberate steps to inure soldiers to killing and even, in some cases, to celebrate it.[25] "Most of the language used in [Marine Corps training] to describe the joys of killing people is bloodthirsty but meaningless hyperbole, and the recruits realized that even as they enjoy it," wrote military historian (and retired naval officer) Gwynne Dyer in the 1980s. "Nevertheless, it does help to desensitize them to the suffering of an 'enemy,' and at the same time they are being indoctrinated in the most explicit fashion (as previous generations were not) with the notion that their purpose is not just to be brave or to fight well; it is to kill people."[26]

In the estimation of one former army colonel, this process of desensitizing soldiers and "deifying" killing amounted to a form of psychological warfare targeting the United States' own troops. And it appears to have been effective, for the nonfire rate in Vietnam was estimated to be around 5 percent, far lower than World War II or Korea. Although the reasons for this reversal were numerous and complex, Jody calls may have been a contributing factor, as they conditioned soldiers to trivialize violence and dehumanize the victims of both sanctioned and unsanctioned killing.[27] Singing cadences, it must be remembered, was not optional. Trainees were *compelled* to make light of the human consequences of wartime carnage as they drilled.

Reflecting on his training in the marines, one Vietnam veteran drew a direct connection between chanting and killing. He explained in a 1982 interview:

> The Vietnam era was, of course, then at its peak, you know, and everybody was motivated more or less towards, you know, the kill thing. We'd run PT [physical training] in the morning and every time your left foot hit the deck you'd have to chant "kill, kill, kill, kill." It was drilled into your mind so much that it seemed like when it actually came down to it, it didn't bother you, you know?

Chanting, in other words, represented an explicit part of the process of conditioning civilians to take enemy lives.[28]

The experience of chanting Jody calls could have profound effects. Mocking authority and reveling in vulgarity and violence, the sense of transgression associated with cadences excited soldiers, bonded them to one another, and underwrote the development of a new identity. This new worldview emphasized a sense of belonging and inclusion based on soldiers' distance from civilian life, as war and violence took the place of a romantic or sexual partner:

> Cindy, Cindy, Cindy Lou,
> Love my rifle more than you.
>
> You used to be my beauty queen,
> Now I love my M-16.

> Send me off to Vietnam
> Goin' to get me some Viet Cong.

Other verses communicated not only the replaceability of women by weapons but also that killing was an act with sexual frisson.[29]

Some of the power of cadences, then, rested too in helping soldiers work through the emotional complications of leaving their old lives behind. Often, this rupture was embodied by the presence of the eponymous "Jody," the good-for-nothing opportunist back home preying upon a soldier's absence, ready to steal his girl, liquor, house, clothes, etc.

> Ain't no use in lookin' back,
> Jody's got your Cadillac.[30]

> I don't know but I've been told
> Jody's wearing your one-button-roll [a type of suit jacket][31]

Detailing Jody's trespasses, such cadences drove a wedge between the military and civilian worlds, signaling to trainees that they could not count on the life they had known back home.

In the Vietnam era, "Jody" was sometimes replaced with "Charlie," G.I.s' personification of the Viet Cong ("VC," or "Victor Charlie" in the military spelling alphabet), as in:

> Tried to write my Suzie Q
> Seems Charlie's got my girlfriend too.

This substitution made cadences more directly relevant to soldiers' immediate circumstances. It also inadvertently obscured Jody's origins in African American prison songs (the name "Jody" is said to be an adaptation of "Joe the Grinder," a recurring character in those songs). Emerging initially in relation to the carceral control of Black male bodies, Jody was brought into the military by Black soldiers in World War II—transposing one state institution based on discipline, conformity, and labor extraction to another. Crucially, though, in the military, Jody's significance shifted. His unscrupulous actions left trainees with a new martial identity—and only that identity.

> Left that girl at home
> Thought was all alone
> Call her on the phone
> Jody had her and gone

You don't give a damn
You work for Uncle Sam
Am I right or wrong?
Hear me if I'm wrong
Hey, hey, what do ya say?
The Delta Demons [i.e., the 187th Airborne] are here to stay.

Where Jody was concerned, female infidelity was guaranteed, but the military, these lyrics suggested, offered absolute loyalty and constancy.[32]

In short, rather than dispiriting recent inductees, Jody's fiendish behavior could help them make a psychological break, and this was one of basic training's essential purposes—to strip away an old identity and cultivate a new one in its place. As a kind of folklore, Jody calls developed organically, but their effect, drawing a clear line between what social scientists would call the in-group (the military) and the out-group (civilians), elevating the soldier above his former peers, was indispensable for the military's institutional wartime goals. If preparing soldiers to go to war involved stripping trainees of their civilian lives and then offering them redemption through military service, Jody calls musicalized this process of dispossession and reconciliation.

Needless to say, the process of turning ordinary citizens into killers entailed more than singing Jody calls, and trainees did not necessarily take the lyrics of the chants at face value.[33] But the psychological effects of singing cadences warrant being taken seriously, including how they affected what trainees were inclined to do or what actions they were capable of taking once they were deployed. Particularly because of the circumstances in which they were sung, it would be a mistake to think that the words that trainees sang had no meaning or impact. The lyrics alone did not produce personal psychological transformation: context mattered a great deal.

The Jody calls belonged to an induction ritual, a practice whose very aim was to mark and effect "a decisive alteration in the . . . status" of participants, as philosopher Mircea Eliade defined such experiences. Its intention was to effect what the psychologist Robert Jay Lifton characterized as a "totalizing" change, involving both renunciation and reeducation, an administered or coerced rebirth enacted through what one student of cadences has called "violently enforced normalization."[34] The socialization of warriors, "now called *basic training*," Lifton wrote, necessitated the eradication or suppression of a person's civil identity, for "only through such a prescribed process can the warrior become psychically numbed toward killing and dying, shielded from complexity, and totalized in his commitment to the warrior role."[35]

Further, the circumstances under which trainees experienced cadences were characterized by near total observation and constraint. Such "milieu control," Lifton found, "[disrupted the] balance between self and outside world," making people unusually impressionable or susceptible to new dogma.[36] Inductees were not just *exposed* to the lyrics; they were compelled to vocalize them themselves—and to do so in a state of heightened suggestibility. As the historian William McNeill recalled, drilling induced a trance-like effect involving intense feelings of outward expansiveness and empowerment, heightened identification with the group, and dulled awareness of oneself as an individual.[37] In this twilight state, as trainees marched and ran, their moving and chanting in unison made them psychically open. This activity, in the words of another scholar, allowed "nowhere for a soldier to withdraw, retreat, or hide from the beliefs of the leader."[38] In practice, the military's effectiveness in instilling new values was no doubt uneven—milieu control was always imperfect—but the military's efforts to propagate a new martial worldview benefited from the fact that all soldiers, regardless of their affinity or aptitude for music, had to emit the words from their own mouths, in circumstances of extreme vulnerability.

Singing cadences was not the same thing as dropping napalm, but it may have made dropping napalm easier. Persuading one human to kill another—even an enemy—is hard. Far easier, from the military's perspective, was convincing a trainee to kill a dehumanized surrogate or image, just as wartime propaganda had long depicted the nation's enemies in grotesque or cartoonish styles. "This dissociation of one's enemy from humanity is a kind of pseudospeciation," Vietnam veteran Karl Marlantes wrote in *What It Is Like to Go to War*. "You make a false species out of the other human and therefore make it easier to kill him."[39] If the lyrics of cadences operated on the level of caricature, this too was part of the formula that made them effective.

At the same time, the larger point is not simply that Jody calls conditioned soldiers to kill. It is that making light of wartime atrocities occupied the same functional space as mocking a staff sergeant, venting complaints about food, and denouncing the offenses of the opportunistic Jody. They were, in effect, interchangeable. As one veteran remembered the cadences years later, "Most of 'em was sexual, slurs, jokes—nothing bad."[40] On this, trainees and military officials generally agreed, for ultimately, the importance of the cadences rested on their dual identity: both an embodiment of the state and an organic folk culture, a synthesis of military officials' need to produce fighters and the rank and file's need to come to terms with (and hopefully endure) their obligations as soldiers. These two agendas were often in tension, if not at odds, but the cadences spoke to them both.

In-Country: More Than a Rock-and-Roll War

Singing cadences made music part of the process of becoming a soldier in the course of countless hours of drilling and marching. It helped shape G.I.s' understanding of the military—what it was for, how it worked—and what they would, and would not, do as soldiers.

When they arrived "in country," however, everything changed. For personnel assigned to combat duties, music was relatively scarce. Soldiers in the jungle needed to be all ears for signs of enemy belligerents, and they avoided extraneous sounds which could betray their own positions. On patrol, listening and being quiet could be matters of life or death. "I don't know where or why the Vietnam War got the nickname 'the rock 'n' roll war,'" wrote W. D. Ehrhart, who served thirteen months in Vietnam in 1967–68. "That certainly wasn't my experience." He then detailed a few musical experiences he did have during his tour but noted such occasions "are so memorable precisely because they are so rare."[41]

But many more soldiers served in positions away from the front lines. Disdained by combat troops as "rear-echelon motherfuckers," or REMFs, noncombat personnel greatly outnumbered combat troops (estimated ratios range from two to one to eleven to one), probably far more so than in any previous war.[42] That is, most G.I.s spent most of the war on military bases near Saigon or elsewhere, living in relative security and comfort, not in the chaos of combat.[43] In the late 1960s, for example, some sixty thousand troops were stationed outside of Saigon at Long Binh Post, whose facilities and amenities included restaurants, Olympic-size swimming pools, air-conditioning units, and lighted baseball diamonds.[44] For them, changes in the logistics of war expanded the times, places, and means by which musical activity was available and therefore complicated the roles that music played in their daily lives.

As in World War II, USO shows and armed forces radio constituted a lot of G.I.s' musical world in Vietnam—neither of which was oriented around rock music. In conjunction with the Entertainment Branch of the army's Special Services Division, the USO staged more than 5,600 live performances for U.S. military personnel in Southeast Asia by 569 different acts from May 1965 to June 1972. Relatively unknown artists made up the greatest number of these, by far, but numerous big-name performers flew over to entertain the troops as well, often skewing toward stars whose fame dated back to—and in some cases had peaked in—the 1940s and '50s and who probably appealed particularly to older military personnel (often career officers). Most famous among these performers was Bob Hope, a World War II stalwart, while Raymond Burr, Xavier Cugat, Sammy Davis Jr., Henry Fonda, Connie Francis, Danny Kaye, George Jessel, Jayne Mansfield, John Wayne, and Jonathan Winters appeared as well.[45] Although younger, more contemporary acts occasionally went on USO tours, too, including Nancy Sinatra and Johnny Cash (neither a rock artist), the military embraced the heritage of older acts. An Entertainment Branch press release about a tour by singer and comedian Martha Raye read (with unabashed racism), "'I may not be very pretty . . . , but at least . . . my eyes are round!' Lines like these have endeared Miss Raye to every soldier since World War II, when . . . Miss Raye toured North Africa."[46]

Another holdover from World War II and the Korean War was the music of armed forces radio. Complementing the USO, whose shows were special events and took place only on secure military bases, the American Forces Vietnam Network (AFVN), an affiliate of the Armed Forces Radio and Television Service, broadcast throughout South Vietnam on both the AM and FM bands, twenty-four hours a day. Accessible to G.I.s every day, all over the country, AFVN made up a much bigger part of soldiers' musical world than USO spectacles did. "Almost everyone listened [to AFVN]," wrote Vietnam veteran Doug Bradley and historian Craig Werner in their book about music in the Vietnam War.[47] Biding their time in a listening area with few other English-language options on the radio, G.I.s tuned in—a lot—regardless of their branch of the military. From 1968 to 1971, the military conducted a series of surveys of the AFVN audience, offering a synoptic picture of who, when, how long, and to what G.I.s were listening. In 1968, 80 percent of respondents listened two or more hours a day, and a third of G.I.s listened to the radio for five hours a day or more.[48] Further, at places like Long Binh Post, the daily averages were often substantially higher, especially among troops aged twenty and younger and those doing administrative or support work. And notably, these numbers remained fairly consistent, even as cynicism increased and support for the war declined in the military. By 1971, disaffection among the troops had grown substantially, yet average listening times to AFVN held rather steady.[49]

On the air, music mattered most. Following the model of armed forces radio in World War II, AFVN tried to imitate stateside commercial broadcasting, with music-themed shows accounting for as much as 65 percent of the program schedule.[50] Although the network also broadcast sports, informational spots on Vietnamese language and culture, and news reports, which were most listeners' main source of information about the war and public affairs, one report noted, "music is the primary radio programming material for the American Forces Vietnam Network."[51]

As for *what* music the AFVN was broadcasting, program schedules and listener surveys offer a picture of preferences and listening habits that complicates the conventional wisdom. Audience members were opinionated—the vast preponderance of mail that AFVN received from listeners concerned music—and to keep soldiers' ears, AFVN had to accommodate diverse tastes and tolerances, with contemporary rock making up only a relatively small proportion of what G.I.s were actually tuning in to. As much as the so-called rock revolution transformed American popular music in the 1960s, radically new sounds were not everyone's cup of tea, or at least primary focus. For most listeners at the time, the cutting edge existed alongside a robust musical mainstream, as much Burt Bacharach as Big Brother and the Holding Company.[52]

In 1970, for example, listeners overwhelmingly ranked "current Top 40" and "oldies but goodies" (defined as songs from 1954 to 1969) as their first and second favorite styles or formats, followed distantly, in order of preference, by "easy listening," "country-western," "acid rock," "soul," "classical," and "jazz."[53] Of course, rock and soul did feature prominently in the Top 40 at the time but in and among other styles, including a considerable amount of easy listening. To put this proclivity for Top 40 in perspective, the five leading recordings on the *Billboard* Hot 100 chart for 1970 commingled the hard-driving rock of "American Woman" by the Canadian band the Guess Who with three decidedly softer numbers— Simon and Garfunkel's "Bridge over Troubled Water"; the Carpenters' "Close to You"; and B. J. Thomas's "Raindrops Keep Fallin' on My Head." The fifth song in the top five was Edwin Starr's "War (What Is It Good For?)," an antiwar soul anthem which the AFVN did not play.[54] Given the number of other top twenty artists that year who fell outside of the rock and soul orbit, including Ray Stevens, Bread, Vanity Fare, Neil Diamond, and Tony Orlando & Dawn, the designation Top 40 was far from synonymous with what today would be called classic rock.

Some of AFVN's music shows were produced in the United States, others in Vietnam. The most popular of the former was *A Date with Chris*, a Top 40 popular-music program hosted by a sultry-voiced pinup, Chris Noel, airing Monday to Friday for one hour in the late afternoon (figure 6.1).[55] Opening each program with her trademark "Hi, love," she cultivated an air of flirtatious intimacy, and her patter emphasized to G.I.s that she was playing the same music their girlfriends and wives were listening to back home. Musically, a typical playlist moved easily between buoyant and soulful pop (the Dave Clark Five, "You Got What It Takes"; Arthur Conley, "Sweet Soul Music"), light, saccharine country (Sandy Posey, "What a

Woman in Love Won't Do"; Roger Miller, "Walkin' in the Sunshine"), and the occasional rock number (the Seeds, "Pushin' Too Hard"), with a penchant for shimmering, string- and horn-soaked production (Andy Williams, "Music to Watch Girls By").[56] If chanting Jody calls in boot camp embodied the rupture G.I.s experienced from the lives they had known before the military, listening to *A Date with Chris* was its opposite: a musical practice offering them the ordinariness of home.

Along similar lines, G.I.s' favorite shows produced in-country were *Dawnbuster* and *Million Dollar Music*. Thanks to the 1987 film *Good Morning, Vietnam*, the *Dawnbuster* morning show is the best-remembered AFVN program today. It aired for three hours Monday to Saturday, featuring primarily Top 40 music interspersed with lively commentary and patter. In 1965 and 1966, it was hosted by Adrian Cronauer (played in *Good Morning, Vietnam* by comedian Robin Williams) and later by future TV game-show emcee Pat Sajak and others. As in the film, the real *Dawnbuster* did present a lot of rapid-fire talk and (nominal) humor, but it rarely strayed outside the bounds of military-approved propriety and generic middle-of-the-road music. The manic, anarchic, on-air antics of Williams in the movie were a Hollywood fiction. (The real-life Cronauer described himself in 2005 as a "lifelong card-carrying Republican" and campaigned for Bob Dole in 1996 and George W. Bush in 2000.)[57]

The second show, *Million Dollar Music*, aired in the midafternoon, Monday to Friday, featuring "oldies but goodies," a category AFVN

Figure 6.1. Chris Noel, host of AFVN's *A Date with Chris*, traveled from the United States to Vietnam eight times to visit the troops (here in 1967). Her daily Top 40 program was one of the network's most listened-to shows.

defined not stylistically but as "pop standards and up-tempo music which continues to sell over a period of years." Anything from the mid-1950s on was permissible, but generally this meant a repertoire of innocuous pop hits of the recent past which avoided any music that even whiffed of transgression. A typical show from 1971, for example, featured Eddie Floyd's "Knock on Wood" (1966), the Beach Boys' "Surfer Girl" (1963), the Chiffons' "He's So Fine" (1963), and the Association's "Along Comes Mary" (1966).[58] In this spirit, when the DJ/producer of another oldies program, Bob Casey, played the Rolling Stones' "Satisfaction"—a song banned by the AFVN for its "sexually suggestive" lyrics—a commanding officer tried to have him pulled off the air and reassigned to a remote location.[59]

From today's vantage, what stands out is this: as antiwar sentiment among the rank and file swelled over time, G.I.s' support for mainstream music formats remained strong. In their book *We Gotta Get Out of the This Place*, Doug Bradley and Craig Werner contended that a sea change took place in G.I.s' tastes in and relationship with music from the early 1960s to the early '70s, becoming more and more politically charged over time. To some degree this was true, but disaffection from the military does not appear to have correlated to alienation from middle-of-the-road American music. Despite growing cynicism among the troops, the AFVN's audience survey of 1971, which had the highest response rate to date (56 percent), found oldies and Top 40 by far the G.I.s' two most preferred musical categories, with easy listening the clear third, followed by acid rock (the military's catchall term for contemporary rock) and country, which were close to tied, and then soul. And a quarter of respondents wanted even more oldies on the air, far ahead of requests for any other format or style.[60] These figures, of course, do not reflect the preferences of *all* G.I.s in Vietnam, but the surveys were based on a statistically randomized sample and do appear to have indicated the tastes of *many*.

Looking outside of the military's own data, we get a more complex and nuanced picture of music among G.I.s, but the contours are similar. In 1968, *Rolling Stone* magazine mailed its own questionnaire to a "select group" of military personnel from across the armed forces. In response to its queries about music and drug use, replies came in from servicemen stationed in nearly fifty locations, ranging from bases within the U.S. and ships at sea to Saigon and the Vietnamese jungle.[61] The ten-thousand-word article summarizing these results, "Is This Any Way to Run the Army?—Stoned?," both complicates and confirms the impressions created by the AFVN surveys. On the one hand, as would be expected of a leading organ of the counterculture, many of *Rolling Stone*'s respondents thought about and experienced music in ways that departed sharply from the AFVN's official findings. Presumably, such G.I.s would have been among the soldiers less likely to have answered an AFVN survey. Numerous accounts, for example, emphasized the chasm between enlisted men and career military personnel, a.k.a. "lifers." "Lifers can't comprehend rock and roll," one low-ranking soldier wrote. "They're completely disoriented doers of the establishment." Another recounted that fans of the Doors, the Grateful Dead, or Bob Dylan were subject to harassment from officers. To them, AFVN programming consisted of "mainly piped in restaurant-type music" and "Big Brother Uncle Sam talking to you with his liferdog propaganda." A corporal who gave his name as "Very Obscure" was blunter: "[AFVN] sucks, as the programming tries to please everyone. The Chris Noel show makes most G.I.s vomit."[62]

Fortunately for rock fans like "Very Obscure," radio listening was not the only option for music. Many G.I.s assembled elaborate hi-fi sound systems, made up of the latest Japanese consumer electronics (Akai amplifiers, Sony turntables, Teac reel-to-reel and, later, cassette-tape players, etc.) purchased at the military post exchange (PX) stores, sometimes before such goods were available domestically in the U.S. Indeed, so great was soldiers' interest in this area, noted historian Meredith Lair, that most unit newspapers featured music columns and offered detailed advice on selecting components, ensuring their compatibility,

Figure 6.2. The latest Japanese electronics were available to purchase at the military post exchange (PX) stores. Here, G.I.s enjoy a Budweiser while listening to a reel-to-reel tape player.

and maximizing audio quality. "The majority of us who come to Vietnam will go home with some piece of hi-fi equipment," an *Army Reporter* columnist wrote in 1970.[63] Statistically speaking, this was an exaggeration (such G.I.s were not the majority), but from 1969 to 1971, PX stores in Vietnam did sell more than 44,000 record players, 80,000 tuners, and 435,000 tape players—alongside 550,000 transistor radios.[64] In this environment, far from the singing of cadence calls in boot camp, these soldiers used the consumer culture available to them to exercise as much control over their musical lives as possible.

When they could, the hard-core rock fans preferred to listen to their own music, not to armed forces radio (see figures 6.2 and 6.3). In some cases, this meant records which they bought at the PX stores, but what soldiers found there varied widely, often having been selected by the uncomprehending wives of lifers who worked there and skewing toward mainstream and country music. A medical officer stationed in the Philippines wrote, "Absolutely no rock records on the island. PX has 50 copies . . . of 'Sing & Skate Along' [a children's record] and all of [country artist] Hank Snow, etc., etc. (So bad, really, I don't want to bum you out any more.) . . . Found Nilsson and Firesign Theatre among the children's records, by luck! We get only shitty records here." Often, however, the preferred medium for rock fans was tapes—initially, reel-to-reel, and then, from around 1971, cassette—which soldiers frequently copied and traded with one another.

Figure 6.3. Rather than tune in to AFVN, some G.I.s preferred to listen to their own music, as much as possible, wherever they were.

"You people [back home] must realize that most people are into tapes," wrote a G.I. from central Vietnam. Another soldier claimed the tapes in circulation outnumbered records. "The true American status symbol here is the tape recorder," he explained. "It parallels the car thing in the States. The tape recorder is more ubiquitous than the radio and the record player because they're so much more practical for the Nam. You're either into rock through tapes or you're into a jukebox 'cause you're in town digging the whores."[65]

On the other hand, such claims about the tastes and habits of "most G.I.s" and "most people" need to be taken with a grain of salt. If some scorned AFVN, others valued it as a weapon against soldiers' great perennial nemesis: boredom. "It's better than listening to the ship rattle in the wind," a petty officer in the navy explained after cataloging how bad AFVN was (figure 6.4). Further, other respondents to *Rolling Stone* suggested the committed partisans of rock accounted for only a relatively small minority of listeners. Another respondent from the navy, whose duties over three years in the service led him to interact with a wide swath of people, offered *Rolling Stone* readers a breakdown of sailors' tastes that

Figure 6.4. Even soldiers who preferred listening to their own music might, at least sometimes, also listen to AFVN. Pictured here, soldiers smoke a joint in their living quarters in South Vietnam in 1971, with a large stereo speaker visible in the rear and a transistor radio on the floor.

fell roughly in line with the AFVN's own figures. Only 10 percent, he thought, were hard-core rock fans—the same proportion as fans of country ("in our idiom, shitkicking music") and folk. Another 20 percent, he believed, liked rock casually and enjoyed "commercial sounds" equally well; 15 percent had "no musical tastes" or did not care; 5 percent favored classical; and 30 percent—the largest single group—were "R&B fanatics."[66] In other words, however important and prominent rock music was at home, it does not necessarily characterize what most G.I.s were listening to most of the time.

While a numerical breakdown offers a loose sense of the relative size of the different fan bases, it also flattens the social and political differences between the groups, which grew increasingly pronounced as the war dragged on. By the late 1960s even military officials recognized that more was at stake in the musical alignments of rock devotees, country music enthusiasts, and R&B fanatics than idiosyncrasies of personal taste. That is, they saw how musical affiliations mapped onto social and political divisions and were interconnected with morale, discipline, and support for the war effort. In this spirit, AFVN tried to connect with counterculture-inclined rock listeners by launching its own "underground" music show, *Sergeant Pepper*, where soldiers might hear edgier sounds like Cream's "White Room" back to back with a cut from the Beatles' "white" album, though more transgressive artists like the Fugs or Frank Zappa still remained off-limits. To an extent, this sop to rock fans represented a strategic effort to rebrand the military (or the AFVN, at least) in the eyes of G.I.s—what historian Michael Kramer has called "hip militarism"—but just as telling is the fact that *Sergeant Pepper* aired only one (later two) hours weekly, on Sunday nights, leaving most of the program schedule intact.[67]

Country music had a presence equal to that of rock, if not greater. According to both *Rolling Stone* and the AFVN surveys, country fans made up roughly the same proportion of soldiers as the hard-core rock crowd. The extensive presence of this music should not be surprising given that a majority of soldiers came from poor or working-class backgrounds, many in the South or rural areas, where country music was widely embraced. "Although it usually plays a secondary role in the music mythology of the sixties," Bradley and Werner have written, "country music probably had as many fans among the troops in Vietnam as rock or soul."[68]

Compared to rock and soul, however, country music enjoyed a much higher profile within the military.[69] It was heard more frequently on the airwaves and featured in USO shows like the Grand Ole Opry Revue; the record bins in the PX stores teemed with Marty Robbins and Porter Wagoner discs; and jukeboxes in enlisted men's clubs were regularly stocked with country hits. This prominence was not a simple reflection of consumer taste. It was also a product of the unusually tight relationship between the government and the music industry in Nashville. As historian Joseph Thompson has shown in a pathbreaking study, for more than a decade Nashville had promoted country music and musicians as the signature sound of both American patriotism and militarism—another example of the deep interconnectedness of government and private institutions evident in World Wars I and II. Starting in the 1950s, the armed forces began to see great public-relations value in cultivating close ties to Nashville, especially for recruitment. Meanwhile, threatened by the rising tide of rock and roll, Nashville latched onto the promotional potential of the military's captive audience and to the free publicity linked to country artists in uniform touring the U.S. and civilian performers playing for G.I.s on military bases. The military publicized country music performers who served, like Faron Young. It used country music in recruitment advertisements. And it ensured country music was widely available to the men in service.[70]

Although in World Wars I and II the music industries had also collaborated with the military, the connection with Nashville in the 1950s and '60s elevated a particular stylistic preference—one long associated with whiteness, nostalgia, and regionalism—and linked it especially to career military personnel.[71] These factors made country music unusually divisive. Equal numbers of write-in comments to AFVN specifically requested *more* country music and *less* of it, and far more listeners expressed a strong dislike of *Town and Country*, a show that featured country music every weekday for two hours, than for any other of AFVN's programs.[72]

As much as rock, then, country music loomed large in the soundscape of the war, but mythologies of the 1960s and '70s have rendered it almost completely invisible. In 2017, for example, PBS aired *The Vietnam War*, a sprawling ten-part documentary series directed by Ken Burns and Lynn Novick, acclaimed upon its release for showing the war "from all sides."[73] The series' promotional materials highlighted the filmmakers' use of more than 120 popular songs from the period, and its website featured both Spotify playlists and an essay about the soundtrack by David Fricke, a well-known music writer. Far from evoking "all sides," however, *The Vietnam War* relied overwhelmingly on rock music, with some folk, R&B, and soul numbers mixed in. For all their putative catholicism, Burns and Novick featured only two country songs over eighteen hours—Johnny Cash's "Big River" from 1958 and Merle Haggard's 1969 anti-hippie anthem "Okie from Muskogee"—neither of which was representative of the "Nashville Sound" and honky-tonk that soldiers heard daily on AFVN or that sparked clashes in bars and clubs, nor did viewers encounter any of the middle-of-the-road Top 40 music that hummed in the background of G.I.s' daily lives.[74]

If the rock-centered narrative gives voice to a cognitive dissonance many people *felt* during the war, this may help us explain why that narrative has become so entrenched and pervasive. It may accord with what many soldiers and civilians experienced even if it departs from what they were listening to most of the time. But the absence of country music distorts our understanding of social relations in the military. In particular, for African American G.I.s the prominence of country music was an affront. Black soldiers in the 1960s were well aware they made up a disproportionate number of draftees and combat troops and were dramatically underrepresented in the officer corps.[75] Yet only a small slice of the music preferred by Black soldiers got airtime on AFVN. In 1968, for example, Motown chart-toppers like Smokey Robinson or Marvin Gaye and Tami Terrell were welcome in the Top 40 mix. But many hits by Black artists that year were not, from the psychedelic sounds of the Temptations ("Cloud Nine") and the Fifth Dimension ("Stoned Soul Picnic") to Johnny Taylor's woman-left-behind-themed "Who's Making Love" to politically tinged soul anthems like James Brown's "Say It Loud—I'm Black and I'm Proud." And although in June 1968 Brown himself performed for ten straight days on military bases in Vietnam (figure 6.5),

Figure 6.5. James Brown, the "Godfather of Soul," performs in Vietnam in 1968 on a tour that he (not the USO) arranged.

his tour grew out of his own efforts, not through an invitation from the military or the USO, and it was only possible because of his personal relationship with Vice President Hubert Humphrey and Brown's role quelling racial tensions in the wake of Martin Luther King Jr.'s assassination two months earlier. (Brown did not perform "Say It Loud—I'm Black and I'm Proud" in Vietnam. It was recorded a few months later.)[76]

The following year, a short-lived underground G.I. magazine called *Your Military Left* noted that despite the disproportionate number of Black soldiers, the USO featured very few Black performers, and an artists' management agency representing mostly Black talent had failed in its efforts to change this. One of that agency's principals, Rodney Savoy, explained, "I have been given excuses by the [USO's] Hollywood Overseas Committee that black performers were not interested in entertaining servicemen because of their general anti-war sentiment; black entertainers might express their anti-war sentiments in a show; and a show with all black people or too many black people would not be 'American.'"[77] As a result, his efforts to get more Black artists performing USO shows were thwarted.

Wherever African American troops were stationed, the military's elevation of country music and its exclusion or marginalization of Black music added insult to injury. In some cases, Black soldiers pushed back with formal demands for more soul records on jukeboxes. In others, social friction about music could spark explosive confrontations—a function of musical genres being social phenomena as much as aesthetic or aural categories.[78] "When trouble broke out over music," historian James Westheider noted, "it almost always involved not rock but country and western." As early as 1966, in the enlisted men's club at Camp Tien Sha, a naval base near Danang, a riot broke out between Black and white troops over whether country music or soul should be played on the jukebox. In 1968 and 1969, clashes erupted in more than a dozen other enlisted men's clubs in Vietnam where country music was prioritized over soul. A year later, in the wake of a "near-riot" between Black and white troops on an air force base in Labrador, Canada, precipitated, again, by music, Black soldiers complained to investigators from the NAACP that soul music was mainly relegated to the workweek in enlisted men's clubs, while country music was featured in the popular weekend and off-duty hours.[79]

•

These clashes between musical cultures did not simply *reflect* division and difference. They enacted it. Musical activity articulated, embodied, and made manifest the social dynamics and underlying material relationships of the armed forces. It was also an exertion of power—a practice for amplifying some voices and silencing others. After a conflict over music mushroomed into a melee between Black and white soldiers in Darmstadt, Germany, in 1971, journalist Wallace Terry explained the feelings of frustrated Black soldiers to the Congressional Black Caucus: "If Blacks can account for up to twenty-two percent of the dying, they should at least have twenty-two percent of the jukebox or the music on armed forces radio."[80] Indeed, from 1969 to 1971, the Department of Defense and Congress both launched investigations into racial conflict in the military—with music repeatedly identified as an intensely disputed terrain and catalyst for physical confrontation.[81]

Given that "base clubs . . . were viewed as alien and often hostile places for blacks," as an NAACP report put it in 1971, many African American G.I.s sought other destinations for socializing and relaxing.[82] In this, music and racial politics likewise shaped where soldiers went to unwind off-base, with Black and white troops often frequenting different areas with jukeboxes stocked with different kinds of records. In Saigon, for example, white soldiers tended to go to Tu Do Street, an area of bars featuring mostly rock and country music, while Black troops would hang out in the Khanh Hoi section of the city at establishments serving American-style soul food, with soul music on the jukebox. "I get so tired of the goddamn hillbilly music," one soldier recalled about why he preferred to hang out in Khanh Hoi. In other cities, however, Black soldiers might have to search for a while to find a place where they felt comfortable. "A group of us would walk around to find a joint that would be playin' some soul music, some Temptations, Supremes, Sam and Dave," a Black army specialist Harold Bryant recalled about his time near An Khe. "I would want to do my drinking somewhere where I'd hear music that I liked rather than hillbilly."[83] In other places, however, relations with off-base communities could be fraught. In 1971, adjacent to Camp Humphreys in South Korea, a hundred Black servicemen reportedly attacked a neighborhood bar after it replaced its soul music offerings with country and western, jeopardizing the military's relationship with the local population.[84]

Other grievances of Black G.I.s involved PX stores, which soldiers complained lacked products from home that they sought, including music. They also objected to hair regulations, which they claimed officers enforced inconsistently, disregarding the length of white soldiers' hair but prohibiting Black soldiers from wearing Afros. At the same time, military officials saw racial conflict as a threat to national security and, consequently, they were forced to consider making cultural accommodations at odds with the military's institutional logic of complete uniformity and standardization. Ultimately, they struggled to work out a clear and consistent policy pertaining to hair length, but they did make accommodations at the PXs, which quelled some of the tension. As a result, Black soldiers could purchase *Jet* magazine, Black hair-care products, and a wider selection of soul recordings. If the purpose of PX stores was to sustain morale, under these circumstances adjustments to what the stores stocked had operational implications.[85] Soul records alone did not defuse the powder keg of racial conflict, but given the drop in the number of violent clashes that followed these accommodations, they may have contributed to this outcome.

The Resonance of Rock

Chanting cadences, tuning into Top 40 and oldies shows on armed forces radio, and fighting over country and soul music—taken together, these practices among G.I.s decenter rock and roll in our understanding of the war. This is not to say, however, that rock did not resonate—increasingly—over the course of the hostilities. It did, in both recorded and live forms. Tape trading functioned as a valuable, if tenuous, connection to the currents of stateside musical culture for some G.I.s. Meanwhile, outside of the occasional USO concerts that featured rock, many soldiers enjoyed performances by live cover bands both on- and off-base. In order to keep "American soldiers and their dollars" (as General William Westmoreland put it) from upsetting delicate relations with the local economies and to reduce the temptation of what were considered disreputable local night spots, the military tried to provide adequate entertainment for G.I.s in servicemen's clubs and messes on base. To do so, it worked with independent booking agencies to arrange a variety of suitable acts, which spanned from country singers to accordionists but mostly featured rock bands.[86]

Known as Commercial Entertainment Units in military-speak, these musical artists were not actually sponsored by or affiliated with the government, as USO performers were, and consequently, groups performing on military bases had to audition before a Special Services board that evaluated talent and set the fee they could charge. Most of the acts were "girl" bands, comprised of young, miniskirted Filipino, Korean, or Vietnamese women, whose accommodations, transportation within the country, and usually airfare to and from home were paid for by the booking agent. Officially, Special Services permitted only "wholesome" entertainment, but in practice "partial strips," as the military referred to them, were tolerated as well.[87] According to Jonathan Randal of the *New York Times*, one of these groups, the four-member Filipino band called the Paulettes, was responsible in 1967 for reviving "We Gotta Get Out of This Place" by the Animals, which Randal described as "half-forgotten" at the time but quickly became a G.I. favorite and subsequently one of the war's anthems. Originally released two years earlier, "We Gotta Get Out of This Place" soon appeared on all the bands' set lists, often as a finale with a rousing sing-along chorus, its ubiquity and popularity reminiscent of "A Hot Time in the Old Town Tonight" in the Philippines or "It's a Long Way to Tipperary" in World War I, but far less cheery. "If you don't know it, the G.I.s request it," explained Luzviminda Reyes, the twenty-year-old leader of the Reynettes, a recently arrived Filipino band.[88]

If the majority of G.I.s did not align themselves with the contemporary rock culture, those who did could enjoy a music scene off-base worthy of Haight-Ashbury—though more cosmopolitan. In 1970, many went to an area of Saigon they called Plantation Road, where they frequented establishments like the Kim Kim Club, which had a Chinese owner and an Indian manager and catered to young people both American and Vietnamese. The *Grunt Free Press*, a semipornographic humor magazine for G.I.s, published a vivid description of the scene there. Throbbing with psychedelic energy, the article warrants quoting at length:

> On stage there are five young Vietnamese musicians, none over 21, all unisexed with long hair. Behind them is a bright orange and red peace symbol, psychedelic posters selected at random, showing the finger V for peace, a black militant, a cereal box marked "weedies" and the Jefferson Airplane. Black light flashes on the players and the signs, giving half-second slow motion glimpses of the long haired swaying musicians, naked from the waist up and the brilliant red-orange of the posters. On the stage itself and in ten rows of stools in front of it are about 200 G.I.s in fatigues, Army and Air Force mainly, all between 18 and 25 and none over the rank of buck sergeant. There are also about 50 Vietnamese teenagers in the crowd. The volume is turned full blast and the music bounces off the ceiling and walls, cool and hot music, right off the top of the charts and played with Woodstock intensity.
>
> The grunts dig it all the way, swaying, head bobbing, finger tapping, foot stomping, and when a special number is finished, they get to their feet and clap and yell while the players ham it up. There is an empathy between these young Vietnamese and young Americans found nowhere else in Vietnam. The vibrations are there in the flashing lights and the cool music and the hot air and smoke and crowding.

Played with "Woodstock intensity," the music evidently structured a unique social experience, and in the view of at least one soldier, the pleasure to be found in this countercultural utopia even canceled out the unpleasantness of being in Southeast Asia. "Some G.I.s bitch and moan about being in Vietnam, but, man, it ain't as bad as all that," he said. "Gimme a place like this and it don't matter [if] I'm in Saigon or Sioux City. There's some good thing[s] going for us here."[89]

In this respect, rock offered a sensibility, an affect, and occasionally a critique. For some G.I.s, it may even have provided a valuable site of identity formation.[90] What it did not do was develop a systemic analysis of the war, nor did it disrupt military operations. From the point of view of the armed forces, it was soul, not rock, that posed a greater threat to business as usual. If the songs and the sounds of artists like Jimi Hendrix and Creedence Clearwater Revival had special meaning for many G.I.s—which undoubtedly they did—in the bigger picture, the emotional and political relationship soldiers had with rock music could obscure as much it revealed.

Making Music

G.I.s themselves also made music, and, mythologies of the 1960s notwithstanding, much of it was not at cross-purposes with the war effort at all. Not every song was cynical, not all musicians alienated. As powerfully as music could express ambivalence and disapprobation, it also contributed to maintaining the status quo. Broadly speaking, musical activity offered G.I.s a means to question and critique what the United States was doing in Vietnam. It also kept the war going.

This duality was evident on every level. On the one hand, some of the songs that soldiers wrote and sang articulated a vitriolic commentary on the military and the war in general. When the *New York Times Magazine* ran a profile of soldier life in Vietnam in 1966, for example, it highlighted "The Battle of the Co Van My," a song mocking the military's rear-echelon planners and decision-makers (*cố vấn mỹ*, or American advisers). A parody of "The Wabash Cannonball," it ridiculed these officials as aggressive, detached, and ignorant deskbound pencil pushers, with verse after verse indicting their offhand indifference to the destruction and casualties their decisions produced. A typical verse:

> His intelligence is six months old, his native wit is nil,
> For him, the trees teem with VC and regiments crowd each hill.
> He has no kinfolk in the woods, there's naught for him to lose,
> So if in doubt, he'll always shout, "Send in B-52's!"[91]

Portraying officials as equally ill qualified and trigger-happy, such songs scorned those who shaped what happened on the front lines from afar (figure 6.6).

Other songs took aim at the social dynamics within the military, as in this splenetic parody of the official song of the army, "The Caissons Go Rolling Along," sung by a group of conscripts in the mid-1960s. Directing their invective at lifers, they sang together:

Over hill, over dale, as we hit the dusty trail,
As the lifers go stumbling along,
Watch them drink, watch them stink,
Watch them even try to think,
As the lifers go stumbling along.

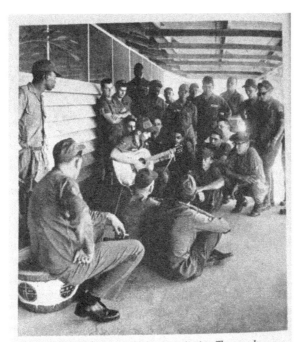

SONG TIME—Every outfit has a guitarist. The war has produced a large body of songs, some of them printable.

Figure 6.6. This image (by the well-known photographer Jill Krementz) accompanied a profile of soldier life in Vietnam published in the *New York Times Magazine* in 1966. As the article explained, "almost every club has a resident musician, usually a guitar player, whom the men crowd around, singing songs about their lives in a strange country and the war they are fighting. The songs are laced with cynicism and political innuendos and they echo the frustrations of the 'dirty little war' that has become a dirty big one."

With even more bite, the same unit parodied the World War I–era pop song "I Want a Girl (Just Like the Girl That Married Dear Old Dad)": "I want a war, just like the war / That mutilated dear old Dad."[92] This kind of creative refashioning was at once a legacy of earlier wars, of the folk revival of the 1950s and early '60s, and of the Jody calls in basic training, and it thrived alongside soldiers' listening to records, tapes, and armed forces radio.

On the other hand, it would be a gross mistake to assume that all G.I.s with acoustic guitars were singing antiwar protest songs. There was nothing inherently oppositional or politically progressive about folk song in Vietnam. A remarkable set of recordings compiled by Edward Lansdale, a senior liaison officer of the CIA, made this clear. Considered one of the ten best spies of all time by former CIA director William Colby, Lansdale had an unusual interest in folk culture as a channel for tapping into popular opinion. Earlier, as an operative of the Office of Strategic Services (OSS) in World War II, he had pushed for the use of Japanese proverbs as an instrument of psychological warfare. He continued to explore the power of folk culture in the Philippines after World War II and then in Vietnam, where he arrived in 1954. Starting in 1962, he began making tapes of the singing at gatherings in his home in Saigon by a range of people connected to the war in some way—soldiers; journalists and visiting dignitaries; civilians working for the CIA, the United States Information Service (USIS), the Agency for International Development (AID), and other groups; Vietnamese musicians; visitors from Korea and the Philippines; and so on—and he continued to collect songs about Vietnam at his home in Virginia upon his return to the United States. In 1967, before he left Vietnam, he made a mix tape of the war with fifty-one of these recordings and sent copies to Lyndon Johnson, Hubert Humphrey, Robert McNamara, William Westmoreland, and other top American officials in order to convey to them the political and psychological complexity of the situation in Vietnam itself. (He received nothing but form letters in response.)[93]

In a musical mode more Kingston Trio than Bob Dylan, most of the Lansdale recordings reflect a folk song culture quite distinct from the protest tradition, being better characterized instead as patriotic and militaristic. In addition to some drinking ballads and cautionary tales about beautiful, thieving Vietnamese women, most of the performances by members of the military consisted of "occupational folklore"—music related to a particular line of work. "All the traditional themes of military folk song can be found in [this collection]," scholar Lydia Fish has written, including "praise of the great leader, celebration of heroic deeds, laments for the dead comrades, disparagement of other units, and complaints about incompetent officers and vainglorious rear-echelon troops."[94] Some of the songs were cynical or ironic, but they were not pacifistic. "Saigon Warrior" was a send-up of pencil pushers in the spirit of "The Battle of the Co Van My" but not an attack on the war itself. The title of one song proclaimed, "I'm Proud to Be an American," while another, about South Vietnam, hailed the "Birth of a Nation."[95]

All of these military performers appear to have been officers ("lifers," in the lexicon of the grunts). And nearly all were aviators—that is, soldiers who generally saw themselves as an elite class in the military and who, whether they flew helicopters or airplanes, were somewhat removed from the carnage and destruction on the ground. This distance left at least some of them feeling consciously detached from their actions, whose consequences could feel abstract. "You never could see the people," recalled Captain Randy Floyd, who flew ninety-eight bombing missions:

> You never heard the explosion, you never saw any blood or [heard] any screams. It was very clean. You're doing a job. You're an expert at what you do. I was a technician. . . . The reality of the screams or of people being blown away or their homeland being destroyed just was not a part of what I thought about.[96]

Certainly, being airmen did not make these soldiers singers, but it may well have influenced the kinds of songs they sang.

Indeed, the difference between the aviators' music and the left-wing protest tradition emerges clearly from more than seventy extant songbooks from this period. Compiled by airmen from the various branches of the military, these songbooks often featured a repertoire unfit to perform at formal military functions, but their contents may have been belted out at weekly song and ballad competitions which the commanding officers of some air bases organized to boost morale.[97] A considerable number of these songs echoed the violence and sadism of the cadences sung in boot camp. Occasionally, these songs, some of which were inherited from earlier wars, concerned sex ("The Great Bloody Wheel," a.k.a. "The Fucking Machine"; "O'Reilly's Daughter").[98] Others celebrated the devastating effects of napalm. In "Isn't Napalm Pretty to Watch," they sang:

> Fire, fire, fire, it looks like the end
> Singes the hair and burns the skin
> Burn, burn, burn, people burned and marred
> By pretty red flames, their bodies well scarred
> Isn't napalm pretty to watch

Isn't napalm pretty to watch
Isn't napalm pretty to watch
It's a gas for you and me.

A different song, to the tune of "The Good Ship Titanic," presented the dropping of napalm as a mock tragedy ("It was sad when my napalm went down!"), while the tone of another, to the melody of the folk song "Get Along Home, Cindy," was giddy:

Oh, chocolate-covered napalm is raining from the sky,
Chocolate-covered napalm is made for you and I;
It's so much fun to drop it, and here's the reason why,
When it finally hits the ground, it makes the people fry.

Although the singers may have intended the upbeat lyrics of such songs ironically, these words also represented—and perhaps facilitated—an aloofness from the impact of these soldiers' work.[99]

Just as important, if the songbooks are any indication, songs such as these were casually slipped in among dozens of others about many other subjects, part of a bigger whole, and they appear to have been sung from early in the war straight through to the end. They did not decline (or increase) in popularity as disaffection among the troops in general grew. In short, the repertoire of songs G.I.s sang was complicated, diverse, and contradictory.[100] If, later in the war, some cynically sang this lampoon of "Camptown Races"—

Your son was killed in Vietnam,
Doo dah, doo dah . . .

or belted out a nihilistic parody of the Wisconsin state song—

Fuck, fuck, fuck, fuck
Fuck, fuck, fuck, fuck
Fuck, fuck, fuck, fuck

a much greater number of songs in the many extant songbooks concerned other subjects besides Vietnam ("The Whiffenpoof Song," "Ode to Shit-Hot Spud Wives"), valorized the airmen's service ("I Fly the Line," "I've Been Everywhere"), made light of destroying villages and killing civilians ("Dashing through the Hooch," "Strafin' round the Mountain"), and bemoaned the risks aviators faced ("Give Me Operations," "I Wanted Wings")—bypassing judgment on the war generally.[101]

·

Outside of singing and guitar strumming, G.I.s also made their own music in a different way when they chose to listen to radio outside of AFVN. For example, they were under no illusions about the propagandistic nature of Radio Hanoi, but many were intrigued or entertained by it, especially given the scarcity of alternatives to AFVN on the dial. In particular, they tuned into the broadcaster known as Hanoi Hannah, whose thirty-minute program was repeated several times a day. Sometimes they listened for laughs, late at night, perhaps after a few beers. In other cases, they might have been allured by what she had to say. As with the legendary propaganda broadcasters of World War II (Tokyo Rose, Lord Haw Haw), soldiers were intrigued by information Hannah had about the war (or was rumored to have), such as news of Viet Cong offensives or welcoming a specific U.S. military unit to Vietnam. Many also had good things to say about the music she played, which featured songs that were banned on AFVN or laced with critical irony (e.g., Connie Francis singing "I Almost Lost My Mind"). Hannah, whose real name was Trinh Thi Ngo, also made special appeals to Black soldiers, claiming the American war had racist underpinnings, as well as announcing the names of G.I.s killed in battle in the previous month and reading newspaper clippings about antiwar demonstrations in the U.S.[102]

In other instances, G.I.s pushed back against AFVN via unsanctioned radio broadcasting by soldiers themselves. Generally this meant unauthorized transmissions over the "bullshit band" (unused military radio channels), but these fly-by-night communications mostly existed for soldiers to air their grievances, not for playing music. By contrast, the most brazen example in alternative broadcasting was Radio First Termer, a short-lived music-focused station launched in early 1971 by air force sergeant C. David DeLay Jr., under the pseudonym "Dave Rabbit." Emanating from a makeshift studio allegedly located on the top floor of a Saigon brothel, Radio First Termer operated with the secret assistance of a few military engineers over AFVN transmitters and relay towers and is said to have been heard widely across South Vietnam. DeLay later claimed that to publicize Radio First Termer he briefly even took control of the AFVN airwaves, redirecting its listeners to his own station. He also promoted it with placards around Saigon and with hand-painted T-shirts he had made.[103]

G.I.s tuning into Radio First Termer heard a lot of heavy acid rock in the vein of what many stateside FM stations had on their playlists at the time—e.g., Iron Butterfly's "In-a-Gadda-Da-Vida" or Carlos Santana's "Evil Ways"—intermixed with irreverent DJ patter and humorous skits.

Looking back, it is tempting to see Radio First Termer as a form of antiwar protest, striking out against what DeLay called the "bullshit that was constantly cranking out on AFVN." As the historian Michael Kramer noted, however, the reality was more complex, for the humor—ironic, profane, and, above all, crude—undercut a coherent ideological position, offering an outlet for G.I. disaffection without making an explicit critique of the war. Hanoi Hannah this was not. And if the lone surviving air check tape is any indication, the patter and skits were often misogynistic, homophobic, and racist.[104]

There is a danger, therefore, in keeping the spotlight on musical dissent. While these examples of radio listening beyond AFVN demonstrate the limits of the military's monopoly of the airwaves and G.I.s' yen for broadcasting beyond what the armed forces offered, their importance should not be exaggerated. Radio First Termer was cynical but not seditious, and it broadcast only a few hours a day, over a period of about three weeks, relatively late in the conflict. In the long history of the war, only a tiny fraction of G.I.s heard it. Arguably, other musical practices, including the chanting of cadences in boot camp, reveal more about the experience of soldiering in the so-called rock-and-roll war. As for Radio Hanoi, which was a permanent institution on a much larger scale than Radio First Termer, its audience among G.I.s appears to have been sporadic, and Hanoi Hannah's influence does not seem ever to have been much of a concern to U.S. military officials.

•

Perhaps the most troubling example of musical activity sustaining the war as much as hindering it was found in the Command Music Touring Shows (CMTS), a special unit launched by the army's Entertainment Branch to bring live music and theater to smaller outposts and areas too dangerous for USO performers or the civilian acts furnished by independent booking agents. From 1966 to 1971, CMTS put on performances by soldiers in remote, high-risk areas throughout South Vietnam, from the Mekong Delta in the south to the demilitarized zone in the north, in a wide range of styles (figure 6.7). As the military saw it, these shows marked a distinct logistical achievement, surpassing even its programs with professional musicians. "They go where the pros can't," boasted Major Edward J. Jones in 1969.[105] And their impact was acute. "It is impossible to be over-emphatic about the value of the military entertainment program from an idealistic angle," one military official wrote in 1967.[106]

Performers were volunteers from the ranks who, after passing a rigorous audition, were temporarily reassigned to CMTS for a specific tour.

Over the course of six years, 119 acts went out on the road, in diverse genres, playing thousands of gigs to audiences spanning from a few dozen servicemen to several thousand. In 1967, for example, CMTS included such artists as the Traildusters playing country and western, the Vagabonds belting out show tunes, the Barons doing straight-ahead pop, Monday's Children strumming "conventional folk tunes," and the Happy Our featuring musical variety, as well as an act simply called "Rock & Soul." And this diversity persisted through the later years of the program even when rock and soul were at their apex. In 1970–71, CMTS acts included country, jazz and blues, folk, soul, acid/heavy rock, a musical variety show, and a male-female duet.[107] Moreover, judging from the "after-action reports" which a military coordinator was required to file following each performance, all different kinds of artists received enthusiastic responses from audiences. (The same goes for the theatrical performances, which spanned from *You're a Good Man, Charlie Brown* to Neil Simon's three-act comedy *Star-Spangled Girl* to Samuel Beckett's *Krapp's Last Tape*.[108])

Tellingly, the military cared more about form than content, remaining conspicuously indifferent to repertoire. What the Entertainment Branch was concerned about was logistics, favorable audience reaction,

Figure 6.7. The Command Music Touring Shows program sent soldier-musicians to remote and dangerous locations. Here, the Coastal Crusaders perform in early 1969.

the absence of obscenity, and musicians conducting themselves professionally. Thus, contradictions notwithstanding, in 1970 the band the Soul Chordinators' preapproved set closer was Edwin Starr's antiwar anthem "War." Likewise, although military officials were seriously concerned about drug abuse by G.I.s, the Peace-Pac's preapproved set list featured the Steppenwolf song "The Pusher," which had featured in the film *Easy Rider*, the ne plus ultra of counterculture cinema.[109]

As curious as it sounds today that the military sponsored a band performing "mostly show tunes" or whose official biography name-checked the Mothers of Invention and Buffalo Springfield, CMTS belonged to the long history of the military's commitment to furnishing troops with music in war zones.[110] Justified on the basis of its benefit to morale, the program built on a legacy which included everything from nightly brass-band concerts in the Civil War to supplying soldiers with harmonicas and kazoos in World War II. In this case, CMTS cut across musical genres to appeal to a variety of tastes and sought to reach soldiers in extreme locations, sometimes at grave risk to the musicians themselves. The story of one band suggests the persistence and popularity of music besides rock even in the early 1970s and illustrates the danger involved for individual performers.

Priscilla Mosby was an Army stenographer and amateur singer and keyboardist who went to Vietnam in 1970 at age twenty. After auditioning for the military in Saigon, she found herself both the leader of and only woman in a nine-piece band, playing both covers (Frank Sinatra, Barbra Streisand) and originals written in styles ranging from pop ballads to jazz to country. For eight months, Mosby and her group toured support camps known as fire bases, often forced to play under straitened circumstances. In some cases, a lack of electricity prevented the musicians from plugging in their instruments, but they adhered to a show-must-go-on ethic and the band improvised as best possible. "So we had to just rough it," Mosby remembered fondly a quarter century later, "and that was even more fun." Yet her memories of the eight-month tour in the field also convey a palpable threat of sexual violence:

> The main thing I kept in mind was to be decent and dedicated and determined and to let them know that it was going to be all right. They could let off steam, singing and dancing and pouring beer on me, whatever—[my bottom line was] just don't rape me.

Fortunately, she notes, none did rape her, but the threat she perceived was quite real. Reports filed by other female personnel, such as those in the Nurse Army Corps, attest to the considerable risk of sexual assault that women in the military faced.[111]

Moreover, Mosby's CMTS tour still ended tragically. Out for a walk one afternoon in a small city in the Mekong Delta, Mosby returned to barracks to find her entire band had been killed by incoming enemy artillery.[112] For all the show-business professionalism and spectacular escapism that CMTS bands offered, ultimately they still embodied the intersection of the joy of music and the violence of war.

•

Military officials in the 1960s and '70s understood how important music was for making and maintaining the American soldiery, building into military life Jody calls, armed forces radio, USO shows, and other band performances on military bases. They sent CMTS bands to remote and dangerous locations, and in some cases, they staged songwriting contests. At the same time, in G.I.s' daily lives, many soldiers supplemented the official musical activities with initiatives of their own. Tapes were traded. Lyrics were written. Songs were sung. Underground radio programs were broadcast. The military never fully administered what music did to and for soldiers, never restricted all of the ways music functioned in their lives, never prescribed or contained what music meant to them.

Amid the menacing cacophony of the war, "sounds were as precious as water," wrote journalist Michael Herr about music in his landmark book *Dispatches*. Indeed, musical activity was frequently an invaluable means for G.I.s to express themselves and connect with others, both their comrades in arms and those they longed for back home. For some soldiers, in some circumstances, music sanctioned and endorsed what they were doing in the war—buoying, reassuring, and perhaps even galvanizing them. For others, music was a medium through which feelings of hostility, resistance, and critique took shape and found release. Transcending—or at least contesting—the dehumanizing environment of the military, music touched people personally and affirmed their social, cultural, and political identities. In this respect, music's effects could be therapeutic, offering comfort or distraction or escape, a psychic refuge and the affect of alternative possibilities, especially when it was combined with drug use, which, for some listeners, was often. "Being stoned and listening to music helps you 'get away,'" an army private explained to *Rolling Stone* in 1968. Underscoring the feeling of listening through headphones, a field medic later recalled, "Music was definitely an escape thing, a way of turning inward," a form of what scholars would later call "mobile privatization."[113] This intentional experience of interiority and the production of a virtual privatized, individuated space marked a sea change in the way musical listening was mediated over the course of the twentieth century, with headphones doing a very different kind of work in the military than, say, the mass "sings" of World War I.

Military officials, therefore, did not exercise complete control over musical activity—nor did they seek to. Total authority over music was, in some respects, beside the point. Drawing on older practices in the military, the general importance of music in the ranks from the institutional perspective was as a force that may have aided the prosecution of the war by making it more tolerable. Making and listening to music were, for most soldiers, a means of expression and psychic safety valve whose end was survival, not rebellion. This included rock, which, sixties clichés notwithstanding, was not a revolutionary or pacifistic force in Vietnam.

One veteran recalled that rock music "made me feel I could make it through anything" and then took pains to explain the anti-radical implications of this:

> Despite what some may choose to think, rock & roll was never fundamentally *anti*war; it was a soundtrack for the entire process [of the war], of which opposition was only a part. Rock also served to let civilians forget about the war, just as it allowed those who were in Vietnam or had somebody there to make it through just one more day without doing anything about the situation.[114]

Music could stir up trouble, but more often it did not. Where musical activity did cultivate emergent, oppositional political identities, usually these got traction only after a G.I. left the service, manifest in groups like Vietnam Veterans against the War. A demystified picture of the work that music was made to do in the American armed forces in Vietnam shows that neither rock nor any other prominent genre was a tinderbox of insubordination. In the big picture of the war, even the clashes over soul and country music were exceptions, not the rule.

There is no question music was important to waging war in Vietnam, as it had been in other American wars. And as in other conflicts, there are contradictions in what it did and meant there. Over the course of the war, the military had to contend with declining morale and discipline, and music was an essential expression of the psychological and emotional dissonance many soldiers experienced, part of the complex of feelings that was also manifest in the increase in desertions and going AWOL as the war dragged on.[115] In one instance, a conflict over music between Black soldiers and a white officer is even reported to have escalated into an incident of fragging, or killing a commanding officer. On the one hand, some unsanctioned musical activity in the armed forces increased friction in the gears of the war machine, causing it to operate less smoothly than it would have otherwise. On the other hand, such music did not gum up the works completely. Only occasionally did it interfere with the daily operations of waging war. For the most part, it lubricated those gears, enabling, not undermining, the pursuit of American war aims. When the army's Entertainment Branch asked G.I.s to name their favorite song performed by the CMTS bands, Edwin Starr's "War" (refrain: "War / What is it good for? / Absolutely nothing") came in first place. Yet the program continued.[116] Here, then, was the ultimate paradox: in some cases, music worked *for* the military even when it was *against* it.

CHAPTER SEVEN

Shoot to Thrill

The music blared out of loudspeakers attached to the Humvee's gun turret where normally a machine gun would have been. The singer wailed:

> Shoot to thrill, play to kill
> Too many women, too many pills
> Shoot to thrill, play to kill
> I got my gun at the ready gonna fire at will.

The song "Shoot to Thrill" by the Australian rock band AC/DC dated from 1980, but in November 2004, it rang out through darkened, empty Iraqi streets on the eve of the Second Battle of Fallujah. And when it ended, a different song began—then another and another—reverberating off the walls. The music was provided by the U.S. Army's psychological operations (psyops) team, which, in the run-up to the military assault, sought to harass and intimidate Iraqi insurgents with sound, just as the army and marines had done before the First Battle of Fallujah the previous April. Indeed, so relentlessly did American military forces pound the city with hard rock and heavy metal that the marines took to calling the city "Lollafallujah," after the music festival Lollapalooza.[1]

Far from cowed, Iraqis responded in kind. Through loudspeakers and amplifiers powered by generators, defiant mullahs retaliated with recordings of Islamic chants and prayers and Arab music. Before the bullets flew, the fight for Fallujah was waged in sound. Whether or not the Iraqis within earshot of the Americans understood the songs' lyrics made little difference. The message came through loud and clear. "It's not so much the music as the sound," U.S. Army spokesman Ben Abel said during the Second Battle. "It's like throwing a smoke bomb. The aim is to disorient and confuse the enemy to gain a tactical advantage. If you can bother the enemy through the night, it degrades their ability to fight." As early as World War II, the U.S. military had conducted experiments on ways that sound could be used as a tactical weapon. In twenty-first-century Iraq, it was.[2]

Did it work? The U.S. military did not conduct controlled studies to determine whether blaring raucous rock music weakened the insurgency, but if nothing else, it appears to have affected the American forces. "Oh, last night on watch, they played the Arabic translation of our 'warning and ultimatums' over loud speakers in the city and afterwards played 'Let the Bodies Hit the Floor' [i.e., "Bodies," by Drowning Pool], some Pantera, Aerosmith, CCR, Jimi Hendrix, Disturbed, etc.," a young marine, Seth Conner, recorded in his journal in April 2004. This weaponization of heavy metal and rock struck Conner as ironic but not without effect— "kind of funny and motivating," as he put it. Moreover, in his estimation the destruction of Islamic houses of worship and the blaring of Western popular music were a one-two punch in the battle against Iraqi insurgents. "If blowing up their mosque doesn't piss them off," he concluded, "playing some American rock 'n' roll while they try to sleep would!"[3]

What makes sonic assaults like these especially striking is that, compared to Vietnam, the recent wars in Iraq and Afghanistan do not usually conjure strong musical associations. In the popular imagination, these conflicts do not have a ready-made soundtrack. Perhaps this is because they have not featured in music-saturated makeovers by Hollywood like *Apocalypse Now* or *Full Metal Jacket*. Or perhaps the lack of an anthem or two is attributable to the absence of a cohesive antiwar movement like that of the 1960s and '70s, or simply to music not carrying the political and cultural weight that it did then.

Whatever the reason, the tuneless popular narrative gets it wrong. Not only did music course through American war-making in the early twenty-first century, it was as consequential as ever. For soldiers in the "war on terror," music was widely recognized as a *weapon*—culture as a cudgel, sound a medium of force.[4] Whether it involved "intimidation playlists" blasted by psyops units through city streets or individual tracks repeated for hours at high volume in secret detention facilities, music functioned as matériel, a potent addition to the military arsenal. And these represent only some of the ways that war-making and music-making were entwined in the early twenty-first century. From beginning to end—recruitment to reentry into the civilian world—music was integral to the "life cycle" of soldiering in the first decades of the new millennium. Indeed, through initiatives from both above and below, musical activity inflected more of the spectrum of military service than ever before.

Admittedly, the heyday of "military music" as such has passed. Many soldiers now have difficulty recalling the official songs of their branch or unit, and when mourners hear taps at a military funeral, it is now most likely not the sound of a live bugler but of a recording.[5] Yet the American military remains a musical institution. With at least 130 dedicated musical ensembles, the U.S. armed forces employ more professional musicians than any other institution in the world. Furthermore, beyond the six thousand soldiers whose official military classification is "musician," chanting "Sound off!" and other Jody calls continues as an integral part of basic training. Officially, the military no longer tolerates the lyrical excesses of violence and misogyny in cadences as it once did, but singing remains woven into the process of transforming civilians into warriors. In addition, many soldiers still sing informally, and some write and perform music as well. Documentary films like *Gunner Palace* (2005) and *Soundtrack to War* (2006) show that in Iraq these soldier-musicians ranged widely, from hip-hop freestylers and beatboxers to country-tinged singer-songwriters and heavy-metal guitar shredders.[6]

The use of music to attract, train, maintain, and rehabilitate the military personnel who fought in Afghanistan and Iraq built on important legacies, the inheritance of at least a century and a half of American warmaking. It also reflected the emergence of a social landscape in which militarism suffused American popular culture and the armed forces were enmeshed with the popular entertainment industries in new ways. If musical activity persisted as a time-honored part of military service, it did so in novel conditions with unprecedented implications, in a feedback loop involving movies, television, and video games and fogging the distinctions between war and commercial amusement. Meanwhile, with country music songs like Darryl Worley's "Have You Forgotten?" and Toby Keith's "Courtesy of the Red, White, and Blue (The Angry American)" sounding the drumbeats of war on the home front, stylistically diverse musical activity in the ranks served a wide range of functions, spanning from readying soldiers for battle to helping veterans heal war's deep psychic wounds.[7]

That's Militainment!

In the early twenty-first century, the presence of music in the wars in Afghanistan and Iraq grew out of several specific conditions. First was the fusion of militarism and popular entertainment in contemporary American life—what the communications scholar Roger Stahl has called "militainment"—whereby the values, logics, language, and technologies of the armed forces spread throughout popular culture. Although the roots of militainment extend back to the brass-band movement of the nineteenth century, the current phenomenon took shape in the 1980s and accelerated in the '90s after the end of the Cold War, produced by a "military-entertainment complex," first analyzed by Bruce Sterling in the first issue of *Wired* magazine in 1993.[8] Throughout the twentieth century, the military and the commercial entertainment industries had cooperated closely, from the creation of Liberty Theaters in World War I to the War Department's collaboration with Hollywood and the radio industry in World War II to the military's partnership with Nashville in the 1950s and '60s.[9] But in light of the military's conversion to an "all-volunteer force" after the draft ended in 1973, what took shape in the age of Reagan and which grew in the '90s and early '00s differed in scope, subtlety, and substance. With input and coordination from the Department of Defense (and, after 2001, the Department of Homeland Security), for example, movies and TV dramas glorified, romanticized, and eroticized the military and national security. Films like *An Officer and a Gentleman* (1982) and *Top Gun* (1986) and the long-running television series *24* (2001–10) not only made military life and antiterrorism work sexy and thrilling but did so with the active cooperation of the government.[10]

Not all aspects of militainment were musical, but many were. CNN added music to its coverage of the 9/11 attacks as early as two o'clock in the morning on September 12, 2001, introducing an original composition which musicologist James Deaville called the network's "fear and anger" theme. Played repeatedly over the days that followed, it featured "martial snare drums, a driving string part, and a concluding plagal cadence and bell sound, referencing the drums and attack of war, the urgent, leaping strings of action and danger, the unresolved cadence of open-ended conflict, and the bell of death and of a call to arms."[11] Other networks soon followed with musical themes of their own. Subsequently, when the United States invaded Iraq in March 2003, news programs often included bespoke theme music, although for the Iraq War, it was commissioned days or even months in advance. Moreover, since the shift to the all-volunteer force, the military was increasingly reliant on advertising and consumer-marketing campaigns to fill its ranks—and these appeals often involved a notable musical component as well. A prominent element of the military's television commercials, for example, was their musical themes, most famously the army's catchy jingle "Be All That You Can Be" in the 1980s and '90s, followed in the first decade of the 2000s by spots with pounding heavy-metal numbers and soaring orchestral themes resembling the soundtrack of action movies.[12]

Complementing the emergence of the military-entertainment complex was the militarization of American life more broadly. Municipal police departments were increasingly outfitted with surplus military hardware, high school officials welcomed military recruiters to their assemblies, and audiences cheered military flyovers at NASCAR races and sporting events. In some cases, parents even sent their children to summertime "spy camps." More and more, the perspectives and priorities of the armed forces were normalized in culture, society, and foreign policy—a trend historian Andrew Bacevich called in 2005 the "new American militarism." The result was not only a growing number of civilians who saw the military as the best or only vehicle for solving international problems but also, more generally, a blurring of the line between military and civilian, between war and not-war, and between entertainment and state violence.[13]

Alongside the growth of the military-entertainment complex and militarization more broadly were changes in the political economy of music and the ever more seamless way that music and the music *business* were integrated into the fabric of daily life. Most narratives of the commerce and culture of music at the turn of the twenty-first century focus on the proliferation of nonmonetized exchange of music (i.e., file sharing) as a leisure activity among consumers and its consequences for record companies. Unquestionably, these were important developments, but at the same time, the business of music was also being reinvented and music itself put to new ends. This involved the creation of new revenue streams like ringtones, a multi-billion-dollar-a-year industry in the early 2000s, which made popular music integral to the new soundscape of cell phones. And it involved the transformation of older revenue streams, like the metamorphosis of Muzak, which ceased to be a producer of saccharine instrumental remakes of popular hits and instead became a broker of existing familiar recordings to be played in commercial spaces. The products of the "new" Muzak in the early twenty-first century had the same function as that of the old, that is, to enliven and stimulate workers and shoppers, but they were now indistinguishable from nonprogrammed music. Manipulating listeners remained the goal, but Muzak no longer had a telltale sonic signature.[14]

The upshot was that the young people who entered the armed forces in the new millennium had a different relationship to popular music and to the popular-music industry in particular than their counterparts had in the 1960s and '70s. More than ever, they were acculturated to music as an industrial commodity, with songs and sound recordings circulating as yet another economic dimension of everyday life. Musical activity in the military, meanwhile, both paralleled and intensified the granular-level changes occurring in the civilian domain. File sharing was not limited to suburban teenage bedrooms and college campuses, and shifts in the aural experience of musical listening reached far outside of cell phone culture and the aural environment of the mall. For soldiers, rather than a background soundtrack to shopping, music functioned as the active soundtrack to war-making. Military service in the twenty-first century involved music in new and old forms and contexts, from video games to actual military operations—some fairly pedestrian, others quite spectacular. Thus, the musical dimensions of making and maintaining American warriors both drew on the legacies of earlier wars and integrated songs and sound recordings into military life in entirely new ways.

Playing Games

The two most remarkable characteristics of musical activity in the military in the twenty-first century were its range—involving not only recreational making of and listening to music, which were practices of long standing, but also video games, music videos, motivational listening, weaponized musical assaults, and music therapy—and the degree to which this musical activity blurred the line between the military and civilian worlds. Arguably, this blurring had begun roughly a century earlier, when Sousa-inspired military bands became the model for legions of high school and college ensembles (many of which live on today, performing spectacular halftime shows at football games) and the community singing movement inspired new training protocols in World War I. In the Second World War, the effort to use the USO, V-Discs, and armed forces radio as tools for normalizing military life also shrank the distance between military and civilian cultures. What occurred around the turn of the twenty-first century, however, elided the distinction between these two worlds more completely and with greater nuance than in previous conflicts.

Beyond the movies and television shows, this shift began in the 1990s with attempts by the military to utilize video games (in which sound played a big part) for training purposes and the development of a reciprocal relationship between the military, private defense contractors, and the gaming industry. In 1997, the U.S. Marine Corps modified a popular commercial first-person-shooter game called *Doom* to create *Marine Doom*, a vehicle for teaching teamwork, attack planning, and other skills. The U.S. Navy adapted a commercial game called *Fleet Command* for its own simulations two years later. Other training simulation games were built from scratch, as with a simulator developed by the gaming giant Sega for Lockheed Martin (which in turn manufactured chips for Sega game modules). For its part, defense heavyweight McDonnell Douglas contributed to the development of *Apache*, a helicopter simulator game for the commercial market, and another defense contractor, OC, Inc., produced a complex military-strategy simulation game for the Joint Chiefs of Staff called *Joint Force Employment*, in which players engaged in everything from deployment of conventional ground and air forces to psychological operations (e.g., leaflet dropping), propaganda, and media campaigns. This game was released commercially as *Real War* in September 2001 only weeks after the 9/11 attacks. So promising did this relationship with the gaming industry appear to the Department of Defense that in 2000, at a cost of $45 million, the DoD launched a new think tank, the Institute for Creative Technologies, at the University of Southern California to harness the talent and imaginations of Hollywood, academics, toy makers, and game designers.[15]

For the military, more was at stake in its relationship with the gaming industry than just training soldiers in its ranks. This collaboration also concerned appealing to civilians, for in the era of the all-volunteer force, the military had to sell itself to prospective recruits and entice them to enlist. In addition to the creation of games for training and education (sometimes called "serious games"), military officials saw great potential in games as a means of advertising, inserting the military into the cultural landscape where young people's ideas about war and the military were formed. Given that recruiters could not sign anyone up until the age of seventeen, the creation of so-called advergames represented an effort to connect with young people, thirteen and above, to compensate for what the military deemed "market failures that increased the national cost of manning the army with quality soldiers."[16] The implication was that the Pentagon could lower costs by expanding its outreach to gamers before they were old enough to enlist. At the same time, such games would also shape young people's imaginations about what the military was—and sound, we shall see, was a big part of this.

Nothing represented this new approach to recruitment better than *America's Army*, the game that the U.S. Army launched with considerable fanfare on the Fourth of July, 2002, after the 9/11 attacks and the invasion of Afghanistan and during the run-up to the Iraq War. Developed at a cost of $7.5 million—a drop in the bucket of the Pentagon's $700 million advertising budget but three times the average for comparable games—it marked the military's most aggressive sally into the gaming field yet. And its invasion of the gaming industry was not merely metaphorical. In May 2003, ten months after the game was made available as a free download and platform for online play, the army's Special Forces descended on an unlikely target: the annual trade show of the gaming industry, the Electronic Entertainment Exposition in downtown Los Angeles. There, soldiers slid down zip ropes from a Black Hawk helicopter hovering outside the Staples Center and then rappelled down the walls inside. Meanwhile, camouflage-clad members of a Stryker brigade stood armed and at the ready beside an armored vehicle outside the convention hall. At a cost of around $500,000, this effort to shock and awe the gaming industry was as meticulously planned as any operation in the field.[17]

It seems to have worked. Initially, the gaming community had greeted *America's Army* with some skepticism, influenced perhaps by the staid formality of the military's stated goals ("to educate the American public about the U.S. Army and its career opportunities, high-tech involvement, values, and teamwork"). But the game proved astoundingly popular.[18] Not only did the part-role-playing, part-first-person-shooter game rank as one of the top five online action games played worldwide on the Internet in 2003, it spawned at least eight sequels, along with a console game for Xbox (2005), a cell phone game (2007), and a coin-operated arcade game (2007)—as well as plastic G.I. Joe–like action figures and a series of graphic novels.[19] In 2009, seven years after the game's initial release, the Guinness franchise awarded it five "world records," all of which seem to have been dreamed up specifically as accolades for *America's Army* but which nonetheless attest to the project's staggering success. They included "World's Largest Virtual Army" (9.7 million registered users, about seven times the size of the entire active-duty U.S. military in 2008), "Most Downloaded War Video Game" (42 million downloads), and "Most Hours Spent Playing a Free Online Shooter Game" (231 million hours as of August 2008).[20]

One of the game's selling points was its verisimilitude: the equipment that avatars were outfitted with, the tasks players had to perform, and the sounds of different grenades and firearms were all based on real-world characteristics. Empty shell casings, for example, made a different sound when they fell on sand than on cement. At the same time, *America's Army* was still a game and had to be entertaining to succeed—and here's where the music and sound design came in. Unlike many other first-person-shooter games, *America's Army* had no music when players were "in action," but, as with many other games, a musical theme greeted players each time they began, and music punctuated play itself, signaling to a player that he (or, less often, she) had killed all the enemies in a certain round.[21] As such, music structured how players moved through the game, welcoming them every time they started anew, then celebrating the end of a task and cuing them to move on to the next chapter.

Players thus became intimately familiar and connected with the game's musical themes, and many were conscious of the music's affective significance. According to a study of *America's Army* by ethnomusicologist Matthew Sumera, this sentiment from an online post was widely shared: "Now, what [the designers of the game] chose to do was perfect: music at the menu to ignite you to want to play again, [and] brief emotional music at the end of each round/match." Another player characterized the musical effect this way: "The music in the main menu is . . . serene, but makes you want to go back into combat." In other words, music appeared in the game only intermittently, but its impact was far from negligible. It was an integral part of the game's interface, framing gameplay and reenergizing players to keep going—a digital variation on the way music had long been used to reenergize soldiers, stretching back to brass-band concerts in the Civil War and earlier.[22]

Notably, other players praised the sounds of gunshots, explosions, and other sound effects as the game's "music," and this represented one of the subtle but essential ways that the military-entertainment complex promoted war as spectacle and amusement to potential recruits. In *America's Army* (and games like it), the sounds of war—the click of firearms, the whiz of bullets, the boom of ordnance—became linked to pleasure and play. Of course, generally this "gamification" of war sounds was unconscious, but it was amplified by the musical theme and interludes. In other words, if music (in the conventional sense) was marginal to the "real" substance of the game, this is exactly what made it crucial: at the periphery, music framed the ever more realistic representations of state violence rendered as entertainment, distraction, and fun.[23]

In this way, the immersive environment of the game made players virtual soldiers in both senses of the word *virtual*—"digital" and "almost." The ludic violence took place only on two-dimensional screens, but at least some of the physical effects—the sweat, elevated blood pressure, and mental fatigue, all studied by the army—were real.[24] As the line between civilian and soldier blurred, *America's Army* did its work.

From the government's perspective, this kind of targeted marketing also appealed to officials because it was more cost-effective than expensive mainstream television commercials. At the time, the Department of Defense spent, on average, around $15,000 to woo each new enlistee, which meant the game needed only yield three hundred new soldiers per year to recoup development costs over two years. In fact, enlistments swelled following the game's release in 2002. It would be foolish, of course, to suggest that *America's Army* alone produced this increase, but survey data suggest the game may well have contributed to it. In 2003, Colonel Casey Wardynski, the army official who had launched the project, boasted that the game was the fourth-ranked factor creating "favorable awareness" of the army, topped only by the war in Iraq, homeland security, and tensions with North Korea. Two years later, around 40 percent of enlistees reported having played the game before signing up.[25] That said, as far as the military was concerned, the measure of the game's value could not be reduced to recruitment numbers. The army did not expect every player of the game to enlist. "There are people who would like to ask me, well, how many people came into the army because of the game?" Wardynski explained. "That's not exactly why we did it. What we did it for was . . . to put the army in pop culture." As the military saw it, propagating the values, logics, and norms of the army, especially among young people, would pay off in the kinds of people who signed up.[26]

Beyond Entertainment

Gamers or not, when recruits began basic training, they had to put their personal items in storage, and at that point, anything like the individualized experience of video games was superseded by the collective chanting of cadences during drills. In many respects, this chanting echoed military training since the closing years of World War II. Now, however, women made up a sizable proportion of the soldiery, and in the wake of the Tailhook sexual-assault scandal in 1991, military officials generally restricted the kinds of Jody calls that were permissible, prohibiting those that were misogynistic or sexually graphic. That said, evidence also suggests that out of earshot of commanding officers, drill instructors occasionally reprised the older, more offensive material—making it feel all the more transgressive. In any case, by this time Jody calls were such a staple of popular culture that virtually all recruits anticipated that chanting would be part of their experience in the service. Many were familiar with this chanting from movies and television shows—spanning from *Stripes* and *Full Metal Jacket* in the 1980s to *The Simpsons* and *SpongeBob SquarePants* in the 1990s and 2000s. Some had also seen cadences sung in a 2001 recruitment video, *212 Ways to Be a Soldier*. Far from the screens of video games, chanting Jody calls was, as we have seen, fundamental to the process of transforming civilians into warriors.[27]

Once soldiers were deployed, their musical lives changed yet again, in multiple ways and perhaps to greater effect than ever before. By and large, this came from soldiers' own initiative. In Afghanistan and Iraq, far less of the musical activity among the rank and file was orchestrated from above than in earlier wars (although the military had never exercised exclusive control over music anyway). Large-scale organized singing had long since disappeared, and armed forces radio attracted many fewer listeners, who now had more options at their disposal.[28] The USO again staged concerts on military bases, but these were relatively infrequent and, however popular, received far less attention than they had in World War II or even in Vietnam.

Vernacular musical activity, though, was everywhere, and more than in previous wars, its presence in soldiers' lives was widely recognized by contemporary journalists, filmmakers, and social critics. Hip-hop freestyling, shredding on electric guitars, blasting music from psyops speaker trucks—all these featured prominently in the 2005 documentary

Gunner Palace, directed by Michael Tucker and Petra Epperlein, about U.S. soldiers occupying a former pleasure palace built by Saddam Hussein. Music in the Iraq War was also the subject of George Gittoes's 2005 documentary *Soundtrack to War: A Film* (made during 2003–4), numerous clips of which also appeared in Michael Moore's *Fahrenheit 9/11*, which came out in 2004 before Gittoes's own film was released. Elsewhere, newspapers, music magazines, tech websites, and radio profiles documented the widespread presence of music in the wars as well. Even cartoonist Garry Trudeau offered his own wry comment on it in his nationally syndicated comic strip *Doonesbury*.[29]

Domestically, some of this coverage had the effect of sentimentalizing soldiers and normalizing the war. For example, the PRX radio documentary series *Soldiers' Soundtracks to War* featured short profiles of individual service members talking about their musical tastes and listening habits, like the staff sergeant who expressed his fondness for gospel music or the army specialist who relished techno and "anything with a beat." In essence, these portraits were an exercise in "supporting the troops," detached from the larger context of the war. With the exception of George Gittoes's documentary film, most of the contemporary coverage of soldiers' music missed the nuances in how deliberately and consciously soldiers used music for many different ends. Mobilized for everything from self-care to accompaniment for tactical operations, their musical activity was far more diverse and complicated than labels like "entertainment" and "recreation" would suggest.[30] This complexity was also indicated by a number of parodies of Apple's 2003 advertising campaign for the iPod. Done by two unrelated art collectives, Forkscrew Graphics and Copper Greene, the parodies appeared on posters in New York and Los Angeles starting in 2004. These guerrilla-art images depicted war-related silhouettes wearing iPods, such as the hooded detainee in the Abu Ghraib prison who was wired for mock electrocution (figure 7.1). Although not about music and soldiers explicitly, this antiwar *détourement* redirected Apple's iconic advertising campaign as an oblique critique of the American military operation at a time when many service personnel were coming to see MP3 playback devices as essential pieces of equipment.[31]

In 2004, the *New York Times* reported that a new characteristic of soldiers in the twenty-first century was their unbroken connection to American popular culture, thanks to the electronics they brought with them and to the internet. Indeed, in hindsight, one of the first things that stands out about the wars in Afghanistan and Iraq for our purposes is that they occurred at a pivotal moment in the history of music technology. At the start of the Iraq War in 2003, CDs were still the norm among

Figure 7.1. This was one of numerous posters which appeared around New York and Los Angeles starting in 2004 parodying Apple's famous iPod advertisements at the time iPod use was becoming widespread in the military.

military personnel. "Almost everyone had a CD player," recalled Sergeant C. J. Grisham about the initial invasion of Iraq.[32] By 2006, though, this older technology was superseded by iPods and laptop computers. This had profound consequences for when and where soldiers listened to music, what they did with it, and how it affected them.[33]

As it had since World War I, recorded music functioned as a medium of sociality among soldiers, but in the MP3 era, recordings circulated in new ways. Reducing recorded sound to small digital files enabled soldiers to build huge music libraries which they could carry with them wherever they were deployed. This conversion also became the basis for a mass sharing economy, as soldiers traded not just individual recordings (as some Vietnam-era G.I.s had) but whole collections of music, via thumb drives and external hard drives or by downloading files from a shared server. Colby Buzzell, a Stryker brigade machine-gunner, claimed to have transferred 942 hours of music to his iPod from friends and acquaintances. Another soldier, Staff Sergeant Erik Holtan, said he acquired some thirty thousand songs from a friend.[34] At least one base in Iraq had a shared computer server which soldiers called the base's "morale drive"—a shared resource for music, videos, movies, and pornography.[35]

Alongside the countless MP3s, soldiers were also trading another new music medium of the twenty-first century: DIY war-themed music videos. Splicing together still photographs, cell phone video, and documentary footage from government and news sources, the videos generally showed soldiers, military hardware, representations of terrorism, and images of Muslims or the Middle East. Some of the videos were made by soldiers themselves; many were made by civilians; all were accompanied by music. Moreover, beyond informal file sharing, they were also exchanged on websites such as MiltaryVideos.net, CombatVids.com, RealWarVideos.com, MilitaryWarVideos.com, and especially, after its launch in 2005, YouTube.

The progenitor of the genre was "Taliban Bodies." Made by an IT specialist in Florida, Ryan Hickman, the video was released only a few weeks after the 9/11 attacks and immediately "went viral" (a phrase which took off around 2005) as well as being featured on television news programs. The video began with intertitles addressed to the Taliban, warning it of the power of the U.S. military. It then presented a barrage of hundreds— perhaps thousands—of rapid-fire still images and video snippets, meticulously edited to follow the musical structure of the song "Bodies," by the heavy-metal band Drowning Pool (which was soon to become the de facto anthem of soldiers in Afghanistan and Iraq). Guided by the propulsive music, viewers saw a split-second series of pictures—the Twin Towers, unidentified Middle Eastern men, U.S. soldiers, military equipment, explosions, etc.—carefully timed to match the rhythm and breaks of the song. In other words, the music was hardly incidental. More than just giving the video its structure, it enriched the images in a way that made their meaning appear "natural" or self-evident, giving the (false) impression that the soundtrack was unnecessary or redundant (a mode of perception that film theorist Michel Chion has called "audiovision").[36]

What made "Taliban Bodies" remarkable, however, was not only its content but also its circulation. It spread rapidly among military personnel worldwide through informal channels, and it was also adopted by every branch of the U.S. military into official settings, from orientation in basic training to briefings during deployments abroad. As one soldier put it, "This was like the quintessential indoctrination video for new trainees . . . lol." Others noted that the video continued to be exchanged back and forth among soldiers for years, and one subsequently recalled, "Even just about ten years later, . . . it remains a beloved classic of every single person I know who is deployed or has deployed since 9/11."[37]

The video also epitomized the military-civilian feedback loop. After its creator moved "Taliban Bodies" and similar videos (some created by him, others not) to his personal website, grouchymedia.com, that site became so popular among military personnel that soldiers repeatedly sent him pictures of bombs on which they had written "Thanks Grouchy" in big letters across the side—pictures that he included in follow-up videos, which became yet another motivation for soldiers. Such videos, Matthew Sumera noted, were less *about* war than they were literally part *of* it.[38]

·

The sharing economy of MP3s exposed many soldiers to unfamiliar kinds of music, as did living in cramped quarters closely with people from different backgrounds. Such exposure could lead to new social bonds. "You could stand in one place and listen to thirty-three different kinds of music in most cases," National Guardsman David "JR" Schultz recalled approvingly. Army specialist and hip-hop emcee Richmond Shaw concluded, "I guess I don't even see the difference between rap and country anymore, except the beat." In his estimation,

> we're talking about the same things . . . out here in the middle of this oven. . . . I might be part of the Tupac generation, but we're all trying to avoid getting shot, and we're all wondering whether people will remember us and . . . trying to make a difference before we die. Isn't that what country music is about, too?[39]

To be sure, there were musical subcultures and cliques and sometimes arguments erupted, but they were not as fraught, culturally and racially, as they had been in Vietnam, and they had none of the same explosive consequences. There were many reasons for this. For one thing, the fan base of hip-hop, the style most preferred by African American soldiers, extended far beyond Black troops. For another, country music, while still often identified with whiteness, had become so widely associated with a fervent American patriotism and support for the military (particularly since the revival of Lee Greenwood's 1984 hit "God Bless the U.S.A." during the Gulf War of 1990–91) that its presence was now largely taken for granted. On another level, more of these soldiers had grown up going to racially integrated schools than their counterparts in Vietnam, and in the age of the all-volunteer force, the military was no longer the tinderbox of racial resentments that it had been in the 1960s and early '70s, when disagreements about jukeboxes uncorked much deeper animosities.[40]

The shift from CDs to MP3s did more than cultivate sociality and fuel the development of a vast sharing economy, however. The advent of iPods also transformed the circumstances in which soldiers could listen to music and the range of different ends, both collective and individual, to which it was put. To some degree, the design of the technology enabled and even encouraged this, for beyond its storage capacity, the iPod also had the new feature of allowing users to create custom playlists, which for G.I.s meant the easy ability to make mixes calibrated for different purposes. Ubiquitous today, bespoke playlists at that time were a novelty. This comes across clearly in army machine-gunner Colby Buzzell's 2005 memoir, *My War: Killing Time in Iraq*. An enthusiastic early adopter of the device, Buzzell could not assume his readers were familiar with it: "The iPod comes with a 'playlist' feature, on which you can organize and create different themed playlists, and it even has a feature that allows you to name the playlists."[41] The new technology made customization possible on the fly, with very little effort, as opposed to the painstaking process of making mix tapes or CDs.

On the most basic level, recorded music offered diversion and fought boredom, which, of course, was a long-standing function of musical activity in the military. It was, as one scholar has written of music in factories, "a way of preventing the senses from being dominated by the monotonous." "Everybody had their MP3 player," the infantryman David Schultz recalled, "It was a way to pass the time." Sergeant Neal Saunders put it more bluntly: "Guys over there are just trying to listen to music to keep their minds off of what the fuck it is that they're going through on a daily basis."[42]

More than in previous conflicts, though, music played a direct role in operations as well. This began with listening either collectively or individually (i.e., through earphones) as part of psychological preparation for going out on a mission. Almost every account of music among soldiers in Afghanistan and Iraq attests to this. "Music got me in the mood," Colby Buzzell recalled; "[it] gets you pumped up." Generally, this meant heavy metal or hip-hop, and often, units adopted particular songs as "their" theme.[43] Drowning Pool's "Bodies" was mentioned more than any other track (chorus: "Let the bodies hit the floor / Let the bodies hit the floor / Let the bodies hit the floor / Let the bodies hit the floor"), but each unit had its favorites. "War is heavy metal," one soldier explained. "It's fast-paced, heavy, and emotional." In this, he acknowledged that soldiering rested not only on physical acts but also on an enormous amount of emotional labor. "Metal," he concluded, "helps you feel what you gotta feel."[44]

Other soldiers emphasized its functional value. "[Music is] the ultimate rush," one said, "because you know you're going into the fight to begin with and you've got a good song playing in the background, and that gets you real fired up."[45] That is, music was something soldiers used consciously and deliberately in preparation for conflict, an exogenous psychological agent enabling them to commit unnatural acts of violence. "Listening to music would artificially make you aggressive when you needed to be aggressive," another soldier, C. J. Grisham, noted, even as "[you hoped] you wouldn't have to use that aggression." Describing his unit's adoption of Eminem's "Go to Sleep" as its de facto anthem (chorus: "Now go to sleep, bitch! / Die, motherfucker, die! Ugh, time's up, bitch, close ya eyes"), Grisham later said, "I'm almost embarrassed to say it was our theme song. But, hey, that's what happens in war. You've gotta become inhuman to do inhuman things . . . [like] shoot a weapon at a living person."[46]

In many instances, the music did not end when the soldiers left the base—thanks, in part, to the available technology. Besides storage and playlists, another advantage of iPods was that they did not skip or stop when jostled, which allowed them to be used in many more situations than prior music-playback devices. With these features, numerous soldiers reported listening to iPods in their vehicles, a practice which ranged from playing songs through portable, battery-powered speakers to plugging the device into the onboard audio communication system and listening through either speakers or helmets. They never had music on where hearing ambient sounds was essential, of course, but under some circumstances, soldiers found that having music playing actually heightened their alertness and awareness by reducing talk and other distractions.[47]

After operations, soldiers often had other playlists, "cool-down music," which they put on individually to unwind. In this context, they turned away from what Sergeant William Thompson ironically referred to as "let's-go-kill-people music" and cued up everything from Dave Matthews Band to Jeff Buckley to Diana Krall to Arvo Pärt.[48] In this way, iPod listening—and, for some soldiers, making music themselves—functioned as a resource to modulate their moods and express their emotions. These musical practices were, as ethnomusicologist J. Martin Daughtry put it, a means of "creating and sustaining ontological security." Soldiers valued musical activity as a safe, sanctioned outlet and a means of formulating feelings that might otherwise be inchoate, unacceptable, or threatening. Staff Sergeant Terrance Staves, who participated in recording a rap album, *Live from Iraq*, with several other soldiers, explained, "I had a lot of [emotionally difficult] stuff happen to me. . . . For me to . . . be able to get in the [makeshift recording] booth and let all my anger out was wonderful, because sometimes you can't let all your anger out there because you might endanger yourself, your brothers, or do something you're not supposed to do. It was a beautiful outlet."[49]

Another soldier who explained this with particular insight was Specialist Jennifer Atkinson, who did a one-year tour of duty in Iraq in 2005. "Even if you don't go outside the wire [i.e., security perimeter], and a lot of folks don't, you're still in a place where things blow up," she noted. Music was not only "a good way to bleed off some of the stress," it also permitted soldiers to "express things that you don't always know how to say." And it did so in an accessible way, within acceptable limits:

> I could express myself through my musical choices in a way that I might not have otherwise been able to do, because it's a very controlled environment, and if you're frustrated, you have to be careful how you express it because, one, you're armed, and two, everyone else around you is armed. You don't lose your temper. So [music] allows me to express a lot of different emotions in a safe and controlled manner.

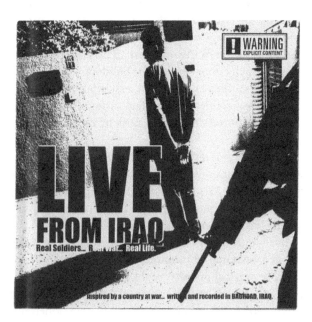

Figure 7.2. Cover of the CD *Live from Iraq*, a hip-hop collaboration between six soldiers in Iraq.

Not all soldiers were as self-aware as Atkinson about what music did for them, but certainly she was not alone in finding that music helped keep her "a bit more balanced." Others concluded things like "if it wasn't for music, I don't think I would've made it through the last fifteen months . . . in Iraq" and "I think music saved my life during my deployment."[50]

The effects of this musical activity were complex. One reason soldiers valued iPods was that listening to them produced what one scholar called a "privatized auditory bubble." In Iraq, such bubbles encompassed either individuals (using earphones) or small groups (listening inside an armored vehicle), in both cases detaching listeners from their surroundings.[51] This aural isolation cut in two directions. On the one hand, musical recordings had the power to conjure other worlds and transport listeners to imagined psychological spaces and idealized emotional states, which music scholar Josh Kun has called "audiotopias." For a homesick soldier, particular songs or playlists could make a loved one far away feel closer. Or the bubble produced a feeling of just being "somewhere else"—a utopian "nowhere"—by oneself. On the other hand, this kind of listening could also have the effect of deprecating the outside world, severing the connections an individual or group felt to those outside the bubble, and diminishing the status of the space the bubble moved through.[52] This detachment could be good for an individual's mental health, but it was more problematic when it concerned U.S. soldiers rolling over foreign soil, seeing and hearing local conditions as a world apart. Such privatized listening, a scholar of headphone use has written, can be a means of creating or maintaining a "safe space" free of racial or ethnic Others.[53]

Thinking about what soldiers did with music *for themselves*, then, requires we also consider what they did with music *to others*. One of the war's most novel features, the weaponization of music, both reflected and contributed to the ongoing process of blurring the line between reality and virtuality, war and not-war, spectacle and state violence. In the civilian domain, the media and culture industries peddled war as entertainment, while in the military domain, entertainment commodities reshaped the waging of war. This feedback loop was never more evident than in the employment of Hollywood-inspired music in the enactment of real violence. When machine-gunner Colby Buzzell included Louis Armstrong's "What a Wonderful World" on the custom playlist he made for his Stryker brigade combat team in 2003–4, he riffed on the song's ironic appearance in the film *Good Morning, Vietnam*—an allusion that would not have been lost on his comrades in arms.[54]

In other cases, music was weaponized as an instrument of intimidation and harassment, either by psyops units or on an improvised basis. One inspiration for this was the widely publicized aural assault on Manuel Noriega in Panama by U.S. psyops forces in 1990, featuring, among other songs, Kenny Loggins's hit "Danger Zone" from the soundtrack of the military-glorifying film *Top Gun*.[55] Another inspiration was the now-iconic scene in *Apocalypse Now*, in which helicopters blasted Wagner's "Ride of the Valkyries" during an aerial attack on a Vietnamese jungle, reenacted on the ground in Iraq through speakers originally intended to convey spoken messages to local populations. Whether the Wagnerian theme came from a convoy driving ten miles per hour into Baghdad or a small unit storming the house of suspected insurgents, soldiers were acting out, over and over, a script written by the American culture industry (based loosely on actual psyops activities in Vietnam). In other words, it was not simply the power of Wagner fueling their actions but also that of Hollywood.[56]

Buzzell himself was explicit about the staging of war as (musical) spectacle. Listening to a custom iPod playlist before going out on operations, he said, was "like having your own soundtrack, to your own movie, your own war. If you watch a movie and they have a war scene or a shoot-'em scene it's not the same without some cool music [playing] on top of it. When you're out there in real life, you know, hey, this is your movie. So [if] this is my movie, then this is my soundtrack and this is what I'm listening to, and it just gets you pumped up for it."[57] War inspires Hollywood fabulations, which in turn inspire actual military operations—and around and around, it goes.

While it is tempting to dismiss blasting music and creating "soundtracks" for operations as incidental to the operations themselves, these musical practices could have material ramifications. Inspired by movies, "service members open themselves to the temptation of aestheticizing violence," the ethnomusicologist J. Martin Daughtry noted, "and hence trivializing it, and desensitizing them to it." And it could have bad optics. One of Daughtry's informants, an Iraqi familiar with life in wartime Baghdad, reported that homemade videos showing American military personnel and private security contractors engaging in gun battles with music blaring circulated widely on the internet and on DVDs sold in local markets. It is impossible to track the impact of such videos, but their intent, the Iraqi said, was to show the callous and amoral character of the American fighters.[58]

Music as Torture

Alongside the use of hard rock, heavy metal, and Wagner to frighten and intimidate local populations, the fusion of warfare and popular culture was also manifest in another form of weaponization: music as an instrument of torture. As early as 2003, reports began to emerge of loud music being employed as part of a system of practices that the U.S. government euphemistically called "enhanced interrogation techniques." High-volume playback of sound recordings, often repeating a single track for hours at a time or sometimes playing two recordings at once, was combined with strobe lights, sleep deprivation, uncomfortably cold or hot temperatures, and other conditions—all intended to overwhelm prisoners with feelings of powerlessness and helplessness and forcing them to lose a sense of their own identity.[59] If, in other circumstances, soldiers cued up their cool-down playlists to achieve feelings of "ontological security," in this environment they had different playlists and musical practices whose purpose was to destroy the ontological security of others.[60]

While interrogators decided which sounds to play and how to play them, it was not they who devised this tactic. Rather, it derived from numerous American experiments in psychological abuse spanning from the late nineteenth century to the Cold War. The techniques resulting from these experiments made up a single complex weapon system which Alfred McCoy, the leading historian of American torture, called "a counterintuitive breakthrough—the first real revolution in the cruel science of pain in more than three centuries."[61] One component of the system, waterboarding, had first been used by the U.S. military against Philippine insurgents a century earlier. Other techniques grew out of CIA-funded research to "break" prisoners psychologically in the 1950s and '60s, some of which drew on the experiments by Nazi doctors at Dachau. Still others derived from protocols devised after the Korean War to condition American military personnel to withstand abuse if captured (known as Survival, Evasion, Resistance, and Escape, or SERE, training). That is, these techniques, which had been developed to *resist* torture, were now being used to *inflict* it. Taken together, these practices make up what has been known to scholars and policy officials since the 1990s as "no-touch torture."[62]

Sometimes, these methods involved forcing prisoners to listen through headphones which they could not remove. More often, though, detainees were subjected to this "futility music" (as interrogators called it) through very loud sound systems. The latter technique had far more profound effects, for the vibrations attacked not only the prisoner's ears but his entire body, forcing his skin, bones, and viscera to resonate with the music. Under these conditions, the pathbreaking musicologist Suzanne Cusick has written, sound "is no longer a metaphor for power, no longer only a medium by which prison authorities can reconfigure their wards' experiences of space and place so as to obviate any illusion of privacy . . . , not a metaphor for power but power itself."[63]

In the press and the academic literature, much has been made of the song selections used for this type of torture—lots of hard rock and heavy metal (again, Drowning Pool's "Bodies" was a favorite), the *Barney & Friends* theme song, the Meow Mix jingle, Neil Diamond's "America," etc.—and it is likely that most prisoners disliked these songs. Arguably, however, what affected prisoners the most was less the character of the songs than the sheer acoustic energy—the vibrational force—combined with the repetition and duration of sound. This was both a conceptual innovation and a technological one: playing individual tracks over and over, for hours at a time, would have been impractical without the "repeat" function on every CD and MP3 player.[64] When former detainees were interviewed about their conditions, they seldom dwelled on the content of the music. In some cases, they were unfazed by it. One, Murat Kurnaz, had even been a bouncer at a dance club in Germany prior to his detention, where his exposure to Western music had been extensive.[65]

In more cases, former detainees focused on the effects of the sound, which, according to government regulations, could be maintained at ninety decibels—the equivalent of a loud motorcycle or lawnmower—for eight hours at a time but which anecdotal evidence suggests often exceeded such levels.[66] In the words of another ex-detainee, "You feel like your body is being bombarded with something. . . . Really, literally, so it was much more harmful [than the dark prison], physically, mentally, and intrusively. . . . In Guantánamo the music affects your mind, your body, your senses. . . . It's like you're being hit with a hammer, din din din din. When it stops, it's like a beating has stopped."[67] Other accounts were remarkably similar. Former Guantánamo prisoner Ruhal Ahmed recalled, "It makes you feel like you are going mad. You lose the plot and it's very scary to think that you might go crazy because of all the music, because of the loud noise, and because after a while you don't hear the lyrics at all, all you hear is heavy banging."[68]

Today, the word *torture* has lost much of the power it had before 9/11. Debates in the early twenty-first century about what is or isn't torture, about whether or not torture "works," and so on have robbed the word of its force. It no longer stops us dead in our tracks. It's been normalized. This is particularly unfortunate in relation to psychological mistreatment, which has sometimes been dismissed as "torture lite."[69]

Of all these various techniques, music especially has been the subject of mockery, particularly in relation to children's music and jingles. This was anticipated by Hollywood films like Billy Wilder's *One, Two, Three* (1961) and Woody Allen's *Bananas* (1971), in which political prisoners were forced to listen, over and over, to "Itsy Bitsy Teenie Weenie Yellow Polka Dot Bikini" and a Victor Herbert operetta, *Naughty Marietta*, respectively. These films were comedies, and the musical selections signified that this kind of torture was funny. In reality, however, the effects of these practices were far from trivial or humorous and may have been comparable to bodily torture. According to a 2007 clinical study of nearly three hundred Bosnian victims of torture, "ill treatment during captivity, such as psychological manipulations and forced stress positions does not seem to be substantially different from physical torture in terms of the severity of mental suffering . . . and their long-term psychological outcome."[70]

Approval and acceptance of the use of music as torture has waxed and waned. In September 2003, the U.S. military commander in Iraq, Lieutenant General Ricardo Sanchez, authorized the use of music as one of the practices intended "to create fear, disorient [prisoners,] . . . and prolong capture shock." In 2010, however, after years of intense criticism by human rights activists, musical artists, and others, Kevin Bybee, coauthor with John Yoo of the Justice Department's infamous memos asserting that federal laws against torture did not apply overseas, testified before the House Judiciary Committee that interrogations involving high-volume music and noise (among other techniques) went far beyond what the original guidelines intended. Officially, the government no longer endorsed wielding music as a tool of torture. Military officials and the troops, meanwhile, have hardly disavowed the music. In 2017, the band Drowning Pool went on at least its fifth USO tour since 2005, culminating in "Freedom Fest," a July Fourth show for troops stationed at Guantánamo. According to spokesperson Colonel Lisa Garcia, military leadership was likely unaware that the band's song "Bodies" had been used for torture in the prison nearby.[71]

Conclusion: Music on the Back End

Military musical activity in the early twenty-first century did not end in the interrogation room with high-volume sound systems. It ended somewhere quieter, with the process of transforming soldiers back into civilians. Music therapy has held an important place in the rehabilitation of military personnel returning from Iraq and Afghanistan, and the range of initiatives launched in the past two decades reflects the enthusiasm that exists for work in this area. As we have seen, music has long been part of making and maintaining soldiers, and increasingly, it has been part of healing them too. Building on music therapy's roots treating veterans of World Wars I and II, initiatives over the past two decades reflect much about the work that music has done in the waging of America's wars.[72]

Both doctors and patients since ancient times have observed music's salutary and even salubrious effects on the ill and injured, but only recently did music therapy emerge as a recognized profession. In the Civil War and World War I, military bands regularly played at hospitals, and reports indicate their performances were appreciated. It was not until after World War I, however, that musicians and medical practitioners sought to use music in a systematically therapeutic manner, and nearly all of the pioneers of the field in the interwar years cut their teeth on the rehabilitation of soldiers returning from the Great War. Their work, in turn, influenced the widespread use of music in army hospitals in World War II, leading to the professionalization of the field in the postwar decades.[73] Although skeptics questioned whether clinical evidence supported claims of the healing powers of musical activity, in recent decades more experimental data has given credence to the field, thanks especially to fMRI and other brain-imaging technologies.[74]

The significance of music therapy today also rests on shifts in warfare. While musicians and medical practitioners did work with returning soldiers in earlier conflicts, the high survival rate for military personnel wounded in combat today sets our era apart. Because of changes in how wars are fought and advances in lifesaving medical technology, approximately 91 percent of soldiers wounded in battle in Afghanistan and Iraq returned home alive. In World War II, only 50 percent did, and in World War I, only 4 or 5 percent.[75] Returning home alive, however, did not mean returning intact. An additional reason for interest in music therapy is the widespread incidence of post-traumatic stress disorder (PTSD) and traumatic brain injury (TBI). In 2008, a major study by the RAND Corporation found that 19 percent of soldiers experienced TBI when deployed and roughly 20 percent returned with PTSD, and consequently, the long-term mental health costs of war have been more widely recognized than in previous generations.[76] These conditions make rehabilitation more important than ever.

Because the invisible wounds of trauma are so difficult to heal, the military has found that turning soldiers back into civilians can be as difficult as turning civilians into soldiers. Music appears to help. Or at least this is what is suggested by the interest in and support for numerous initiatives. Some music therapy is offered through the Department of Veterans Affairs (VA), which includes programs in individual, group, and community-based musical activity, as it has since World War II. The bedrock of these programs is active music-making, most often with drums and percussion, guitar, keyboard or piano, and voice. Other common techniques involve both interactive activities and structured listening aiming at emotional, psychological, neurological, and cognitive benefits. Falling into a broad range of practices, these include songwriting, lyric analysis, music-assisted relaxation, guided listening, music and movement exercise, neurologic music therapy, and music-based cognitive training.[77] Music also factors into Creative Forces, a major partnership between the VA, the Department of Defense, and the National Endowment for the Arts launched in 2011, which connects arts therapy to a range of rehabilitative services and integrative mind-body care. Administered at more than a dozen VA facilities around the country, from Washington, DC, to Anchorage, Alaska, its aim has been to weave songwriting, performance, and listening into care for service personnel who have experienced brain trauma or suffer from psychological health conditions. Research based on this work has yielded at least nineteen scholarly publications.[78]

Complementing these federally sponsored initiatives have been numerous independent, nonprofit projects. Guitars for Vets, for example, was established in 2007 to provide guitars and instruction to returning military personnel struggling with physical or emotional distress. Similar but broader is the Warrior Cry Music Project, established in 2012, which also provides instruments and instruction but is not guitar-specific. More unusual is SongwritingWith:Soldiers, a project of Texas-based singer-songwriter Darden Smith which pairs veterans with professional songwriters to craft songs that might lessen the impact of trauma.[79] By 2019, Smith had initiated more than four hundred collaborations.

What really set this last undertaking apart was that its apparent success inspired two faculty members of the Harvard Medical School, Ronald Hirschberg and Louisa Sylvia, to study its impacts clinically. To do this, they gave each of the ten participants in the study a thumb drive with their collaboratively written song on it and instructed them to listen to the recording daily for four weeks. Each also took home a Fitbit device to track physiological variables, like heart rate, activity level, and hours of sleep. The results were notable: four weeks after the songwriting sessions, study participants reported a 33 percent drop in PTSD symptoms and a 22 percent decline in depression. While the data did not allow the clinicians to explain what it was *about* the collaboratively written songs that produced these effects, their findings suggest that music could lead to measurable material benefits.[80]

·

In the context of this book, the focus on music in the rehabilitation of military personnel for civilian life does more than bring closure to the life span of soldiering. It also stands for a bigger story: the ongoing efforts to channel the power of making and listening to music into the complex process of war-making, which encompasses everything from recruiting warriors to easing their transition back into postwar life. Looking back to the nineteenth century, we see myriad attempts to harness music's emotional and aesthetic charge to discipline, stimulate, entertain, and soothe soldiers' bodies and minds. Technologies and musical styles have differed. IPods and hip-hop are worlds away from tattered songbooks and parlor ballads. Musical activity has been present, though, with remarkable consistency—whether initiated from above by top brass or from below by the rank and file.

As an instrument of war, what *has* changed about music is the degree to which the songs soldiers heard and sang are part of an enormous commercial entertainment industry that has profited from and sometimes promoted this interconnectedness with war-making. Popular music today cannot be separated from the military-entertainment complex.[81] Another transformation is the greater degree to which musical activity has become synonymous with listening, rather than singing or other active music-making. To be sure, in the Civil War, after a day of fighting or marching many soldiers were content to listen quietly to a regimental brass band, but there was a much greater likelihood then compared to today that they might also have been singing along. And different too are the ever more calculated and inventive ways that music has been instrumentalized in state violence, from video games to torture to soldier rehabilitation. This is not to say that the fighting of America's wars *could* not have occurred without all this music. The point is: it did not. If musical activity coursed through a century and a half of U.S. war-making, much is at stake in coming to terms with what this music involved and why it mattered.

Seven Elegies

"One of the main ways that war transforms you has to do with your sense of hearing," musician Henry Threadgill writes in his recent memoir. Having carried both a saxophone and an M-16 when he served in Vietnam from 1967 to 1968, Threadgill details a change that soldiers of many wars would recognize. "It's partly an expansion of your aural palette, all the new stuff you become attuned to in the new environment," In his case, this meant the sounds of weapons firing, of course, as well as the ribald banter of comrades in arms, the voices of indigenous mountain people, the unfamiliar patter of rain in the jungle, and the tuneful cries of Saigon street-food vendors.[1]

"But it's not simply a matter of hearing more," Threadgill continues. "It makes you hear *differently*, too. You acquire a heightened sensitivity to sound. Your body learns quickly that listening can be a matter of life or death. Your ears start to pick up things you wouldn't even have noticed back at home, because in the war missing the slightest signal at the wrong moment could get you killed. Your body learns to hear things with great precision even while you're asleep, and to jolt you awake at any hint of a threat."[2]

A bandleader, multi-instrumentalist, and Pulitzer Prize–winning composer, Threadgill concludes by elaborating on the effects of this change in hearing as they resonated over a lifetime. "For any artist, such a profound transformation of your understanding and perception can't help but find its way into what you're doing," he explained. "It's like I grew a set of antennae over there. When I returned, my reception equipment was different. And even if the war messed up my head in a million other ways at the same time—and even if I didn't ask for any of it—I'd have to admit that that heightened sensitivity became one of the main things that shaped me into the composer I've become."[3] By the time Threadgill was discharged from the military in 1969, his experience in the war had planted in him the seeds of a new creative practice.

These remarks do more than lend insight into Threadgill's impressive body of work. They also remind us that wars do not end when bullets stop flying and armies return home. Indeed, wars never conclude so neatly. Wars reverberate. They echo. They remain unsettled. They are felt for generations in the physical destruction, loss of life, and trauma they involve for soldiers and civilians, abroad and at home. They continue in the stories we tell about them.

"All wars are fought twice, the first time on the battlefield, the second time in memory," the novelist and essayist Viet Thanh Nguyen has written.[4] If this is true (as I believe it is), music has a place in the second fight too, no less than the first. As a means of influencing popular memory, a war's musical legacies, the sounds it leaves behind and the sounds it inspires, help shape social understandings of the past. At the time of this writing, the United States is marking the twentieth anniversary of the invasion of Iraq, an inflection point in historical remembrance. Two decades on, few true believers remain, but domestic narratives of what happened diverge and clash. As skeptics predicted in the run-up to the war, the weapons of mass destruction that the George W. Bush administration used to justify the invasion were never found. Conservatives maintain the war was prosecuted in good faith, on the basis of flawed intelligence. Progressives generally see it as either an oil grab, a bid for revenge against Saddam Hussein after the Gulf War of 1990–91, an outgrowth of a Manichean, post-Vietnam, post–Cold War neoconservative worldview, or some combination of these.

The causes of the Iraq War, in other words, remain unsettled, open to interpretation. Its consequences do too, recalled in other kinds of stories—written in sound. Reflecting on the significance of music in waging war over time, we gain additional insight from the recent wars' complex musical legacies. By turns brash, elegant, and troubling, these inheritances can influence how the conflicts in Iraq and Afghanistan are remembered. If culture is a process through which people make meaning out of what they are doing in the world (and what's being done to them), it never speaks only in a single, dominant voice. Rather, it always contains within it residual elements from the past and emergent impulses reaching toward the future.[5] It is polyphonic and at least some of it heterodox. A survey of these diverse sonic traces can help us appreciate wars' long-term repercussions.

Such a survey begins in the crucible of war itself. Despite its title, the underground hip-hop album *Live from Iraq* (2005) by the group 4th25 is not any kind of concert document. It was "live from Iraq" in the sense of voicing the experiences of at least some American soldiers serving there, where all the tracks were recorded. Over heavy, jagged beats, rhymes like bullets barrage listeners with the emotional strain of soldiering in Iraq. Through fifteen tracks, the record refracts a spectrum of feelings,

from the pain of leaving families ("The Deployment"), to fears of infidelity ("Dirty"), to resentment of comrades seen as selfish and unmanly
("Pussy"). One splenetic cut ("I Ride") defends relentless killing as retri-
bution for American casualties:

> This is for them soldiers that not gonna make it home . . .
> Shoot em dead in y'all memory . . .
> We are not fuckin around here
> We don't get much sleep
> When we on the blocks all night
> Exchanging bullets for peace
> And once we start pulling these triggers
> We don't stop 'til the whole block leaks
> Til there's not a live body in the streets.

The stakes for these boots on the ground, in other words, are personal:
"For them families that are now grieving / . . . There will be a whole lot
of fuckers in return who stop breathing."[6]

Notably, many of the songs are addressed to civilians back home, especially those who question or criticize soldiers or the war. "Testament
of a Soldier," for example, pushes back against condemnation by people
who take their own security for granted:

> If it wasn't for war, you wouldn't be able to live the life you live
>   now . . .
> Wouldn't have shit
> If it wasn't for soldiers like us . . .
> I don't think y'all understand what y'all doin
> Or what y'all sayin
> You got to be kiddin me
> What did you think it cost to be living free?
> For our country we will bleed
> While you run your mouth . . .
> No, you don't have to agree
> But you could at least support us
> Stand behind us if not for us.

Fulminating against stateside naysayers, the song connects political debates over the war itself to the experience of soldiers putting their lives on
the line. It is a perspective even the war's sharpest critics must reckon with.[7]

In both form and content, *Live from Iraq* stands in sharp contrast
to *Rifles & Rosary Beads* (2018), a record by the singer-songwriter Mary

Gauthier comprised of songs she penned with veterans through the Song-writingWith:Soldiers initiative. As with *Live from Iraq*, this album, which was nominated for a Grammy Award, is a testament of the emotional world of soldiers, but it focuses primarily on the torment, disappointment, and frustrations they experienced after they returned stateside and on the toll their service took on their interpersonal relations. "What saves you in the battle / Can kill you at home," Gauthier sings in the record's opening cut, "Soldiering On." The lyrics confront warriors' ambivalence about suppressing their emotions. "Suck it up, shut it down, it don't matter how you feel," begins the song's bridge, "Mission first, just drive on, a soldier's a cog inside a wheel." Another cut, "Still on the Ride," explores survivors' guilt and the feeling of closeness of comrades lost in battle. Other songs concern the effects of war on loved ones. In "The War after the War," the song's protagonist asks, "Who's gonna care for the ones who care for the ones who went to war?" Elsewhere on the record, "It's Her Love" pays tribute to a partner who remains steadfast "when . . . I'm drowning in a river of pain."[8]

By design, *Live from Iraq* and *Rifles & Rosary Beads* channel the unruly psychology of soldiers' wartime service into conventional generic forms. With nuance and pathos, they use established musical styles to explore and express difficult, unfamiliar, unwelcome feelings in order to render them legible to outsiders. Other musical legacies approach the complexity of the war in less conventional ways. Boring deeper into the messy terrain of the mind, for example, is *Holding It Down: The Veterans' Dreams Project* (2013) by pianist Vijay Iyer and the poet and emcee Mike Ladd, an unclassifiable record whose lyrics are based on interviews with veterans of color about their dreams during and after their service in Afghanistan and Iraq.[9] It represents the third work in Iyer and Ladd's trilogy about life in the post-9/11 world, following an album about the experience of people of color in airports since 2001 (*In What Language*) and another about the twenty-four-hour news cycle (*Still Life with Commentator*). Unlike the oblique approach to the post-9/11 world taken in the first two installments, *Holding It Down* zeroes in on the visceral experience of military personnel, a disproportionate number of whom were people of color engaged in conflicts abroad in which the United States' enemies were often cast as racialized Others.[10]

Working with a group of respected instrumentalists, Iyer and Ladd collaborated also with two veterans. One, Maurice Decaul, was a former marine who took up writing poetry after he left the military to help cope with his complicated, unresolved emotional distress, while the other, Lynn Hill, was a poet and onetime drone pilot for the air force who fought the war from a command center in Nevada. An acclaimed composer and performer, Iyer here keeps the music in a supporting role—a swirl of acoustic instruments and live electronics and effects, complementing, commenting on, and sometimes in tension with the vocals, which span from rapping to spoken-word poetry to excerpts from interviews. The combined effect is to open a window on the anxiety, anguish, and guilt haunting the lives of many who participated in the wars, in musical moods that move from discordant to somber to seething and searching. Iyer and Ladd call this idiom "irritainment"—art made "out of stuff that no one wants to talk about"—and Iyer has noted the commercial "jazz business" showed little interest in the project aside from giving the duo a "pat on the back for doing good work."[11] More evocative than didactic, the pieces call to mind the gritty materiality and ethereal evanescence of dreams inflected by war, with bullets that "cackle" ("My Fire"), mermaids that walk ("There Is a Man Slouching in the Stairway"), and the polyphony of "Arabic, Kurdish, English in ten different accents" ("Dream of an Ex-Ranger").[12]

In contrast to both *Live from Iraq*, which sounds insistent and urgent, and *Rifles & Rosary Beads*, which feels sentimental, Iyer and Ladd's *Holding It Down* is discomfiting. It sets listeners on edge. Looking back on the wars through the gauzy veil of nocturnal dream imagery, it reels us into a twilight world of restless torment. As Decaul sings in one song:

> I've been talking in my sleep again, mumbling in Arabic, pounding my chest, a prayer ritual reflex.
> I've been talking in my sleep again, incoherent rantings, snipers, traffic control points, suicide bombers.
> I've been talking in my sleep again, tense hands form fists, I fight an invisible enemy.

Here, the repetition of "I've been talking in my sleep again" becomes a metaphor for ongoing distress, with the mumbling, incoherent ranting, and tense fists signaling a mental state now incapable of relaxation.[13]

Holding It Down flips the script on thank-you-for-your-service pieties. With its undertow of bottomless anxiety and psychic injury which resists healing, it leaves us with the unnerving sense of the wars as an open wound, a conflict in search of a resolution. Meanwhile, in the waking world, government bureaucracy made the absence of closure a permanent condition. Iyer and Ladd sought to follow *Holding It Down* with a new project about the war from the perspective of Iraqis, but that project, titled *Sleep Song*, stalled when U.S. government officials denied visas to the Iraqi participants—ensuring that the voices of the war's victims abroad would remain marginalized.[14]

The tension between voices present and absent runs through another of the wars' unconventional musical legacies as well. *Baghdad Music Journal* is a 2006 CD by William A. Thompson IV (a.k.a. WATIV), a New Orleans jazz musician who joined the National Guard in 1999 to help pay for college and ended up serving in Iraq as a counterintelligence specialist in 2004–5. Before deploying, Thompson took pains to ensure he would be able to continue making music overseas. He arranged to bring with him an eighty-eight-key electronic synthesizer, a click-wheel iPod with a recording attachment, and a laptop computer loaded with the latest music-production software (Reason, Logic, Ableton Live). These devices became the focus of all his free time. At night, while comrades watched DVDs or passed the time drinking (banned) alcohol, Thompson crafted a series of experimental compositions evoking the densely layered soundscapes of wartime Baghdad. Although he had never owned a computer previously, this erstwhile piano player ended up making work of striking originality, unlike anything to come directly out of a theater of war before.[15]

The pieces weave together field recordings from street markets, news reports from Iraqi radio, excerpts from Arabic-language instruction records issued by the military, drum tracks a musician friend had snuck onto his iPod, and musical themes Thompson played on his keyboard. The album closes with several excerpts from a hastily arranged improvisatory recording session in New Orleans when Thompson was home on leave in the middle of his tour. Throughout the CD, one hears a contrapuntal relationship between ambient sounds and musical invention, between technological mediation and liveness, between the foreign and the familiar. Many of the tracks crackle with static. Some feature beats made from looped mechanical noises. One is sprinkled with Arabic-language radio commentary on the results of the 2004 U.S. presidential election. On another, a sampled acoustic bass line unfurls against the high-pitched whine of an air-conditioner window unit. The combined effect is an eerie, airless interplay between listening and being heard. There is beauty, and there is menace.

In its affect, the record feels remarkably true to life. It preserves individual voices, both musical and spoken, while also evoking (sonic) manipulation and the restricted, coercive conditions under which those voices might be audible. As a record of the war (in both senses of *record*), it rests on a paradox, the contradiction between voicing and silencing, a symbol of the ambivalence of music in the process of making war. Living under the cloud of constant mortal danger, Thompson has said, invigorated his creative practice. The constant threat of car bombs, snipers, and ambushes was artistically liberating, opening up for him an unfettered world of sonic possibility. "It sounds weird and dark," he told me in 2023, but the hazardous, violent conditions empowered him to make a different kind of music than he ever had before. "It's freeing. . . . I had no shortage of ideas and inspiration at all."[16]

At the same time, Thompson's "day job" was working as a "tactical human intelligence" specialist. He kept his beard long and did not wear a regular military uniform. Much of his job involved interrogating Iraqis detained for questioning—most only briefly, on minor matters, and in a conversational manner. As he described this work, doing interrogations was "not as horrible as it sounds—although sometimes it was." Given that much of his work may still be classified, he is reluctant to elaborate on it, except to say that he found playing "nice guy" the most effective means of getting information.[17] Still, intimidation and force loom in the background, the undertow of this novel creative output. (He gave no indication of having used music in his interrogations.)

The flip side of *Baghdad Music Journal*, figuratively speaking, is Drew Baker's composition *Stress Position* (2008), a solo work for piano with electronic amplification and delay.[18] If Thompson was a composer serving in the military whose music remained silent about detention, Baker was a civilian composer of roughly the same age with the opposite goal: exploring the relationship between private music-making and the abuse of detainees. That is, *Stress Position* connects the experience of pianists with that of prisoners—one group spending endless hours confined in small practice rooms for the sake of their artistic training, the other forced to spend endless hours in small rooms of a different sort for the sake of interrogations.[19]

More specifically, *Stress Position* explicitly and implicitly homes in on the practice of "enhanced interrogation techniques"—torture—to which many detainees were subjected. The title *Stress Position* refers to the procedure of compelling prisoners to direct the weight of their bodies for a prolonged period of time onto one or two muscle groups—the physical strain of which is invoked in the composition by the extreme demands required of the pianist. The performance of the piece lasts (one might say "endures") around nine minutes, in which the musician is forced to strike the piano keys in a continual, barely changing monotonous rhythmic pattern, with arms outstretched at the lowest and highest ends of the keyboard. The feeling is all tension and no release. Meanwhile, the volume increases in increments and gradually the discrete pitches are replaced by clusters. In performance, the sound of the piano grows louder and louder and is eventually amplified electronically, ratcheting it up beyond the level of comfort. Then, in the middle of the piece, the lights are extinguished. A wall of sound assaulting them, audience members are plunged into darkness. The pressure mounts—and then it is over. There is no crescendo. Like interrogations, the performance ends abruptly, without warning.

"This stressful conception of the work, its anxiety-evoking form, and the use of the pedal and amplifier create strange acoustic phenomena," a witness to one performance recalled. "The high pitches start to sound like wailing sirens, and the low pitches like an airplane engine or other extremely slashing noise."[20] Thus, the piece does in music that which cannot be done in words, at once suggesting and embodying both physical and mental abuse. With arms stretched wide to the lowest and highest notes on the keyboard over the entire length of the piece, the strained position of the pianist's body recalls the torture victim, such as the hooded prisoner with arms extended in the most infamous of the Abu Ghraib photographs. The incessant sixteenth notes, growing mass of sound, and surges in pianistic attack conjure the insistent, monotonous repetition of questioning and the concomitant effect on the prisoner's mental state. In the music, the feeling of helplessness swells, the sense of agitation creeps ever higher, and the darkness intensifies the experience of the sound and reenacts the sensory deprivation to which many detainees were subjected. The performance is a provocation, forcing us to ask whether the experience of torture can even be represented and, if so, to what effect.

Like war, however, musical conversations are never one-sided. Music is a social phenomenon, and the protean nature of musical activity guarantees many kinds of interlocutors. Part of the value of thinking about music and war in the same frame comes from the fact that music resists boundaries, refuses one-dimensional interpretation, connects us to others, whether we intend it to or not. Always, polyphony persists—in wartime and its aftermath, myriad musical voices strain to be heard. If music belongs to the process of making soldiers (as this book has shown) and helps us know better the toll of waging war (as this coda has suggested), it can also enable us to hear war's victims. Shifting our attention from American to Iraqi musicians, the documentary film *Heavy Metal in Baghdad* (2007) tracks the activity of Iraq's lone heavy-metal band, Acrassicauda, celebrating the small subculture of musicians and fans who remained steadfast despite grave wartime risks. In focusing on heavy metal, the film challenges Western assumptions about what Iraqi music is. At the same time, it pays homage to the defiant spirit of young Iraqis, which persisted even as the band members were forced into exile in Syria. By contrast, all sorts of musicians and enthusiasts who remained in Iraq were subject to intimidation, harassment, detention, and sometimes murder.[21]

Where Acrassicauda is loud and exuberant, another musical artist in exile has offered perspective on the war's victims in a style delicate and poignant. In 2017, the oud virtuoso Rahim AlHaj released *Letters from Iraq*, a CD of instrumental compositions for oud and string quartet, inspired by letters written by Iraqi women and children living under the U.S. occupation. A world-class master of one of civilization's oldest stringed instruments, AlHaj followed a different path than the heavy-metal musicians. Born in 1968, he is somewhat older than them and had an elite musical training in Baghdad, and after twice having been imprisoned under Saddam Hussein for his peace activism, he fled Iraq during the Gulf War of 1990–91. After stints in Jordan and Syria, he eventually resettled in Albuquerque, New Mexico, not returning to Iraq until 2004, when he was able to visit family and friends he had not seen for years.[22] By the time he recorded *Letters from Iraq* more than a decade later, the war's toll on human lives had reshaped his homeland.

In Western terms, *Letters from Iraq* represents a kind of "program music," that is, instrumental compositions written about extramusical subjects. The liner notes for the recordings (in the booklet accompanying the CD and available as a free download) recount the stories AlHaj transposed of Iraqi life during and after the invasion and detail the feelings that the composer sought for each piece to convey. Among the most moving is "Running Boy," about his nephew Fuad's experience when a car bomb exploded near the barbershop where he was getting his hair cut. Born with a physical disability which made it difficult for him to walk, Fuad ran and fell—and ran and fell again—in pursuit of safety while people screamed, bullets buzzed, and fires crackled around him. The music feels intense and anxious, accented by the addition of percussion, the deep bass voice of a cajon (a wooden Latin American box drum). Another piece, "Forbidden Attraction," paints a musical picture of two young lovers, a Shi'ite man and a Sunni woman, separated by sectarian violence, the oud and violin representing the two voices, trading parts that move from playful to forlorn. In "Unspoken Word," a violin expresses the grief felt by a boy who loses his mother to an explosion in an open-air market, played out over a cello and bass with percussion ostinato. Spanning a wide range of moods, "the eight compositions here aim deep into human feelings that come out in times of crisis," the program notes explain. Calling to mind not only conditions in Iraq but also elsewhere in the world, they ask: "Can we do better?"[23]

AlHaj's oud playing has a warmth and elegance that brings light to what might otherwise be a pall of darkness. Through the sounds of barbarity and violence, the capacity of love and hope to inspire remains intact. "Music can make us laugh, make us cry, make us march into war," he says in the notes' conclusion. "I want to make music to make us realize peace."[24]

This ambition is woven into the very design of the project. Despite the destruction and carnage which the U.S. invasion brought to Iraq, AlHaj holds fast to an ecumenical strain of wonder, not a naive optimism but an unbowed belief in the benevolent possibilities of art to forge meaningful human connections. If a film about heavy metal in the Middle East symbolizes one kind of cultural syncretism, AlHaj's compositions for oud and string quartet mark another. Performed by musicians from the United States, Europe, and the Middle East, they embody a seamless fusion of Arabic and Western classical musics. Underscoring this complementarity, the liner notes are printed in both English and Arabic and are themselves a multimedia counterpart to the program music, mixing text with color reproductions of vivid paintings by artist Riyadh Neama. In pictures, words, and music, the *Letters from Iraq* project recalls a couplet by Lynn Hill, the air force veteran featured on *Holding It Down*:

> When I dream, I dream of normalcy
> I dream the color of peace.[25]

That dream looks backward and forward. If music can be part of wars' past, perhaps it can be part of peace's future.

Acknowledgments

This book was many years in the making and never would have come to fruition without all the assistance and encouragement I received along the way. It is a great pleasure to acknowledge my gratitude publicly now that this work is entering into the world.

I came to this project with experience writing about history and music, but I have never served in the military. My first thanks are to the many current and former military personnel I communicated with who shared their experiences with me and generously offered feedback on my interpretations of what military life involved. In particular, I learned a great deal from my conversations with Pamela Ahearn, Ross Caputi, Ron McClure, and William A. Thompson IV, and I am indebted to their patient answers to my many questions, some of which probably sounded quite odd.

I am fortunate to have great colleagues and students at the University of Delaware, and many of them, current and former, aided this project in some way. The resulting book has been enriched by comments, questions, provocations, and suggestions I received from Zara Anishanslin, Kayle Avery, Anne Boylan, Jim Brophy, Rebecca Davis, Erica Armstrong Dunbar, Darryl Flaherty, Peter Kolchin, Rudi Matthee, Arwen Mohun, Dael Norwood, Alison Parker, Tyler Putman, Ram Rawat, Rachael Storm, Jai Virdi, and Owen White. Mehdi Mousavi, who aided with the illustrations, was as conscientious and indefatigable a research assistant as one could hope for.

Throughout the project, I was helped, heartened, and inspired by the generosity of other scholars and the tireless, often unsung work of archivists and librarians. Jonathan Pieslak shared with me the raw audio of interviews he conducted for his book *Sound Targets: American Soldiers and Music in the Iraq War*. Paul Miles drew on his deep knowledge of the armed forces and U.S. historiography to assist me in analyzing tooth-to-tail ratios. William Davis pointed me to music-therapy sources I never would have found otherwise. Megan Harris showed me how to navigate the Library of Congress's Veterans History Project and directed me to other valuable material. Dan Del Fiorentino made it possible for me to access interviews in the National Association of Music Manufacturers' rich oral-history library.

When it came to crafting my ideas, I received invaluable critical feedback on many facets of this project in the course of its development. At a crucial early stage, I benefited from the sharp insights of Emily Thompson and Douglas Kahn. People who read and offered productive critiques of parts of the manuscript include Andrea Bohlman, Jeremy Braddock, Greg Daddis, Andrew Friedman, Roger Horowitz, Sophie Maisonneuve, Emily Marker, Charles McGovern, Rebecca McKenna, Jeff Melnick, Erik Rau, Elena Razlogova, Eileen Ryan, and Phil Scranton. Other interlocutors who helped me at various points include Beth Bailey, Lisa Gilman, Sumanth Gopinath, Stefan Helmreich, Alix Hui, Nick Kapur, Karl Hagstrom Miller, Mara Mills, David Novak, Sergio Ospina Romero, Marina Rustow, Joey Thompson, Barry Shank, Jennifer Stoever, Fred Turner, Neil Verma, Jacques Martin Vest, Elijah Wald, and Gayle Wald.

I am grateful to have had the opportunity to present parts of this work publicly on numerous occasions. My thanks to the organizers and participants of the Hagley Museum and Library research seminar; the Lees Seminar at Rutgers University–Camden; the Popular Music Books in Process series; the Haverford College Faculty Working Group in American Studies; the Sonologia conference in São Paulo, Brazil; the Indiana University Music Department; the Cornell University English Department; the Sound Instruments and Sonic Cultures conference sponsored by the National Science and Media Museum, Bradford, U.K.; the Productive Sounds in Everyday Spaces workshop at the Max Planck Institute in Berlin; the Sound in Theory, Sound in Practice symposium at Bard College; Periods and Waves: A Conference on Sound and History at Stony Brook University; and the Pop Conference.

This project was also sustained by the love and support I got from Ed Boland, Erik Brunar, Michael Carter, Lara Cohen, Michael Dorian, Ben Harley, Chisa Hidaka, Marion Immerman, Richard Immerman, Semyon Khokhlov, Dave King, Joe McKoy, Heidi Nakashima, Ed Park, Tracy Rolling-Brunar, Derrick Rossi, Margaret Ryan, David Sampliner, Mike Sappol, Anshu Srivastava, Jill Stauffer, Charlie Suisman, Ingrid Suisman, Richard Suisman, Frank Tartaglione, Juliet Whelan, and Sam Zalutsky. Thank you for all the meals, hugs, and countless other ways you energized me.

Joyce Seltzer helped me figure out how to turn this work into a book. My editor at the University of Chicago Press, Timothy Mennel, expressed excitement about this project from the moment I approached him with it, and the book benefited greatly from all his astute suggestions. Andrea Blatz answered my countless inquiries about illustrations and editorial protocols. Greg Daddis was an ideal outside reader for the press—thoughtful in evaluating the book's arguments, careful in his critiques, generous with his encouragement and suggestions, and helpful in alerting me to sources I otherwise would have overlooked. Thanks, too, to the other outside reader, who remained anonymous.

I cannot count the number of hours I spent discussing this project with Jeremy Braddock, Gus Stadler, and Susan Strasser, and the latter two read and offered comments on the entire manuscript. It is an understatement to say I appreciate their incisive challenges, comments, aperçus, and creative approaches to this work.

My sister Sherry Suisman cheered me on without fail, never questioning if I was on the right track. My parents Janet and Michael Suisman did not live to see this book completed, but I think every day about all the tools they gave me to make my way in the world, not the least of which was a love of reading. My final thanks goes to Eileen Ryan, who never flagged in her enthusiasm for this book, never complained about the odd hours I kept writing it, and never hesitated to make time to talk about it with me. In every way, she helped me keep this project in perspective. I am grateful for her insights and wit, awed by the depth of her compassion, and inspired by her curiosity and open-mindedness to adventures of any kind. Her love and thoughtfulness enrich my life in more ways than I have words for.

Illustration Credits

Chapter One

Figure 1.1 courtesy of Wikimedia Commons; figure 1.2 public domain; figure 1.3 courtesy of Massachusetts Historical Society; figure 1.4 courtesy of Frederick R. Selch Collection of American Music History, Oberlin Conservatory Library; figure 1.5 courtesy of Library of Congress, Prints & Photographs Division, Civil War Photographs, LC-DIG-ppmsc-02781.

Chapter Two

Figure 2.1 courtesy of University of Minnesota Libraries; figures 2.2 and 2.7 public domain; figures 2.3 and 2.5 courtesy of Minnesota Historical Society; figure 2.4 courtesy of Indiana Historical Society P0357; figure 2.6 courtesy of Library of Congress; figure 2.8 courtesy of Denver Public Library, Western History Collection, Z-3007; figure 2.9 courtesy of Charles H. Templeton, Sr., Sheet Music Collection, Manuscripts Unit, Archives & Special Collections, Mississippi State University Libraries.

Chapter Three

Figures 3.1, 3.3, 3.4, 3.7, 3.11, 3.14, and 3.16–3.18 courtesy of National Archives, photo nos. 165-WW-473G-2, 165-WW-473D-12, 165-WW-473G-49, 111-SC-10389, 165-WW-473A-1, 165-WW-262A-92, 165-WW-46D-37, and 165-WW-473E-29; figures 3.2 and 3.10 courtesy of Library of Congress, Prints & Photographs Division, LC-USZC4-8068, LC-USZC4-10035; figures 3.5, 3.8, and 3.9 from author's collection; figures 3.6, 3.12, 3.13, and 3.15 courtesy of Kautz Family YMCA Archives, University of Minnesota Libraries; figure 3.11 courtesy of James Francis Driscoll Collection of American Sheet Music, Illinois University Library.

Chapter Four

Figures 4.1–4.3 from author's collection; figures 4.4 and 4.5 courtesy of Library of Congress; figures 4.6 and 4.7 courtesy of San Diego Air and Space Museum Archives; figure 4.8 courtesy of J. W. Pepper and Son, Inc.; figures 4.9, 4.11, and 4.13 courtesy of National Archives, photo nos. 208-NP-8T-2, 111-SC-210796, and 342-FH-3A45250-67818AC; figure 4.10 courtesy of Kautz Family YMCA Archives, University of Minnesota Libraries; figure 4.12 courtesy of Wikimedia Commons; figure 4.14 public domain.

Chapter Five

Figure 5.1 courtesy of Robin Caldwell and Norma Brown; figures 5.2–5.4 and 5.6 courtesy of Kautz Family YMCA Archives, University of Minnesota Libraries; figure 5.5 courtesy of University of North Texas Digital Library.

Chapter Six

Figure 6.1 courtesy of Wikimedia Commons; figure 6.2 courtesy of Doug Bradley; figures 6.3–6.5 courtesy of Bettmann Archive; figure 6.6 courtesy of Jill Krementz; figure 6.7 courtesy of National Archives.

Chapter Seven

Figure 7.1 courtesy of the Center for the Study of Political Graphics; figure 7.2 from author's collection.

Abbreviations Used in the Notes

JANCWR	Joint Army and Navy Committee on Welfare and Recreation Papers, Music Division, Library of Congress
JHC	Jack Horntip Collection, Military Songbooks, https://www.horntip.com/html/songs_sorted_by_informant/military_songbooks/index.htm
LC-AFC	American Folklife Center, Library of Congress
LC-VHP	Veterans History Project, Library of Congress
NAMM	Oral History Program, National Association of Music Merchants
NARA-RG330	Record Group 330, Records of the Office of the Secretary of Defense, National Archives and Records Administration
NARA-RG472	Record Group 472, Records of the U.S. Forces in Southeast Asia, National Archives and Records Administration
NYT	*New York Times*
USAHEC	Veterans Survey Collection, U.S. Cavalry 1st Regiment, Spanish American War Papers, U.S. Army Heritage and Education Center, Carlisle Barracks, Pennsylvania
UMN-YMCA	Kautz Family YMCA Archives, University of Minnesota

Notes

Prologue

1. Dave Philipps, "Military Is Asked to March to a Less Expensive Tune," *NYT*, July 1, 2016; "Make Your Passion Your Profession," U.S. Army Bands, accessed August 22, 2020, https://www.bands.army.mil/careers/. For another unusual military music group, see Andrew R. Martin, *Steelpan Ambassadors: The US Navy Steel Band, 1957–1999* (Jackson: University Press of Mississippi, 2017).

2. Betty McCollum, "Congresswoman McCollum's Remarks on the Amendment to Reduce Spending on Military Bands and the Deficit," Congresswoman Betty McCollum, July 18, 2012, https://mccollum.house.gov /taxonomy/statements-for-the-record/congresswoman-mccollums-remarks -amendment-reduce-spending; Philipps, "Military Is Asked to March to a Less Expensive Tune"; Brian Dix, "Stop Scaling Back Military Bands," *San Diego Union-Tribune*, July 21, 2016. Dix was former director of the Marine Drum and Bugle Corps.

3. Ellen Mitchell, "The Pentagon's Battle of the Bands," *Politico*, May 22, 2016, https://www.politico.com/story/2016/05/pentagons-bands-battle-223435.

4. Philipps, "Military Is Asked to March to a Less Expensive Tune." "The Stars and Stripes Forever" was made the official National March of the United States by an act of Congress in 1987.

5. Wood quoted in Edward Frank Allen and Raymond B. Fosdick, *Keeping Our Fighters Fit: For War and After* (Washington, DC: Commissions on Training Camp Activities, 1918), 69–70.

6. "'Victory Sings' All over Our Land," *NYT*, November 24, 1918. On Bell in the Philippines, see, e.g., Andrea Pitzer, *One Long Night: A Global History of Concentration Camps* (New York: Little, Brown, 2017), 44–52.

7. Frank B. Tiebout, *A History of the 305th Infantry* (New York: The 305th Infantry Auxiliary, [1919]), 12; Elliott White Springs, *Letters from a War Bird: The World War I Correspondence of Elliott White Springs*, ed. David K. Vaughan (Columbia: University of South Carolina Press, 2012), 112.

8. Sly and the Family Stone, "I Want to Take You Higher," on *Stand!*, Epic, 1969; Josh Kun, *Audiotopia: Music, Race, and America* (Berkeley: University of California Press, 2005); The Mekons, "Memphis, Egypt," on *The Mekons*

Rock 'n' Roll, Blast First, 1989. A single footnote cannot do justice to the enormous range of books exploring the force of music to move people politically and libidinally, but important recent work includes Barry Shank, *The Political Force of Musical Beauty* (Durham, NC: Duke University Press, 2014); Ann Powers, *Good Booty: Love and Sex, Black and White, Body and Soul in American Music* (New York: Dey Street, 2018); Gustavus Stadler, *Woody Guthrie: An Intimate Life* (Boston: Beacon Press, 2020); Daphne Brooks, *Liner Notes for the Revolution: The Intellectual Life of Black Feminist Sound* (Cambridge, MA: Belknap, 2021); Alexandra T. Vazquez, *Listening in Detail: Performances of Cuban Music* (Durham, NC: Duke University Press, 2013); Eric Weisbard, ed., *Pop: When the World Falls Apart* (Durham, NC: Duke University Press, 2012). Older but also essential is the work of George Lipsitz, including his "Popular Culture: This Ain't No Sideshow," in *Time Passages: Collective Memory and American Popular Culture* (Minneapolis: University of Minnesota Press, 1990), 3–20; *Footsteps in the Dark: The Hidden Histories of Popular Music* (Minneapolis: University of Minnesota Press, 2007); and *Dangerous Crossroads: Popular Music, Postmodernism, and the Poetics of Place* (London: Verso, 1994).

9. On "capillary" power, see, e.g., Michel Foucault, "Two Lectures," in *Power/Knowledge: Selected Interviews and Other Writings 1972–1977*, ed. Colin Gordon (New York: Pantheon, 1980), 96.

10. Josiah Marshall Favill, *The Diary of a Young Officer Serving with the Armies of the United States during the War of the Rebellion* (Chicago: R. R. Donnelley & Sons, 1909) 96.

11. On emotional labor, see Arlie Russell Hochschild, *The Managed Heart: Commercialization of Human Feeling* (Berkeley: University of California Press, 1983). On soldiers as laborers, see Roger Horowitz, "It Is 'the Working Class Who Fight All the Battles': Military Service, Patriotism, and the Study of American Workers," in *American Exceptionalism?: US Working-Class Formation in an International Context*, ed. Rick Halpern and Jonathan Morris (New York: St. Martin's, 1997), 76–100; Joshua B. Freeman and Geoffrey Field, "Labor and the Military: Introduction," *International Labor and Working-Class History*, no. 80 (2011): 3–5, and the articles in special issue "Labor and the Military"; Beth L. Bailey, *America's Army: Making the All-Volunteer Force* (Cambridge, MA: Harvard University Press, 2009).

12. Jeremy Montagu et al., "Military Music," Grove Music Online, https://www.oxfordmusiconline.com/subscriber/article/grove/music/44139; Sun Tzu, *The Art of War*, trans. Lionel Giles (n.p.: Project Gutenberg, 1994 [1910]), http://www.gutenberg.org/ebooks/132; Thucydides, *The History of the Peloponnesian War*, trans. Richard Crawley (n.p.: Project Gutenberg, 2003 [1903]), http://www.gutenberg.org/files/7142/7142-h/7142-h.htm; Arthur Koestler, *Janus: A Summing Up* (New York: Vintage, 1979), 2. On the history of military music in the West, see, e.g., Henry George Farmer, *The Rise & Development of Military Music* (London: Wm. Reeves, 1912); Henry George Farmer, *Military Music* (London: Parrish, 1950).

13. See, e.g., Brian Balogh, *The Associational State: American Governance in the Twentieth Century* (Philadelphia: University of Pennsylvania Press, 2015).

14. I am using the term "culture industry" in a generic sense, to refer to the commercial infrastructure organized around popular amusement and creative expression, more in line with what sociologist Paul Hirsch called the "cultural industries" than the phenomenon Theodor Adorno and Max Horkheimer theorized in the 1940s. See, e.g., Paul M. Hirsch, "Processing Fads and Fashions: An Organization-Set Analysis of Cultural Industry Systems," *American Journal of Sociology* 77, no. 4 (1972): 639–59; Max Horkheimer and Theodor W. Adorno, "The Culture Industry: Enlightenment as Mass Deception," in *Dialectic of Enlightenment* (Stanford, CA: Stanford University Press, 2007), 94–136.

15. Some of the works that *have* addressed music and war include Trevor Herbert and Helen Barlow, *Music & the British Military in the Long Nineteenth Century* (Oxford: Oxford University Press, 2013); Trevor Herbert, ed., *The British Brass Band: A Musical and Social History*, rev. ed. (New York: Oxford University Press, 2000); and Emma Hanna, *Sounds of War: Music in the British Armed Forces During the Great War* (New York: Cambridge University Press, 2020). Some books focusing on music on the home front include John Bush Jones, *The Songs That Fought the War: Popular Music and the Home Front, 1939–1945* (Waltham, MA: Brandeis University Press, 2006); Kathleen E. R. Smith, *God Bless America: Tin Pan Alley Goes to War* (Lexington: University Press of Kentucky, 2003).

16. One exception would be the volume edited by Sarah Kraaz, *Music and War in the United States* (New York: Routledge, 2018).

17. James A. Davis, "Music and Gallantry in Combat during the American Civil War," *American Music* 28, no. 2 (2010): 144. On the military as a "musical institution," see Trevor Herbert and Helen Barlow, "The British Military as a Musical Institution, c. 1780–c. 1860," in *Music and Institutions in Nineteenth-Century Britain*, ed. Paul Rodmell (Farnham, U.K.: Ashgate, 2012), 247–66.

18. R. Nash and James E. Wentz, *American Forces Vietnam Network: Audience Opinion Research and Analysis* (Saigon: [American Forces Vietnam Network], 1969), 21.

19. Christopher Small, *Musicking: The Meanings of Performing and Listening* (Middletown, CT: Wesleyan University Press, 1998). Small's work recalls the analysis of the complex of interdependent actors in sociologist Howard Becker's influential *Art Worlds* (Berkeley: University of California Press, 1982).

20. Bruno Latour, *Science in Action: How to Follow Scientists and Engineers through Society* (Cambridge, MA: Harvard University Press, 1987); Tia DeNora, *After Adorno: Rethinking Music Sociology* (Cambridge: Cambridge University Press, 2003), 46.

21. Small, *Musicking*, 183.

22. On the notion of sonic displacement, see Martin Kaltenecker, "'What Scenes! What Sounds!': Some Remarks on Soundscapes in War Times," in

Music and War in Europe from French Revolution to WW1, ed. Étienne Jardin (Turnhout, Belgium: Brepols, 2016), 9.

23. Geneva R. Belton, "The Contribution of Negro Music and Musicians in World War II" (MM thesis, Northwestern University, 1946), 34.

24. See Michael Bull, "War, Cognition and the Media: Training the Senses in a Fully Mediated World," in *The Auditory Culture Reader*, ed. Michael Bull and Les Back, 2d ed. (New York: Routledge, 2015), 303–17, esp. 315.

25. Thanks to Andrew Friedman for helping me think about the limits of this metaphor.

26. Although it falls outside the scope of this work, it may be fruitful to consider how war itself can function as a kind of music. War too can be emancipatory or libidinal. It too can be a means of contesting or circumventing power. Were we to consider the unconscious drives that propel human societies into war, we might say it too can take us to that "secret place we all want to go." See, e.g., Barbara Ehrenreich, *Blood Rites: Origins and History of the Passions of War* (New York: Metropolitan, 1997).

Chapter One

1. H. E. Gerry, *Camp Fire Entertainment and True History of R.H. Hendershot, the Drummer Boy of the Rappahannock* (Chicago: Hack & Anderson, 1900); William Sumner Dodge, *Robert Henry Hendershot; or, the Brave Drummer Boy of the Rappahannock* (Chicago: Church and Goodman, 1867), 172–73.

2. Francis A. Lord and Arthur Wise, *Bands and Drummer Boys of the Civil War* (New York: T. Yoseloff, 1966), esp. 100–117; Perry Byam, "A Nine-Year-Old Warrior," *Harper's Weekly*, June 12, 1909, 24–25. For drummer boys in popular culture, see J. T. Trowbridge, *The Drummer Boy: A Story of Burnside's Expedition* (Boston: J. E. Tilton, 1863); "The Drummer Boy's Burial," *Harper's New Monthly Magazine* 29, no. 170 (July 1864): 145–46; "The Drummer Boy of Our Regiment," *Harper's Weekly*, December 19, 1863; Samuel J. Muscroft, *The Drummer Boy; or, the Battle-Field of Shiloh, a New Military Allegory in Five Acts.* (Worcester, MA: C. Hamilton, 1888); Kenneth E. Olson, *Music and Musket: Bands and Bandsmen of the American Civil War* (Westport, CT: Greenwood, 1981), 126; Albert Boime, "Thomas Couture's Drummer Boy Beating a Path to Glory," *Bulletin of the Detroit Institute of Arts* 56, no. 2 (1978): 108–31.

3. J. J. Sutton, *History of the Second Regiment West Virginia Cavalry Volunteers, during the War of the Rebellion* (Portsmouth, Ohio: n.p., 1892), 225 and opposite 228; E. M. Woodward, *History of the One Hundred and Ninety-Eighth Pennsylvania Volunteers* (Trenton, NJ: MacCrellish & Quigley, 1884), 58; John M. Gibson, *Those 163 Days: A Southern Account of Sherman's March from Atlanta to Raleigh* (New York: Coward-McCann, 1961), 239–42. See also Frederick Fennell, "The Civil War: Its Music and Its Sounds," *Journal of Band Research* 6, no. 1 (1969): 53; Olson, *Music and Musket*, 45–50, 247–50. "The past is a foreign country" comes from L. P. Hartley, *The Go-Between* (New York: Knopf, 1954), 9.

4. Charles B. Haydon, *For Country, Cause & Leader: The Civil War Journal of Charles B. Haydon*, ed. Stephen W. Sears (New York: Ticknor & Fields, 1993), 323; Thomas T. Ellis, *Leaves from the Diary of an Army Surgeon: Or, Incidents of Field, Camp, and Hospital Life* (New York: John Bradburn, 1863), 182; Josiah M. Favill, *The Diary of a Young Officer Serving with the Armies of the United States during the War of the Rebellion* (Chicago: R. R. Donnelley & Sons, 1909), 96; Wilder Dwight, *Life and Letters of Wilder Dwight: Lieut.-Col. Second Mass. Inf. Vols* (Boston: Ticknor, 1891), 196. Another soldier, who rose from corporal to colonel over the course of the war put it this way: "[Music] makes this life pleasant and even enjoyable, and we are better men and soldiers for cultivating a taste for finer things." Robert Hunt Rhodes, ed., *All for the Union: The Civil War Diaries and Letters of Elisha Hunt Rhodes* (New York: Orion, 1991), 213.

5. For example, the database *The American Civil War: Letters and Diaries* contains more than 3,700 references to music in documents from 2,009 different authors, using the search terms *music, musician, singing, song, drum, drummer, bugle,* and *bugler.* The use of such sources is of course biased toward soldiers who were literate, but there is no reason to believe that the experience of illiterate soldiers would have been different. Moreover, literacy rates appear to have been high: greater than 90 percent among white soldiers from the North and above 80 percent for Confederate soldiers. On soldiers' literacy rates, see James M. McPherson, *For Cause and Comrades: Why Men Fought in the Civil War* (New York: Oxford University Press, 1997), 11. For military manuals that mention music, see Orville J. Victor, *The Military Hand-Book and Soldier's Manual of Information* (New York: Beadle, 1862); Daniel Butterfield, *Camp and Outpost Duty for Infantry: With Standing Orders, Extracts from the Revised Regulations for the Army, Rules for Health, Maxims for Soldiers, and Duties of Officers* (New York: Harper & Brothers, 1863); William Gilham, *Manual of Instruction for the Volunteers and Militia of the Confederate States* (Richmond, VA: West and Johnson, 1862); *The Soldier's Guide: A Complete Manual and Drill Book for the Use of Volunteers, Militia, and the Home Guard* (Philadelphia: T. B. Peterson, [1861]); *The Soldier's Companion: For the Use of All Officers, Volunteers, and Militia in the Service of the United States, in the Camp, Field, or on the March* (Philadelphia: T. B. Peterson, 1861).

6. Campbell Dalrymple, *A Military Essay* (London: D. Wilson, 1761), 229; Trevor Herbert and Helen Barlow, *Music & the British Military in the Long Nineteenth Century* (Oxford: Oxford University Press, 2013), 33; Raoul F. Camus, *Military Music of the American Revolution* (Chapel Hill: University of North Carolina Press, 1976), 78, 59–60; Friedrich Wilhelm Ludolf Gerhard Augustin Steuben, *Regulations for the Order and Discipline of the Troops of the United States* (Exeter, NH: Henry Ranlet, 1794).

7. Richard English, *Modern War: A Very Short Introduction* (Oxford: Oxford University Press, 2013), 11 (emphasis in original); Martin Van Creveld, *Technology and War: From 2000 B.C. to the Present*, rev. ed. (New York: Touchstone,

1991). On "total war," see John Bennett Walters, "General William T. Sherman and Total War," *Journal of Southern History* 14, no. 4 (1948): 447–80; Stig Förster and Jorg Nagler, eds., *On the Road to Total War: The American Civil War and the German Wars of Unification, 1861–1871* (New York: Cambridge University Press, 1997); Hew Strachan, "Essay and Reflection: On Total War and Modern War," *International History Review* 22, no. 2 (2000): 341–70; Lance Janda, "Shutting the Gates of Mercy: The American Origins of Total War, 1860–1880," *Journal of Military History* 59, no. 1 (1995): 7–26; Joseph G. Dawson, "The First of the Modern Wars?," in *Themes of the American Civil War: The War Between the States*, ed. Susan-Mary Grant and Brian Holden Reid, 2nd ed. (New York: Routledge, 2010), 64–80. For a contrasting views, see David A. Bell, *The First Total War: Napoleon's Europe and the Birth of Warfare as We Know It* (Boston: Houghton Mifflin, 2007); Wayne Wei-Siang Hsieh, "Total War and the American Civil War Reconsidered: The End of an Outdated 'Master Narrative,'" *Journal of the Civil War Era* 1, no. 3 (2011): 394–408.

8.   On soundscapes and keynotes, see R. Murray Schafer, *The Tuning of the World* (New York: Knopf, 1977). For a critique of "soundscapes," see Ari Y. Kelman, "Rethinking the Soundscape: A Critical Genealogy of a Key Term in Sound Studies," *Senses and Society* 5, no. 2 (2010): 212–34. Problems notwithstanding, I believe the term retains some descriptive and analytical value if used judiciously.

9.   As the eminent military historian John Keegan put it, smoke and noise were the "two most oppressive characteristics of the [nineteenth-century] battlefield." See John Keegan, *The Face of Battle: A Study of Agincourt, Waterloo and the Somme* (New York: Viking, 1976), 139–43, quotation at 139. Keegan was writing about the Napoleonic Wars, but the same black powder was used for muskets and artillery in the U.S. in the 1860s. On the effects of smoke in the Civil War, see Russell L. Johnson, *Warriors into Workers: The Civil War and the Formation of the Urban-Industrial Society in a Northern City* (New York: Fordham University Press, 2003), 178.

10. J. Martin Daughtry, *Listening to War: Sound, Music, Trauma, and Survival in Wartime Iraq* (New York: Oxford University Press, 2015), 19 and 123–58. The notion of "embodied knowledge" is associated with Pierre Bourdieu's theory of habitus; see p. 129. Soldiers developed a facility for listening in different ways. Whether in camp or in battle, they had to be aurally on their guard all the time—an ongoing state of alertness that other scholars have called "listening-in-readiness" or "monitory" listening. Yet when enjoying the music of a band or singing songs, they also often practiced a more active kind of listening, at the same time. These "modes" of listening, however distinct, worked in concert, jointly and concurrently. See Barry Truax, *Acoustic Communication* (Norwood, NJ: Ablex, 1984), 19–21; Alexandra Supper and Karin Bijsterveld, "Sounds Convincing: Modes of Listening and Sonic Skills in Knowledge Making," *Interdisciplinary Science Reviews* 40, no.

2 (June 2015): 124–44. On modes of listening, see also see Ola Stockfelt, "Adequate Modes of Listening," in *Keeping Score: Music, Disciplinarity, Culture*, ed. David Schwarz, Anahid Kassabian, and Lawrence Siegel (Charlottesville: University of Virginia Press, 1997), 129–46; Anahid Kassabian, *Ubiquitous Listening: Affect, Attention, and Distributed Subjectivity* (Berkeley: University of California Press, 2013); Theodor W. Adorno, *Introduction to the Sociology of Music*, trans. E. B. Ashby (New York: Seabury, 1976), 1–20. For theorizations of listening, see, e.g., Jean-Luc Nancy, *Listening* (New York: Fordham University Press, 2009); Adrienne Janus, "Listening: Jean-Luc Nancy and the 'Anti-Ocular' Turn in Continental Philosophy and Critical Theory," *Comparative Literature* 63, no. 2 (2011): 182–202; Brian Kane, "Jean-Luc Nancy and the Listening Subject," *Contemporary Music Review* 31, nos. 5–6 (2012): 439–47; Peter Szendy, *Listen: A History of Our Ears* (New York: Fordham University Press, 2008); Georgina Born, "Listening, Mediation, Event: Anthropological and Sociological Perspectives," *Journal of the Royal Musical Association* 135, no. S1 (2010): 79–89, and other articles in special issue "Listening: Interdisciplinary Perspectives"; Sander van Maas, ed., *Thresholds of Listening: Sound, Technics, Space* (New York: Fordham University Press, 2015); Angus Carlyle, ed., *On Listening* (Axminster, U.K.: Uniformbooks, 2013). For historical approaches to listening, see James H. Johnson, *Listening in Paris: A Cultural History* (Berkeley: University of California Press, 1995); Alain Corbin, *A History of Silence: From the Renaissance to the Present Day*, trans. Jean Birrell (Cambridge: Polity, 2018); Mark M. Smith, *Listening to Nineteenth-Century America* (Chapel Hill: University of North Carolina Press, 2001).

11. Paul A. Cimbala, *Soldiers North and South: The Everyday Experiences of the Men Who Fought America's Civil War* (New York: Fordham University Press, 2010), 156; Charles C. Nott, *Sketches of the War: A Series of Letters to the North Moore Street School of New York* (New York: William Abbatt, 1911), 12; Wilbur Fisk, *Hard Marching Every Day: The Civil War Letters of Private Wilbur Fisk, 1861–1865*, ed. Emil Rosenblatt and Ruth Rosenblatt (Lawrence: University Press of Kansas, 1992), 226.

12. Hillel Schwartz, *Making Noise: From Babel to the Big Bang and Beyond* (New York: Zone, 2011), 264–66; Franc B. Wilkie, *Pen and Powder* (Boston: Ticknor, 1888), 168; Nott, *Sketches of the War*, 12; Robert Krick, "An Insurmountable Barrier between the Army and Ruin: The Confederate Experience at Spotsylvania's Bloody Angle," in *The Spotsylvania Campaign*, ed. Gary W. Gallagher (Chapel Hill: University of North Carolina Press, 1998), 105. Typhus, Schwartz notes, was another cause of deafness. See also the website Civil War Artillery, https://civilwarartillery.com/.

13. Staples quoted in Johnson, *Warriors into Workers*, 179. Although not himself a Civil War veteran, novelist Stephen Crane (born 1871) captured this effect memorably in *The Red Badge of Courage*: "The noises of the battle were like stones; he believed himself liable to be crushed." Quoted in Schwartz, *Making Noise*, 327.

14. One other sound that Union soldiers may have encountered is the "rebel yell," said to have been the Confederate war cry. Although its ubiquity and impact have been exaggerated and embellished by the lore of the "Lost Cause," it may not be entirely fictive. See, e.g., Craig A. Warren, *The Rebel Yell: A Cultural History* (Tuscaloosa: University of Alabama Press, 2014); Andrew S. Hasselbring, "The Rebel Yell," *Louisiana History* 25, no. 2 (1984): 198–201; H. Allen Smith, *The Rebel Yell, Being a Carpetbagger's Attempt to Establish the Truth Concerning the Screech of the Confederate Soldier Plus Lesser Matters Appertaining to the Peculiar Habits of the South* (Garden City, NY : Doubleday, 1954).

15. Schwartz, *Making Noise*, 265–66; Peter Cozzens, *This Terrible Sound: The Battle of Chickamauga* (Urbana: University of Illinois Press, 1994), 283. For more on pre- and post-battle soundscapes, see, e.g., Cozzens, *This Terrible Sound*, esp. chaps. 6 and 15.

16. Indeed, the sheer number of war memoirs that mention the sound before, during, and after battle attests to this lasting impact—though it may also say something about sound as a trope in war memoirs. Powell quoted in Schwartz, *Making Noise*, 286.

17. Communication *between* units was the responsibility of the newly established Signal Corps, but communication *within* units was dependent on field music. On the history of the Signal Corps, see Kathy Coker and Carol Stokes, *A Concise History of the U.S. Army Signal Corps* (n.p.: U.S. Army Signal Center and Fort Gordon, 1991); Rebecca Robbins Raines, *Getting the Message through: A Branch History of the U.S. Army Signal Corps* (Washington, DC: Center of Military History, U.S. Army, 1996).

18. On marching in step, see Trevor Herbert and Helen Barlow, *Music & the British Military in the Long Nineteenth Century* (Oxford: Oxford University Press, 2013), 24. On the history of drilling (by the Dutch military in the 1590s), see William H. McNeill, *Keeping Together in Time: Dance and Drill in Human History* (Cambridge, MA: Harvard University Press, 1995), 3. On manuals, see, e.g., Orville J. Victor, *The Military Hand-Book and Soldier's Manual of Information* (New York: Beadle, 1862), 96–97. For a similar description in a Confederate military manual, see William Gilham, *Manual of Instruction for the Volunteers and Militia of the Confederate States* (Richmond, VA: West and Johnson, 1862), 483–84, 489–90. Other manuals include Daniel Butterfield, *Camp and Outpost Duty for Infantry: With Standing Orders, Extracts from the Revised Regulations for the Army, Rules for Health, Maxims for Soldiers, and Duties of Officers* (New York: Harper & Brothers, 1863); *The Soldier's Guide: A Complete Manual and Drill Book for the Use of Volunteers, Militia, and the Home Guard* (Philadelphia: T. B. Peterson, [1861]); *The Soldier's Companion: For the Use of All Officers, Volunteers, and Militia in the Service of the United States, in the Camp, Field, or on the March* (Philadelphia: T. B. Peterson, 1861).

19. Lawrence Sangston *The Bastiles* [*sic*] *of the North* (Baltimore: Kelly, Hedian, & Piet, 1863), 37. On regulating time with bells and whistles in factories and

factory towns, see E. P. Thompson, "Time, Work-Discipline, and Industrial Capitalism," *Past & Present* 38, no. 1 (1967): 56–97; Michael O'Malley, *Keeping Watch: A History of American Time* (Washington, DC: Smithsonian, 1996). On bells in factories and on antebellum plantations, see Smith, *Listening to Nineteenth-Century America*, 113, 128, 136–41. See also Johnson, *Warriors into Workers*, 169–70.

20. John D. Billings, *Hardtack and Coffee* (Boston: George M. Smith, 1887), 186.

21. "Interesting Career of John F. Stratton," *Music Trades*, September 19, 1908, 36–37; "John F. Stratton and Son," in *General History of the Music Trades of America* (New York: Bill & Bill, 1891), 81; Robert E. Eliason, "John F. Stratton: Musician, Manufacturer, and Merchant," *Journal of the American Musical Instrument Society* 38 (2012): 106. Other notable suppliers included John F. M. Joerdans in New York, Klemm Brothers in Philadelphia, and John Church Jr. in Cincinnati. See Chris Nelson, "Collecting Civil War Bugles," *North South Trader's Civil War* 29, no. 4 (2003): 49–50; Robert Joseph Garofalo and Mark Elrod, *A Pictorial History of Civil War Era Musical Instruments & Military Bands* (Charleston, WV: Pictorial Histories, 1985).

22. The figure of forty thousand comes from Lord and Wise, *Bands and Drummer Boys of the Civil War*, 100. The Union army had slightly more than two thousand individual regiments, according to Willard A. Heaps and Porter Heaps, *The Singing Sixties: The Spirit of Civil War Days Drawn from the Music of the Times* (Norman: University of Oklahoma Press, 1960), 130. On older field musicians, see, e.g., Roger Norland, "Bugler of the 1st Minnesota: The Life of Ernst Meyer," *Military Images* 17, no. 3 (1995): 27–37.

23. Bruce P. Gleason, "Military Music in the United States: A Historical Examination of Performance and Training," *Music Educators Journal* 101, no. 3 (March 2015), 39. George B. Bruce and Daniel D. Emmett's *The Drummer's and Fifer's Guide: Or Self-Instructor, Containing a Plain and Easy Introduction of the Rudimental Principles for the Drum and Fife* was first published by Firth, Pond & Company in New York in 1862, although Emmett's name was omitted from the title page of some early editions. On standardization, see also William Nevins and A. J. Vaas, *Army Regulations for Drum, Fife, and Bugle: Being a Complete Manual for These Instruments, Giving All the Calls for Camp and Field Duty, to Which Is Added Suitable Music for Each Instrument* (Chicago: Root & Cady, 1864).

24. Norton, *Army Letters*, 179; Delavan S. Miller, *Drum Taps in Dixie; Memories of a Drummer Boy, 1861–1865* (Watertown, NY: Hungerford-Holbrook, 1905), 131; William Bircher, *A Drummer-Boy's Diary: Comprising Four Years of Service with the Second Regiment Minnesota Veteran Volunteers, 1861 to 1865* (St. Paul, MN: St. Paul Book and Stationery, 1889), 177–78.

25. Norton, *Army Letters*, 327–29; Jari A. Villanueva, "24 Notes That Tap Deep Emotions: The Story of Taps" (Washington, DC: U.S. Department of Veterans Affairs, n.d.), https://va.gov/opa/publications/celebrate/taps.pdf; Eugene C. Tidball, *No Disgrace to My Country: The Life of John C. Tidball* (Kent, OH: Kent State University Press, 2002), 250–51.

26. This definition can be found in Melvin Kranzberg, "At the Start," *Technology and Culture* 1, no. 1 (1959): 1–10, esp. 8–9.

27. Foucault defined four types of technology: (1) technologies of production, (2) technologies of sign systems, (3) technologies of power, and (4) technologies of the self. Arguably, music also functioned as a technology of sign systems, but this category I would contend, has less bearing on concrete military outcomes. Michel Foucault, "Technologies of the Self," in *Technologies of the Self: A Seminar with Michel Foucault*, ed. Luther H. Martin, Huck Gutman, and Patrick H. Hutton (Amherst: University of Massachusetts Press, 1988), 16–49; David Rooney, "A Contextualising, Socio-technical Definition of Technology: Learning from Ancient Greece and Foucault," *Prometheus* 15, no. 3 (1997): 399–407. On music and semiotics, see, e.g., Steven Feld, "Communication, Music, and Speech About Music," *Yearbook for Traditional Music* 16 (1984): 1–18.

28. "Civil War Soldiers—SNL," YouTube, https://www.youtube.com /watch?v=eIdXxDARU_0. Thanks to Gregory Daddis for referring me to this video.

29. Tia DeNora, "Music as a Technology of the Self," *Poetics* 27, no. 1 (1999): 31–56; Tia DeNora, *Music in Everyday Life* (New York: Cambridge University Press, 2000). See also Daniel C. Semenza, "Feeling the Beat and Feeling Better: Musical Experience, Emotional Reflection, and Music as a Technology of Mental Health," *Sociological Inquiry* 88, no. 2 (2018): 322–43.

30. James A. Davis, ed., *"Bully for the Band!": The Civil War Letters and Diary of Four Brothers in the 10th Vermont Infantry Band* (Jefferson, NC: McFarland, 2012), 121–22. On instruments, see Billings, *Hardtack and Coffee*, 69; Christian McWhirter, *Battle Hymns: The Power and Popularity of Music in the Civil War* (Chapel Hill: University of North Carolina Press, 2012), 112, 118–19.

31. See, e.g., *Touch the Elbow Songster* (New York: Dick & Fitzgerald, 1862); *Beadle's Dime Union Song Book No. 2* (New York: Beadle, 1861); *Songs for Our Soldiers and Sailors* (n.p.: United States Christian Commission, 1862); *John Brown, and "The Union Right or Wrong" Songster: Containing All the Celebrated "John Brown" and "Union Songs" Which Have Become so Immensely Popular throughout the Union.* (San Francisco: D. E. Appleton, 1863). For an analysis of Confederate songsters in particular, see Kristen Schultz, "The Production and Consumption of Confederate Songsters," in *Bugle Resounding: Music and Musicians of the Civil War Era*, ed. Mark A. Snell and Bruce C. Kelley (Columbia: University of Missouri Press, 2004), 133–68.

32. James Stone, "War Music and War Psychology in the Civil War," *Journal of Abnormal and Social Psychology* 36, no. 4 (1941): 543–60; Heaps and Heaps, *The Singing Sixties*, passim, esp. 132; Susan J. Matt, *Homesickness: An American History* (New York: Oxford University Press, 2014), 87.

33. Dena J. Epstein, *Music Publishing in Chicago Before 1871: The Firm of Root & Cady, 1858–1871* (Detroit: Information Coordinators, 1969); David Suisman,

Selling Sounds: The Commercial Revolution in American Music (Cambridge, MA: Harvard University Press, 2009), 22–23. On "John Brown's Body" and "The Battle Cry of Freedom," see McWhirter, *Battle Hymns*, 41–55.

34. Alfred M. Williams, "Folk-Songs of the Civil War," *Journal of American Folklore* 5, no. 19 (1892): 273–73.

35. Keith P. Wilson, *Campfires of Freedom: The Camp Life of Black Soldiers during the Civil War* (Kent, OH: Kent State University Press, 2002), 165–68.

36. Quoted in Wilson, *Campfires of Freedom*, 148.

37. Thomas Wentworth Higginson, *Army Life in a Black Regiment* (Boston: Lee and Shepard, 1890), 218; Wilson, *Campfires of Freedom*, 147–75. It bears noting that I have seen no references to white soldiers singing abolitionist songs, although it was enough of an issue that in 1862 the abolitionist singing group the Hutchinson Family Singers were banned from performing for the Union army. See Scott Gac, *Singing for Freedom: The Hutchinson Family Singers and the Nineteenth-Century Culture of Reform* (New Haven, CT: Yale University Press, 2007), 20. On songs of the enslaved and the recently free, see, e.g., William Francis Allen, Charles Pickard Ware, and Lucy McKim Garrison, eds., *Slave Songs of the United States* (New York: A. Simpson, 1867); Ronald Radano, *Lying up a Nation : Race and Black Music* (Chicago : University of Chicago Press, 2003); Lawrence W. Levine, *Black Culture and Black Consciousness: Afro-American Folk Thought from Slavery to Freedom* (New York: Oxford University Press, 1977); Sterling Stuckey, *Slave Culture: Nationalist Theory and the Foundations of Black America* (New York: Oxford University Press, 1987); Mat Callahan, *Songs of Slavery and Emancipation* (Jackson: University Press of Mississippi, 2022).

38. Higginson, *Army Life in a Black Regiment*, 222; Wilson, *Campfires of Freedom*, 148, 150–53, 162.

39. Armstrong quoted in Wilson, *Campfires of Freedom*, 157.

40. Dena J. Epstein, *Sinful Tunes and Spirituals: Black Folk Music to the Civil War* (Urbana: University of Illinois Press, 1977); Higginson, *Army Life in a Black Regiment*, 252. On subalterns' secretive oppositional culture, see James C. Scott, *Domination and the Arts of Resistance: Hidden Transcripts* (New Haven, CT: Yale University Press, 1990).

41. Walter Clark, ed., *Histories of the Several Regiments and Battalions from North Carolina in the Great War 1861–'65* (Goldsboro, NC: Nash, 1901), 2:399.

42. In the seventeenth and eighteenth century, the designation "band of music" was a general term for what we would call an orchestra. By the late eighteenth century, however, it came to be associated in both Britain and the United States with social and ceremonial music for the military. See Herbert and Barlow, *Music & the British Military in the Long Nineteenth Century*, 38.

43. Bård Mæland and Paul Otto Brunstad, *Enduring Military Boredom: From 1750 to the Present* (New York: Palgrave Macmillan, 2009), 9; Matt, *Homesickness*, 85.

44. Olson, *Music and Musket*, 7, 25-37. On brass band directors discarding earlier repertoires, see Camus, "The Early American Wind Band," 57. On the evolution of military bands from the seventeenth to the nineteenth century, see, e.g., Henry George Farmer, *Military Music* (London: Parrish, 1950), 18–22; Henry George Farmer, *The Rise & Development of Military Music* (London: Wm. Reeves, 1912), 56–66; Raoul Camus, "The Early American Wind Band: Hautboys, Harmonies, and Janissaries," in *The Wind Ensemble and Its Repertoire: Essays on the Fortieth Anniversary of the Eastman Wind Ensemble*, ed. Frank J. Cipolla and Donald Hunsberger (Rochester, NY: University of Rochester Press, 1994), 57–76.

45. Richard Crawford, *America's Musical Life: A History* (New York: Norton, 2001), 275–81; Donald Hunsberger, "Foreword," in *The Wind Band in and around New York ca. 1830–1950*, ed. Frank J. Cipolla and Donald Hunsberger (n.p.: Alfred Music, 2007), iii. The regular army, the navy, and the marines also established bands starting around the turn of the nineteenth century, growing more formal in the 1830s and '40s. Olson, *Music and Musket*, 13–17.

46. Dwight quoted in Jon Newsom, "The American Brass Band Movement," *Quarterly Journal of the Library of Congress* 36, no. 2 (1979): 17.

47. [John Sullivan Dwight,] "Military Music," *Dwight's Journal of Music* 16, no. 26 (March 24, 1860), 412. On the growth of band music in this era, see Margaret Hindle Hazen and Robert M. Hazen, *The Music Men: An Illustrated History of Brass Bands in America, 1800–1920* (Washington, DC: Smithsonian Institution Press, 1987), 1–14.

48. Union infantry and artillery units typically had around twenty-four players, while cavalry units had bands of sixteen. Confederate bands generally fell in the range of eight to sixteen players. Bruce P. Gleason, "Military Music in the United States: A Historical Examination of Performance and Training," *Music Educators Journal* 101, no. 3 (March 2015): 39; Lord and Wise, *Bands and Drummer Boys of the Civil War*, 30.

49. Lord and Wise, *Bands and Drummer Boys of the Civil War*, 135. For private funding of instruments, see, e.g., Zenas T. Haines, *Letters from the Forty-fourth Regiment M.V.M.: A Record of the Experience of a Nine Month's Regiment in the Department of North Carolina in 1862-3* (Boston: Herald Job Office, 1863), 110; Davis, *"Bully for the Band!,"* 6, 68.

50. Jack H. Felts, "Some Aspects of the Rise and Development of the Wind Band During the Civil War," *Journal of Band Research* 3, no. 2 (1967), 32; "Orchestras for the Army," *NYT*, January 6, 1862; Dwight, *Life and Letters of Wilder Dwight*, 196.

51. Alonzo H. Quint, *The Potomac and the Rapidan* (Boston: Crosby and Nichols, 1864), 96.

52. Lord and Wise, *Bands and Drummer Boys of the Civil War*, 29–30, 33.

53. Olson, *Music and Musket*, 154–55; McWhirter, *Battle Hymns*, 134–35. For an example of a regimental band that did not muster out, see, e.g., Dwight A. Gardstrom, "A History of the Fourth Regimental Band and Musicians of the

Fourth Minnesota Infantry Volunteers during the War of the Great Rebellion, 1861–1865" (PhD diss., University of Minnesota, 1989).

54. McWhirter, *Battle Hymns*, 134–35; James A. Davis, "Regimental Bands and Morale in the American Civil War," *Journal of Band Research* 38, no. 3 (2003): 4.

55. Davis, "Regimental Bands and Morale in the American Civil War," 4. While not all soldiers heard as much music after 1862 as before, it appears most did. For one exception, though, see Eric A. Campbell, "Civil War Music and the Common Soldier," in *Bugle Resounding: Music and Musicians of the Civil War Era*, ed. Mark A. Snell and Bruce C. Kelley (Columbia: University of Missouri Press, 2004), 207.

56. Chauncey Herbert Cooke, *Soldier Boy's Letters to His Father and Mother, 1861–5* (n.p.: News-Office, 1915), 66–67; Burt Green Wilder, *Practicing Medicine in a Black Regiment: The Civil War Diary of Burt G. Wilder, 55th Massachusetts*, ed. Richard M. Reid, (Amherst: University of Massachusetts Press, 2010), 93; Benedict, *Army Life in Virginia*, 36; John Gardner Perry, *Letters from a Surgeon of the Civil War*, comp. Martha Derby Perry (Boston: Little, Brown, 1906), 79; George H. Allen, *Forty-Six Months with the Fourth R.I. Volunteers in the War of 1861 to 1865* (n.p.: J. A. & R. A. Reid Printers, 1887), 154.

57. Joseph T. Wilson, *The Black Phalanx: A History of Negro Soldiers of the United States in the Wars of 1776–1812, 1861–1865* (Hartford, CT: American Publishing Company, 1888), 506; James Monroe Trotter, *Music and Some Highly Musical People* (Boston: Lee and Shepard, 1878), 315; Wilson, *Campfires of Freedom*, 173 and 147–75 passim. See also Keith Wilson, "Black Bands and Black Culture: A Study of Black Military Bands in the Union Army during the Civil War," *Australasian Journal of American Studies* 9, no. 1 (1990), 35.

58. Benny Pryor Ferguson, "The Bands of the Confederacy: An Examination of the Musical and Military Contributions of the Bands and Musicians of the Confederate States of America" (North Texas State University, 1987), esp. 475, 486; Garofalo and Elrod, *A Pictorial History of Civil War Era Musical Instruments & Military Bands*, 55–56; E. Lawrence Abel, *Singing the New Nation: How Music Shaped the Confederacy, 1861–1865* (Mechanicsburg, PA: Stackpole Books, 2000), 182–95; McWhirter, *Battle Hymns*, 115; J. W. Reid, *History of the Fourth Regiment of South Carolina Volunteers, from the Commencement of the War Until Lee's Surrender* (Greenville, SC: Shannon, 1892), 60.

59. Bell Irvin Wiley, *The Life of Johnny Reb, the Common Soldier of the Confederacy* ([Indianapolis]: Bobbs-Merrill, 1943), 156–57; McWhirter, *Battle Hymns*, 65–82; Heaps and Heaps, *The Singing Sixties*; Abel, *Singing the New Nation*; Carlton McCarthy, *Detailed Minutiae of Soldier Life in the Army of Northern Virginia, 1861–1865* (Richmond, VA: Carlton McCarthy, 1882), 52; Ferguson, "The Bands of the Confederacy," 483. On Confederate bands, see also Lord and Wise, *Bands and Drummer Boys of the Civil War*, 56–81, 118–21; Harry H. Hall, *A Johnny Reb Band from Salem: The Pride of Tarheelia* (Raleigh: North Carolina Confederate Centennial Commission, 1963); George B. Lane,

"Brass Instruments Used in Confederate Military Service during the American Civil War," *Historic Brass Society Journal* 4 (1992): 71–86.

60. See, e.g., Davis, *"Bully for the Band!,"* 7; Bircher, *A Drummer-Boy's Diary*, 73, 176.

61. Charles E. Davis, *Three Years in the Army*, quoted in Henry Steele Commager, ed. *The Blue and the Gray* (New York: New American Library, 1973), 1:285. James A. Davis has questioned the degree to which bands played on the march, but as I discuss below, sources do suggest this occurred regularly, however onerous and exhausting such playing may have been. See Davis, "Regimental Bands and Morale in the American Civil War," 6.

62. Davis, *"Bully for the Band!,"* 7. For an example of a hospital detachment, see Bircher, *A Drummer-Boy's Diary*, 78. On bands playing for funerals and executions, see, e.g., Richard C. Spicer, "'An Inspiration to All': New Hampshire's Third Regiment and Hilton Head Post Bands in Civil War North Carolina," in *Bugle Resounding: Music and Musicians of the Civil War Era*, ed. Mark A. Snell and Bruce C. Kelley (Columbia: University of Missouri Press, 2004), 92–100.

63. Davis, *"Bully for the Band!,"* 119, 183.

64. See, e.g., Davis, *"Bully for the Band!,"* 2. Heaps and Heaps, *The Singing Sixties*, 133, also makes mention of this phenomenon but without identifying a source for this information.

65. See, e.g., Spicer, "'An Inspiration to All,'" 96–98; Davis, *"Bully for the Band!,"* 8; Lord and Wise, *Bands and Drummer Boys of the Civil War*, 211. Notably, bandsmen serving as stretcher-bearers appears to have continued even after the organization of the Ambulance Corps in the Union army, which took place in stages from 1862 to 1864.

66. Davis, *"Bully for the Band!,"* 229; Bruce Catton, *A Stillness at Appomattox* (Garden City, NY: Doubleday, 1953), 347; Arthur James Lyon Fremantle, *The Fremantle Diary: Being the Journal of Lieutenant Colonel James Arthur Lyon Fremantle, Coldstream Guards, on His Three Months in the Southern States*, ed. Walter Lord (Boston: Little, Brown, 1954), 208. For other accounts of bands playing during battle, see James A. Davis, "Music and Gallantry in Combat during the American Civil War," *American Music* 28, no. 2 (2010): 141–72; Davis, "Regimental Bands and Morale in the American Civil War," 12; Olson, *Music and Musket*, 206–7; McWhirter, *Battle Hymns*, 131–32; Bruce P Gleason, *Sound the Trumpet, Beat the Drums: Horse-Mounted Bands of the U.S. Army, 1820–1940* (Norman: University of Oklahoma Press, 2016), 49–51; Bruce P. Gleason, "The Mounted Band and Field Musicians of the U.S. 7th Cavalry during the Time of the Plains Indian Wars," *Historic Brass Society Journal* 21 (2009): 69–92; Augustus Meyers, *Ten Years in the Ranks, U. S. Army* (New York: Sterling, 1914), 248; Edward P. Tobie, *History of the First Maine Cavalry 1861–1865* (Boston: Emery and Hughes, 1887), 402, quoted in Robert Joseph Garofalo and Mark Elrod, *A Pictorial History of Civil War Era Musical Instruments & Military Bands* (Missoula, MT: Pictorial Histories, 2002), 57.

67. James A. Davis, "Musical Reconnaissance and Deception in the American Civil War," *Journal of Military History* 74, no. 1 (January 2010): 79–105, esp. 93–94; Davis, "Music and Gallantry in Combat During the American Civil War." See also Charles D. Ross, "Sight, Sound, and Tactics in the American Civil War," in *Hearing History: A Reader*, ed. Mark M. Smith (Athens: University of Georgia Press, 2004), 267–78.

68. Quoted in Tobie, *History of the First Maine Cavalry*, 392. For a similar incident prior to the Siege of Yorktown in 1862, see McWhirter, *Battle Hymns*, 129.

69. Thomas F. Toon, "Twentieth Regiment," in *Histories of the Several Regiments and Battalions from North Carolina in the Great War 1861–'65*, ed. Walter Clark (Goldsboro, NC: Nash, 1901), 2:113. While it would be easy to think that exchanges such as these were merely the stuff of lore, the evidence for them is extensive. See, e.g., McWhirter, *Battle Hymns*, 243nn41–42; Davis, "Music and Gallantry in Combat During the American Civil War," 161–62; Abel, *Singing the New Nation*, 190–91.

70. Frank Rauscher, *Music on the March, 1862–'65: With the Army of the Potomac* (Philadelphia: Wm. F. Fell, 1892), 264–65.

71. Christopher Small, *Musicking: The Meanings of Performing and Listening* (Middletown, CT: Wesleyan University Press, 1998).

72. See, e.g., Simon Frith, "Music and Identity," in *Questions of Cultural Identity*, ed. Stuart Hall and Paul Du Gay (Thousand Oaks, CA.: Sage, 1996), 108–27; John Blacking, *How Musical Is Man?* (Seattle: University of Washington Press, 1974); Alfred Schütz, "Making Music Together: A Study in Social Relationship," *Social Research* 18, no. 1 (1951): 76–97. On the Civil War specifically, see James A. Davis, *Music along the Rapidan: Civil War Soldiers, Music, and Community during Winter Quarters, Virginia* (Lincoln: University of Nebraska Press, 2014); Deane L. Root, "Music and Community in the Civil War Era," in *Bugle Resounding: Music and Musicians of the Civil War Era*, ed. Mark A. Snell and Bruce C. Kelley (Columbia: University of Missouri Press, 2004), 37–53.

73. William H. McNeill, *Keeping Together in Time: Dance and Drill in Human History* (Cambridge, MA: Harvard University Press, 1995), 2–3 passim. Hanna quoted at 8. For a more scientific approach to the same issues, see Walter Freeman, "A Neurobiological Role of Music in Social Bonding," in *The Origins of Music*, ed. Nils L. Wallin, Björn Merker, and Steven Brown (Cambridge, MA: MIT Press, 2001), 411–24.

74. Lydia Minturn Post, ed., *Soldiers' Letters, from Camps, Battle-Field and Prison* (New York: Bunce & Huntington, 1865), 212; George B. Clark, ed., *Devil Dogs Chronicle: Voices of the 4th Marine Brigade in World War I* (Lawrence: University Press of Kansas, 2013), 41; Wilson, *The Black Phalanx*, 506.

75. Frank Rauscher, *Music on the March, 1862–'65: With the Army of the Potomac* (Philadelphia: Wm. F. Fell, 1892). 264; David H. Donald, ed. *Gone for a Soldier: The Civil War Memoirs of Private Alfred Bellard* (Boston: Little, Brown,

1975), 37; Charles B. Haydon, *For Country, Cause & Leader: The Civil War Journal of Charles B. Haydon*, ed. Stephen W. Sears (New York: Ticknor & Fields, 1993), 323.

76. Dwight, *Life and Letters of Wilder Dwight*, 196. Dwight quotes Saxe in the original French; translation mine.

77. Carlton McCarthy, *Detailed Minutiae of Soldier Life in the Army of Northern Virginia* (Richmond, VA: Carleton McCarthy, 1882), 52. For an overview of contemporary research on music's effect on bodies, see Donald Hodges, "Bodily Responses to Music," in *Oxford Handbook of Music Psychology*, ed. Susan Hallam, Ian Cross, and Michael Thaut (Oxford: Oxford University Press, 2011), 183–96.

78. Les Cleveland, *Dark Laughter: War in Song and Popular Culture* (Westport, CT: Praeger, 1994), 3; Arlie Russell Hochschild, *The Managed Heart: Commercialization of Human Feeling* (Berkeley: University of California Press, 1983); Amy S. Wharton, "The Sociology of Emotional Labor," *Annual Review of Sociology* 35, no. 1 (2009): 147–65. When a substantial misalignment exists between what workers feel and what they can express, they often try to change their feelings ("deep acting") or at least change those feelings that are publicly displayed ("surface acting"). Failure to square one's feelings with the world (what Hochschild calls "emotional dissonance") can lead to a kind of (self-)estrangement and disconnection from one's environment: "When we do not feel emotion, or disclaim an emotion, we lose touch with how we actually link inner to outer reality." (Hochschild, 90, 223, quoted in Wharton at 149.) Emotional management, then, can entail *not feeling* as much as conditioning what is felt.

79. Of course, soldiers never lose their individuality completely, in that they, like other workers, retain some control over how well they perform their jobs. This control is sharply delimited, however, by the fact that a soldier who fails to follow orders is subject to serious punishment, including incarceration and execution. Horowitz, "It Is 'the Working Class Who Fight All the Battles,'" 80. On alienation, see Karl Marx, *Economic and Philosophic Manuscripts of 1844* (Moscow: Progress, 1977), 67–80.

80. Marek Korczynski, *Songs of the Factory: Pop Music, Culture, and Resistance* (Ithaca, NY: ILR, 2014). On musical experience, see Jeanette Bicknell, *Why Music Moves Us* (New York: Palgrave Macmillan, 2009).

81. Barbara Rosenwein, *Emotional Communities in the Early Middle Ages* (Ithaca, NY: Cornell University Press, 2006), 24–26. See also Christian Bailey, "Social Emotions," in *Emotional Lexicons: Continuity and Change in the Vocabulary of Feeling 1700–2000*, ed. Ute Frevert et al. (Oxford: Oxford University Press, 2014), 201–29.

82. Frith, "Music and Identity," 110–11. See also John A. Sloboda, "At the Interface of the Inner and Outer World: Psychological Perspectives," in *Handbook of Music and Emotion: Theory, Research, Applications*, ed. Patrik N. Juslin (New York: Oxford University Press, 2010), 73–98. The idea that emotions are not self-contained, preexisting entities prior to their expression

is developed in Monique Scheer, "Are Emotions a Kind of Practice (and Is That What Makes Them Have a History)? A Bourdieuian Approach to Understanding Emotion," *History and Theory* 51, no. 2 (May 2012): 193–220.

83. On the word *emotion*, see Monique Scheer, "Topographies of Emotion," in *Emotional Lexicons: Continuity and Change in the Vocabulary of Feeling 1700–2000*, ed. Ute Frevert et al. (Oxford: Oxford University Press, 2014), n.p.

84. Allen, *Forty-Six Months with the Fourth R.I. Volunteers in the War of 1861 to 1865*, 64; George C. Underwood, "Twenty-Sixth Regiment," in *Histories of the Several Regiments and Battalions from North Carolina in the Great War 1861–'65*, ed. Walter Clark (Goldsboro, NC: Nash, 1901), 399; Delavan S. Miller, *Drum Taps in Dixie: Memories of a Drummer Boy, 1861–1865* (Watertown, NY: Hungerford-Holbrook, 1905), 106–7; Perry, *Letters from a Surgeon of the Civil War*, 119; Rauscher, *Music on the March*, 265.

85. "Review of the Armies," *NYT*, May 24, 1865; "Military Pageants in History," *Philadelphia Inquirer*, May 26, 1865.

86. Gardstrom, "A History of the Fourth Regimental Band and Musicians of the Fourth Minnesota Infantry Volunteers during the War of the Great Rebellion, 1861–1865," 296–98; Alonzo L. Brown, *History of the Fourth Regiment of Minnesota Infantry Volunteers during the Great Rebellion, 1861–1865* (St. Paul, MN: Pioneer, 1892), 423.

Chapter Two

1. George F. Root, *The Story of a Musical Life* (Cincinnati: J. Church, 1891), 132–33; Christian McWhirter, *Battle Hymns: The Power and Popularity of Music in the Civil War* (Chapel Hill: University of North Carolina Press, 2012), 50–55; Albert E. Gardner, "The Watter Cure in the P.I.," in pocket notebook, folder 10, box 38, Veterans Survey Collection, U.S. Cavalry 1st Regiment, Spanish American War Papers, USAHEC. Commentary on this song appears in Glenn Anthony May, *Battle for Batangas: A Philippine Province at War* (New Haven, CT: Yale University Press, 1991), 147–49; and Paul Kramer, *The Blood of Government: Race, Empire, the United States, & the Philippines* (Chapel Hill: University of North Carolina Press, 2006), 141. For discussion of the smiling and thumbs-up gesture in the Abu Ghraib photograph, see Philip Gourevitch and Errol Morris, "Exposure," *New Yorker*, March 17, 2008, https://www.newyorker.com/magazine/2008/03/24/exposure-5.

2. This same mordant irony is evident in another diary entry, titled "A Testimonial," a parody of a commercial endorsement for a patent medicine:

> A Testimonial. Lemery, P.I., 1902.
>
> My dear Dr. Uncle Sam,
>
> For a long time I was suffering from lots of memory, loss of speach [*sic*] and other symptoms of Insurrectos. In fact my memory was so bad that I had forgotten where I placed my Bolo [knife] and my rifle. I took

only one treatment of your wonderful water cure and my speech and memory at once came back to me. Since then I have no trouble to remember and telling where I had placed my Bolo and rifle.

Yours gratefully, Mariano Gugu.
PS: No hombre's shack is complete without a barrel of it. M.G.

3. The undated manuscript is titled "Odds and Ends" and also includes "A Testimonial." It can be found in folder 10, box 38, USAHEC.

4. Walter Pater, *The Renaissance* (New York: Modern Library, 1873), 114. Dwight is quoted in Michael Broyles, *Music of the Highest Class: Elitism and Populism in Antebellum Boston* (New Haven, CT: Yale University Press, 1992), 255.

5. Approximately 275,000 served in Cuba and 125,000 in the Philippines. Richard Stewart, ed., *American Military History*, vol. 1 (Washington, DC: Center for Military History, United States Army, 2004), 344, 359.

6. "President's Call to Arms," *NYT*, April 24, 1898; Trevor Herbert, "Sousa, the Band and the 'American Century,'" *Journal of the Royal Musical Association* 135, no. 1 (2010), 183. See also Frank J. Cipolla, "Patrick S. Gilmore: The Boston Years," *American Music* 6, no. 3 (1988): 281–92; Marwood Darlington, *Irish Orpheus, the Life of Patrick S. Gilmore, Bandmaster Extraordinary* (Philadelphia: Olivier-Maney-Klein, 1950), 60–61; P. S. Gilmore, *History of the National Peace Jubilee and Great Musical Festival Held in the City of Boston, June, 1869, to Commemorate the Restoration of Peace Throughout the Land* (Boston: P. S. Gilmore, 1871); Jon Seymour Nicholson, "Patrick Gilmore's Boston Peace Jubilees" (EdD diss., University of Michigan, 1971); Frank S. Cipolla, "Gilmore, Patrick S(arsfield)," *Oxford Music Online*, https://doi-org .udel.idm.oclc.org/10.1093/gmo/9781561592630.article.11152.

7. Neil Harris, "John Philip Sousa and the Culture of Reassurance," in *Perspectives on John Philip Sousa* (Washington, DC: Library of Congress, 1983), 11–40. On Sousa's nationalism, see, e.g., Herbert, "Sousa, the Band and the 'American Century,'" 183–90; Carol A. Hess, "John Philip Sousa's El Capitan: Political Appropriation and the Spanish-American War," *American Music* 16, no. 1 (1998): 1–24; Patrick Warfield, *Making the March King: John Philip Sousa's Washington Years, 1854–1893* (Urbana: University of Illinois Press, 2013).

8. Jon Newsom, "The American Brass Band Movement," *Quarterly Journal of the Library of Congress* 36, no. 2 (1979): 114–39; Leon Mead, "The Military Bands of the United States," *Harper's Weekly*, September 28, 1889, 785–88; Harris, "John Philip Sousa and the Culture of Reassurance," 28.

9. "Over $30,000 Worth of the J. W. Pepper Premier—Own Make—Band Instruments Purchased by the U. S. Government Since May, 1891," [advertisement, 1896], box 1, J. W. Pepper Archive, Exton, Pennsylvania; Peter M. Lefferts, "U.S. Army Black Regimental Bands and the Appointments of Their First Black Bandmasters," *Black Music Research Journal* 33, no. 2 (2013), 153.

10. "John H. Brandhorst of St. Paul in Barracks at Manila," photograph, Minnesota Historical Society, http://collections.mnhs.org/cms/display?irn =10664050. Volunteer regiments were distinct from those of the regular

army. Initially, volunteer regiments were organized by the states, but this system was superseded in 1899 by the establishment of the system of U.S. Volunteers. See Stewart, ed., *American Military History*, 356.

11. Kyle Ward, "The 13th Minnesota Volunteer Regiment and the Spanish-American and Philippine-American Wars, 1898–1899" (MA thesis, St. Cloud State University, 1998), 48; Brian McAllister Linn, *The Philippine War, 1899–1902* (Lawrence: University Press of Kansas, 2000), 14.

12. Stephen D. Coats, *Gathering at the Golden Gate: Mobilizing for War in the Philippines, 1898* (Fort Leavenworth, KS: Combat Studies Institute Press, 2006), 151; "Troops Off for Philippines," *Washington Post*, March 27, 1901. On bandsmen's duties, see, e.g., Camp, *Official History of the Operations of the First Idaho Infantry*, 2, 27, 28–9; Alfred O. Anderson, "Band Concerts: They Are a Pleasant Part of Camp Life—They Make the Volunteer Homesick, However," *Cleveland Press*, June 3, 1898.

13. John H. Parker, *History of the Gatling Gun Detachment, Fifth Army Corps, at Santiago, with a Few Unvarnished Truths Concerning That Expedition* (Kansas City, MO: Hudson-Kimberly, 1898), 55 and 172; Ward, "The 13th Minnesota Volunteer Regiment and the Spanish-American and Philippine-American Wars," 46; Coats, *Gathering at the Golden Gate*, 32, 96, 151, and 205.

14. Franklin F. Holbrook, ed., *Minnesota in the Spanish-American War and the Philippine Insurrection* (St. Paul: Minnesota War Records Commission, 1923), 49 and 58; Gardner's "Scribble-In" notebook, folder 10, box 38, USAHEC; Pandia Ralli, "Campaigning in the Philippines with Company I of the First California Volunteers," *Overland Monthly*, February 1899, 158–59.

15. Adelbert M. Dewey, *The Life and Letters of Admiral Dewey* (Akron, OH: Werner, 1899), 195; Marrion Wilcox, *A Short History of the War with Spain* (New York: F. A. Stokes, 1898), 191; Edward W. Harden, "Dewey at Manila: One Year's Retrospect," *Frank Leslie's Popular Monthly* 48, no. 1 (May 1899): 21–38.

16. Gregory Dean Chapman, "Taking Up the White Man's Burden: Tennesseans in the Philippine Insurrection, 1899," *Tennessee Historical Quarterly* 47, no. 1 (1988), 32. See also Holbrook, ed., *Minnesota in the Spanish-American War and the Philippine Insurrection*, 49.

17. George F. Telfer, *Manila Envelopes: Oregon Volunteer Lt. George F. Telfer's Spanish-American War Letters*, ed. Sara Bunnett (Portland: Oregon Historical Society Press, 1987), 29. Sargent is quoted in Albert G. Robinson, *The Philippines: The War and the People, a Record of Personal Observations and Experiences* (New York: McClure, Phillips, 1901), 287 and 289. On "fiesta politics," see Kramer, *The Blood of Government*, 285–91.

18. Henry Watterson, *History of the Spanish-American War: Embracing a Complete Review of Our Relations with Spain* (New York: Werner, 1898), 603.

19. Robinson, *The Philippines*, 175. On piano ownership in America at this time, see Craig H. Roell, *The Piano in America, 1890–1940* (Chapel Hill: University of North Carolina Press, 1989).

20. Marian M. George, *A Little Journey to Hawaii and the Philippines* (Chicago: A. Flanagan, 1901), 46; Telfer, *Manila Envelopes*, 29; Mary Talusan, *Instruments*

of Empire: Filipino Musicians, Black Soldiers, and Military Band Music During Us Colonization of the Philippines (Jackson: University Press of Mississippi, 2021), 6–8.

21. *Harper's Pictorial History of the War with Spain* (New York: Harper & Brothers, 1899), 2:361; Trumbull White, *Pictorial History of Our War with Spain for Cuba's Freedom* (Chicago: J. S. Ziegler, 1898), 520; Tom C. Davis, "A Chronology of the 1st United States Cavalry: The Diary of Tom Davis," The Spanish American War Centennial Website, 1898, https://www.spanamwar.com /1stUScav.htm; Sarah Mahler Kraaz, "The Spanish-American War," in *Music and War in the United States*, ed. Sarah Kraaz (New York: Routledge, 2018), 95–96.

22. On Black performers' creative manipulation of opportunities in the entertainment business, see, e.g., David Gilbert, *The Product of Our Souls: Ragtime, Race, and the Birth of the Manhattan Musical Marketplace* (Chapel Hill: University of North Carolina Press, 2015); Karen Sotiropoulos, *Staging Race: Black Performers in Turn of the Century America* (Cambridge, MA: Harvard University Press, 2006); Lynn Abbott and Doug Seroff, *Ragged but Right: Black Traveling Shows, "Coon Songs," and the Dark Pathway to Blues and Jazz* (Jackson: University Press of Mississippi, 2007); Louis Onuorah Chude-Sokei, *The Last "Darky": Bert Williams, Black-on-Black Minstrelsy, and the African Diaspora* (Durham, NC: Duke University Press, 2006); W. T. Lhamon Jr., "Whittling on Dynamite: The Difference Bert Williams Makes," in *Listen Again: A Momentary History of Pop Music*, ed. Eric Weisbard (Durham, NC: Duke University Press, 2007), 7–25; Daphne Brooks, *Liner Notes for the Revolution: The Intellectual Life of Black Feminist Sound* (Cambridge, MA: Belknap, 2021).

23. Lefferts, "U.S. Army Black Regimental Bands and the Appointments of Their First Black Bandmasters," 152n3; Marvin Fletcher, *The Black Soldier and Officer in the United States Army, 1891–1917* (Columbia: University of Missouri Press, 1974), 100.

24. John Philip Sousa, *A Book of Instruction for the Field-Trumpet and Drum* (Cleveland: Ludwig Music, 1985 [1886]). Fifes were replaced by trumpets and bugles during the Civil War.

25. Damon Runyon, "To the Colors!" in *Rhymes of the Firing Line* (New York: Desmond FitzGerald, 1912), 64. See also "Outpost, 4 A.M." and "Bugle Calls" in Damon Runyon, *The Tents of Trouble: Ballads of the Wanderbund and Other Verse* (New York: Desmond FitzGerald, 1911), 74, 79–81.

26. Erwin C. Garrett, "Bugles Calling" in *Army Ballads and Other Verses* (Philadelphia: John C. Winston, 1916), 86–88; "Three Calls," in *From Field and Camp: Verses to the Twenty-Eighth Regiment, U.S.V.* (San Francisco: F. H. Abbott, 1901), n.p.; [J. C. O. Redington,] "The Glorious Roll of the American Drum," in *Old War Songs and New and Old Patriotic and National Songs* (Syracuse, NY: J. C. O. Reddington, 1900), 1. See also Erwin C. Garrett, "Taps" in *My Bunkie, and Other Ballads* (Philadelphia: J. B. Lippincott, 1907), 60–61; William Edward Biederwolf, *History of the One Hundred and Sixty-First*

Regiment Indiana Volunteer Infantry (Logansport, IN: Wilson, Humphreys, 1899), 38.

27. Parker, *History of the Gatling Gun Detachment*, 181.

28. Italics in original. Damon Runyon, "The Song of the Bullet," in *The Tents of Trouble*, 71. Descriptions such as these were not uncommon. Another poet, a member of the Tenth Pennsylvania Volunteers, called attention to the ways the "Mauser cracked / And the whistling balls came near," and a song, "Explosions from a Tropical Language" referred to "the barking of a Krag [i.e., Krag–Jørgensen rifle]." J. A. Harshman, "Battle of Malate," in J. D. Mitchell, ed., *Souvenir Song Book: 25 Original Songs and Poems Written by Members of the 8th Army Corps* (Manila: Carmelo y Bauermann, 1898), 12; The Trident Society of the United States Naval Academy at Annapolis, Maryland, *The Book of Navy Songs* (Garden City, NY: Doubleday, Page, 1926), 122.

29. On the emergence of "hits" and Tin Pan Alley, see David Suisman, *Selling Sounds: The Commercial Revolution in American Music* (Cambridge, MA: Harvard University Press, 2009), 18–89. On "Home, Sweet Home," see Charles H. Sylvester, "John Howard Payne and *Home, Sweet Home*," in *Journeys through Bookland*, ed. Charles H. Sylvester (Chicago: Bellows-Reeve, 1922), 6:221–28.

30. Patricia R. Schroeder, "Passing for Black: Coon Songs and the Performance of Race," *Journal of American Culture* 33, no. 2 (2010): 139–53; James H. Dormon, "Shaping the Popular Image of Post-Reconstruction American Blacks: The 'Coon Song' Phenomenon of the Gilded Age," *American Quarterly* 40, no. 4 (1988): 450–71.

31. Charles Johnson Post, *The Little War of Private Post* (New York: New American Library, 1961), 98.

32. Deirdre O'Connell, "Howling 'A Hot Time': The Paradoxical Anthem of the Progressive Age," *Journal of American Studies* 55, no. 3 (July 2021), 596–619, esp. 596 and 609–12.

33. Benjamin E. Neal Diaries, entry for February 28, 1902, Benjamin E. Neal Papers, Special Collections, Syracuse University Library, quoted in Andrew J. Rotter, "Empires of the Senses: How Seeing, Hearing, Smelling, Tasting, and Touching Shaped Imperial Encounters," *Diplomatic History* 35, no. 1 (January 1, 2011): 11n14.

34. O'Connell, "Howling 'A Hot Time,'" 604. *The Music Trades* (January 25, 1908) is quoted in "A Hot Time in the Old Town," in *Encyclopedia of Great Popular Song Recordings*, ed. Steve Sullivan (Lanham, MD: Scarecrow, 2013), http://www.credoreference.com/book/rowmanpopular.

35. Kraaz, "The Spanish-American War," 98; Joe Hayden and Theodore Metz, "A Hot Time in the Old Town" (New York: Willis Woodward, 1898).

36. "The Keynote," *Music Trade Review* (August 6, 1898), 8; O'Connell, "Howling 'A Hot Time,'" 604; Tom Hall, *The Fun and Fighting of the Rough Riders* (New York: Frederick A. Stokes, 1899), 59; Herschel V. Cashin, *Under Fire with the Tenth U.S. Cavalry* (Niwot: University Press of Colorado, 1993 [1899]), 272; Parker, *History of the Gatling Gun Detachment*, 55; O'Connell, "Howling 'A Hot Time,'" 613; inscription on verso of photo of the First Infantry Regiment

of Colorado Volunteers regimental band, image file ZZR711003007, Denver Public Library; Edward S. Paterson, "Three Cheers for All," in J. D. Mitchell, ed., *Souvenir Song Book: 25 Original Songs and Poems Written by Members of the 8th Army Corps* (Manila: Carmelo y Bauermann, 1898), 19–20; Runyon, "August 13—'98," in *The Tents of Trouble*, 101–3; Pandia Ralli, "Campaigning in the Philippines—[Part] II—with Company I of the First California Volunteers," *Overland Monthly*, March 1899, 231.

37. Quoted in Edward A. Johnson, *History of Negro Soldiers in the Spanish-American War* (Cincinnati: W. H. Ferguson, 1899), 87–88.

38. See "Songs of '98" songbook (1932), folder 10, box 38, USAHEC.

39. Thomas P. Walsh, *Tin Pan Alley and the Philippines: American Songs of War and Love, 1898–1946: A Resource Guide* (Lanham, MD: Scarecrow, 2013), xviii and 33; Marshall Everett, ed., *Exciting Experiences in Our Wars with Spain and the Filipinos* (Chicago: Educational Co, 1900), 215 and 222. I am indebted to Walsh's *Tin Pan Alley and the Philippines*, an outstanding reference work without which I doubt this chapter could have been written.

40. Willard B. Gatewood Jr., *"Smoked Yankees" and the Struggle for Empire: Letters from Negro Soldiers, 1898–1902* (Urbana: University of Illinois Press, 1971), 174, 244; *Hero Tales of the American Soldier and Sailor as Told by the Heroes Themselves and Their Comrades: The Unwritten History of American Chivalry* (Rochester, IN: Rochester Book Concern, 1899), 125.

41. Sidney A. Witherbee, ed., *Spanish-American War Songs: A Complete Collection of Newspaper Verse During the Recent War with Spain* (Detroit: Sidney A. Witherbee, 1898). Although this book explicitly contained only verse, others included both or did not distinguish between song and verse, e.g., George M. Moreland, *Idle Songs of an Idle Soldier* (Monterey, CA: Press of the Monterey New Era, 1909); Mitchell, ed., *Souvenir Song Book*.

42. Walsh, *Tin Pan Alley and the Philippines*, 1–7. The Thirteenth Minnesota, it should be noted, was not unique. Walsh's compendium contains an equal number of songs about the Oregon Volunteers, for example. See Walsh, *Tin Pan Alley and the Philippines*, 1–7, 31, 41, 68. On Otis's ineptitude, see Linn, *The Philippine War*, 27.

43. For an example of a unit-specific songbook, see Mitchell, ed., *Souvenir Song Book*.

44. Mitchell, ed., *Souvenir Song Book*, n.p. See also Walsh, *Tin Pan Alley and the Philippines*, 131.

45. Walsh, *Tin Pan Alley and the Philippines*, 68–70; Military Order of the Carabao, *Historical Sketch, Constitution, and Register of the Military Order of the Carabao, Together with Songs That Have Been Sung at "Wallows" in Various Places* (Washington, DC: W. F. Roberts, 1914), 125; Trident Society of the United States Naval Academy, *The Book of Navy Songs*, 128–29; "Along the Waterfront," *Honolulu Republican*, Sep 12, 1901. According to "Naval Officers and Men May Damn Little Brown Men in Song to Their Hearts' Content," *Washington Post*, August 5, 1906, the rumors that the song was banned were untrue. Some sources incorrectly identify its source melody as "Gilligan

the Lodger," and Otis, it should be noted, was not actually the governor-general; he was the military governor.

46. Charles Ingram, "Cotten, Lyman Atkinson," in *Dictionary of North Carolina Biography*, ed. William S. Powell (Chapel Hill: University of North Carolina Press, 1979), 437–38; Trident Society of the United States Naval Academy, *The Book of Navy Songs*, 116. On Philippinitis, see Warwick Anderson, *Colonial Pathologies: American Tropical Medicine, Race, and Hygiene in the Philippines* (Durham, NC: Duke University Press, 2006), 130–57.

47. The song appears in one of Gardner's notebooks, folder 10, box 38, USAHEC.

48. Barbara Ehrenreich, *Blood Rites: Origins and History of the Passions of War* (New York: Metropolitan, 1997); Theodore Roosevelt, *The Strenuous Life: Essays and Addresses* (New York: Century, 1902); Kristin L. Hoganson, *Fighting for American Manhood: How Gender Politics Provoked the Spanish-American and Philippine-American Wars* (New Haven, CT: Yale University Press, 1998); Gail Bederman, *Manliness and Civilization: A Cultural History of Gender and Race in the United States, 1880–1917* (Chicago: University of Chicago Press, 1996), esp. 170–216. On specific songs, see Edward Arthur Dolph, *"Sound Off!": Soldier Songs from the Revolution to World War II* (New York: Farrar & Rinehart, 1942), 222; "An International Affair," in *From Field and Camp*, n.p.

49. Sean Dennis Cashman, *America Ascendant: From Theodore Roosevelt to FDR in the Century of American Power, 1901–1945* (New York: New York University Press, 1998), 126.

50. Military Order of the Carabao, *Historical Sketch, Constitution, and Register of the Military Order of the Carabao*, 126.

51. See, e.g., James H. Blount, *The American Occupation of the Philippines, 1898–1912* (New York: G. P. Putnam's Sons, 1913), 266, 270, which uses this title and refers to it as "that old familiar song." (Blount's account has negligibly different lyrics.)

52. Walsh, *Tin Pan Alley and the Philippines*, 102–3; Blount, *The American Occupation of the Philippines*, 266. Rather than banning the song outright, the Department of the Navy instead called singing it a violation of its official code of conduct, in effect a distinction without a difference. See "'Damn' Song Not Barred," *(New York) Sun*, August 5, 1906.

53. Military Order of the Carabao, *Historical Sketch, Constitution, and Register of the Military Order of the Carabao*, 7, 154–85; Edward Arthur Dolph, *"Sound Off!": Soldier Songs from Yankee Doodle to Parley Voo* (New York: Cosmopolitan. 1929); Dolph, *"Sound Off!": Soldier Songs from the Revolution to World War II*, vii.

54. Quoted in Michael Fellman, *In the Name of God and Country: Reconsidering Terrorism in American History* (New Haven, CT: Yale University Press, 2010), 214.

55. Dolph, *Sound Off!: Soldier Songs from the Revolution to World War II*, 210; Military Order of the Carabao, *Historical Sketch, Constitution, and Register of the Military Order of the Carabao*, 176. On the origins of the epithet *gugu*, see

Charles Freeman, "Yankee Music in the Far East," *American Oldtimer* 3, no. 1 (1935): 31.

56. Military Order of the Carabao, *Historical Sketch, Constitution, and Register of the Military Order of the Carabao*, 133, 169–70; Fellman, *In the Name of God and Country*, 213; Dolph, *Sound Off!: Soldier Songs from the Revolution to World War II*, 206. The lyrics of "The Little Brown Brothers" were also reprinted in Jack Manska's privately printed history of his war service in Cuba and the Philippines, *The Dog Robber Goes to War* (Lebanon, SD: n.p., n.d.), 49, folder 10, box 38, USAHEC.

57. Fellman, *In the Name of God and Country*, 186–87. See also, e.g., Daniel Immerwahr, *How to Hide an Empire: A History of the Greater United States* (New York: Farrar, Straus and Giroux, 2019).

58. "Nebraska Boys in the Trenches," in Mitchell, ed., *Souvenir Song Book*, 26.

59. David W. Blight, *Race and Reunion: The Civil War in American Memory* (Cambridge, MA: Belknap, 2002); Nina Silber, *The Romance of Reunion: Northerners and the South, 1865–1900* (Chapel Hill: University of North Carolina Press, 1993); Moreland, *Idle Songs of an Idle Soldier*, 15.

60. Dolph, *Sound Off!: Soldier Songs from the Revolution to World War II*, 186–87. Other songs exemplifying what Dolph calls the "Kipling vogue" include "At Naic" and "On the Road to Old Luzon."

61. "Drink to the Members of the Carabao," in Military Order of the Carabao, *Historical Sketch, Constitution, and Register of the Military Order of the Carabao*, 136.

62. Antonio C. Hila, *Music in History, History in Music* (Manila: University of Santo Tomas Publishing House, 2004), 71–72; Kramer, *The Blood of Government*; Paul A. Kramer, "Race-Making and Colonial Violence in the U.S. Empire: The Philippine-American War as Race War," *Diplomatic History* 30, no. 2 (2006): 169–210. Sousa is quoted in Talusan, *Instrument of Empire*, 3.

63. Talusan, *Instrument of Empire*, 67–118, esp. 105–6; Kramer, *The Blood of Government*, 109–10. "Benevolent assimilation" was a policy based on the notion of the U.S. intervening in the Philippines, in McKinley's words, "not as invaders or conquerors, but as friends" (quoted in Kramer, *The Blood of Government*, 110).

Chapter Three

1. Photograph, ID no. 165-WW-473G-2, folder "Recreation—Music—Miscellaneous," series "American Unofficial Collection of World War I Photographs," record group 165, National Archives and Records Administration, https://catalog.archives.gov/id/45541767.

2. "Lend the Way They Fight," photograph, 1917, Prints and Photographs Division, Library of Congress, https://www.loc.gov/pictures/item/00652849/.

3. On Progressive support for the war, see, e.g., David M. Kennedy, *Over Here: The First World War and American Society* (New York: Oxford University Press, 1982), 38–40, 49–53.

4. G. Stanley Hall, *Morale: The Supreme Standard of Life and Conduct* (New York: D. Appleton, 1920), 74–76; "Adjuvant, adj. and n.," *OED Online*, Oxford University Press, https://www-oed-com.udel.idm.oclc.org. Hall's treatise was a revised and expanded version of ideas first appearing in G. Stanley Hall, "Morale in War and After," *Psychological Bulletin* 15, no. 11 (1918): 361–426.

5. Daniel W. La Rue, "Morale in the Making," *Infantry Journal* 15, no. 7 (January 1919): 561–62; David C. Shanks, *Management of the American Solider* (n.p.: n.p., 1918), 64; Lincoln C. Andrews, *Leadership and Military Training* (Philadelphia: J. B. Lippincott, 1918), 28. See also Straub, *A Sergeant's Diary in the World War*, 153; Frank B. Tiebout, *A History of the 305th Infantry* (New York: The 305th Infantry Auxiliary, 1919), 41.

6. *History of the Seventy Seventh Division: August 25th, 1917–November 11th, 1918* (New York: W. H. Crawford, 1919), 22; James H. Hallas, *Doughboy War: The American Expeditionary Force in World War I* (Boulder, CO: Lynne Rienner, 2000), 197. "While marching, nothing will so effectively keep up the spirits of the men and prevent them from straggling as the singing of marching songs," Scott told the *New York Times* in 1918. "The soldier's mind is thus stimulated, and instead of thinking of the weight of his equipment or his physical weariness he develops a dogged and cheerful determination." "Singing Meets War Needs," *NYT*, Nov. 18, 1918.

7. As Miller put it, "Let a man break out in song near the end of a weary march and others pick it up. Watch the eyes brighten, the steps quicken." Arthur H. Miller, *Leadership : A Study and Discussion of the Qualities Most to Be Desired in an Officer, and of the General Phases of Leadership Which Have a Direct Bearing on the Attaining of High Morale and the Successful Management of Men* (New York: G. P. Putnam's Sons, 1920), 153. See also Tiebout, *A History of the 305th Infantry*, 51; Edward A. Dolph, *"Sound Off!": Soldier Songs from Yankee Doodle to Parley Voo* (New York: Cosmopolitan, 1929), ix.

8. On the Morale Division, see Thomas M. Camfield, "'Will to Win'—The U.S. Army Troop Morale Program of World War I," *Military Affairs* 41, no. 3 (1977): 125–28.

9. Edward L. Munson, *The Management of Men: A Handbook on the Systemic Development of Morale and the Control of Human Behavior* (New York: Henry Holt, 1921), 185, 205-0=6, 526, 541. See also 470, 538, 542–45.

10. La Rue, "Morale in the Making," 555. For other positions on music and morale, see John J. Pershing, *My Experiences in the World War*, 2 vols. (New York: Frederick A. Stokes, 1931), 2:236; United States Adjutant-General's Office, *The Army Band: A Vital Necessity to the Military Establishment in Peace & War* (Washington, DC: Government Printing Office, 1919); Russell V. Morgan, "Music and Morale," *Music Supervisors' Journal* 6, no. 3 (1920): 24; Miller, *Leadership*, 153.

11. United States Army, *Infantry Drill Regulations, 1911: Text Corrected to Include Changes 23, Sept. 10, 1918, and Appendix D, U.S. Rifle Model 1917* (New York: Army and Navy Journal, 1918), 192–208; William Nevins and A. J. Vaas, *Army*

Regulations for Drum, Fife, and Bugle: Being a Complete Manual for These Instruments, Giving All the Calls for Camp and Field Duty (Chicago: Root & Cady, 1864); War Department, *Cavalry Drill Regulations: United States Army* (Washington, DC: Government Printing Office, 1918), 396–97.

12. On the day-to-day responsibilities of bandsmen, see Harold Bachman, *The Million Dollar Band: The Story of the Band of the 116th Regiment of Engineers, 41st (Sunset) Division, American Expeditionary Forces. The Original Million Dollar Band in World War I and the Professional Concert Band Which Succeeded It* (Chicago: Educational Music Bureau, 1962), 19; *The 346th Infantry Historical Notes, 1917–1919* (Nantes, France: Imprimerie du Commerce, 1919), 38–39; Elmer Frank Straub, *A Sergeant's Diary in the World War* (Indianapolis: Indiana Historical Commission, 1923), 34; Chalmer Richardson, *Here Comes the Band!: Unofficial History of the 345th Infantry Band in the Great War* (North Platte, NE: Hemphill Printery, 1928); Ralph C. Huffer, Diary, Ralph C. Huffer Papers, box 3, folder 39, U.S. Army Heritage and Education Center, Carlisle Barracks, Pennsylvania; Thomas C. Key, "Diary of Thomas C. Key," 1918, Kenneth Spencer Research Library, University of Kansas Libraries; "Diary of a World War I Musician, 1918 July 30–Aug. 24," Chicago History Museum, Chicago; George B. Clark, ed., *Devil Dogs Chronicle: Voices of the 4th Marine Brigade in World War I* (Lawrence: University Press of Kansas, 2013), 71.

13. There were 390 bands in the military of 4.7 million soldiers. The size of each band grew from twenty-eight players before the war to forty-eight. Navy bands had twenty-two players, marine bands twenty-eight. Russell V. Morgan, "Music and Morale," *Music Supervisors' Journal* 6, no. 3 (1920): 26; Bruce P. Gleason, "Military Music in the United States: A Historical Examination of Performance and Training," *Music Educators Journal* 101, no. 3 (March 2015): 39–40.

14. Benedict Crowell, *America's Munitions 1917–1918: Report of Benedict Crowell, the Assistant Secretary of War, Director of Munitions* (Washington, DC: Government Printing Office, 1919), 475; William Carter White, *A History of Military Music in America* (Westport, CT: Greenwood, 1975 [1944]), chap. 18; "Better Band Music to Inspire Troops," *NYT*, August 24, 1918. For context on band education at this time, see Michael D. Martin, "Band Schools of the United States: A Historical Overview," *Journal of Historical Research in Music Education* 21, no. 1 (1999): 41–61.

15. Crowell, *America's Munitions*, 475–76.

16. Luther H. Gulick, *Morals and Morale* (New York: Association Press, 1919), 66. On music and Progressivism, see Derek Vaillant, *Sounds of Reform: Progressivism and Music in Chicago, 1873–1935* (Chapel Hill: University of North Carolina Press, 2003).

17. A. A. Clappé, "Music as a Moral Force on Morale," *Infantry Journal* 15 (March 1919): 729–36.

18. Baker quoted in Raymond B. Fosdick, *Chronicle of a Generation: An Autobiography* (New York: Harper, 1958), 143.

19. E. Christina Chang, "The Singing Program of World War I: The Crusade for a Singing Army," *Journal of Historical Research in Music Education* 23, no. 1 (2001): 19–21. On the CTCA, see Allan M. Brandt, *No Magic Bullet: A Social History of Venereal Disease in the United States Since 1880* (New York: Oxford University Press, 1985), 52–95, esp. 59–60.

20. *Summary of World War Work of the American YMCA* (n.p.: International Committee of Young Men's Christian Associations, 1920), 119–24.

21. May Stanley, "Wanted: Singing Leaders for Army Camps," *Musical America* 26 (August 14, 1917): 3–4; Fosdick, *Chronicle of a Generation*, 154–57. Fosdick, who takes credit for initiating the singing program, calls singing an activity "in which I was especially interested" (154), explaining that he had been inspired in promoting it in the camps after seeing its effect on German soldiers during a visit to Europe four years earlier.

22. "Making Singing Sailors for Uncle Sam's Navy," *Musical America* 27 (January 26, 1918): 3; "Teaching Uncle Sam's Soldiers and Sailors to Sing," *Music Supervisors' Journal* 4, no. 2 (1917): 30; "Music in War," *Music Supervisors' Journal* 4, no. 1 (1917): 26.

23. On song leaders, see Frances F. Brundage, *Music in the Camps* (Washington, DC: Government Printing Office, 1919); Chang, "The Singing Program of World War I," 19–45; Christina Gier, "The 'Song Leaders' of the American Expeditionary Forces, 1917–18," *Journal of Musicological Research* 33, nos. 1–3 (July 2014): 130–44. On the resentment some soldiers felt for song leaders, see Robert Kodosky, "Musical Mêlée: Twentieth Century America's Contested Wartime Soundtrack," in *Routledge History of Social Protest in Popular Music*, ed. Jonathan Friedman (New York: Routledge, 2013), 74. On the deviation between War Department–endorsed songs and those soldiers sang for themselves, see John Jacob Niles and Douglas Moore, *The Songs My Mother Never Taught Me* (New York: Macaulay, 1929); John Jacob Niles, *Singing Soldiers* (New York: C. Scribner's Sons, 1927); and Maci Reed, "'A Singing Army Is a Fighting Army': American Soldiers' Songs and the Training Camp Experience in World War I," *Voces Novae* 8, no. 1 (April 2018), 124.

24. Kenneth Gow, *Letters of a Soldier* (New York: H. B. Covert, 1920), 71.

25. Edward Frank Allen and Raymond B. Fosdick, *Keeping Our Fighters Fit for War and After* (Washington, DC: Commissions on Training Camp Activities, 1918), 68; Shanks, *Management of the American Solider*, 72.

26. Chang, "The Singing Program of World War I," 23. On community singing, see, e.g., Peter W. Dykema, "The Spread of the Community Music Idea," *Annals of the American Academy of Political and Social Science* 67, no. New Possibilities in Education (September 1916): 218–23; Cora Conway, "Community Songs and Singing," *Music Supervisors' Journal* 5, no. 1 (September 1918): 26 and 28; Esther M. Morgan-Ellis, "'Making the Many-Minded One': Community Singing at the Peabody Prep in 1915," *Musical Quarterly* 102, no. 4 (Winter 2020): 361–401; Esther M. Morgan-Ellis, *Everybody Sing!: Community Singing in the American Picture Palace* (Athens: University of Georgia Press, 2018).

27. Commission on Training Camp Activities, "War Songs in the Schools," *Music Supervisors' Journal*, November 1918, 25–26. For a detailed study of the CTCA's singing program, see see Christina Gier, *Singing, Soldiering, and Sheet Music in America During the First World War* (Lanham, MD: Lexington, 2019), chaps. 3–5.

28. "Music an Essential for Soldiers," *Chicago Daily Tribune*, June 8, 1918; "Owen Wister Praises Singing among Soldiers," *NYT*, May 12, 1918.

29. *Army Song Book*. See also Kenneth S. Clark, comp., "Camp Songs of the United States Army and Navy," ca. 1917, Manuscript Collection SC 2138, Indiana Historical Society Library.

30. Brundage, *Music in the Camps*, 12; Marshall Bartholomew, ed., *Military Singing: A Short Drill in Fundamental Principles for the Training of Song Leaders in the Army, Navy and Marines* (New York: Music Committee of the National War Work Council, 1918), 22; Allen and Fosdick, *Keeping Our Fighters Fit For War and After*, 74; "To Standardize All Music for Army and Navy," *Musical America* 26 (September 8, 1917): 1. The quotation "nucleus of songs" comes from Bartholomew, *Military Singing*, 22. On Americanizing influence of the singing, see, e.g., "Owen Wister Praises Singing among Soldiers."

31. Bernard Lentz, "The Army as an Americanization Agency" (Washington, DC: Moore, 1919), 5, http://archive.org/details/armyasamericanizoolent.

32. Lorenz to his wife, September 4, 1918, quoted in Carrie A. Meyer, *Letters from the Boys: Wisconsin World War I Soldiers Write Home* (Madison: Wisconsin Historical Society Press, 2018), 63. "On, Wisconsin" became the official state song in 1959.

33. Gulick, *Morals and Morale*, 59 and 61.

34. Domestically, the YMCA outfitted 952 buildings with musical and other equipment at training camps and bases. Overseas, its record was similar. In France, for example, it stocked 491 huts and 1,045 tents. *Summary of World War Work of the American YMCA*, 9, 17, 26, 45, 124; William H. Taft and Frederick Harris, eds., *Service with Fighting Men: An Account of the Work of the American Young Men's Christian Associations in the World War* (New York: Association Press, 1922), 1:437, 1:524–25, 2:189.

35. These gifts are detailed in the two scrapbooks that comprise the Helen Culver Kerr Papers, Manuscript Division, Library of Congress. On Kerr's discretion, see, e.g., Kerr to Alice Carpenter, April 25, 1918, in the first volume of these scrapbooks.

36. See, e.g., Mark Hauser, "All the Comforts of Hell: Doughboys and American Mass Culture in the First World War" (PhD diss., Carnegie Mellon University, 2019), 206.

37. "15,000 Enroll in Phonograph Drive," *NYT*, October 27, 1918. See also, e.g., "Musicians to Aid 'Records for Fighters' Campaign," *Musical America*, (October 19, 1918): 31. On soldiers buying musical equipment themselves, see Hauser, "All the Comforts of Hell," 32.

38. Pershing quoted in James W. Evans and Gardner L. Harding, *Entertaining the American Army: The American Stage and Lyceum in World War* (New York: Association Press, 1951), 88.

39. Weldon B. Durham, *Liberty Theatres of the United States Army, 1917–1919* (Jefferson, NC: McFarland, 2006), 13, 15, 45, 62, 86, 88–93, 182–83; Fosdick, *Chronicle of a Generation*, 152–53; Hauser, "All the Comforts of Hell," 106–7.

40. Thomas McLane interview, typescript, folder "War Historical Bureau, interview with Thomas McLane," Box 41, Armed Services: World War I, UMN-YMCA; James Forbes interview, typescript, folder "War Historical Bureau, interview with James Forbes," Box 41, Armed Services: World War I, UMN-YMCA; Taft and Harris, eds., *Service with Fighting Men*, 1:621; Hauser, "All the Comforts of Hell," 111–58; *Summary of World War Work of the American YMCA*, 125.

41. Gier, "The 'Song Leaders' of the American Expeditionary Forces," 132–34; Taft and Harris, eds., *Service with Fighting Men*, 1:307, 1:368, 1:623.

42. Taft and Harris, eds., *Service with Fighting Men*, 1:306, 1:623, 2:190; *Popular Songs of the A.E.F.* (Paris: YMCA, 1918); *Army Song Book* (Washington, D.C.: War Department Commission on Training Camp Activities, 1918); *Summary of World War Work of the YMCA*, 42, 49.

43. Loving quoted in Hauser, "All the Comforts of Hell," 53.

44. Hauser, "All the Comforts of Hell," 53; photograph of hut with Black soldiers, box 141AV, Armed Services: World War I, UMN-YMCA.

45. Jennifer D Keene, *Doughboys, the Great War, and the Remaking of America* (Baltimore: Johns Hopkins University Press, 2001), 94, 102; Taft and Harris, eds., *Service with Fighting Men*, 1:309. Under Raymond Fosdick, the CTCA took no steps to oppose racism in the military either. Hauser, "All the Comforts of Hell," 53–54.

46. Allen and Fosdick, *Keeping Our Fighters Fit For War and After*, 73. Emphasis in original.

47. In his pathbreaking work on the aural experience of the U.S. war in Iraq, the ethnomusicologist J. Martin Daughtry called the audible spectrum of war "belliphonic" sound (from the Latin words for "war," *bellum*, and "voice," *phone*). Daughtry was concerned specifically with the aural experience of the combat environment, but I would contend a more complete inventory of belliphonic sounds would include other aspects of war-making as well, including military environments far from the battlefield and on the home front. See J. Martin Daughtry, *Listening to War: Sound, Music, Trauma, and Survival in Wartime Iraq* (New York: Oxford University Press, 2015), 3.

48. Suisman, *Selling Sounds*, 195–200; Herman H. B. Meyer, comp., *A Check List of the Literature and Other Material in the Library of Congress on the European War* (Washington, DC: Government Printing Office, 1918), 211–93.

49. Glenn Watkins, *Proof through the Night: Music and the Great War* (Berkeley: University of California Press, 2003), 290–92, 298–307. See Barbara L. Tischler, "One Hundred Percent Americanism and Music in Boston during World War I," *American Music* 4, no. 2 (1986): 164–76; Edmund A. Bowles, "Karl Muck and His Compatriots: German Conductors in America during World War I (and How They Coped)," *American Music* 25, no. 4 (2007): 405–40; Alan H. Levy, "The American Symphony Orchestra German: American Musicians and Federal Authorities during World War I," *Mid-America: An*

Historical Review 71 (1989): 5–13; Matthew Mugmon, "Patriotism, Art, and 'The Star-Spangled Banner' in World War I: A New Look at the Karl Muck Episode," *Journal of Musicological Research* 33, nos. 1–3 (July 3, 2014): 4–26; E. Douglas Bomberger, "Taking the German Muse Out of Music: The Chronicle and US Musical Opinion in World War I," *Journal of the Society for American Music* 14, no. 2 (May 2020): 141–75; Melissa D. Burrage, *The Karl Muck Scandal: Classical Music and Xenophobia in World War I America* (Rochester: University of Rochester Press, 2019).

50. Anonymous, *The Cannoneers Have Hairy Ears: A Diary of the Front Lines* (New York: J. H. Sears, 1927), 130. For other accounts of World War I sound, see Douglas Kahn, *Noise, Water, Meat: A History of Sound in the Arts* (Cambridge, MA: MIT Press, 2001), 64; Gow, *Letters of a Soldier*, 343; Hillel Schwartz, *Making Noise: From Babel to the Big Bang and Beyond* (New York: Zone, 2011), 572, 574–77, 583; Michael Bull, "Into the Sounds of War: Imagination, Media, and Experience," in *The Oxford Handbook of Sound and Imagination*, ed. Mark Grimshaw-Aagaard, Mads Walther-Hansen, and Martin Knakkergaard (New York: Oxford University Press, 2019), 1:175–202; Kassandra Hartford, "Listening to the Din of the First World War," *Sound Studies* 3, no. 2 (July 2017): 98–114; Tyler Whitney, *Eardrums: Literary Modernism as Sonic Warfare* (Evanston, IL: Northwestern University Press, 2019); Axel Volmar, "In Storms of Steel: The Soundscape of World War I and Its Impact on Auditory Media Culture during the Weimar Period," in *Sounds of Modern History: Auditory Cultures in 19th- and 20th- Century Europe*, ed. Daniel Morat (New York: Berghahn, 2014), 229–30; Gascia Ouzounian, *Stereophonica: Sound and Space in Science, Technology, and the Arts* (Cambridge, MA: MIT Press, 2021); Raviv Ganchrow and Alan Jones, "An Improbable Dimension," *Res: Anthropology and Aesthetics* 49–50 (March 2006): 204–21; Raviv Ganchrow, "Perspectives on Sound-Space: The Story of Acoustic Defense," *Leonardo Music Journal* 19 (2009): 71–75. On underwater listening, see, e.g., C. V. Drysdale, "Listening under Water," *Engineering and Industrial Management* 6 (December 1921): 45–53; Willem D. Hackmann, "Sonar Research and Naval Warfare 1914–1954: A Case Study of a Twentieth-Century Establishment Science," *Historical Studies in the Physical and Biological Sciences* 16, no. 1 (1986): 83–110.

51. On shell shock, see, e.g., Trevor Dodman, *Shell Shock, Memory, and the Novel in the Wake of World War I* (New York: Cambridge University Press, 2015); Edgar Jones and Simon Wessely, *Shell Shock to PTSD: Military Psychiatry from 1900 to the Gulf War* (New York: Psychology Press, 2005). A useful interpretation of the difference between shell shock and PTSD appears in Daniel Roberts, "'Shellshock' and 'PTSD': Two Different Conditions, Two Different Ways of Understanding and Handling War Trauma," *Essex Student Journal* 9, no. 1 (January 2017).

52. The novelty and alienness of these sounds even led the British phonograph giant HMV in December 1918 to issue a record of a gas shell bombardment. Produced by the British American recording engineer Will Gaisberg, whose brother Fred had cut some of the most important discs of the

early phonograph industry, the recording was purportedly recorded live by Gaisberg in the field in France—which would have been considered a technological marvel at the time. Recent scholars have raised doubts about the authenticity of the record, but HMV presented it as the real item, "an historical record which should be in every home." The record remained in HMV's catalog until 1945. Louis Goddard, "'A Few Feet of Film Run Backwards': Tracing the Sonic Construction of Shellfire, 1914–30," in *The Auditory Culture Reader*, ed. Michael Bull and Les Back, 2nd ed. (New York: Routledge, 2015), 293; Brian Hanrahan, "Reproducing Traces of War: Listening to Gas Shell Bombardment, 1918," *Sounding Out!* (blog), July 7, 2014, https://soundstudiesblog.com/2014/07/07/listening-to-traces-of-war-gas-shell-bombardment-1918/. On the noisiness of modernity, see, e.g., John M. Picker, *Victorian Soundscapes* (New York: Oxford University Press, 2003); Emily Thompson, *The Soundscape of Modernity: Architectural Acoustics and the Culture of Listening in America, 1900–1933* (Cambridge, MA: MIT Press, 2002). On the soundscapes of World War I and their unrepresentability, see Michael Bull, "Into the Sounds of War: Imagination, Media, and Experience," in *The Oxford Handbook of Sound and Imagination*, ed. Mark Grimshaw-Aagaard, Mads Walther-Hansen, and Martin Knakkergaard (New York: Oxford University Press, 2019), 1:175–202; Kassandra Hartford, "Listening to the Din of the First World War," *Sound Studies* 3, no. 2 (July 2017): 98–114; Tyler Whitney, *Eardrums: Literary Modernism as Sonic Warfare* (Evanston, IL: Northwestern University Press, 2019).

53. Kaltenecker, "'What Scenes! What Sounds!'"; Daughtry, *Listening to War*; Barry Truax, *Acoustic Communication* (Norwood, NJ: Ablex, 1984).

54. Tiebout, *A History of the 305th Infantry*, 77; Josh Kun, *Audiotopia: Music, Race, and America* (Berkeley: University of California Press, 2005), 2.

55. Elliott White Springs, *Letters from a War Bird: The World War I Correspondence of Elliott White Springs*, ed. David K. Vaughan (Columbia: University of South Carolina Press, 2012), 112; Taft and Harris, eds., *Service with Fighting Men*, 1:384.

56. On the popularity of band performances at hospitals, see, e.g., Richardson, *Here Comes the Band!*, 77.

57. Quoted in Suisman, *Selling Sounds*, 198. For another Canadian perspective on the importance of phonographs at the front, see John W. Beattie and Duncan McKenzie, "At the Front. Two Letters from France," *Music Supervisors' Journal* 5, no. 1 (1918): 4–12. On the significance of phonographs for British, French, and German troops, see Elodie A. Roy, "Worn Grooves," *Media History* 24, no. 1 (January 2018): 26–45.

58. "'Mademoiselle Miss': Letters from an American Girl Serving with the Rank of Lieutenant in a French Army Hospital at the Front," World War I: The Medical Fronts, http://www.vlib.us/medical/MMiss.htm; Eva Dobell, "In a Soldiers' Hospital II: Gramophone Tunes," in *The Penguin Book of First World War Poetry*, ed. George Walter (New York: Penguin, 2007), 208; Roy, "Worn Grooves," 33–35.

59. A. E. Reschke-Hernandez, "Paula Lind Ayers: 'Song-Physician' for Troops with Shell Shock during World War I," *Journal of Music Therapy* 51, no. 3 (September 2014): 276–91; Munson, *The Management of Men*, 633. See also William B. Davis, "Ira Maximilian Altshuler: Psychiatrist and Pioneer Music Therapist," *Journal of Music Therapy* 40, no. 3 (October 2003): 247–63.

60. John Dos Passos, *Three Soldiers* (New York: George H. Doran, 1921); Dorlea Rikard, "Patriotism, Propaganda, Parody, and Protest: The Music of Three American Wars," *War, Literature & the Arts: An International Journal of the Humanities* 16, no. 1 (2004): 129–44; John Trombold, "Popular Songs as Revolutionary Culture in John Dos Passos' 'U.S.A.' and Other Early Works," *Journal of Modern Literature* 19, no. 2 (1995): 289–316; Dolph, *"Sound Off!": Soldier Songs from Yankee Doodle to Parley Voo,"* 95–96.

61. Army field clerk Will Judy drove this point home: "The Star-Spangled Banner was sung very seldom, never of our own accord." Judy quoted in Hallas, *Doughboy War*, 199.

62. Robert B. Westbrook, "'I Want a Girl, Just Like the Girl That Married Harry James': American Women and the Problem of Political Obligation in World War II," *American Quarterly* 42, no. 4 (1990): 587–614; Hall, *Morale*, 76–78.

63. Elsie Janis, *The Big Show: My Six Months with the American Expeditionary Forces* (New York: Cosmopolitan, 1919), 186. Emphasis and the masking of "G—d——" in original.

64. According to John and Alan Lomax, one private collection contained more than six hundred pornographic or obscene stanzas. See John A. Lomax and Alan Lomax, *American Ballads and Folk Songs* (New York: Macmillan, 1934), 557–58. For an example of an expurgated version of "Hinky Dinky," see, e.g., Evans and Harding, *Entertaining the American Army*, 208.

65. Ed Cray, *The Erotic Muse: American Bawdy Songs*, 2nd ed. (Urbana: University of Illinois Press, 1999), 392.

66. Ettinger quoted in Hallas, *Doughboy War*, 197. I have been unable to locate the article he referred to.

67. Niles and Moore, *The Songs My Mother Never Taught Me*, 12, 13; Niles, *Singing Soldiers*; Reed, "'A Singing Army Is a Fighting Army,'" 124.

68. Niles and Moore, *The Songs My Mother Never Taught Me*, 211.

69. Roi Ottley, "Negroes Are Saying . . . ," in *Reporting World War II: Part One, American Journalism 1938–1944* (New York: Library of America, 1995), 443.

70. On first black bandleaders, see Peter M. Lefferts, "U.S. Army Black Regimental Bands and the Appointments of Their First Black Bandmasters," *Black Music Research Journal* 33, no. 2 (2013): 151–75.

71. The story of Europe and the Harlem Hellfighters Band has now been told many times, contextualized in terms of both the discrimination that the Hellfighters and other black American soldiers faced and the early development and dissemination of jazz. See Reid Badger, *A Life in Ragtime: A Biography of James Reese Europe* (New York: Oxford University Press, 1995); Stephen L. Harris and Rod Paschall, *Harlem's Hell Fighters: The African-American 369th Infantry in World War I* (Washington, DC: Potomac, 2005);

Peter N. Nelson, *A More Unbending Battle: The Harlem Hellfighter's Struggle for Freedom in WWI and Equality at Home* (New York: Civitas, 2009); William A. Shack, *Harlem in Montmartre: A Paris Jazz Story between the Great Wars* (Berkeley: University of California Press, 2001); R. Reid Badger, "James Reese Europe and the Prehistory of Jazz," *American Music* 7, no. 1 (1989): 48–67. For recordings, see *Lieutenant Jim Europe's 369th U.S. Infantry "Hell Fighters" Band: The Complete Recordings* (Memphis Archives, 1996).

72. Peter Lefferts, "Black US Army Bands and Their Bandmasters in World War I," 22, Faculty Publications: School of Music, March 2, 2018, digitalcommons. unl.edu/musicfacpub/67; Mark Tucker, "In Search of Will Vodery," *Black Music Research Journal* 16, no. 1 (1996): 134. Note: Lefferts gives slightly different numbers in his "Black US Army Bands and Their Bandmasters," 35–36.

73. Emmett J. Scott, *Scott's Official History of the American Negro in the World War* (New York: Underwood and Underwood, 1919), 310. Scott was Special Assistant for Negro Affairs in the War Department, a journalist, and Booker T. Washington's chief aide at the Tuskegee Institute.

74. Lefferts, "Black US Army Bands and Their Bandmasters in World War I," 12. Du Bois quoted at 26. For a survey of Black bands other than James Reese Europe's, see Dan Vernhettes, *Commemoration of the Centenary of the Arrival of the African-American Military Bands in France during World War I: A Historical and Musical Approach* (Saint-Etienne-du-Rouvray, France: Jazzedit, 2017), 40–52.

75. Wilson quoted in Craig H. Roell, *The Piano in America, 1890–1940* (Chapel Hill: University of North Carolina Press, 1989), 189.

76. "America's Greatest Musical Opportunity," *Etude*, January 1919, 9; Charles D. Isaacson, "A New Musical Outlook—and the War," *Musical Quarterly* 6, no. 1 (January 1920): 1; Laurence Bergreen, "Oh! How We Hated to Get Up in the Morning," *MHQ: The Quarterly Journal of Military History* 2, no. 4 (Summer 1990): 72–81.

77. On "cultural apparatus," see Kim Sawchuk, "The Cultural Apparatus: C. Wright Mills' Unfinished Work," *American Sociologist* 32, no. 1 (2001): 27–49.

78. Munson, *The Management of Men*, 542.

Chapter Four

1. "Fourth Anniversary Luncheon," December 11, 1945, box 3, *U.S. Camp Shows, Inc.*, 3:1646–49, quotation at 3:1648, Record Group 407, Records of the Adjutant General's Office, Special Service Division, Records of Camp Shows, Inc., 1941–1957, National Archives and Records Administration; E. J. Kahn Jr., "The Quiet Guy in Lindy's," *New Yorker*, April 20, 1946, 43. Byron's nasal voice can be heard on V-Disc 298B ("Hark! The Herald Angels Sing" and "Oh, Come, All Ye Faithful"), available at https://www.youtube.com /watch?v=pHt4s4PskXY.

2. Annegret Fauser, *Sounds of War: Music in the United States during World War II* (New York: Oxford University Press, 2013), 106–7.

3. Officially, the Morale Division went through a series of different names before it became the Special Services Division in July 1943. On the evolution from one to the other, see "Records of the Information and Education Division," National Archives, https://www.archives.gov/research/guide-fed -records/groups/165.html, accessed December 7, 2022. The Music Section was rechristened the Music Branch in March 1945. For the sake of simplicity, I will refer to it as the Music Section throughout the chapter.

4. Otto H. Helbig, *A History of Music in the U.S. Armed Forces during World War II* (Philadelphia: M. W. Lads, 1966), 6 and 36; Fowler V. Harper, "Report of the Joint Army and Navy Committee on Welfare and Recreation" (n.p.: n.p., 1942), https://www.google.com/books/edition /Report_of_the_Joint_Army_and_Navy_Commit/WBVQAQAAMAAJ.

5. The other six subcommittees were devoted to athletics, army newspaper, education, hostesses, radio, and religious activities.

6. The official was Colonel Theodore Bank, who was involved in the army's athletics and recreation programs, quoted by Howard Bronson, in Richard S. Sears, *V-Discs: A History and Discography* (Westport, CT: Greenwood, 1980), xxv.

7. Helbig, *A History of Music in the U.S. Armed Forces During World War II*, 9, 13; Agnes Nolan Underwood, "Folklore from G.I. Joe," *New York Folklore* 3, no. 1 (1947): 291. The Nimitz quote comes from *New York Herald Tribune*, April 2, 1941, quoted in Homer Pearson, *Music at War* (Poughkeepsie, NY: Vassar College, 1943), 82.

8. *Army Song Book* (Washington, DC: Government Printing Office, 1941); Howard C. Bronson, "Music in the Army," *Music Educators Journal* 28, no. 6 (1942): 58; Howard C. Bronson, "The Musical Activities of the Morale Branch," in *Volume of Proceedings of the Music Teachers National Association*, ed. Theodore Finney (Pittsburgh: Music Teachers National Association, 1942), 19; Fauser, *Sounds of War*, 113.

9. Fauser, *Sounds of War*, 115; M. Claude Rosenberry, "The Army Music Program," *Music Educators Journal* 30, no. 5 (1944): 18; "Music Section," memorandum, n.d., box 25, folder "Report Notes," JANCWR; Helbig, *A History of Music in the Armed Forces during World War II*, 23–25.

10. "Digest of Reports from Music Advisors," n.d., box 11, folder 9, JANCWR, 2.

11. Helbig, *A History of Music in the Armed Forces during World War II*, 12; Jim Tranquada and John King, *The 'Ukulele: A History* (Honolulu: University of Hawai'i Press, 2012), 140–41; Richard K. Lieberman, *Steinway & Sons* (New Haven, CT: Yale University Press, 1995), 227; Henry Z. Steinway, oral history, January 20, 2006, NAMM, https://www.namm.org/library/oral-history /henry-z-steinway.

12. Lieberman, *Steinway & Sons*, 227–28; "How Do You Get a Piano onto the Battlefront? Push It Out of an Airplane" (Michigan Radio, November 10, 2017), https://www.michiganradio.org/arts-culture/2017-11-10/how-do-you -get-a-piano-onto-the-battlefront-push-it-out-of-an-airplane; George Lukas, oral history, February 8, 2004, NAMM, https://www.namm.org/library /oral-history/george-lukas.

13. Helbig, *A History of Music in the U.S. Armed Forces during World War II*, 25–27, 236; Rosenberry, "The Army Music Program," 19.

14. The army alone had nearly 500 bands. The navy had 285, and the marines 45. See "Army Bands," U.S. Army, https://cybercemetery.unt.edu/archive /oilspill/20121009233743/http://www.goarmy.com/band/about-army-bands /history.html; Patrick M. Jones, "A History of the Armed Forces School of Music" (PhD diss., Pennsylvania State University, 2002), 88; "Marine Corps," *National Music Council Bulletin* 4, no. 2 (December 1943): 12. The number of bands may have decreased over the course of the war as some army bands were deactivated and their members reassigned to other duties. See "Music in the Army," *National Music Council Bulletin* 4, no. 2 (December 1943): 12.

15. Kelly Von Lunen, "A Glorious Time for Songs and Fighter Pilots," *VFW Magazine* (December 2011): 27; "The Forgotten First: U.S. Navy B-1 Band and the Integration of the Modern Navy," Calvin Frank Morrow Papers, f. 5, MSS Box 1115, LC-VHP; Caleb P. Maher III, "Former Black Navy Musicians Receive Belated Recognition," press release, [1981], Navy Public Affairs Center, Norfolk, VA, Calvin Frank Morrow Papers, folder 2, MSS Box 1115, LC-VHP.

16. Patrick M. Jones, "A History of the Armed Forces School of Music" (PhD diss., Pennsylvania State University, 2002), 36 and 62; Rhea Smith, "Rhea's Journal," n.d., Rhea Smith Papers, MSS Box 499, LC-VHP; Jill M. Sullivan, "Parading Women: The Commodification of Women's Military Bands during World War II," in *Women's Bands in America*, ed. Jill M. Sullivan (Lanham, MD: Rowman & Littlefield, 2017); Jill M. Sullivan, *Bands of Sisters: U.S. Women's Military Bands during World War II* (Lanham, MD: Scarecrow, 2011); Jill M. Sullivan, "Women's Military Bands in a Segregated Army: The 400th and 404th WAC Bands," *Journal of Band Research* 41, no. 2 (Spring 2006): 1–35; Carrie Hagen, "Seventy-Five Years Ago, the Military's Only All-Black Female Band Battled the War Department and Won," *Smithsonian Magazine*, March 28, 2019, https://www.smithsonianmag.com/history /seventy-five-years-ago-militarys-only-all-black-female-band-won-victory -against-war-department-180971815/.

17. Joseph G. Mason, "Music and Mud (or) through World War II with Trumpet and Transit," 2003, Joseph G. Mason Papers, AFC 2001/001/8233, LC-VHP; Richard Burt, "Oral History of Cpl. Richard Burt," on *746th Far East Air Force Band: Sentimental Journey*, comp. Jason Burt (J&L Historical, 2020). See also "Jungle Band," *Life* 19 (November 5, 1945), 134 and 137; Geneva R. Belton, "The Contribution of Negro Music and Musicians in World War II" (MM thesis, Northwestern University, 1946), 27–28; Ellis E. Leighty and Alan W. Walker, *A History of the 106th Infantry Division Band* ([Urbana, IL]: n.p., [1948]), USAHEC, 10.

18. Richard C. Lancaster, *Serving the U.S. Armed Forces, 1861–1986: The Story of the YMCA's Ministry to Military Personnel for 125 Years* (Schaumburg, IL: Armed Services YMCA of the USA, 1987), 149. "Quasi-state agency" comes from Meghan K. Winchell, *Good Girls, Good Food, Good Fun: The Story of*

USO Hostesses During World War II (Chapel Hill: University of North Carolina Press, 2008), 5.

19. The number of canteens domestically peaked at 3,035 in 1944. Winchell, *Good Girls, Good Food, Good Fun*, 2; "History," WW2 USO Preservation Association, https://ww2uso.org/history.html.

20. "Soldier Opinion about USO Clubs," May 1944, folder "Soldier Opinion about USO Clubs," box 97, Armed Services, UMN-YMCA; Sherrie Tucker, *Dance Floor Democracy: The Social Geography of Memory at the Hollywood Canteen* (Durham, NC: Duke University Press, 2014), xv–xvi. See also Winchell, *Good Girls, Good Food, Good Fun*; James J. Cooke, *American Girls, Beer, and Glenn Miller: GI Morale in World War II* (Columbia: University of Missouri Press, 2012). For a description of racially segregated and unequal USO facilities, see Deton J. Brooks Jr., "Morale Sags at Camp Forrest as Jim Crow Rules," in *Reporting World War II: Part One, American Journalism 1938–1944*, 2 vols. (New York: Library of America, 1995), 1:663.

21. Emily Yellin, *Our Mothers' War: American Women at Home and at the Front during World War II* (New York: Free Press, 2005), 86–87; Sam Lebovic, "'A Breath from Home': Soldier Entertainment and the Nationalist Politics of Pop Culture during World War II," *Journal of Social History* 47, no. 2 (2013): 263; M. Paul Holsinger, "United Service Organization (USO)," in *War and American Popular Culture: A Historical Encyclopedia*, ed. M. Paul Holsinger (Westport, CT: Greenwood, 1999), 320; Winchell, *Good Girls, Good Food, Good Fun*; E. J. Kahn Jr., "The Quiet Guy in Lindy's," *New Yorker*, April 20, 1946, 35.

22. Kahn, "The Quiet Guy in Lindy's," 35–37, quotation at 37.

23. Kahn, "The Quiet Guy in Lindy's," 35, 38, 40; Frank Coffey, *Always Home: 50 Years of the USO: The Official Photographic History* (Washington, DC: Brassey's, 1991), 25; E. J. Kahn, "The Quiet Guy in Lindy's—Part II," *New Yorker*, April 27, 1946, 27.

24. Kahn, "The Quiet Guy in Lindy's," 35. On the range of performers: USO–Camp Shows, Inc., *USO-Camp Shows, Inc.: A Guide to the Foxhole Circuit* (New York: USO–Camp Shows, Inc., 1944), reproduced in Lynn O'Neal Heberling, "Soldiers in Greasepaint: USO-Camp Shows, Inc., during World War II" (PhD diss., Kent State University, 1989), 186–216.

25. Kahn, "The Quiet Guy in Lindy's," 38; Lebovic, "'A Breath from Home,'" 271, 279–80.

26. Kahn, "The Quiet Guy in Lindy's," 36, 37, 40, 44.

27. Sears, *V-Discs*, xxvii–xxix, xliii–xliv. Vincent deserves a book by himself. In 1916, Vincent (then fifteen years old), after many years of collecting voice recordings, went by ship to Europe to record voice tracks on wax cylinders in the middle of World War I. In England he tried unsuccessfully to enlist in the British Army, then served as a dispatch rider for the French infantry until he was sent back to the U.S. in 1917 because he was underage. In 1918, Vincent enlisted in the U.S. Army, went to Officer Candidate School, and was commissioned a lieutenant, at seventeen. He returned to France, again

taking his portable recording equipment, and he remained in Europe after the war, making additional voice recordings.

He came back to the U.S., graduated from Yale in 1922, after which he got a job at Thomas A. Edison Labs (West Orange, NJ) doing recording and sound research. When Edison lost interest in sound recording, he apparently gave Vincent his personal collection of wax cylinders. Vincent then went out on his own, setting up a commercial transcription lab (the National Vocarium) in New York City.

After Pearl Harbor, Vincent, then forty-one, was turned down by the army when he tried to enlist again, but he then received government approval to make a trip for the USO along the East Coast, recording the sounds involved with the military preparations underway in many camps and bases in the run-up to U.S. entry into World War II. These recordings circulated widely, leading him to be invited to the White House, where he played his recordings for the Roosevelts. Finally, he got a commission as a lieutenant and was assigned to the Radio Service of the Army's Morale Services Division, where he launched the V-Disc program.

Eventually, Vincent was promoted to major, left the army, and became the chief sound engineer at the Nuremberg trials, responsible for translation and communication systems (November 1945–October 1946). He later joined the fledgling United Nations as chief of sound and recording, after which he reestablished his own recording studio, did some film work, and ultimately donated his collection of more than ten thousand voice recordings to Michigan State University.

28. Sears, *V-Discs*, xiii–xvii, xxxii–xxiii, and lxxvii.

29. "Palitz Handling Recording for Army 'V Discs,'" *Billboard*, October 30, 1943, 14; Sears, *V-Discs*, xxiii, xlix; Helbig, *A History of Music in the U.S. Armed Forces during World War II*, 191; Douglas E. Collar, "'Hello, Posterity': The Life and Times of G. Robert Vincent, Founder of the National Voice Library" (PhD diss., Michigan State University, 1988), 170; "Swingin' on a V-Disc," Program 329, Riverwalk Jazz, http://riverwalkjazz.stanford.edu/program /swinging-v-disc-jazz-wwii.

30. "Swingin' on a V-Disc"; Collar, "'Hello, Posterity,'" 173, Jones quoted at 179.

31. War Department, *Basic Field Manual FM 28-105* (Washington, DC: Government Printing Office, 1944), 15, 52. On development of the B-Kit by Hittenmark, see Theodore Stuart DeLay, "An Historical Study of the Armed Forces Radio Service to 1946" (PhD diss., University of Southern California, 1951), 77–79.

32. Sears, *V-Discs*, xxxi.

33. Sears, *V-Discs*, lxxx–lxxxvi.

34. Sears, *V-Discs*, lxxv–lxxvi; Helbig, *A History of Music in the U.S. Armed Forces during World War II*, 20–23.

35. Elodie A. Roy, "Worn Grooves: Affective Connectivity, Mobility and Recorded Sound in the First World War," *Media History* 24, no. 1 (January 2018), 33, 35. Roy was writing of World War I, but her point holds for World War II as well.

36. Sears, *V-Discs*, xviii.

37. *History of AFRTS: The First 50 Years* ([Alexandria, VA]: American Forces Information Service and Armed Forces Radio and Television Service, n.d.), 6–11, Lewis quoted at 19; DeLay, "An Historical Study of the Armed Forces Radio Service to 1946," 36–65. On radio and national community, see, e.g., Jason Loviglio, *Radio's Intimate Public: Network Broadcasting and Mass-Mediated Democracy* (Minneapolis: University of Minnesota Press, 2005); Michele Hilmes, *Radio Voices: American Broadcasting, 1922–1952* (Minneapolis: University of Minnesota Press, 1997).

38. Charles J. Rolo, *Radio Goes to War: The "Fourth Front"* (New York: G. P. Putnam's Sons, 1942), 3 and 11 (italics in original); Edward Frank Allen, "Radio Offensives in Total War," *New York Times*, January 25, 1942; "Charles J. Rolo, Author and Securities Analyst," *New York Times*, October 29, 1982. On the *War of the Worlds* panic, see, e.g., David Goodman, *Radio's Civic Ambition: American Broadcasting and Democracy in the 1930s* (New York: Oxford University Press, 2011), 245–85.

39. "S189: Radio Study," October 1944, *The American Soldier in World War II*, https://americansoldierww2.org/surveys/s/S189/q-0/tab-1, accessed December 18, 2022; "S35: Trend Study and Special Services Facilities," January 1943, *The American Soldier in World War II*, https://americansoldierww2.org/surveys/s/S35/q-0/tab-1, accessed December 18, 2022.

40. Quoted in Gerd Horten, *Radio Goes to War: The Cultural Politics of Propaganda During World War II* (Berkeley: University of California Press, 2003), 116–17.

41. *History of AFRTS*, 14–18.

42. For example, the Program Section of AFRS was run by Mann Holiner, formerly of Benton & Bowles, then by Austin Peterson, formerly of Young & Rubicam (where he had worked with Lewis). See *History of AFRTS*, chap. 13. Barnouw quoted in DeLay, "An Historical Study of the Armed Forces Radio Service to 1946," 115.

43. See "Radio Habits of Enlisted Men," folder 6, box 15, JANCWR.

44. Lewis quoted in DeLay, "An Historical Study of the Armed Forces Radio Service to 1946," 108–9. Emphasis in original.

45. Edward M. Kirby, "References and Recollections of Historic Highlights: American Broadcasting in World War II" (1964), Wisconsin Historical Society, 21 and 23.

46. DeLay, "An Historical Study of the Armed Forces Radio Service to 1946," 109.

47. See "Interview with Roger Rooney," folder "Interviews by Dr. Larry Suid: transcripts (folder 2)," box 11, NARA-RG330.

48. On Lewis's disdain for the style of propaganda favored by the Office of War Information, see Martin Hadlow, "The Mosquito Network: American Military Broadcasting in the South-West Pacific 1944–1946," in *The Military and the Media*, ed. Peter Dennis and Jeffrey Grey (n.p.: Australian History Military Publications, 2008), 77. It should be noted, however, that Voice of

America became more subtle in its approach to propaganda in the Cold War. On radio operations aimed at foreign listeners, see, e.g., Alan L. Heil, *Voice of America: A History* (New York: Columbia University Press, 2003); Robert William Pirsein, *The Voice of America: An History of the International Broadcasting Activities of the United States Government, 1940–1962* (New York: Arno, 1979); Lawrence C. Soley, *Radio Warfare: OSS and CIA Subversive Propaganda* (New York: Praeger, 1989); Arch Puddington, *Broadcasting Freedom: The Cold War Triumph of Radio Free Europe and Radio Liberty* (Lexington: University Press of Kentucky, 2015).

49. DeLay, "An Historical Study of the Armed Forces Radio Service to 1946," 110–11. The literature on Axis propaganda broadcasting and broadcasters is extensive. For a concise critique, see Ann Elizabeth Pfau and David Hochfelder, "'Her Voice a Bullet': Imaginary Propaganda and the Legendary Broadcasters of World War II," in *Sound in the Age of Mechanical Reproduction*, ed. David Suisman and Susan Strasser (Philadelphia: University of Pennsylvania Press, 2010), 47–68.

50. See DeLay, "An Historical Study of the Armed Forces Radio Service to 1946."

51. DeLay, "An Historical Study of the Armed Forces Radio Service to 1946," 250–51; Samuel Brylawski, "Armed Forces Radio Service: The Invisible Highway Abroad," *Quarterly Journal of the Library of Congress* 37, nos. 3–4 (1980): 441. The exact number of radio stations at any given time is difficult to pinpoint. According to *History of AFRTS*, there were 154 in March 1945. DeLay, "An Historical Study of the Armed Forces Radio Service to 1946," 313, says there were 179 in summer 1945. The "comparable number" and the million come from *History of AFRTS*, chap. 14. DeLay, "An Historical Study of the Armed Forces Radio Service to 1946," 500, also estimates there were 845 AFRS outlets, circa 1942–46, around the world, including AFRS stations, commandeered stations, and sound systems.

52. *History of AFRTS*, chap. 12; Hadlow, "The Mosquito Network," 74–95. The AFRS also broadcast over shortwave via transmitters in the United States, but because shortwave signals had poorer sound quality and were more vulnerable to fluctuating atmospheric conditions, they were less reliable and consistent than longwave signals and were used mostly for news, sports, and special events. On shortwave, see DeLay, "An Historical Study of the Armed Forces Radio Service to 1946," 502–69; *History of AFRTS*, chap. 13; David Culbert, "Erik Barnouw's War: An Interview Concerning the Armed Forces Radio Services' Education Unit, 1944–1945," *Historical Journal of Film, Radio and Television* 22, no. 4 (October 2002): 485.

53. DeLay, "An Historical Study of the Armed Forces Radio Service to 1946," 285.

54. "S227: Radio Study," July 1945, *The American Soldier in World War II*, https://americansoldierww2.org/surveys/s/S227/q-0/tab-1, accessed December 19, 2022; DeLay, "An Historical Study of the Armed Forces Radio Service to 1946," 285.

55. *History of AFRTS*, chap 14; DeLay, "An Historical Study of the Armed Forces Radio Service to 1946," 285–300.

56. DeLay, "An Historical Study of the Armed Forces Radio Service to 1946," 59–62; "Radio Programs Served on a Platter," *Bureau of Naval Personnel Information Bulletin*, no. 331 (October 1944): 9.

57. DeLay, "An Historical Study of the Armed Forces Radio Service to 1946," 163–37, Lewis quoted at 167; Jim Grubbs, "Women Broadcasters of World War II," *Journal of Radio Studies* 11, no. 1 (June 2004): 40–54; Robert B. Westbrook, "'I Want a Girl, Just like the Girl That Married Harry James': American Women and the Problem of Political Obligation in World War II," *American Quarterly* 42, no. 4 (1990): 587–614; "Radio Programs Served on a Platter," 8.

58. Hilmes, *Radio Voices*, 263; Lauren Rebecca Sklaroff, "Variety for the Servicemen: The 'Jubilee' Show and the Paradox of Racializing Radio during World War II," *American Quarterly* 56, no. 4 (2004): 945–73; Lauren Sklaroff, *Black Culture and the New Deal: The Quest for Civil Rights in the Roosevelt Era* (Chapel Hill: University of North Carolina Press, 2014), 159–92, esp. 176–78; Jeff A. Webb, "VOUS-Voice of the United States: The Armed Forces Radio Service in Newfoundland," *Journal of Radio Studies* 11, no. 1 (May 2004): 93. The "militarization of swing" comes from David W. Stowe, *Swing Changes: Big-Band Jazz in New Deal America* (Cambridge, MA: Harvard University Press, 1994), 73–74, 152–53. See also DeLay, "An Historical Study of the Armed Forces Radio Service to 1946," 149–52.

59. DeLay, "An Historical Study of the Armed Forces Radio Service to 1946," 672–73.

60. Brylawski, "Armed Forces Radio Service," 452. The impact of AFRS on this shift is debated. Cf. DeLay, "An Historical Study of the Armed Forces Radio Service to 1946," 244.

61. Ray Green, "Veterans Administration Hospital Music," *Hospital Music Newsletter* 1, no. 1 (May 1948): 3. The 130,000 involved in active music-making broke down as follows: approximately 32,000 in musical performing groups such as bands, orchestras, choirs, glee clubs, concerts, and recitals; 83,121 in ward sings and community sings; 13,110 in instrumental and vocal instruction; 1,800 in creative music activities, such as songwriting, arranging, and harmony.

62. William B. Davis and Susan Hadley, "A History of Music Therapy," in *Music Therapy Handbook*, ed. Barbara L. Wheeler (New York: Guilford, 2015), 17–28; William B. Davis and Kate E. Gfeller, "Music Therapy: Historical Perspective," in *An Introduction to Music Therapy: Theory and Practice*, ed. William B. Davis, Kate E. Gfeller, and Michael Thaut, 3rd ed. (Silver Spring, MD: American Music Therapy Association, 2008), 17–39, esp. 22–26; Ted Gioia, *Healing Songs* (Durham, NC: Duke University Press, 2006).

63. Ruth Boxberger, "A Historical Study of the National Association for Music Therapy," in *Music Therapy 1962: Twelfth Book of Proceedings of the National Association for Music Therapy*, ed. Erwin H. Schneider (Lawrence, KS: National Association for Music Therapy, 1963), 139 and 141–47; "Columbia University to Heal Wounded by Music," *Literary Digest* 60, no. 9 (March 1, 1919):

59 and 62; "How Music Is Saving Thousands from Permanent Mental Breakdown: Willem Van de Wall," *Etude*, September 1925, n.p.; William B. Davis, "Keeping the Dream Alive: Profiles of Three Early Twentieth Century Music Therapists," *Journal of Music Therapy* 30, no. 1 (March 1993): 42; Davis and Gfeller, "Music Therapy," 30, 32.

64. Helbig, 37. For an account of the dizzying range of activities associated with convalescent soldiers, see Guy V. R. Marriner, "Report on Music in Reconditioning Program at Fitzsimmons General Hospital, Denver 8, Colorado," July 24, 1944, box 25, folder "Report notes—music related," JANCWR, and the report "Musical Activities," [9–10], March 1, 1946, box 15, folder 6, JANCWR. On the emergence of music therapy in the postwar period, see Lori F. Gooding and Diane G. Langston, "Music Therapy with Military Populations: A Scoping Review," *Journal of Music Therapy* 56 (November 2019): 1–33; William B. Davis, "Ira Maximilian Altshuler: Psychiatrist and Pioneer Music Therapist," *Journal of Music Therapy* 40, no. 3 (October 2003): 247–63.

65. Quoted in "Musical Activities," memorandum, March 1, 1946, box 15, folder 6, JANCWR. On the implementation of radio in hospitals, see DeLay, "An Historical Study of the Armed Forces Radio Service to 1946," 277, 484–97; "Interview with Roger Rooney," folder "Interviews by Dr. Larry Suid: transcripts (folder 2)," box 11, NARA-RG330; "Music in Reconditioning in Army General Hospitals," *National Music Council Bulletin* 5, no. 2 (January 1945): 14–15.

66. Fauser, *Sounds of War*, 127–34, Spivacke quoted at 130 and 131.

67. Kendall quoted in Fauser, *Sounds of War*, 131.

68. As the surgeon general saw it, in Marriner's words, the goal of this rehabilitation program was "to produce a more effective soldier, or if the patient is to be discharged, to equip and orient him as a civilian for effective work in the war effort." Guy V. R. Marriner, "Music in Reconditioning in Army Service Forces Hospitals," *Notes* 2, no. 3 (1945): 161.

69. Marriner, "Music in Reconditioning in Army Service Forces Hospitals," 162; Fauser, *Sounds of War*, 132.

70. War Department, "TB MED 187: Music in Reconditioning in ASF Convalescent and General Hospitals" (Washington, DC, July 26, 1945), 1; Spivacke to Marriner, box 10, folder 2, JANCWR; Fauser, *Sounds of War*, 127–34; "Summarized Report on Music and Reconditioning in General Hospitals, October to December 1943," memorandum, December 13, 1944, box 10, folder 2, JANCWR.

71. Mark Wilson, *Destructive Creation: American Business and the Winning of World War II* (Philadelphia: University of Pennsylvania Press, 2016).

72. See, e.g., Hiromu Nagahara, *Tokyo Boogie-Woogie: Japan's Pop Era and Its Discontents* (Cambridge, MA: Harvard University Press, 2017); Suzanne Ament, *Sing to Victory!: Song in Soviet Society during World War II* (Boston: Academic Studies Press, 2019); Derek W. Vaillant, *Across the Waves: How the United States and France Shaped the International Age of Radio* (Urbana: University of

Illinois Press, 2017); Robert E. Herzstein, *The War That Hitler Won: Goebbels and the Nazi Media Campaign* (New York: Paragon House, 1986); Alan E. Steinweis, *Art, Ideology, and Economics in Nazi Germany: The Reich Chambers of Music, Theater, and the Visual Arts* (Chapel Hill: University of North Carolina Press, 2017); Kerim Yasar, *Electrified Voices: How the Telephone, Phonograph, and Radio Shaped Modern Japan, 1868–1945* (New York: Columbia University Press, 2018); Christina L. Baade, *Victory through Harmony: The BBC and Popular Music in World War II* (New York: Oxford University Press, 2012).

Chapter Five

1. Lilian Rixey, "Soldiers Still Sing," *Life*, September 27, 1943,46. See also "Songs the Soldiers Sing," *Life*, August 30, 1943, 127–28.
2. Erving Goffman is generally credited with defining the concept. See "On the Characteristics of Total Institutions," in *Asylums: Essays on the Social Situation of Mental Patients and Other Inmates*, by Erving Goffman (Garden City, NY: Anchor, 1961), 1–124. For its application to the military, see David Vine, *Base Nation: How U.S. Military Bases Abroad Harm America and the World* (New York: Henry Holt, 2015), 158–59.
3. James Scott, *Domination and the Arts of Resistance: Hidden Transcripts* (New Haven, CT: Yale University Press, 1990), esp. 17–44.
4. *Selective Service and Victory: The 4th Report of the Director of Selective Services* (Washington, DC: Government Printing Office, 1948), 187; Thomas D. Morgan, "Native Americans in World War II," *Army History*, no. 35 (Fall 1995): 22; "Japanese Americans at War," World War II Memorial, https:// www.nps.gov/wwii/learn/historyculture/japanese-americans-at-war.htm. For Mexican Americans, estimates vary widely. The 500,000 number comes from "Latinos in World War II: Fighting on Two Fronts," National Park Service, https://www.nps.gov/articles/latinoww2.htm.
5. Studs Terkel, *"The Good War": An Oral History of World War II* (New York: New Press, 1997); Elizabeth D. Samet, *Looking for the Good War: American Amnesia and the Violent Pursuit of Happiness* (New York: Farrar, Straus and Giroux, 2021), 31–32.
6. Samet, *Looking for the Good War*, 25–26; Paul Fussell, *Wartime: Understanding and Behavior in the Second World War* (New York: Oxford University Press, 1989); Michael C. C. Adams, *The Best War Ever: America and World War II*, 2d ed. (Baltimore: Johns Hopkins University Press, 2015); Matthew F. Delmont, *Half American: The Epic Story of African Americans Fighting World War II at Home and Abroad* (New York: Viking, 2022). See also Kenneth Rose, *Myth and the Greatest Generation* (New York: Routledge, 2007).
7. Gustave O. Arlt and Chandler Harris, "Songs of the Services," *California Folklore Quarterly* 3, no. 1 (1944): 36.
8. Eric Posselt, *Give Out! Songs of, by, and for the Men in Service* (New York: Arrowhead, 1943), [4]; Edgar A. Palmer, *G.I. Songs: Written, Composed and/or Collected by the Men in the Service* (Great Neck, NY: Granger, 1978 [1944]), 6.

9. Austin Fife, "Anthology of Folk Literature of Soldiers of the Pacific Theater," 1947, n.p., Austin E. Fife Collection, AFC 1947/002, LC-AFC. For "Extra Songs and Poetry (Pornographic)," see folder 5.

10. Agnes Nolan Underwood, "Folklore from G.I. Joe," *New York Folklore* 3, no. 1 (1947): 287. Similarly, in the late 1950s and early '60s, folk-song collector and singer Oscar Brand recorded four albums of servicemen's songs (one for each of the branches of the military, minus the coast guard): *The Wild Blue Yonder* (Elektra, 1956), *Every Inch a Sailor* (Elektra, 1959), *Tell It to the Marines* (Elektra, 1959), and *Cough! Army Songs out of the Barracks Bag* (Elektra, 1963). He claimed in the liner notes of the first of these records not to have bowdlerized any lyrics, yet the songs contain no profanity and elsewhere he explained that he had to rewrite all the songs because "naturally, you could not put them [out] the way they were." See liner notes to the reissue of *Tell It to the Marines* and *Cough!* (Collectors' Choice, 2006) by Richie Unterberger. The most extensive collection of unexpurgated material is volume 2, the "Stag Bar Edition," of C. W. Getz's privately printed two-volume collection of air force songs, *The Wild Blue Yonder: Songs of the Air Force*, (Burlingame, CA: Redwood, 1986). Numerous soldier songs are also contained in [John Walsh,] *Songs of Roving and Raking* (n.p.: n.p., [1962]). Facsimiles of this latter collection and of many of Getz's sources are available online at JHC.

11. Allison McCracken, *Real Men Don't Sing: Crooning in American Culture* (Durham, NC: Duke University Press, 2015). On the association of music with "sissy": Leila A. McKay, "Music as a Group Therapeutic Agent in the Treatment of Convalescents," *Sociometry* 8, no. 3/4 (1945): 235. On the crisis of crooning in the British context, see Christina L. Baade, *Victory through Harmony: The BBC and Popular Music in World War II* (New York: Oxford University Press, 2012), 131–52.

12. Allan Bérubé, *Coming Out under Fire: The History of Gay Men and Women in World War Two* (New York: Free Press, 1990), 49, 101–2, 155, 157.

13. [Harold Spivacke?], "Music in the Armed Forces," memorandum, n.d., folder 3, box 11, JANCWR, 7.

14. Lawrence Tibbett, "Tibbett Sees Flaws in Music for Forces," *Musical America* 63 (January 25, 1943): 7; Martin O. Rauhut et al., "Something to Write Home About," *Music Educators Journal* 32, no. 1 (1945): 56; Everett L. Timm et al., "Something to Write Home About," *Music Educators Journal* 32, no. 2 (1945): 40.

15. Timm et al., "Something to Write Home About," 40; "S63: Morale and AWOL Study," July 1943, *The American Soldier in World War II*, https://americansoldierww2.org/surveys/s/S63/q-0/tab-1/6; "Attitudes of Enlisted Men toward Singing in the Army," August 23, 1943, folder 6, box 15, JANCWR, 2, 7, and 10. See also Fauser, *Sounds of War*, 108.

16. From a 1979 letter to Richard Rodgers, quoted in Todd S. Purdum, *Something Wonderful: Rodgers and Hammerstein's Broadway Revolution* (New York: Henry Holt, 2018), 94–95.

17. "S63: Morale and AWOL Study," July 1943, *The American Soldier in World War II*, https://americansoldierww2.org/surveys/s/S63/q-0/tab-1/6; "From the

Home Front and the Front Lines," Library of Congress, https://www.loc.gov
/exhibits/homefront/correspondence.html#objo63.

18. Otto H. Helbig, *A History of Music in the U.S. Armed Forces during World War
II* (Philadelphia: M. W. Lads, 1966), 25–28; War Department, *OK, USA: A
Soldier Shows "Blueprint" Special*, Pamphlet No. 28-12A, June 1945, a copy of
which can be found in folder 1, Merwyn Eugene Morlan Papers, MSS Box
2123, LC-VHP; Mort Lewis, *Comedy Acts and Minstrel Show Material* (Washington, DC: Infantry Journal, 1943), a copy of which can be found in folder
4, Merwyn Eugene Morlan Papers, MSS Box 2123, LC-VHP. See also War
Department, *Basic Field Manual FM 28-105* (Washington, DC: Government
Printing Office, 1944), 1.

19. Laurence Bergreen, "Oh! How We Hated to Get Up in the Morning," *MHQ*
2, no. 4 (Summer 1990): 72–81; Laurence Bergreen, "Irving Berlin: This Is the
Army," *Prologue* 28, no. 2 (1996): 95–105; "'This Is the Army' a Rousing Hit;
Throng Pays $45,000 at Opening," *NYT*, July 5, 1942.

20. Bérubé, *Coming Out under Fire*, 68–70, 72, 74, and 67–97 passim.

21. Bérubé, *Coming Out under Fire*, 90–91. *Savannah Morning News* quoted at 91.

22. Bérubé, *Coming Out under Fire*, 71–72, 79; "Eisenhower Commends Army
Show in Algiers," *NYT*, October 29, 1943.

23. See, e.g., the lyrics to Irving Berlin's "Blue Skies" in the spiral notebook,
Dominick Anthony Salerno Collection, folder 1, MSS Box 1182, LC-VHP.

24. This was the final verse of the Vera Lynn version, lyrics by Tommie Connor,
reprinted in the liner notes, p. 169, of *Lili Marleen an Allen Fronten: Ein Lied
Geht Um Die Welt: Das Lied, Seine Zeit, Seine Interpreten, Seine Botschaften*
(Bear Family Records, 2005), a seven-CD collection of over two hundred versions of the song. For a broader history of "Lili Marlene," see Liel Leibovitz
and Matthew Miller, *Lili Marlene: The Soldiers' Song of World War II* (New
York: W. W. Norton, 2009).

25. Alan Lomax, "Notes," n.d., folder 12.03.17, Alan Lomax Coll., AFC 2004/004,
LC-AFC, https://www.loc.gov/resource/afc2004004.ms120317.

26. Paul McKenzie, "The Gas House Gang (A Fighting Song of the Chemical
Warfare Svc)," *Chemical Warfare Bulletin* 29 (1943–44): 40–41.

27. The cover of this songbook also bears a curious injunction: "Instructions:
Carry this booklet in the pocket of your fatigue jacket at all times. Refer
all questions and new song suggestions to your Drill Instructor. Sing only
the authorized songs." *Song Book BTC #4*, JHC, https://www.horntip.com
/html/books_&_MSS/1940s/1943ca_BTC_No4_song_book_(mimeo)/1943ca
_btc_no4_song_book.pdf.

28. Technically speaking, the WASP was a civilian organization whose members
were not in the military, though its operations were coordinated with the
Army Air Force.

29. *Women's Army Corps Song Book*, 1944, JHC, https://www.horntip.com/html
/books_&_MSS/1940s/1944-08-01_womens_army_corps_song_book
_(PB)/1944-08-01_womans_army_corps_song_book.pdf; *Songs for the Wom-
en's Army Corps*, 1944, JHC, https://www.horntip.com/html

/books_&_MSS/1940s/1944_songs_for_womens_army_corps/1944_songs_for
_womens_army_corps_(getz_collection_no_110).pdf. See also *WAC Song
Book* (Des Moines, IA: n.p., n.d.) in Norma L. Harris Collection, Women Veterans Historical Project, University of North Carolina, Greensboro, https://
gateway.uncg.edu/islandora/object/wvhp%3A11826.

30. [Hazel Meyers,] *W.A.C. Songs*, (Brooklyn, 1943), Music Division, Library of
Congress; *Camp Monticello 43 Song Book* (n.p.: n.p., n.d.), JHC, https://www
.horntip.com/html/books_&_MSS/1940s/1943ca_camp_montecello_43
_songbook/1943ca_camp_montecello_43_songbook_(getz_collection
_no_115).pdf, 7 and 9; *Marching to Victory* (Northampton, MA: Naval
Reserve Midshipmen's School, 1943), JHC, https://www.horntip.com/html
/books_&_MSS/1940s/1943_marching_to_victory_(PB)/1943_marching
_to_victory_naval_reserve_midshipmens_school.pdf. See also Special
Services, comp., *WAC Song Book* (Fort Lee, VA: Women's Army Corps Training Center, [ca. 1945]), JHC, https://www.horntip.com/html/books_&_MSS
/1940s/1945ca_WAC_songbook_(mimeo)/1945ca_WAC_songbook_(fort_lee
_va)_(getz_collection_no_116).pdf; *HQ & HQ Company* (Camp Lee, VA:
Women's Army Corps Training Center, [ca. 1945], JHC, https://www
.horntip.com/html/books_&_MSS/1940s/1945ca_HQ_HQ_company
_womens_army_corps/1945ca_HQ_HQ_company_womens_army_corps
_(getz_collection_no_121).pdf; *WASP "Songbook"* (n.p.: n.p., [ca. 1943]),
JHC, https://www.horntip.com/html/books_&_MSS/1940s/1943ca_WASP
songbook(mimeo)/1943ca_wasp_songbook.pdf; [Marine Corps Women's
Reserve,] *Semper Fidelis* (n.p.: n.p., 1946), JHC, https://www.horntip
.com/html/books_&_MSS/1940s/1946-02-13_semper_fidelis_(marine_corp
_womens_reserve_song_book)_(mimeo)/1946-02-13_semper_fidelis
_(marine_corp_womens_reserve_song_book).pdf; "The Army Air Corps
Song Lyrics," n.d., Suzette Van Daell Douglas Collection, University of
North Texas Libraries, https://texashistory.unt.edu/ark:/67531
/metapth870724/.

31. *WAC Song Book*, 12, Norma L. Harris Collection, University of North Carolina
Greensboro, https://gateway.uncg.edu/islandora/object/wvhp%3AWV0309.

32. Meyers, [*W.A.C. Songs*], 6.

33. Meyers, [*W.A.C. Songs*], 9, 12.

34. Carol Burke, "'If You're Nervous in the Service . . .': Training Songs of
Female Soldiers in the '40s," in *Visions of War: World War II in Popular Liter-
ature and Culture*, ed. M. Paul Holsinger and Mary Anne Schofield (Bowling
Green, OH: Popular Culture Press, 1992), 127–37.

35. Meyers, [*W.A.C. Songs*], 5.

36. Quoted in Burke, "'If You're Nervous in the Service," 129. A WAVES version
of this song appears in *Marching to Victory Songbook* (Northampton, MA:
Naval Reserve Midshipmen's School, 1943), Virgilia Williams Collection,
University of North Carolina Greensboro, https://gateway.uncg.edu
/islandora/object/wvhp%3A11935#page/48/mode/1up.

37. Burke, "'If You're Nervous in the Service," 131–32.

38. "A Guy to Tie My Tie," in the WAVES songbook *Marching to Victory* (Northampton, MA: Naval Reserve Midshipmen's School, 1943). This verse was not included in the version printed in the songbook *Dedicated to the United States Marine Corps Women's Reserve*, n.d., Tennessee Virtual Archive, https://teva.contentdm.oclc.org/digital/collection/p15138coll18/id/2244/.

39. *WASP "Songbook,"* n.p., Dorothy Hoover Collection, University of North Carolina Greensboro, https://gateway.uncg.edu/islandora /object/wvhp%3A18863?islandora_paged_content_page=001. See also *SPAR Song Book*, U.S. Department of Defense, https://media.defense .gov/2020/Aug/20/2002481103/-1/-1/0/SPAR_SONG_BOOK.PDF; Marine Corps Women's Reserve, *Semper Fidelis*. On WASP, see "Women Airforce Service Pilots and Their Fight for Veteran Status," U.S. Air Force, https://www.af.mil/News/Article-Display/Article/2838960 /women-airforce-service-pilots-and-their-fight-for-veteran-status/.

40. Samuel Hynes, *Flights of Passage: Reflections of a World War II Aviator* (New York: Frederic C. Beil, 1988), 127–28; Les Cleveland, "Soldiers' Songs: The Folklore of the Powerless," *New York Folklore* 11 (1985): 79, 81.

41. "By far" is from Rixey, "Soldiers Still Sing," 54. "All" airmen's favorite is from Palmer, *G.I. Songs*, 136–37. This version of the song is transcribed from: unidentified singer, ["I Wanted Wings,"] n.d., recording afc2004022 _sr07a, AFC 2004/022: Edward Bell Collection of Ruth Mae Gasper Bell and Margot Mayo Recordings, LC-AFC. See also the navy songbook *Bawdy Bar Room Ballads* (n.p.: n.p., [ca. 1944]), JHC, https://www.horntip.com/html /books_&_MSS/1940s/1944ca_bawdy_bar_room_ballads/1944ca_bawdy_bar _room_ballads_(getz_collection_no_063).pdf.

42. Alan Lomax to Harold Spivacke, April 17, 1943, box 9, folder 44, Army/Navy Sub-Comm. on Music, Correspondence, JANCWR.

43. Hynes, *Flights of Passage*, 195.

44. Roy Palmer, *What a Lovely War: British Soldiers' Songs from the Boer War to the Present Day* (London: M. Joseph, 1990), 142; Cleveland, "Soldiers' Songs," 81–82. See also Rixey, "Soldiers Still Sing," 51.

45. *Women's Army Corps Song Book* (n.p.: War Department, 1944), 41, JHC, https://www.horntip.com/html/songs_sorted_by_informant/military _songbooks/index.htm.

46. Pete Seeger, "Report from the Marianas: Notes of an Innocent Bystander," no. 11, September 16, 1945, https://archive.org /details/1945reportfromthemarianas/.

47. *Aloha Jigpoha* (n.p.: n.p., 1945), in JHC, https://www.horntip.com/html /books_&_MSS/1940s/1945-02-00_aloha_jigpoha_(mimeo)/1945-02-00_aloha _jigpoha.pdf. Critiques of rear-echelon soldiers were legion. For another, see, e.g., "Army Chair Corps Song," a parody of the anthem of the Army Air Corps, dated January 16, 1944, in miscellaneous materials, JHC, https:// www.horntip.com/html/books_&_MSS/1940s/1940s_NASM_archives/nasm _archives_(need_dark_photocopy_of_last_page).pdf, accessed January 16, 2023.

48. [Alan Lomax,] "Notes," n.d., folder 12.03.17, Alan Lomax Coll., AFC 2004/004, LC-AFC, https://www.loc.gov/resource/afc2004004.ms120317/. Lomax identifies the song as "Fuck 'Em All," not "Bless 'Em All." See also the twenty-five verses reproduced in the untitled marine songbook, ca. 1943, in JHC, https://www.horntip.com/html/books_&_MSS/1940s/1943ca_untitled _marine_songbook_(mimeo)/1943ca_untitled_marine_songbook.pdf, 63–67.

49. Fussell, *Wartime*, 79–95, 268 and passim. Heller quoted on back cover of paperback edition of *Wartime*. Fussell's work recalls that of John Jacob Niles and Douglas Moore, whose World War I song collection *The Songs My Mother Never Taught Me* aimed to "[tell] a tale the histories will try to untell for a good many years." John Jacob Niles and Douglas Moore, *The Songs My Mother Never Taught Me* (New York: Macaulay, 1929), 13.

50. J. Douglas Harvey, *Boys, Bombs, and Brussels Sprouts: A Knees-Up, Wheels-Up Chronicle of WWII* (Toronto: McClelland and Stewart, 1983), 148; Fussell, *Wartime*, 264.

51. The collection *Songs of Roving and Raking* features a section titled simply "Songs Which Should Not Be Sung."

52. On "national memory," see Sherrie Tucker, *Dance Floor Democracy: The Social Geography of Memory at the Hollywood Canteen* (Durham, NC: Duke University Press, 2014), xv.

53. See, e.g., Fussell, *Wartime*, 129–43. Others arriving at this view include Samuel A. Stouffer et al., *The American Soldier*, Studies in Social Psychology in World War II, 2 vol. (New York: Wiley, 1965).

54. Robert B. Westbrook, "'I Want a Girl, Just like the Girl That Married Harry James': American Women and the Problem of Political Obligation in World War II," *American Quarterly* 42, no. 4 (1990): 588. Emphasis in original.

55. Westbrook, "'I Want a Girl, Just like the Girl That Married Harry James,'" 599, 600, 611. The title of Westbook's article is an (unexplained) play on the title of a well-known popular song of the era (published in 1911), "I Want a Girl (Just like the Girl That Married Dear Old Dad)," which was included in several wartime songbooks.

56. Rixey, "Soldiers Still Sing," 48; Palmer [pseudonym of Eric Posselt], *G.I. Songs*, 106–9; Arthur Weithas, "The Low-Down on Dirty Gertie," *Yank*, September 10, 1943, 10. On the song's background, see also "Lt. William Russell '27 Wrote Lyrics for Song 'Dirty Gertie from Bizerte,'" *Cornell Sun* 64, no. 21 (August 17, 1943): 5. Later in the war, Alan Lomax found that "without question" the most popular songs among soldiers in Europe were "Lily Marlene" and a horny ditty called "Roll Me Over (in the Clover)." The only lyrics I have located for the latter song, whose origins were likely British, are sexual but not graphic ("Roll me over, lay me down / Do it again"). If Lomax was correct that this was one of the most popular songs among G.I.s in Europe, it is likely there were other, more explicit verses or versions which have not survived. See Alan Lomax, "Notes," n.d., folder 12.03.17, Alan Lomax Coll., AFC 2004/004, LC-AFC, https://www.loc.gov/resource /afc2004004.ms120317/.

57. Rixey, "Soldiers Still Sing," 51; [Dick Boutelle?], comp., *The Three Hats*, 2 vols. (n.p.: Drunken Press, 1949–50), 1:11; *Aloha Jigpoha*, 16.

58. Typescript, Miscellaneous Lore and Broadsides, ca. 1943, JHC, https:// www .horntip.com/html/books_&_MSS/1940s/1943ca_bawdy_xerox-lore_and _broadsides_(MSS)/1943ca_bawdy_xerox_lore_and_broadsides.pdf. Emphasis in original.

59. *The Three Hats*, 2:13.

60. "Bell-Bottom Trousers," n.d., in folder 5, AFC 1947/002, Anthology of Folk Literature, Austin Fife Collection, LC-AFC. Variants include "He'll screw the women" and "He'll climb the riggin.'" This song and several others discussed in this section also appear in Anthony Hopkins, *Songs from the Front & Rear: Canadian Servicemen's Songs of the Second World War* (Edmonton: Hurtig, 1979).

61. See *The Three Hats*, 1:7; untitled marine songbook, ca. 1943, JHC; Arlt and Harris, "Songs of the Services," 39–40. The WASP version, titled "Zoot Suits and Parachutes," appears in *WASP "Song Book,"* Dorothy Hoover Collection.

62. *Bawdy Bar Room Ballads*. Also in *Three Hats*, 2:26–27.

63. Martin Page, ed., *Kiss Me Goodnight, Sergeant Major: The Songs and Ballads of World War II* (London: Hart-Davis, MacGibbon, 1973), 11.

64. Rixey, "Soldiers Still Sing," 54.

65. This transcription is adapted from the epitaph on the tombstone of Willie Lee Duckworth, who is credited with inventing the "Duckworth Chant." "Private Willie Lee Duckworth Sr.," *Historical Marker Database*, https://www .hmdb.org/m.asp?m=103232.

66. For an earlier observation about the effects of singing on marching and cadence exercises, see remarks by General Hugh L. Scott of Camp Dix in "Singing Meets War Needs," *NYT*, November 18, 1918.

67. The V-Disc recording, which includes a retelling of this origins story, can be heard at "Duckworth Chant 1944 on V-Disc," YouTube, http://www.youtube .com/watch?v=4SgUE-6Ewtw, accessed January 19, 2023. See also Bernard Lentz, *The Cadence System of Teaching Close Order Drill*, 5th. rev ed. (Harrisburg, PA: Military Service Pub. Co., 1951), n.p. (preface).

68. Alan Lomax to Harold Spivacke, [September 1944], Alan Lomax file, Army/ Navy Sub-Comm. on Music, Correspondence, JANCWR. See also James Andrew Hardy, oral history, James Andrew Hardy Collection, LC-VHP, https://www.loc.gov/item/afc2001001.84871/.

69. Alan Lomax, *The Folk Songs of North America* (Garden City, NY: Doubleday, 1960), 595.

70. From the military manual of Wei Liao-Tzu, circa 400 BC: "Beat the drum once and the left [foot steps forward]; beat it again and the right [foot advances]. . . . If the drummer misses a beat, he is executed. Those that set up a clamor are executed. Those that do not obey the gongs, drums, bells, and flags, but move by themselves, are executed." *The Seven Military Classics of Ancient China*, trans. Ralph Sawyer with Mei-Chun Sawyer (New York: Basic

Books, 1993), 266–67; Jennifer Lee Ladkani, "Sweating, Swearing and Singing: Cadences as United States Military Culture" (MM thesis, University of Cincinnati, 1997), 2.

71. Bernard Lentz, *The Cadence System of Teaching Close Order Drill*, 3rd ed. ([Menasha, WI]: George Banta, 1925), 1. The basic principles of Lentz's system first appeared in Bernard Lentz, "Helpful Hints in Close Order Drill," *Infantry Journal* 14, no. 10 (April 1918): 743–47; Bernard Lentz, "The Minutiae of Close Order Drill," *Infantry Journal* 15, no. 6 (December 1918), 451–69; Michel Foucault, *Discipline and Punish: The Birth of the Prison* (New York: Vintage, 1979).

72. Travis Salley, "Sound-Off! An Introduction to the Study of American Military Marching Cadences" (MM thesis, University of Massachusetts–Amherst, 2015), 21; Lizabeth Cohen, *A Consumers' Republic: The Politics of Mass Consumption in Postwar America* (New York: Knopf, 2003).

Chapter Six

1. *Apocalypse Now*, directed by Francis Ford Coppola, 1979; John Leonard, "Books of the Times," *NYT*, October 28, 1977.

2. Charlie Clark, "The Tracks of Our Tears: Looking Back on Vietnam and Its Music," *VVA Veteran* 6, no. 2 (February 1986): 11; James Olson, *Dictionary of the Vietnam War* (New York: Greenwood, 1988), 519.

3. Quoted in Doug Bradley and Craig Werner, *We Gotta Get Out of This Place: The Soundtrack of the Vietnam War* (Amherst: University of Massachusetts Press, 2015), 1.

4. Brian McAllister Linn, *Elvis's Army: Cold War GIs and the Atomic Battlefield* (Cambridge, MA: Harvard University Press, 2016), 1, 334–35, quote at 335.

5. The length of boot camp was increased from eight to nine weeks over the course of the war.

6. Joseph Pessenda, oral history, Joseph Pessenda Collection, LC-VHP, https://www.loc.gov/resource/afc2001001.102295.sr0001001/.

7. Christian G. Appy, *Working-Class War: American Combat Soldiers and Vietnam* (Chapel Hill: University of North Carolina Press, 1993), 86, 88.

8. Appy, *Working-Class War*, 96.

9. Fagan, quoted in Carol Burke, "Marching to Vietnam," *Journal of American Folklore* 102, no. 406 (1989): 430. Fagan was interviewed in 1989, but his remarks are equally applicable to the era of the war in Vietnam.

10. William H. McNeill, *Keeping Together in Time: Dance and Drill in Human History* (Cambridge, MA: Harvard University Press, 1995), 2.

11. Bernard Lentz, *The Cadence System of Teaching Close Order Drill*, 3rd ed. ([Menasha, WI]: George Banta, 1925), 1. This manual was published in many editions from 1920s to 1950s.

12. Neither the 1956 nor the 1968 edition of the field manual *FM 22-5 Drills and Ceremonies* for drill instructors mentioned cadence chants, although they did have sections on cadence, voice control, and other aspects of vocal command. The 1958 version of the manual *FM 21-18 Foot Marches* encouraged diversions on the march, including "counting cadence, singing, conversation, or humor in almost any form," but this disappeared in the 1962 revision and later editions. See Department of the Army, *FM 22-5 Drill and Ceremonies* (Washington, DC: Department of the Army, 1956); Department of the Army, *FM 22-5 Drill and Ceremonies* (Washington, DC: Department of the Army, 1968); Department of the Army, *FM 21-18 Foot Marches* (Washington, DC: Department of the Army, 1958); Department of the Army, *FM 21-18 Foot Marches* (Washington, DC: Department of the Army, 1962).

13. Sandee Shaffer Johnson, ed., *Cadences: The Jody Call Book*, 2 vol. (Canton, OH: Daring, 1983–86). See also Sandee Shaffer Johnson, comp., *The New American Cadences Jody Call Handbook*, ed. Robert W. Morgan (Sebring, OH: Talisman, 1994).

14. On cadences as music, see Jennifer Lee Ladkani, "Sweating, Swearing and Singing: Cadences as United States Military Culture" (MM thesis, University of Cincinnati, 1997), 14–26.

15. Henry Threadgill with Brent Hayes Edwards, *Easily Slip into Another World: A Life in Music* (New York: Knopf, 2023), 92.

16. Available sources include a patchwork of verses collected between 1955 and 1964 from interviews with veterans by Ed Cray and numerous chants collected by Carol Burke at the United States Naval Academy in the 1980s, brought there since Vietnam by "prior-enlisted marines and sailors," as well as from active-duty marines and sailors and from students at Virginia Military Institute and the Citadel. George Carey ran alongside trainees. See Ed Cray, *The Erotic Muse: American Bawdy Songs*, 2nd ed. (Urbana: University of Illinois Press, 1999), 392–96; Carol Burke, "Pernicious Cohesion," in *It's Our Military Too: Women and the US Military*, ed. Judith Stiehm (Philadelphia: Temple University Press, 1996); Carol Burke, "Inside the Clubhouse," *Women's Review of Books* 10, no. 5 (1993): 20–21; Carol Burke, "Marching to Vietnam," *Journal of American Folklore* 102, no. 406 (1989): 424–41; Carol Burke, "Dames at Sea," *New Republic* 207, nos. 8–9 (August 17, 1992), 16–20; George G. Carey, "A Collection of Airborne Cadence Chants," *Journal of American Folklore* 78, no. 307 (1965): 52–61.

17. Burke, "Marching to Vietnam," 424, 427; Carey, "A Collection of Airborne Cadence Chants," 54, 57, 59; Agnes Nolan Underwood, "Folklore from G.I. Joe," *New York Folklore* 3, no. 1 (1947), 287. For many other examples, see Johnson, *Cadences.*

18. Burke, "Marching to Vietnam," 425.

19. Memorably depicted on screen in *Full Metal Jacket*, directed by Stanley Kubrick (1987), with Vietnam-era trainees grasping their rifles with one hand and genitals with the other, this was a "truly universal marching chant, one that has crossed all service lines," according to Burke, "Marching to Vietnam," 427.

20. Carey, "A Collection of Airborne Cadence Chants," 55.

21. Burke, "Marching to Vietnam," 425 and 438n4. From interviews with veterans conducted between 1955 and 1964, folklorist Ed Cray collected numerous cadences such as these, each of which would have been followed by "Sound off / One, two / Sound off / Three, four / Cadence, count / One, two, three, four":

> I don't know but I been told
> Eskimo pussy is mighty cold.
>
> I got a gal in Baltimore.
> She's got a red light on her door.
>
> I know a gal named Frisco Lil.
> Touch her tit and get a thrill.
>
> If I die on the Russian front,
> Box me up with a Russian cunt.

Cray, *The Erotic Muse*, 395–96.

22. Appy, *Working-Class War*, 27; Mapheus Smith, "Populational Characteristics of American Servicemen in World War II," *Scientific Monthly* 65, no. 3 (1947): 246–52.

23. TemetNosce, "[NSFW] Anyone remember some 'dirty' cadence calls?," Reddit, February 15, 2014, https://www.reddit.com/r/Military/comments/1xzqfk/nsfw _anyone_remember_some_dirty_cadence_calls/, retrieved July 10, 2021.

24. Burke, "Marching to Vietnam," 434–35 and 440. Napalm appears to have inspired an unusual number of cadences. Another (from Burke, "Marching to Vietnam," 440) went:

> See the VC in the jungle,
> Running down into their tunnel.
> Agent Orange is quite the funnel.
> Yo Oh, Napalm it sticks to kids.
>
> See the children within the brush
> Watchin' their village get all crushed.
> My M-16 will make them mush.
> Yo, Oh, Napalm it sticks to kids.
>
> See the kiddies in the street
> Cryin' and lookin' for som'in to eat.
> Drop trick toys that look real neat
> Blow up in their face and make 'em all meat.
>
> Napalm, napalm sticks like glue.
> Sticks to women and children, too.

25. Dave Grossman, *On Killing: The Psychological Cost of Learning to Kill in War and Society* (Boston: Little, Brown, 1995), 250–52. Journalist (and World War I veteran) S. L. A. Marshall reported a nonfire rate of 80–85 percent in World

War II, and although methodologies and data have subsequently been challenged, his general claims have largely been affirmed and widely endorsed. Marshall's findings appeared in *Men Against Fire: The Problem of Battle Command in Future War* (Washington: Infantry Journal, 1947). For a potent critique of Marshall's findings, see Roger J. Spiller, "S. L. A. Marshall and the Ratio of Fire," *RUSI Journal* 133, no. 4 (1988): 63–71. For a summary of the historiography Marshall's work spawned, see Kelly C. Jordan, "Right for the Wrong Reasons: S. L. A. Marshall and the Ratio of Fire in Korea," *Journal of Military History* 66, no. 1 (2002): 135–62. Other assessments of Marshall's assertion appear in Michael D. Doubler, *Closing with the Enemy: How G.I.s Fought the War in Europe, 1944–1945* (Lawrence: University Press of Kansas, 1994), 289–91; Kenneth Rose, *Myth and the Greatest Generation* (New York: Routledge, 2007), 66–68.

26. Gwynne Dyer, *War* (New York: Crown, 1985), 121. On the impact of S. L. A. Marshall's findings, the increased focused on lethality, and changes in basic training over time, see Conrad Crane et al., *Learning the Lessons of Lethality: They Army's Cycle of Basic Combat Training, 1918–2019* (n.p.: United States Army War College, 2019), esp. 38.

27. At least since the 1980s, other cadences have found macabre humor in animal cruelty, from torturing and crushing birds to clubbing baby seals. I have not been able to confirm that these or similar cadences were sung in the era of the war in Vietnam. See Burke, "Marching to Vietnam," 436; Phillip Gibson, "Warsong: Dynamics of the Cadence in Military Training" (PhD diss., Pacifica Graduate Institute, 2011); and TemetNosce, "[NSFW] Anyone remember some 'dirty' cadence calls?"

28. Gwynne Dyer, *War* (New York: Crown, 1985), 121; on transforming civilians into killers, see 108–21.

29. Burke, "Marching to Vietnam," 427.

30. Burke, "Marching to Vietnam," 431.

31. Carey, "A Collection of Airborne Cadence Chants," 59.

32. Burke, "Marching to Vietnam," 431; Bruce Jackson, "What Happened to Jody," *Journal of American Folklore* 80, no. 318 (1967): 387–96; Carey, "A Collection of Airborne Cadence Chants," 58; Susan L. Carruthers, *Dear John: Love and Loyalty in Wartime America* (Cambridge: Cambridge University Press, 2022). 246–47; Gibson, "Warsong," 55.

33. This section is indebted to Gibson, "Warsong."

34. Ladkani, "Sweating, Swearing and Singing," 64; Eliade, *Rites and Symbols of Initiation* (1958), quoted in Gibson, "Warsong," 14; Robert Jay Lifton, *Thought Reform and the Psychology of Totalism: A Study of "Brainwashing" in China* (New York: W. W. Norton, 1961). Gibson uses the phrase "violently enforced normalization" in "Warsong" on 71.

35. Robert Jay Lifton, *Home from the War: Vietnam Veterans: Neither Victims nor Executioners* (New York: Simon and Schuster, 1973), 28–29.

36. Gibson, "Warsong," 78. Lifton discusses "milieu control" in relation to so-called "brain washing" in China, not basic training, but, as Phillip Gibson

has shown, it is applicable to Lifton's analysis of basic training too. It also bears emphasizing that "milieu control" was only one of eight dimensions of "thought reform" that Lifton identified, along with mystical manipulation, the demand for purity, the cult of confession, the sacred science, the loading of the language, doctrine over person, and the dispensing of existence. Gibson detailed how American soldiers were subject to all eight of these (though not specifically in the Vietnam era). See Lifton, *Thought Reform and the Psychology of Totalism*, 421 and 419–37ff; Gibson, "Warsong," 69–82.

37. McNeill, *Keeping Together in Time*, 2. On the neurophysiology of rhythm, a subject which has received more scientific attention since McNeill's book was published, see 160n10.

38. Gibson, "Warsong," 53.

39. Karl Marlantes, *What It Is Like to Go to War* (New York: Atlantic Monthly Press, 2011), 40–41. Alexander Lowen (1985) makes a related point about the ease of killing dehumanized surrogates in his *Narcissism: Denial of the True Self*, 51, quoted in Gibson, "Warsong," 66.

40. Roger Allen Fain, oral history, 2002, Roger Allen Fain Collection, LC-VHP, https://www.loc.gov/item/afc2001001.06524/.

41. Bradley and Werner, *We Gotta Get Out of This Place*, 63, 147–49.

42. Officials, commentators, and historians all agree that noncombat troops made up a clear majority of American military personnel in Vietnam, but estimates of the ratio of combat to support troops vary widely and often rest on little more than speculation. Christian Appy claimed it "was at least five to one, and some sources put it at ten to one." Other estimates span from 2:1 to 11:1. The most conservative of these (2:1) comes from John McGrath, the most transparent and exacting commentator on this issue, whose conclusions are based on actual data but only from the army (the biggest but not the only branch of the military) and only from 1968 (when the size of U.S. forces in Vietnam peaked). McGrath contends that this ratio was roughly the same as in the Korean War but a radical break from World War I and World War II, when the ratio had been reversed in favor of combat troops, roughly 1:2. Other sources, however, such as Paul Fussell, suggest a majority of noncombat troops in World War II. See John J. McGrath, *The Other End of the Spear: The Tooth-to-Tail Ratio (T3R) in Modern Military Operations*, The Long War Series Occasional Paper 23 (Fort Leavenworth, KS: Combat Studies Institute, 2007); Meredith H. Lair, *Armed with Abundance: Consumerism and Soldiering in the Vietnam War* (Chapel Hill: University of North Carolina Press, 2014), 249n3; Appy, *Working-Class War*, 167; Robert L. Goldich, "U.S. Army Combat-to-Support Ratios: A Framework for Analysis," report CRS-1989-FND-0073 (Washington, DC: Congressional Research Service, June 26, 1989). The ratio of 11:1 in Vietnam comes from military analyst (and Vietnam veteran) David Hackworth, cited in McGrath, *The Other End of the Spear*, 28. On World War II, see Paul Fussell, *Wartime: Understanding and Behavior in the Second World War* (New York: Oxford University Press, 1989), 283.

One problem with all these figures is that they tend to distinguish only between combat troops and support troops when, in fact, there is also a third category: *combat-support*, i.e., troops providing direct support for combat operations. For example, some units in the Army Corps of Engineers or Signal Corps work directly with combat formations, while others operate behind the lines. Thanks to Paul Miles for calling this distinction to my attention.

43. See, e.g., Lawrence Rock, *The Tooth and the Tail: An Oral History of American Support Troops in Vietnam* (n.p.: n.p., 2013).

44. Lair, *Armed with Abundance*, 85, 119, 121; Steve R. Waddell, *United States Army Logistics: From the American Revolution to 9/11* (Santa Barbara, CA: Praeger, 2010), 165.

45. Ronald Jay Rexilius, "Americans without Dog Tags: United States Civilians in the Vietnam War, 1950–1975" (PhD diss., University of Nebraska, Lincoln, 2000), 48. On the predominance of unknown artists, see, e.g., the files in box 23, Entry #P181 Records Regarding United Svc Org (USO) Tours in Vietnam, NARA-RG472.

46. "The Sweetheart of the Special Forces: Miss Martha Raye," n.d., folder "General Historical Records Related to the Entertainment Branch, 1970–72," box 61, Entertainment Branch History files, 1969–1972, NARA-RG472.

47. *History of AFRTS: The First 50 Years* ([Alexandria, VA]: American Forces Information Service and Armed Forces Radio and Television Service, 1993), n.p. (chaps. 20–21); Bradley and Werner, *We Gotta Get Out of This Place*, 150.

48. The sample for these surveys included personnel from all branches of the military, in proportion to their presence in Vietnam, from privates to generals (or the equivalent). However imperfect, these surveys represented far more than impressionistic observations, and the AFVN took pains to explain that its randomized sampling, response rate (ranging from 48 percent in 1968 to 56 percent in 1971), computer tabulation, and methodology were generally consistent with the kind of public-opinion polling that accurately predicted the winners of presidential elections. See R. Nash and James E. Wentz, "American Forces Vietnam Network: Audience Opinion Research and Analysis" (Saigon: [American Forces Vietnam Network], 1969); Francis K. Price and Stephen L. Wiltsie, "American Forces Vietnam Network: 1970 Audience Opinion Research and Analysis" (Saigon: [American Forces Vietnam Network], November 1970); Gunar Grubaums, "American Forces Vietnam Network: 1971 Audience Survey" (Saigon: [American Forces Vietnam Network], 1971). These will be referred to henceforth as "1968 Survey," "1970 Survey," and "1971 Survey," respectively. (The 1968 survey was completed and tabulated in January 1969.) The average listening times come from "1968 Survey," 20.

49. "1970 Survey," 16. On Long Binh Post, see Lair, *Armed with Abundance*, 31–39. According to the 1971 survey, more than 70 percent listened to *at least* one to two hours daily, but actual AFVN listening was probably substantially

higher. The survey inquired specifically about average listening to AFVN's AM broadcasting, but by this time armed forces radio was also broadcasting extensively on FM, which 19 percent of combat respondents and 31 percent of noncombat respondents preferred. A considerable percentage (16 and 17 percent, respectively) listened to AM and FM equally. "1971 Survey," 16. Note: unlike FM radio in the U.S. at the time, which featured a great deal of experimental and "underground" programming, AFVN-FM consisted largely of automated prerecorded audio provided by Armed Forces Radio and Television Service ("1971 Survey," 3).

50. "AFVN Historical Summary, Second Quarter, FY 68," January 15, 1968, folder 1, box 1, AFVN Organizational History, 1962–73, NARA-RG472; Ovid L. Bayless, "The American Forces Vietnam Network," *Journal of Broadcasting* 13, no. 2 (1969): 150.

51. "1968 Survey," 16, 20. Most G.I.s relied on AFVN for news even though increasingly they took its updates with a grain of salt, especially after a scandal erupted around censorship of the news in 1970. By 1971 only a small percentage considered AFVN news "complete and honest," according to surveys conducted by the AFVN of its military audience. See "1971 Survey," 27. On the news censorship scandal, which received extensive coverage in the U.S., see Michael Maxwell, "Fired GI Tells of Censorship on TV in Saigon," *National Catholic Reporter* 6, no. 11 (January 14, 1970): 1, 7; Randall J. Moody, "The Armed Forces Broadcast News System: Vietnam Version," *Journalism Quarterly* 47, no. 1 (March 1970): 27–30; Charles B. Moore, "Censorship of AFVN News in Vietnam," *Journal of Broadcasting* 15, no. 4 (1971): 387–96; Stacy Takacs, "Radio, Television, and the Military," in *A Companion to the History of American Broadcasting*, ed. Aniko Bodroghkozy (Newark, NJ: Wiley, 2018), 264–65.

52. "1968 Survey," 20–22. On the rock revolution, see, e.g., Arnold Shaw, *The Rock Revolution* (New York: Crowell-Collier, 1969); Jonathan Eisen, ed., *The Age of Rock, Sounds of the American Cultural Revolution: A Reader* (New York: Random House, 1969). On the persistence of mainstream tastes in relation to musical innovation, see Elijah Wald, *How the Beatles Destroyed Rock 'n' Roll: An Alternative History of American Popular Music* (New York: Oxford University Press, 2009).

53. "1970 Survey," 18 and appendix B, p. 3. The data from the 1971 survey also show Top 40 and oldies with by far the greatest popularity, though the order differs somewhat from 1970: oldies, Top 40, easy listening, acid rock, country, soul, jazz, classical, and show tunes. "1971 Survey," 18.

54. Edwin Starr's "War" (flip side: "Stop the War Now") represented only one of numerous explicit critiques of the war by Black musicians in the early 1970s. Others include the Temptations' "Ball of Confusion" (1970), which reached number 3; Marvin Gaye's "What's Goin' On" (1971), which hit number 2; and Freda Payne's "Bring the Boys Home" (1971), which reached number 12. Likewise, reggae star Jimmy Cliff condemned the war in his "Vietnam" (1970), as did jazz artists Freddie Hubbard on *Sing Me a Song of Songmy* (1971)

and the Revolutionary Ensemble on *Vietnam* (1973). In a few other cases, Black musicians had begun to speak out earlier, including jazz saxophonist Archie Shepp (particularly in his public statements and interviews) and blues artists J. B. Lenoir ("Vietnam Blues," 1966); Junior Wells ("Vietcong Blues," 1966); and John Lee Hooker ("I Don't Want to Go to Vietnam," 1969). See David James, "The Vietnam War and American Music," *Social Text* no. 23 (October 1989), 141n21. Chart rankings for 1970 come from "Year-End Charts: Hot 100 Songs," Billboard, https://www.billboard.com/charts/year-end/1970/hot-100-songs. Officially, the AFVN did not censor the music that was played, but numerous sources indicated that, in practice, there were certain policies in place. See, e.g., Bob Casey, oral history, February 26, 2008, NAMM, https://www.namm.org/library/oral-history/bob-casey; Bradley and Werner, *We Gotta Get Out of This Place*, 155–58; Christopher Sabis, "Through the Soldiers' Ears: What Americans Fighting in Vietnam Heard and Its Effects" (senior honors thesis, University of Rochester, 2000), 28.

55. "1968 Survey," 24.

56. From a 1967 aircheck preserved here "A Date with Chris—1967 Chris Noel Radio Program," YouTube, https://www.youtube.com/watch?v=g-KmFArv488. On Noel, see Chris Noel, oral history, 2011, LC-VHP, https://www.loc.gov/item/afc2001001.79462/6/23/2011; Chris Noel, *Chris Noel: Confessions of a Pin-Up Girl* (n.p.: n.p., 2011); *A History of AFRTS*, chap. 21.

57. "1968 Survey," 25; Bradley and Werner, *We Gotta Get Out of This Place*, 158; Jim Barthold, "The Real Life of Adrian Cronauer," Urgent Communications, March 1, 2005, https://web.archive.org/web/20120509103859/http://urgentcomm.com/mag/radio_real_life_adrian/, accessed November 23, 2019.

58. "1968 Survey," 51; "American Armed Forces Radio Vietnam No 11," https://archive.org/details/314888-b-nha-trang-air-check-6-23-70_202103. On the range of "oldies but goodies," see "1970 Survey," appendix p. 3.

59. Casey, oral history.

60. By 1971 when respondents were asked to identify one or more types of music they "really like[d] to listen to," oldies ranked highest (68 percent), topping Top 40 (54 percent) for the first time, followed by easy listening (39 percent). Next, acid rock and country were close to tied (31 and 29 percent, respectively), followed by soul (22 percent), jazz (18 percent), semi-classical (18 percent), classical (14 percent), and show tunes (13 percent). And when asked what type of music they wanted more of, 25 percent said oldies, and roughly equal percentages said acid rock, easy listening, and country (14, 13, and 13 percent, respectively). "1971 Survey," 18–19.

61. The article did not specify how this "select group" was defined or chosen.

62. Charles Perry, "Is This Any Way to Run the Army?—Stoned?," *Rolling Stone* (November 9, 1968), 1, 6, 8–9; quotations at 6.

63. Quoted in Lair, *Armed with Abundance*, 158.

64. Lair, *Armed with Abundance*, 159. The changing ratio of radio to tape players is interesting. In 1969 and 1970, the ratio of radios to tape recorders (all reel-to-reel) was substantially higher than 2:1. In 1971, when cassette recorders

became available, that ratio was reversed in (data January–November) to approximately 1:3, encompassing roughly 87,000 radios, 37,000 reel-to-reels, and 220,000 cassette recorders. Many factors may have shaped this change, but it could reflect soldiers' increasing interest in listening to their own sounds, rather than to AFVN, a conclusion supported by increase in purchase of record players in same years: 7,000 in 1969 and 1970, 31,000 in 1971. PX stores also sold records, but sales figures are not available.

65. Perry, "Is This Any Way to Run the Army?—Stoned?," 6; Lair, *Armed with Abundance*, 159. Many G.I.s exchanged audio letters home on tapes too, meaning tapes were not exclusively a music medium.

66. Perry, "Is This Any Way to Run the Army?—Stoned?," 1, 6.

67. "AFVN Fact Sheet," [n.p.: n.p., 1972], 11, https://nebula.wsimg.com /deec76088ae8626b737a6c1c7bba7f61?AccessKeyId=867C324947D38D2A0B0A &disposition=0&alloworigin=1; "1970 Survey," 31; Michael J. Kramer, *The Republic of Rock: Music and Citizenship in the Sixties Counterculture* (New York: Oxford University Press, 2013).

68. Appy, *Working-Class War*, 11–27; Bradley and Werner, *We Gotta Get Out of This Place*, 58. This assertion notwithstanding, their book devotes far more attention to rock.

69. Ca. 1968, the AFVN had no specific rock format or category. The 1970 survey indicated stronger support for country than "acid rock." The 1971 survey showed the two categories roughly equivalent but with "acid rock" having a slight lead. See "1968 Survey," 22; "1970 Survey," 18; "1971 Survey," 18; Bradley and Werner, *We Gotta Get Out of This Place*," 58.

70. This intimate interconnectedness is explored in Joseph Thompson, *Cold War Country: Music Row, the Pentagon, and the Sound of American Patriotism* (Chapel Hill: University of North Carolina Press, 2024).

71. This is not to say that the military promoted *all* forms of country music. The decidedly non-Nashville (or anti-Nashville) strain which later became known as "outlaw" country was not included, for example, nor was a Nashville song like "Ruby, Don't Take Your Love to Town," about a disabled veteran, which became a hit in the U.S. in the late 1960s. On whiteness, nostalgia, and regionalism, see Karl Hagstrom Miller, *Segregating Sound: Inventing Folk and Pop Music in the Age of Jim Crow* (Durham, NC: Duke University Press, 2010). On politics of country music, see Peter La Chapelle, *I'd Fight the World: A Political History of Old-Time, Hillbilly, and Country Music* (Chicago: University of Chicago Press, 2019).

72. Roughly a quarter expressed active dislike of *Town and Country*, whereas nearly half either liked it enthusiastically or expressed mild approval. "1970 Survey," 19–20; "1971 Survey," 19.

73. See, e.g., "Ken Burns Documentary 'The Vietnam War' Examines the Conflict from All Sides," ABC News, https://abcnews.go.com/US/video /ken-burns-documentary-vietnam-war-examines-conflict-sides-49799385, and others at "Press and Events," https://www.pbs.org/kenburns /the-vietnam-war/press-events/.

74. See "Vietnam War Music," https://www.pbs.org/kenburns/the-vietnam-war /music/. Cash's "Big River" was recorded and issued by Memphis's Sun Records. Haggard was one of the best known exponents of the deliberately un-Nashville "Bakersfield Sound" from Bakersfield, California.

75. "Black and White in Vietnam," *NYT*, July 18, 2017; James E. Westheider, *The African American Experience in Vietnam: Brothers in Arms* (Lanham, MD: Rowman & Littlefield, 2008), 17–39, 93–95.

76. On Brown's tour, see James Brown, "After They Got the Funk They Went Back and Reloaded," in *Patriots: The Vietnam War Remembered from All Sides*, ed. Christian G. Appy (New York: Viking, 2003), 184–86; "James Brown Entertains the Troops: Explosive James Brown Takes 'Soul' Show to Vietnam," *Ebony* 23, no. 10 (August 1968): 94–98; Bradley and Werner, *We Gotta Get Out of This Place*, 121–22; Rickey Vincent, *Party Music: The Inside Story of the Black Panthers' Band and How Black Power Transformed Soul Music* (Chicago: Lawrence Hill, 2013), 103–4. The arrangements for Brown's tour stood in sharp contrast to the State Department-sponsored musical tours of the 1950s and '60s. See Penny M. Von Von Eschen, *Satchmo Blows Up the World: Jazz Ambassadors Play the Cold War* (Cambridge, MA.: Harvard University Press, 2004).

77. "No Soul, Brother," *Your Military Left* 1, no. 1 (July 1, 1969): 12.

78. "Seamen Demand Jet Soul Tunes on Juke Boxes, Get Them, Other Demands," *Jet*, Aug 12, 1971, 19. On genre, see Charles Kronengold, *Living Genres in Late Modernity: American Music of the Long 1970s* (Oakland: University of California Press, 2022).

79. James E. Westheider, *Fighting on Two Fronts: African Americans and the Vietnam War* (New York: New York University Press, 1997), 76; "Danang Restriction Imposed by the Navy after Racial Unrest," *NYT*, October 21, 1968; Wallace Terry, "Black Power in Vietnam," *Time*, September 19, 1969, repr. in *Reporting Vietnam, Part One: American Journalism, 1959–1969* (New York: Library of America, 1998), 706; "Air Force Jim Crow," *Crisis*, July 1970, 227; Westheider, *The African American Experience in Vietnam*, 52. So closely was music associated with interracial violence that by 1971, an army training film intended to reduce interracial violence through a kind of managed provocation juxtaposed images of a Black Power salute, a Confederate flag, and scenes of white soldiers who were singing country music songs while clashing with Black soldiers who wanted soul music. Beth Bailey, *An Army Afire: How the US Army Confronted Its Racial Crisis in the Vietnam Era* (Chapel Hill: University of North Carolina Press, 2023), 136.

80. Louis Stokes, "Congressional Black Caucus Report," *Congressional Record* 92nd cong., 2nd. sess. (October 14, 1972), 36582; Westheider, *Fighting on Two Fronts*, 100. Regarding Terry's reference to Black soldiers' reaction to casualty rates, ca. late July 1966 African Americans accounted for 22 percent of all American casualties, although they made up only 12 percent of the general population. In 1967, they accounted for 14 percent of all American casualties, a figure which declined until the active fighting stopped in 1972. In

the end, the overall casualty rate of Black soldiers was comparable to their numbers in the general population. See Westheider, *The African American Experience in Vietnam*, 47 and 49. On the racial antagonism between country and soul fans in the army and marines, see Gerald Astor, *The Right to Fight: A History of African Americans in the Military* (Novato, CA: Presidio, 1998), 428 and 465. For a fascinating aural record of the experiences of Black soldiers, see the collage of interviews assembled on *Guess Who's Coming Home: Black Fighting Men Recorded Live In Vietnam* (Black Forum Records, 1972).

81. Beth Bailey, "The U.S. Army and 'the Problem of Race': Afros, Race Consciousness, and Institutional Logic," *Journal of American History* 106, no. 3 (December 2019): 639–61.

82. Quoted in Westheider, *Fighting on Two Fronts*, 76.

83. Westheider, *Fighting on Two Fronts*, 87; Wallace Terry, *Bloods: An Oral History of the Vietnam War by Black Veterans* (New York: Ballantine, 1992), 31. One factor contributing to the relative invisibility of the perspective of Black soldiers in Vietnam is scarcity of published memoirs by Black G.I.s, especially enlisted men. See Jeff Loeb, "MIA: African American Autobiography of the Vietnam War," *African American Review* 31, no. 1 (Spring 1997): 105–23.

84. Bailey, *An Army Afire*, 2.

85. Bailey, "The U.S. Army and 'the Problem of Race,'" esp. 651; Lair, *Armed with Abundance*, 149.

86. Westmoreland quoted in Kara Dixon Vuic, *The Girls Next Door: Bringing the Home Front to the Front Lines* (Cambridge, MA: Harvard University Press, 2019), 195; "The Road: Over There," *Time*, January 6, 1967, 69.

87. Vuic, *The Girls Next Door*, 191; "MACV Directive No. 28-7," April 16, 1967, folder 206-02, box 185, Historians Background Material Files, NARA-RG472; "The Road: Over There," *Time*, January 6, 1967, 69.

88. See Jonathan Randal, "Rock and Roll Song Becoming Vietnam's Tipperary," *NYT*, June 14, 1967, reprinted in *Broadside*, no. 82, (July 1967), 3. Note that this article ran in an early edition of the *Times* but not the final edition and is not archived in the newspaper's historical online database. Thanks to Jack Begg of the *New York Times'* research department for confirming this (personal correspondence, September 14, 2021). On the Reynettes, see "Update at Girl Garage Mayhem," *Bubblegum Soup*, May 30, 2008, https:// bubblegumsoup.blogspot.com/2008/, accessed September 15, 2021. On the popularity and resonance of "We Gotta Get," see Bradley and Werner, *We Gotta Get Out of This Place*, 9–18.

89. "Happiness Is Acid Rock on Plantation Road," *Grunt Free Press* 2, no. 6 (October 1970): 3–4. For a lively profile of one the groups that performed, see Tom Marlow, "Yea, We're the CBC Band and We'd Like to Turn You on We Got a Little Peace Message, Like, Straight from Saigon. Waaaaaaah Yeaaa!," *Rolling Stone*, no. 71 (November 26, 1970): 28–29. On the rock scene in Vietnam, see Kramer, *The Republic of Rock*, 195–218.

90. Kramer, *The Republic of Rock*; Bradley and Werner, *We Gotta Get Out of This Place*.

91. Joseph B. Treaster, "G.-Eye View of Vietnam," *New York Times Magazine* (October 30, 1966), 104–6.

92. Les Cleveland, *Dark Laughter: War in Song and Popular Culture* (Westport, CT: Praeger, 1994), 135–36.

93. Lydia M. Fish, "General Edward G. Lansdale and the Folksongs of Americans in the Vietnam War," *Journal of American Folklore* 102, no. 406 (October 1989): 390–411.

94. Lydia Fish, "Vietnam War—American Songs: The General Edward G. Lansdale Collection," *Folklife Center News* 11, no. 3 (Summer 1989): 4–5.

95. Lydia Fish, notes on Edward Lansdale, comp., *In the Midst of War*, June 1990, Vietnam War Song #2 subject file, LC-AFC. For another collection with a preponderance of patriotic and militaristic songs, see Saul Broudy, "G.I. Folklore in Viet-Nam," MA thesis, University of Pennsylvania, 1969.

96. *Hearts and Minds*, directed by Peter Davis, 1974.

97. On airmen's songbooks, see Joseph F Tuso, *Singing the Vietnam Blues: Songs of the Air Force in Southeast Asia* (College Station: Texas A&M University Press, 1990), and the numerous Vietnam-related songbooks in JHC. On song competitions, see Martin Heuer, "Personal Reflections on the Songs of Army Aviators in the Vietnam War," *New Directions in Folklore* 7 (2003); "Senior Officer's Debriefing Report," July 13, 1972, Defense Technical Information Center, apps.dtic.mil/sti/pdfs/AD0521407.pdf, 74, accessed October 20, 2021. See also C. W. Getz's two-volume collection of one thousand songs sung in the air force from before World War I to after the war in Vietnam, roughly half of which appear in the guaranteed-to-offend "Stag Bar edition." C. W. Getz, *The Wild Blue Yonder: Songs of the Air Force*, 2 vols. (Burlingame, CA: Redwood, 1981–86).

98. On masculinity and stereotypes of Vietnamese women, see Gregory A. Daddis, *Pulp Vietnam: War and Gender in Cold War Men's Adventure Magazines* (New York: Cambridge University Press, 2021).

99. *8 TFW Stag Bar*, JHC, https://www.horntip.com/html/books_&_MSS/1960s/1969ca_8th_TFW_stag_bar/1969ca_8th_TFW_stag_bar_(getz_collection_no_125).pdf; Tuso, *Singing the Vietnam Blues*, 65–67, 129–31, 185–86. On the ambiguity of the meaning of another song about dropping napalm, sung by helicopter pilots, see John E. Woodruff, "It's 'Napalm Sticks to Kids' on Skytroopers' Hit Parade," *Baltimore Sun*, June 15, 1970.

100. I analyze the range, ambiguities, and contradictions of this song culture more extensively in an article in progress.

101. See songbooks *My Golden Songbook of War Songs* (1969), JHC, https://www.horntip.com/html/books_&_MSS/1960s/1969_the_golden_songbook_of_war_songs_(MS)/1969_the_golden_songbook_of_war_songs_(ms_songbook)_(lydia_fish_collection).pdf; *Proud Bird with a Silver Ass*, JHC, https://www.horntip.com/html/books_&_MSS/1970s/1972-1973_proud_bird_with_a_silver_ass/1972-1973_proud_bird_with_a_silver_ass_(need_photocopy_of_pgs_1_and_21)_(lydia_fish_collection).pdf; *Compliments of 347th TAC FTR WG*, JHC, https://www.horntip.com/html

/books_&_MSS/1970s/1970s_complements_of_34th_TAC_FTR_WG/1970s
_complements_of_34th_TAC_FTR_WG_and_the_flying_dutchman_(getz
_collection_no_087).pdf; *The Spud Hymnal*, JHC, https://www.horntip.com
/html/books_&_MSS/1970s/1971_the_SPUD_hymnal_(various)/1971
_the_SPUD_hymnal_1st_edition_(mimeo)/1971_spud_hymnal_1st_edition.
pdf; *Satan's Angels Songbook*, JHC, https://horntip.com/html/books_&_MSS
/1960s/1968ca_satans_angels_songbook/1968ca_satans_angels_songbook
.pdf; *Dirty Dittys*, JHC, https://horntip.com/html/books_&_MSS/1960s/1966ca
_35th_tactical_fighter_wing_songbooks_(PBs)/1968ca-dirty-dittys-[35-tac-ftr
-wg-songbook]-300dpi.pdf.

102. Bradley and Werner, *We Gotta Get Out of This Place*, 165–67; "Vietnam:
Radio First Termer," *All Things Considered*, November 11, 1987, https://www
.interlockmedia.com/productions/viet_radio/images/1%20Audio%20Track
.flv; Philip Shenon, "Hanoi Hannah Looks Back, with Few Regrets," *NYT*,
November 26, 1994; Mike Ives, "Trinh Thi Ngo, Broadcaster Called 'Hanoi
Hannah' in Vietnam War, Dies," *NYT*, October 4, 2016. G.I.s may also have
listened to a series of antiwar programs called "WPAX," produced for Radio
Hanoi in America by Abbie Hoffman and John Giorno in 1971. The series
was much reported on after being denounced by Vice President Spiro
Agnew, but I have not found confirmation that it actually aired in Vietnam.
See Bill DeNoyelles, "John Giorno: Subduing the Demons in America,"
Bill DeNoyelles, July 5, 2008, http://www.billdenoyelles.com/2008/07
/john-giornosubduing-demons-in-america.html.

103. Bradley and Werner, *We Gotta Get Out of this Place*, 64–67; Kramer, *The Republic
of Rock*, 139–40, 152–55; "Vietnam: Radio First Termer, "*All Things Considered*;
Will Snyder, "Radio First Termer," https://ibiblio.org/jwsnyder/rft/rft.html;
Dave Rabbit, "21 Days in the Saigon Underground: The Birth and Death of
Radio First Termer," http://diymedia.net/old/stuff/drabbit021406
.pdf, accessed November 29, 2019.

104. Dave Rabbit, "21 Days in the Saigon Underground"; Kramer, *The Republic of
Rock*, 159–60.

105. Kramer, *The Republic of Rock*, 171. Indeed, seeking to celebrate and cultivate
G.I. talent, by 1970 officials in the Entertainment Branch were envisioning
the establishment of "Entertainment Centers" spread throughout South
Vietnam where, as Michael Kramer noted, soldiers would be able to "check
out electric guitars, form 'rock combos,' rehearse, and entertain themselves
and their fellow servicemen." Kramer, *The Republic of Rock*, 173–74.

106. "After Action Report—The Black Patches, Third Command Military Touring
Show," March 22, 1967, folder "CMTS Tours—The Black Patches #3," box 39,
Entry #P181 Records Regarding Command Military Touring Show (CMTS)
Tours in Vietnam, NARA-RG472.

107. See CMTS tour files, boxes 39 and 45, Entry #P181 Records Regarding
Command Military Touring Show (CMTS) Tours in Vietnam, NARA-RG472.
The name of the band the Soul Chordinators is sometimes written as Soul
Coordinators.

108. Untitled memorandum, folder "'Entertainment Vietnam' Tours, Oct–Dec 1969," box 62, Entertainment Branch History files, 1969–1972, NARA-RG472; Rick Holen et al., "Off-Off-Broadway," *Esopus* 12 (Spring 2009): 11.

109. Untitled set list, folder "CMTS Tours—The Soul Coordinators [*sic*] (78), Aug. 10, 1970," box 45, Entry #P181 Records Regarding Command Military Touring Show (CMTS) Tours in Vietnam, USARV, SSA (Prov)/Athletic, Recreation, and Entertainment Division, Entertainment Branch, NARA-RG472; press release, "CMTS Tours—The Peace Pac," box 45, Entry #P181 Records Regarding Command Military Touring Show (CMTS) Tours in Vietnam, USARV, SSA (Prov)/Athletic, Recreation, and Entertainment Division, Entertainment Branch, NARA-RG472.

110. Poster, folder "CMTS Tours—The Vagabonds," box 39, Entry #P181 Records Regarding Command Military Touring Show (CMTS) Tours in Vietnam, NARA-RG472; memorandum, folder "Phase III," box 48, Entry #P181 Records Regarding Command Military Touring Show (CMTS) Tours in Vietnam, NARA-RG472.

111. Kara Dixon Vuic, *Officer, Nurse, Woman: The Army Nurse Corps in the Vietnam War* (Baltimore: Johns Hopkins University Press, 2010), 143–46.

112. Austin Bunn, "Unarmed and Under Fire: An Oral History of Female Vietnam Vets," *Salon*, November 11, 1999, https://www.salon.com/1999/11/11/women_4/.

113. Herr, *Dispatches* (New York: Knopf, 1977), 234; Clark, "Tracks of Our Tears," 11. On "mobile privatization," see Raymond Williams, *Television: Technology and Cultural Form* (New York: Schocken, 1975); Stephen Groening, "'An Ugly Phrase for an Unprecedented Condition': Mobile Privatisation, 1974–83," *Key Words: A Journal of Cultural Materialism*, no. 11 (2013): 58–74. The significance of this concept is taken up in chap. 7.

114. Lee Ballinger, "Déjà Vu," in *The First Rock & Roll Confidential Report*, ed. Dave Marsh et al. (New York: Pantheon, 1985), 210.

115. On morale, discipline, desertions, and fragging, see, e.g., Yvonne Honeycutt Baldwin and John Ernst, "In the Valley: The Combat Infantryman and the Vietnam War," in *The War That Never Ends*, ed. David L. Anderson and John Ernst, New Perspectives on the Vietnam War (Lexington: University Press of Kentucky, 2007), 311–34; Kurt Lang, "American Military Performance in Vietnam: Background and Analysis," *Journal of Political & Military Sociology* 8, no. 2 (1980): 269–86.

116. Bradley and Werner, *We Gotta Get Out of This Place*, 120–21; Kramer, *The Republic of Rock*, 174.

Chapter Seven

1. Lane DeGregory, "Iraq 'n' Roll," *St. Petersburg Times*, November 21, 2004. See also Jonathan Pieslak, *Sound Targets: American Soldiers and Music in the Iraq War* (Bloomington: Indiana University Press, 2009), 84–85; Bing West, *No*

True Glory: A Frontline Account of the Battle for Fallujah (New York: Random House, 2011), 176–77, 272–73; Juliette Volcler, *Extremely Loud: Sound as a Weapon*, trans. Carol Volk (New York: New Press, 2013), 103–4; Associated Press, "Troops Blast Music in Siege of Fallujah," April 17, 2004, available at https://www.military.com/NewsContent/0,13319,FL_music_041704,00.html. According to West, it was the marines, not the army, who initiated the use of music during attacks in the First Battle of Fallujah in April 2004 and subsequently inspired the army's psyops use of music in the Second Battle of Fallujah in November–December 2004.

2. West, *No True Glory*, 176–77; DeGregory, "Iraq 'n' Roll." On sonic weapons, see Volcler, *Extremely Loud*.

3. Seth A. Conner, *Boredom by Day, Death by Night: An Iraq War Journal*, ed. English Wesley (Wheaton, IL: Tripping Light, 2007), 39.

4. Indeed, in 2001, Disturbed, one of the bands that Seth Conner mentioned, organized a multi-band tour called Music Is a Weapon. It was repeated numerous times with different lineups through 2011.

5. Jonathan Crane, "The Role of Music in Military Culture," in *Music Therapy with Military and Veteran Populations*, ed. Rebecca Vaudreuil (London: Jessica Kingsley, 2022), 35, 39. The author is an officer in the U.S. Army Band program. Gerald Keating, "Buglers and Bugle Calls in the U.S. Army," *Army History*, no. 27 (1993): 17; Jaweed Kaleem, "Taps Plays On at Military Funerals as Bugle Tradition Declines," *Huffington Post*, May 27, 2013, https://www.huffingtonpost.com/2013/05/27/military-funerals-taps_n_3342807.html.

6. Dave Philipps, "Military Is Asked to March to a Less Expensive Tune," *NYT*, July 1, 2016 ; "Make Your Passion Your Profession," U.S. Army Bands, accessed August 22, 2020, https://web.archive.org/web/20201016155606/www.bands.army.mil/careers/; *Gunner Palace*, directed by Michael Tucker and Petra Epperlein (2005); *Soundtrack to War: A Film*, directed by George Gittoes (2006). On cadences, see Richard Allen Burns, "'I Got My Duffel Bag Packed/And I'm Goin' to Iraq': Marching Chants in the Military," *BASIS: Ballads and Songs, International Studies* 2, special issue "Ballad Mediations: Folksongs Recovered, Represented, and Reimagined" (2006): 6–18.

7. On country music jingoism, see, e.g. Peter J. Schmelz, "'Have You Forgotten?': Darryl Worley and the Musical Politics of Operation Iraqi Freedom," in *Music in the Post-9/11 World*, ed. Jonathan Ritter and J. Martin Daughtry (New York: Routledge, 2007), 123–54; Andrew McKevitt, "'Watching War Made Us Immune': The Popular Culture of the Wars," in *Understanding the U.S. Wars in Iraq and Afghanistan*, ed. Beth L. Bailey and Richard H. Immerman (New York: New York University Press, 2015), 238–58, esp. 247–49.

8. Roger Stahl, *Militainment, Inc.: War, Media, and Popular Culture* (New York: Routledge, 2010); Bruce Sterling, "War Is Virtual Hell," *Wired* 1, no. 1 (1993), http://www.wired.com/wired/archive/1.01/virthell.html. Sterling, it should be noted, theorized the "military-entertainment complex" but did not use the term himself. The first instance of the term I am aware of is J. C. Herz,

Joystick Nation: How Videogames Ate Our Quarters, Won Our Hearts, and Rewired Our Minds (Boston: Little, Brown, 1997), 197–214. The same concept is explored under a different name in James Der Derian, *Virtuous War: Mapping the Military-Industrial-Media-Entertainment Network*, 2nd ed. (New York: Routledge, 2009). See also Ed Halter, *From Sun Tzu to XBox: War and Video Games* (New York: Thunder's Mouth, 2006), 185.

9. On Hollywood and WWII, see Frank J. Wetta and Martin A. Novelli, "Good Bombing, Bad Bombing: Hollywood, Air Warfare, and Morality in World War I and World War II," *OAH Magazine of History* 22, no. 4 (2008): 25–29; Claudia Springer, "Military Propaganda: Defense Department Films from World War II and Vietnam," *Cultural Critique*, no. 3 (1986): 151–67; Clayton R. Koppes and Gregory D. Black, "What to Show the World: The Office of War Information and Hollywood, 1942–1945," *Journal of American History* 64, no. 1 (1977): 87–105. On radio, see Gerd Horten, *Radio Goes to War: The Cultural Politics of Propaganda during World War II* (Berkeley: University of California Press, 2003). On country music, see Joseph Thompson, *Cold War Country: Music Row, the Pentagon, and the Sound of American Patriotism* (Chapel Hill: University of North Carolina Press, 2024).

10. David L. Robb, *Operation Hollywood: How the Pentagon Shapes and Censors the Movies* (Amherst, NY: Prometheus, 2004); David Sirota, *Back to Our Future: How the 1980s Explain the World We Live in Now—Our Culture, Our Politics, Our Everything* (New York: Ballantine, 2011), 112–38; *Theaters of War*, directed by Roger Stahl (2022); Alissa Wilkinson, "Hollywood and the Pentagon: A Love Story," *Vox*, May 27, 2022, https://www.vox.com/23141487/top-gun-maverick-us-military-hollywood; McKevitt, "'Watching War Made Us Immune,'" 249–51.

11. James Deaville, "The Sounds of American and Canadian Television News after 9/11: Entoning Horror and Grief, Fear and Anger," in *Music in the Post-9/11 World*, ed. Jonathan Ritter and J. Martin Daughtry (New York: Routledge, 2007), 43–70, quotation at 51.

12. Nicholas Engstrom, "The Soundtrack for War," *Columbia Journalism Review* 42, no. 1 (June 2003): 45–48; James Deaville, "Selling War: Television News Music and the Shaping of American Public Opinion," *Echo: A Music-Centered Journal* 8, no. 1 (2006), http://www.echo.ucla.edu/Volume8-Issue1/roundtable/deaville.html; Pieslak, *Sound Targets*, 27–31; Jordan Newman, "Sounding Military Identity through US and Canadian Recruiting Videos," *Ethnomusicology Review* 18 (2013); Nadine Smith, "From Catchy Commercials to Hollywood Think Tanks, the Evolution of Military Recruitment Ads," *Hyperallergic*, November 2, 2021, http://hyperallergic.com/687248/the-evolution-of-military-recruitment-ads/. For an example of an army recruitment advertisement without music, see "1971 Radio Ad for Army Recruitment," YouTube, https://www.youtube.com/watch?v=FPt8zZNjhMo. On the military's marketing campaigns after the shift to the all-volunteer force, see Beth L. Bailey, *America's Army: Making the All-Volunteer Force* (Cambridge, MA: Harvard University Press, 2009).

13. Catherine Lutz, "Making War at Home in the United States: Militarization and the Current Crisis," *American Anthropologist* 104, no. 3 (2002): 723–35; Henry A. Giroux, "Militarization, Public Pedagogy, and the Biopolitics of Popular Culture," *Counterpoints* 338 (2008): 39–54; Roberto J. González, *Militarizing Culture: Essays on the Warfare State* (Walnut Creek, CA: Left Coast, 2010), 35–56; Andrew J. Bacevich, *The New American Militarism: How Americans Are Seduced by War* (New York: Oxford University Press, 2005).

14. Sumanth S. Gopinath, *The Ringtone Dialectic: Economy and Cultural Form* (Cambridge, MA: MIT Press, 2013), esp. 19–26; Joseph Lanza, *Elevator Music: A Surreal History of Muzak, Easy-Listening, and Other Moodsong*, rev. ed. (Ann Arbor: University of Michigan Press, 2004); David Owen, "The Soundtrack of Your Life," *New Yorker*, April 2, 2006.

15. Roger Stahl, "Have You Played the War on Terror?," *Critical Studies in Media Communication* 23, no. 2 (June 2006): 116–17; Randy Nichols, "Target Acquired: *America's Army* and the Video Games Industry," in *Joystick Soldiers: The Politics of Play in Military Video Games*, ed. Nina Huntemann and Matthew Thomas Payne (New York: Routledge, 2010), 41–42.

16. Nina B. Huntemann, "Interview with Colonel Casey Wardynski," in *Joystick Soldiers: The Politics of Play in Military Video Games*, ed. Nina Huntemann and Matthew Thomas Payne (New York: Routledge, 2010), 179; Nichols, "Target Acquired," 40–47; Stahl, "Have You Played the War on Terror?," 123.

17. Stahl, "Have You Played the War on Terror?," 122; Nichols, "Target Acquired," 39–52.

18. Robertson Allen, *America's Digital Army: Games at Work and War* (Lincoln: University of Nebraska Press, 2017), 6. The goals were identified in a 2002 document of the Army Game Project.

19. Stahl, "Have You Played the War on Terror?," 123; Matthew Michael Sumera, "War's Audiovisons: Music, Affect, and the Representation of Contemporary Conflict" (PhD diss., University of Wisconsin–Madison, 2013), 96; "America's Army Launches Mobile Offensive," GamesIndustry.biz, January 30, 2007, https://www.gamesindustry.biz/articles/americas-army-launches-mobile -offensive; "Global VR to Deploy America's Army at AAMA Gala," Arcade Renaissance, July 20, 2007, https://web.archive.org/web/20230407002318/www .arcade-renaissance.com/2007/07/global-vr-to-deploy-americas-army-at .html, accessed January 19, 2022.

20. Allen, *America's Digital Army*, 7. The other two records were Earliest Military Website to Support a Video Game and Largest Travelling Game Simulator; Military Leadership Diversity Commission, "Demographic Profile of the Active-Duty Enlisted Force," Issue Paper no. 19, September 2008, https:// diversity.defense.gov/Portals/51/Documents/Resources/Commission/docs /Issue%20Papers/Paper%2019%20-%20Demographics%20of%20Active %20Duty%20Enlisted.pdf.

21. Stahl, "Have You Played the War on Terror?," 123; Sumera, "War's Audiovisions," 104ff.

22. Sumera, "War's Audiovisions," 114.

23. Sumera, "War's Audiovisions," 114, 119.

24. Stahl, "Have You Played the War on Terror?," 113; Jason H. Wong, Anh B. Nguyen, and Lauren Ogren, "Serious Game and Virtual World Training: Instrumentation and Assessment," December 10, 2012, Naval Underseas Warfare Division Center, https://apps.dtic.mil/sti/citations/ADA582033.

25. Stahl, "Have You Played the War on Terror?," 123; Stanley A. Miller, "War Game," *Milwaukee Journal Sentinel*, May 13, 2003; Julian E. Barnes, "The New Action Heroes," *U.S. News & World Report* 139, no. 19 (November 21, 2005): 53–54; Stahl, "Have You Played the War on Terror?," 123.

26. Huntemann, "Interview with Colonel Casey Wardynski," 185; Allen, *America's Digital Army*, 6.

27. Kenneth Lineberry, "Cadence Calls: Military Folklore in Motion" (MA thesis, Truman State University, 2003), 2; Burns, "'I Got My Duffel Bag Packed/And I'm Goin' to Iraq,'"13–16; Jennifer P. Brown, "212 Ways to Be a Soldier," *Kentucky New Era*, March 28, 2001, https://www.kentuckynewera.com/article_39413899-ee72-512d-a2ac-bce123a55b55.html, accessed June 14, 2022. On the impact of cadences in the transformation of civilians into soldiers, see chap. 6.

28. See, e.g., Nate Anderson, "IPods at War," *Ars Technica*, August 21, 2006, https://arstechnica.com/gadgets/2006/08/ipods-war/.

29. *Gunner Palace*; *Soundtrack to War*; *Farenheit 9/11*, directed by Michael Moore (2004). The *Doonesbury* strip, which was published November 26, 2007, is reprinted in Pieslak, *Sound Targets*, 4.

30. "Soldiers Soundtracks to War," produced by PRX, 2010, https://exchange.prx.org/series/31644-soldiers-soundtracks-to-war-iraq. For an astute reading of this series, see Sumera, "War's Audiovisons," 3. Scholarly work that has explored music among soldiers includes Pieslak, *Sound Targets*; Lisa Gilman, *My Music, My War: The Listening Habits of U.S. Troops in Iraq and Afghanistan* (Middletown, CT: Wesleyan University Press, 2016); J. Martin Daughtry, *Listening to War: Sound, Music, Trauma, and Survival in Wartime Iraq* (New York: Oxford University Press, 2015).

31. For a fuller, more nuanced discussion of these posters and the iconicity of iPods, see J. Martin Daughtry, "Aural Armor: Charting the Militarization of the iPod in Operation Iraqi Freedom," in *The Oxford Handbook of Mobile Music Studies*, vol. 1, ed. Sumanth Gopinath and Jason Stanyek (New York: Oxford University Press, 2014), 225–26; Daughtry, *Listening to War*, 224–25.

32. Grisham quoted in Pieslak, *Sound Targets*, 3.

33. "G.I.'s in Iraq Tote Their Own Pop Culture," Tom Shanker, *NYT*, April 13, 2004; Anderson, "IPods at War." The first iPods went on sale in 2001 but did not become a presence in the military for several years after that.

34. Daughtry, "Aural Armor," 235; Erik Holtan, interview by Jonathan Pieslak, April 18, 2006, audio recording, author's collection. Thank you to Jonathan Pieslak for generously sharing his interviews with me.

35. Sumera, "War's Audiovisons," 144.

36. Michel Chion, *Audio-Vision: Sound on Screen*, trans. Claudia Gorbman (New York: Columbia University Press, 1994); Sumera, "War's Audiovisons," esp. 9–10.

37. C. J. Grisham, interview by Jonathan Pieslak, May 1, 2006, audio recording, author's collection. The quotations in this paragraph come from Sumera, "War's Audiovisions," 151.

38. Sumera, "War's Audiovisions," 170; Matthew Sumera, "The Soundtrack to War," in *Virtual War and Magical Death: Technologies and Imaginaries for Terror and Killing*, ed. Neil L. Whitehead and Sverker Finnström (Durham, NC: Duke University Press, 2013), 219.

39. Monica Davey, "Fighting Words," *NYT*, February 20, 2005.

40. While people of color made up a higher proportion of the military than of the general population, in the age of the all-volunteer force their presence was no longer linked to explicitly discriminatory policies, like draft exemptions for college students. A greater proportion of soldiers of color served as officers in Iraq than in the Vietnam era as well.

41. Colby Buzzell, *My War: Killing Time in Iraq* (New York: Penguin, 2005), 146.

42. Marek Korczynski, *Songs of the Factory: Pop Music, Culture, and Resistance* (Ithaca, NY: Cornell University Press, 2014), 11; David "JR" Schultz, interview by Jonathan Pieslak, June 22, 2007, audio recording, author's collection; Neal Saunders, interview by Jonathan Pieslak, April 18, 2006, audio recording, author's collection.

43. Interestingly, Buzzell had a roommate whose music of choice was Barry Sadler's "Ballad of the Green Berets" and other Vietnam-era songs.

44. Colby Buzzell, interview by Jonathan Pieslak, April 26, 2006, audio recording, author's collection; *Soundtrack to War*; Pieslak, *Sound Targets*, 46–57.

45. *Soundtrack to War*.

46. Grisham, interview.

47. Daughtry, "Aural Armor," 236; *Soundtrakc to War*; Grisham, interview.

48. William Thompson, interview by the author, March 30, 2023; William Thompson, interview by Jonathan Pieslak, June 7, 2007, audio recording, author's collection; Jennifer Atkinson, interview by Jonathan Pieslak, May 3, 2006, audio recording, author's collection; *Soundtrack to War*.

49. Daughtry, "Aural Armor," 240; Kristie Rieken, "Soldiers Tell War Stories through 'Live from Iraq' Rap Album," *Plainview [Texas] Herald*, May 28, 2005, https://www.myplainview.com/news/article/Soldiers-tell-war-stories-through-Live-from-8615038.php.

50. Atkinson, interview; "Salute to Our Veterans: Hip-Hop Inside Iraq (Flashback 2008)," *The Source* (blog), November 10, 2017, https://thesource.com/2017/11/10/salute-vetrans-hip-hop-inside-iraq-2008/; Thompson, interview by Pieslak. For a dissenting view, Grisham said he would not have died but that "every day would have felt like a week." Grisham, interview.

51. Michael Bull, *Sound Moves: Ipod Culture and Urban Experience* (London: Routledge, 2007). See also Shuhei Hosokawa, "The Walkman Effect," *Popular Music* 4 (January 1984): 165–80.

52. Josh Kun, *Audiotopia: Music, Race, and America* (Berkeley: University of California Press, 2005); Bull, *Sound Move*, 87–88. On the notion of "mobile privatization," see Raymond Williams, *Television: Technology and Cultural Form* (New York: Schocken, 1975). See also Stephen Groening, "'An Ugly Phrase for an Unprecedented Condition': Mobile Privatisation, 1974–83," *Key Words: A Journal of Cultural Materialism*, no. 11 (2013): 58–74.

53. Mack Hagood, *Hush: Media and Sonic Self-Control* (Durham, NC: Duke University Press, 2019), esp. chap. 5.

54. Buzzell, *My War*, 146; Buzzell, interview.

55. See, e.g., Volcler, *Extremely Loud*, 101. A list of the songs played by the psyops team is available in United States Southern Command, "Public Affairs After Action Report Supplement, "Operation Just Cause" Dec. 20, 1989-Jan. 31, 1990" (n.p.: n.d.), 209–10, https://nsarchive2.gwu.edu/news/20091022/Panama%20playlist.pdf.

56. *Gunner Palace*; Grisham, interview.

57. Buzzell, interview; Daughtry, "Aural Armor," 234.

58. Daughtry, "Aural Armor," 238, 248.

59. Other techniques included shaving, stripping, diapering, hooding, isolation, exposure to continuous light or darkness, and shackling in stress positions.

60. On music and torture, see Suzanne G. Cusick, "'You Are in a Place That Is Out of the World . . .': Music in the Detention Camps of the 'Global War on Terror,'" *Journal of the Society for American Music* 2, no. 1 (2008): 1–26; Suzanne G. Cusick, "Music as Torture/Music as Weapon," *Transcultural Music Review* 10 (2006); Suzanne G. Cusick, "Musicology, Torture, Repair," *Radical Musicology* 3 (2008); Suzanne G. Cusick and Branden W. Joseph, "Across an Invisible Line: A Conversation about Music and Torture," *Grey Room* 42 (January 2011): 6–21; Suzanne G. Cusick, "Towards an Acoustemology of Detention in the 'Global War on Terror,'" in *Music, Sound and Space: Transformations of Public and Private Experience*, ed. Georgina Born (New York: Cambridge University Press, 2013), 275–91; Suzanne G. Cusick, "Afterword to 'You Are in a Place That Is out of the World . . .': Music in the Detention Camps of the 'Global War on Terror,'" *Transposition: Musique et Sciences Sociales*, no. 4 (July 2014); U.S. Senate Select Committee on Intelligence, "Central Intelligence Agency's Detention and Interrogation Program," December 9, 2014, https://www.intelligence.senate.gov/sites/default/files/publications/CRPT-113srpt288.pdf; Anna Papaeti, "On Music, Torture and Detention: Reflections on Issues of Research and Discipline," *Transposition: Musique et Sciences Sociales*, special issue "Sound, Music, and Violence" (March 2020); Manfred Nowak, "Music Torture in the 'War on Terror,'" in *The Routledge Companion to Music and Human Rights*, ed. Julian Fifer et al. (New York: Routledge, 2022), 325–31; Christian Grüny, "The Language of Feeling Made into a Weapon: Music as an Instrument of Torture," in *Speaking about Torture*, ed. Julie A. Carlson and Elisabeth Weber (New York: Fordham University Press, 2012), 205–18; Steven M. Friedson, "The Music Box: Songs of Futility in a Time of Torture," *Ethnomusicology* 63, no. 2 (July 2019): 222–46;

Lily E. Hirsch, *Music in American Crime Prevention and Punishment* (Ann Arbor: University of Michigan Press, 2012), 110–31; David Peisner, "War Is Loud," *Spin*, December 2006, 86–92; Mark Danner, "US Torture: Voices from the Black Sites," *New York Review of Books* 56, no. 6 (April 9, 2009); Mark Danner, "The Red Cross Torture Report: What It Means," *New York Review of Books* 56, no. 7 (April 30, 2009).

61. Alfred W. McCoy, *A Question of Torture: CIA Interrogation, from the Cold War to the War on Terror* (New York: Metropolitan, 2006), 8; cf. Morag Josephine Grant, "Pathways to Music Torture," *Transposition* 4, special issue "Musique et Conflits après 1945" (2014): 1–23. My thinking on music as a "single complex weapon system" was aided by Steven M. Friedson, "The Music Box: Songs of Futility in a Time of Torture," *Ethnomusicology* 63, no. 2 (July 2019), 233.

62. Paul Kramer, *The Blood of Government: Race, Empire, the United States, & the Philippines* (Chapel Hill: University of North Carolina Press, 2006), 140–42; Alfred McCoy, "Legacy of a Dark Decade: CIA Mind Control, Classified Behavioral Research, and the Origins of Modern Medical Ethics," in *The Trauma of Psychological Torture*, ed. Almerindo E. Ojeda (Westport, CT: Praeger, 2008), 43 and 40–69 passim; Jane Mayer, "The Experiment," *New Yorker*, July 11, 2005; U.S. Senate Committee on Armed Services, U.S. Senate, "Inquiry into the Treatment of Detainees in U.S. Custody," November 20, 2008, U.S. Senate, https://www.armed-services.senate.gov/imo/media/doc /Detainee-Report-Final_April-22-2009.pdf. As philosopher Peter Szendy put it, the use of music in "no-touch torture" was a means of "pushing in the nail, from afar and without seeming to touch." Peter Szendy, "Music and Torture: The Stigmata of Sound and Sense," in *Speaking about Torture*, ed. Julie A. Carlson and Elisabeth Weber, trans. Allison Schifani and Zeke Sikelianos (New York: Fordham University Press, 2012), 204.

63. Clive Stafford Smith, "Welcome to 'the Disco,'" *Guardian*, June 18, 2008; Suzanne G. Cusick, "Towards an Acoustemology of Detention in the 'Global War on Terror,'" 288. On music, vibration, and bodies, see Steve Goodman, *Sonic Warfare: Sound, Affect, and the Ecology of Fear* (Cambridge, MA: MIT Press, 2010).

64. My thinking about the "repeat" function was aided by Andrea Bohlman and Peter McMurray's discussion of the "rewind" button in "Tape: Or, Rewinding the Phonographic Regime," *Twentieth-Century Music* 14, no. 1 (February 2017): 3–24.

65. Cusick and Joseph, "Across an Invisible Line," 16.

66. The CIA's guidelines for exposure to continuous sound are specified in *Songs of War: Music as a Weapon*, directed by Tristan Chytroschek (2010).

67. Quoted in Cusick, "Towards an Acoustemology of Detention in the 'Global War on Terror,'" 288.

68. Andy Worthington, "A History of Music Torture in the 'War on Terror,'" *Huffington Post*, January 15, 2009, updated May 25, 2011, https://www .huffpost.com/entry/a-history-of-music-tortur_b_151109.

69. See, e.g., Smith, "Welcome to 'the Disco.'"

70. The study by Metin Başoğlu was published in the *Archives of General Psychiatry*, and quoted in McCoy, "Legacy of a Dark Decade," 41.

71. James Sturcke, "General Approved Extreme Interrogation Methods," *Guardian*, March 30, 2005, https://www.theguardian.com/world/2005/mar/30/usa .iraq; Kevin Drumm, "Bybee Says CIA Broke Torture Rules," *Mother Jones*, July 15, 2010, https://www.motherjones.com/kevin-drum/2010/07/bybee -says-cia-broke-torture-rules; Alex Horton, "A Beloved Metal Band Played at Guantánamo—Where Its Music Was Once Used for Torture," *Washington Post*, July 8, 2017.

72. On the origins and development of music therapy, see William B. Davis and Susan Hadley, "A History of Music Therapy," in *Music Therapy Handbook*, ed. Barbara L. Wheeler (New York: Guilford, 2015), 17–28.

73. James A. Davis, "Regimental Bands and Morale in the American Civil War," *Journal of Band Research* 38, no. 3 (2003): 14–15. On music therapy before 1945, see W. B. Davis, "Keeping the Dream Alive: Profiles of Three Early Twentieth Century Music Therapists," *Journal of Music Therapy* 30, no. 1 (March 1993): 34–45.

74. Annegret Fauser, *Sounds of War: Music in the United States during World War II* (New York: Oxford University Press, 2013), 127–34; Justin Francis and Donna Faraone, "The Evolution of Music Therapy in Military Medicine," in *Music Therapy with Military and Veteran Populations*, ed. Rebecca Vaudreuil (London: Jessica Kingsley, 2022), 46.

75. David Vergun, "Survival Rates Improving for Soldiers Wounded in Combat, Says Army Surgeon General," U.S. Army, August 24, 2016, https://www.army.mil/article/173808/survival_rates_improving_for _soldiers_wounded_in_combat_says_army_surgeon_general; Matthew S. Goldberg, "Casualty Rates of US Military Personnel during the Wars in Iraq and Afghanistan," *Defence and Peace Economics* 29, no. 1 (January 2018): 44–61. World War I and II figures from Sara Kass et al., "Creative Forces®: NEA Military Healing Arts Network—Expanding Creative Arts Therapies in the Departments of Defense and Veterans Affairs," in *Music Therapy with Military and Veteran Populations*, ed. Rebecca Vaudreuil (London: Jessica Kingsley, 2022), 94. In Vietnam, the survival rate is estimated to have been 75–87 percent.

76. Terri Tanielian and Lisa H. Jaycox, eds., *Invisible Wounds of War: Psychological and Cognitive Injuries, Their Consequences, and Services to Assist Recovery* (n.p.: RAND, 2008).

77. Lisbeth Woodward and David Otto, "Music Therapy and the Department of Veterans Affairs," in *Music Therapy with Military and Veteran Populations*, ed. Rebecca Vaudreuil (London: Jessica Kingsley, 2022), 65–90, esp. 80.

78. Kass et al., "Creative Forces®," 91–110 passim. The original name of this program was NEA Military Healing Arts Partnership.

79. "About Us," Guitars 4 Vets, https://guitars4vets.org/about-us/; "About Us," Warrior Cry Music Project, https://www.warriorcry.org /about-us; "SongwritingWith:Soldiers," SongwritingWith:Soldiers, https://www.songwriterswithsoldiers.org.

80. Ronald Hirschberg et al., "Collaborative Songwriting Intervention for Veterans with Post-traumatic Stress Disorder," *Journal of Alternative and Complementary Medicine* 26, no. 3 (March 2020): 198–203; Alvin Powell, "Crafting Soldiers' Songs of Pain—and yet Hope," *Harvard Gazette* (blog), February 1, 2019, https://news.harvard.edu/gazette/story/2019/02/crafting-soldiers-songs-of-pain-and-yet-hope/.

81. Geoffrey Winthrop-Young, "Drill and Distraction in the Yellow Submarine: On the Dominance of War in Friedrich Kittler's Media Theory," *Critical Inquiry* 28, no. 4 (June 2002): 825–54.

Coda

1. Henry Threadgill with Brent Hayes Edwards, *Easily Slip into Another World: A Life in Music* (New York: Knopf, 2023), 153.

2. Threadgill with Edwards, *Easily Slip into Another World*, 153.

3. Threadgill with Edwards, *Easily Slip into Another World*, 153.

4. Viet Thanh Nguyen, *Nothing Ever Dies: Vietnam and the Memory of War* (Cambridge, MA: Harvard University Press, 2016), 4.

5. This approach to culture is informed by Raymond Williams, "Base and Superstructure in Marxist Cultural Theory," *New Left Review*, no. 82 (December 1973): 3–16.

6. 4th25, *Live from Iraq* (4th25 Entertainment, 2005)

7. 4th25, "Testament of a Soldier," on *Live from Iraq*.

8. Mary Gauthier, *Rifles & Rosary Beads* (Proper Records, 2018).

9. Vijay Iyer and Mike Ladd, *Holding It Down: The Veterans' Dreams Project* (Pi Recordings, 2013).

10. "Vijay Iyer: Transforming Veterans' Dreams Into Music," WNYC, October 29, 2020, https://www.wnycstudios.org/podcasts/soundcheck/episodes/vijay-iyer-transforming-veterans-dreams-music-archives.

11. Vijay Iyer, Daniel Fischlin, and Eric Porter, "'Opening Up a Space That Maybe Wouldn't Exist Otherwise'/Holding It Down in the Aftermath: Vijay Iyer in Conversation with Daniel Fischlin and Eric Porter," in *Playing for Keeps: Improvisation in the Aftermath*, ed. Daniel Fischlin and Eric Porter (Durham, NC: Duke University Press, 2020), 84–85.

12. Iyer and Ladd, *Holding It Down*.

13. "Shush," by Maurice Decaul, on Iyer and Ladd, *Holding It Down*.

14. Iyer, Fischlin, and Porter, "'Opening Up a Space That Maybe Wouldn't Exist Otherwise,'" 91.

15. WATIV, *Baghdad Music Journal* (High Mayhem, 2006); William A. Thompson with Jeffrey Albert, "Baghdad Music Journal: A Soldier's Move toward Technology in Music," *Leonardo Music Journal* 25 (2015): 68–72.

16. William Thompson, interview with the author, March 30, 2023.

17. Thompson, interview with the author.

18. For a recording, see Drew Baker, *Stress Position* (New Focus, 2012)

19. Liner notes, *Stress Position*.

20. Susanna Välimäki, "Musical Representation of War, Genocide, and Torture: Treating Cultural Trauma with Music," *Acta Translatologica Helsingiensia* (2015): 133. Välimäki attended a performance at the Musica Nova Helsinki festival, February 20, 2009.

21. *Heavy Metal in Baghdad*, directed by Suroosh Alvi and Eddy Moretti (VBS.tv, 2007); J. Martin Daughtry, *Listening to War: Sound, Music, Trauma, and Survival in Wartime Iraq* (New York: Oxford University Press, 2015), 261–70.

22. Rahim AlHaj, *Letters from Iraq* (Smithsonian Folkways, 2017); "Interview: Rahim AlHaj—Letters from Iraq," Radio New Zealand, April 28, 2017, https://www.rnz.co.nz/national/programmes/accessallareas /audio/201841876/interview-rahim-alhaj-letters-from-iraq.

23. Liner notes, *Letters from Iraq*, 10, 14, and 15; D. A. Sonneborn, "A Reflection on Recording Rahim AlHaj's Letters from Iraq," Smithsonian Center for Folklife and Cultural Heritage, December 1, 2017, https://folklife.si.edu /talkstory/reflection-on-recording-rahim-alhaj-letters-from-iraq-running-boy.

24. Liner notes, *Letters from Iraq*, 15.

25. "Dreams in Color," by Lynn Hill, on Iyer and Ladd, *Holding It Down*.

Index

Page numbers in italics refer to figures.